Lecture Notes in Computer Science 11984

More information about this series at http://www.springer.com/series/7409

Elvira Popescu · Tianyong Hao ·
Ting-Chia Hsu · Haoran Xie ·
Marco Temperini · Wei Chen (Eds.)

Emerging Technologies
for Education

4th International Symposium, SETE 2019
Held in Conjunction with ICWL 2019
Magdeburg, Germany, September 23–25, 2019
Revised Selected Papers

 Springer

Editors
Elvira Popescu ⓘ
University of Craiova
Craiova, Romania

Tianyong Hao ⓘ
South China Normal University
Guangzhou, China

Ting-Chia Hsu ⓘ
National Taiwan Normal University
Taipei, Taiwan

Haoran Xie ⓘ
Lingnan University
Hong Kong, Hong Kong

Marco Temperini ⓘ
Sapienza University of Rome
Rome, Italy

Wei Chen
Chinese Academy of Agricultural Sciences
Beijing, China

ISSN 0302-9743 ISSN 1611-3349 (electronic)
Lecture Notes in Computer Science
ISBN 978-3-030-38777-8 ISBN 978-3-030-38778-5 (eBook)
https://doi.org/10.1007/978-3-030-38778-5

LNCS Sublibrary: SL3 – Information Systems and Applications, incl. Internet/Web, and HCI

This Springer imprint is published by the registered company Springer Nature Switzerland AG
The registered company address is: Gewerbestrasse 11, 6330 Cham, Switzerland

Preface

The 4th International Symposium on Emerging Technologies for Education (SETE 2019) was held in conjunction with the 18th International Conference on Web-based Learning (ICWL 2019). The symposium has traditionally been organized together with ICWL since 2016, aiming to gather a variety of tracks and workshops on hot topics in technology enhanced learning.

This year's conference was hosted by the Magdeburg-Stendal University of Applied Sciences, Germany, during September 23–25, 2019. Researchers, scholars, students, and professionals in the field of educational technology from all over the world gathered in the beautiful city of Magdeburg to share and exchange their state-of-the-art outputs and ideas.

A total of 34 submissions were received for the special tracks. After a rigorous review process, in which each paper was evaluated by at least 3 members of the Program Committee (PC), 10 papers were selected as full papers, yielding an acceptance rate of 29%. In addition, 6 more submissions were selected as short papers. These contributions cover latest findings in various areas, such as: virtual reality and game-based learning; learning analytics; K-12 education; language learning; design, model, and implementation of e-learning platforms and tools; digitalization and industry 4.0; pedagogical issues; and practice and experience sharing.

Furthermore, five workshops were organized at SETE 2019: 12th International Workshop on Social and Personal Computing for Web-Supported Learning Communities (SPeL 2019), Third International Symposium on User Modeling and Language Learning (UMLL 2019), Second International Workshop on Educational Technology for Language and Translation Learning (ETLTL 2019), First Workshop on Artificial Intelligence in Education - Teacher's Role for Student-centered Teaching (AIE-TRST 2019), and 'I Search Therefore I Learn' (ISTIL 2019). These workshops included a total of 24 accepted papers.

The conference also featured a distinguished keynote presentation, by Prof. Sabine Graf (Athabasca University, Canada), entitled "Academic Analytics – Analysis and Mining of Educational Data to Support Teaching," as well as two panels on "Women in Engineering – Sharing Statistics, Progress and Positive Experiences" and "Technology-Enhanced Learning for Higher Education in China: Opportunities and Challenges."

Many people contributed to making the conference possible and successful. Firstly, we thank all the authors who considered SETE for their submissions. We also thank the PC members for their evaluations that made possible the selection of the accepted papers. Last but not least, our thanks go to the local organizers, led by

Prof. Michael Herzog (especially Veronika Weiß and Leonore Franz), for their efforts and time spent to ensure the success of the conference.

October 2019

Elvira Popescu
Tianyong Hao
Ting-Chia Hsu
Haoran Xie
Marco Temperini
Wei Chen

Organization

General Co-chairs

Elvira Popescu   University of Craiova, Romania
Tianyong Hao   South China Normal University, China

Technical Program Committee Co-chairs

Ting-Chia Hsu   National Taiwan Normal University, Taiwan
Haoran Xie   Lingnan University, Hong Kong

Workshop Co-chairs

Marco Temperini   Sapienza University, Italy
Wei Chen   Chinese Academy of Agricultural Sciences, China

Publicity Chair

Liang Chen   Fujian Normal University, China

Track Co-chairs

T01: Emerging Technologies for Open Access to Education and Learning

Gabriela Grosseck   West University of Timisoara, Romania
Gwo-Jen Hwang   National Taiwan University of Science
and Technology, Taiwan

T02: Emerging Technologies Supported Personalized and Adaptive Learning

Kyparissia Papanikolaou   School of Pedagogical and Technological Education,
Greece
Sheng-Yi Wu   National Pingtung University, Taiwan

T03: Emerging Technologies of Design, Model and Framework of Learning Systems

Marie-Hélène Abel   Université de Technologie de Compiègne, France
Hui-Chun Chu   Soochow University, Taiwan

T04: Emerging Technologies Support for Game-based and Joyful Learning

Silvia Margarita Baldiris Navarro	Universidad Internacional de La Rioja, Spain
Zhi-Hong Chen	National Taiwan Normal University, Taiwan

T05: Emerging Technologies Enhanced Language Learning and Assessment

Chiu-Jung Chen	National Chia-yi University, Taiwan
Guanliang Chen	Monash University, Australia
Wing Shui Ng	The Education University of Hong Kong, Hong Kong
Di Zou	The Education University of Hong Kong, Hong Kong

T06: Emerging Technologies Supported Big Data Analytics in Education

Hui-Chun Hung	Taipei Medical University, Taiwan
Anna Mavroudi	KTH Royal Institute of Technology, Sweden
Kin Man Leonard Poon	The Education University of Hong Kong, Hong Kong

T07: Emerging Technologies Supported Collaborative Learning

Maria-Iuliana Dascalu	Politehnica University of Bucharest, Romania
Wai Man Winnie Lam	The Education University of Hong Kong, Hong Kong
Chiu-Pin Lin	National Tsing Hua University, Taiwan

T08: Emerging Technologies of Pedagogical Issues

Pao-Nan Chou	National University of Tainan, Taiwan
Zuzana Kubincova	Comenius University Bratislava, Slovakia
Jerry Chih-Yuan Sun	National Chiao Tung University, Taiwan
Qiaoping Zhang	The Education University of Hong Kong, Hong Kong

T09: Emerging Technologies for Affective Learning

Min-Chai Hsieh	Tainan University of Technology, Taiwan
Tak-Lam Wong	Douglas College, Canada

T10: Emerging Technologies for User Modeling

Yi Cai	South China University of Technology, China
Shin-Jia Huang	National Kaohsiung University of Science and Technology, Taiwan
Filippo Sciarrone	Sapienza University, Italy

Workshop Organizers

The 12th International Workshop on Social and Personal Computing for Web-Supported Learning Communities (SPeL 2019)

Elvira Popescu	University of Craiova, Romania
Sabine Graf	Athabasca University, Canada

The Third International Symposium on User Modeling and Language Learning (UMLL 2019)

Di Zou	The Education University of Hong Kong, Hong Kong
Tianyong Hao	South China Normal University, China
Yuanyuan Mu	Hefei University of Technology, China
Tak-Lam Wong	The Education University of Hong Kong, Hong Kong

The Second International Workshop on Educational Technology for Language and Translation Learning (ETLTL 2019)

Shili Ge	Guangdong University of Foreign Studies, China
Ruilin Li	Guangdong University of Foreign Studies, China
Tianyong Hao	South China Normal University, China
Qinghua Li	Southern Medical University, China

The First Workshop on Artificial Intelligence in Education - Teacher's Role for Student-centered Teaching (AIE-TRST 2019)

Andreja Istenic Starcic	University of Ljubljana and University of Primorska, Slovenia
Manolis Mavrikis	University College London, UCL Knowledge Lab, UK
Maria Cutumisu	University of Alberta, Canada
Cristina Alonso Fernández	Complutense University of Madrid, Spain

The International Workshop on 'I Search Therefore I Learn' (ISTIL 2019)

Ralph Ewerth	Leibniz Information Centre of Science and Technology (TIB), Germany
Ujwal Gadiraju	L3S Research Center, Leibniz Universität Hannover, Germany
Ivana Marenzi	L3S Research Center, Leibniz Universität Hannover, Germany
Bernardo Pereira Nunes	PUC-Rio and UNIRIO, Brazil

Contents

UMLL (User Modeling and Language Learning)

ETLTL (Educational Technology for Language and Translation Learning)

AIE-TRST (Artificial Intelligence in Education – Teacher's Role for Student-Centered Teaching)

ISTIL ('I Search Therefore I Learn')

Emerging Technologies for Education

A Case Study on How Greek Teachers Make Use of Big Data Analytics in K-12 Education

Anna Mavroudi[1](✉) and Spyros Papadakis[2]

[1] Norwegian University of Science and Technology, Trondheim, Norway
anna.mavroudi@ntnu.no
[2] Hellenic Open University, Patras, Greece
papadakis@eap.gr

Abstract. Big Data Analytics can help teachers to make better and informed decisions. Several recent articles in the field of technology enhanced learning concern this potential, yet little is known about how teachers actually make use of Big Data Analytics in their school to support themselves and their students. To compensate for this gap, this paper focuses on the actual uses of Big Data Analytics by active schoolteachers. Thirty teachers who live in Greece participated in survey about their usage of (a) Big Data analytics and (b) online learning environments which capture student data. The data were analysed using mixed methods. Main findings reveal that the schoolteachers are storing and actively using student data as well as Big Data which involve the support of the teaching-learning process. Also, it became clear that teachers use Big Data Analytics for two main distinctively different purposes: to cover teaching-learning aspects and to complete administrative tasks. Finally, it emerged that a small number of teachers is archiving digital multimedia. Consequently, a need arises for appropriate analytics and relevant privacy frameworks. Other practical implications of the findings of this work touch upon the design of teachers 'development programs in Big Data and their analytics.

Keywords: Big data analytics in education · Student digital data · Administration of school education · Teachers in K-12

1 Introduction

The abundance of digital traces that students are leaving in the digital learning environments coupled with advances in artificial intelligence, cloud computing, machine learning and data mining, has generated new opportunities in the educational technology field [16, 17], which are epitomised in the support of "evidence-based learning". The growing popularity of online or blended learning coupled with "evidence-based learning" approaches has contributed to the rise of the field of Big Data (BD) Analytics in Education [2]. It exploits a set of tools that can provide insights which can facilitate pedagogical decision-making [18]. Yet, it has been argued that we need to better understand the users' perspectives [7], e.g. students and teachers. This paper focuses on the

© Springer Nature Switzerland AG 2020
E. Popescu et al. (Eds.): SETE 2019, LNCS 11984, pp. 3–9, 2020.
https://doi.org/10.1007/978-3-030-38778-5_1

current uses of BD by teachers in the context of Greek school education. School education is a context which is heavily underrepresented in this topic at the recent literature
[7]. The aim of this study is to understand what types of BD schoolteachers use, where
are these data coming from, and how they use them.

2 Background

2.1 Big Data in Education

One common definition is that BD is data stored in "large and complex datasets collected from digital and conventional sources that are not easily managed by traditional
applications or processes" [16, p. 75]. There is a strong link between BD in Education
and Learning Analytics summarised as follows: "the process of gathering, analyzing
and reporting educational big data is referred to as learning analytics (LA)" [16, p. 76].
A recent review on the application of BD in education reveals several different pedagogical cases of potential exploitation, including performance prediction, attrition risk
detection, data visualisation, intelligent feedback, course recommendation, student skills
estimation, behaviour detection, grouping and collaboration of students [17]. One of the
sources of BD in Education comes from the user tracking and monitoring capabilities
of online Learning Management Systems (LMS).

2.2 Online Educational Technology Environments in Greece Used by Teachers

The educational technology environments described in this section are online and freely
available to the Greek teachers (offered by the Greek Ministry of Education) currently.
"MySchool" is an online platform designed to support the school units mostly on administrative tasks, and has several implications, such as monitoring early school leaving [13].
Another popular environment is called "Photodentro", which is the Greek national learning object repository for primary and secondary education [11]. All the learning objects
of "Photodentro" are offered as Open Educational Resources. The Greek School Network (GSN) [6] is an online environment which safely connects all schools (including
non-Greek educational units), services and entities supervised by the Ministry at central
and regional levels. The e-learning service of GSN [3] is based on the Moodle LMS.
The Learning Design system [9] is another platform integrated in the GSN; it promotes
collaborative learning and it is based on an open source Learning Activity Management System (LAMS) [8]. The Electronic Classroom service [4] is a platform that can
help teachers to create online courses and fully interact with their students. It can also
be used for teacher training and collaboration between teachers. Finally, the Advanced
Electronic Scenarios Operating Platform (A.E.S.O.P.) [1] is a platform for the design,
evaluation and exploitation of quality digital learning scenarios.

3 Method

3.1 Instrument

A questionnaire was used which was comprised of three main categories of questions:
basic participants' demographics, participants' usage of BD analytics (related either

to students or to the learning process), and participants' usage of online educational technology environments (which capture some users data).

The first category included three questions with predefined options about the teachers' gender, age group, and educational sector (primary or secondary education). The second category included three questions, two open- and one closed-ended. The open-ended questions involved the types of student data kept and used in a digital format, and the ways in which these data are being used, respectively. The closed-ended question had predefined options (Yes/No/I don't know) and was asking whether their school captures and actively uses data which support any aspect of the teaching-learning process, in addition to student data. The third category comprised two questions, one closed- and one open-ended. The former provided predefined options of online educational technology environments that are popular among Greek educators, such as "MySchool" and "Photodentro". The latter was asking about the ways that the participant teachers use these online educational technology tools.

3.2 Procedures and Participants

Teachers who are active in primary or secondary education in Greece were contacted via email asking them to complete the questionnaire anonymously. The link to the online questionnaire was included in the email message. Another prerequisite regarding the teachers' participation in the research was that their school was storing and using digital archives that contain student data. After a time period of a month, the answers were collected and analysed. The demographics data were analysed manually. The text that corresponded to the participants' answers in the open-ended questions was analysed using a software for qualitative analyses and content analysis as the main analysis method.

4   Results

In total, 30 teachers answered the questionnaire, 13 females and 17 males. One third of them works in primary education while the remaining two thirds are active in secondary education. With respect to age, one participant belongs in the 21–35 age group, nine participants belong to the 36–45 age group and the remaining twenty participants belong to the 46–65 age group. All participants declared that their school is storing and actively using digital archives containing student data; also, the majority of them (22 out of 30) declared that their school does the same for data which involve the support of the teaching-learning process. In this question, four participants answered negatively and the remaining four answered that they were not aware of whether such data are being collected in their school unit.

With respect to the student data kept in a digital format, Table 1 depicts the main data categories and the associated frequency of occurrence in the participants' answers. Grades and students' attendance are the data types kept most frequently, along with personal data like contact details (address and phone), and parents' names. In addition, it seems that the teachers capitalise on the affordances of educational technology systems in keeping in a digital format other student data such as: progress, awards, artifacts (created as part of educational activities and stored in e-portfolios), participation in educational programs or activities (usually funded by national or European grants). Interestingly, a small number of participants are aware that their school keeps videos from social events, field trips and excursions. Thus, we can conclude that the BD are being nowadays kept in a multimodal format or in various different formats, which can combine text, videos, and photos.

Table 1. Student data gathered and used in the Greek schools.

Student data	Frequency of occurrence
Grades	19
Personal data	13
Attendance	8
Student progress	5
Awards	5
Student artifacts	4
Participation	3
Multimedia	3

Following, in the question "in what ways are these data used?" the main answer in ten cases is quite generic (e.g. "in ways that help us covering the needs of the school unit"); or variations of that answer, without specifying more though. These variations revolve around: better organisation of the school life, educational, administrative or functional needs of the school. Four cases point out that they are keeping student data in line with national regulations (in one case this is explicitly mentioned) and consequently they are used in accordance with it. For example, to monitor absence of students from school, to issue grade certificates at the end of the semester or certificates of completion of an educational program. Other reasons mentioned are: monitoring of and providing feedback in the teaching-learning process, as well as archiving decisions made by the local educational policymakers.

With respect to online educational technology tools or resources used, Fig. 1 depicts the teachers' answers. The "MySchool" environment and online OERs are the most popular options among teachers, since they are supported by the Ministry of Education and are freely available. Following, four types of learning environments received the same attention from the participant teachers: the use of social media, LMS, Google Docs or similar, and applications that can support mobile learning. Less popular is the use of e-portfolios and finally, a considerable percentage of teachers makes use of other, additional tools.

Finally, the question "how do you use online educational technology tools?" was asking for more in-depth information. The response rate in this question was low, receiving 13 answers in total. Some answers were describing tool-specific usage, whereas others were more abstract and orientated towards the description of pedagogical methods that can be supported by the educational technology tools. Two main emerging themes are the improvement of the teaching-learning process and the administration of education. Examples of the former include visual learning, practice knowledge via test items, and communication skills development. Examples of the latter include communication with parents, and improving the visibility of the school activities among stakeholders. These examples were mentioned by the participants.

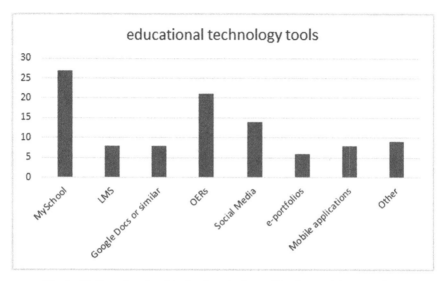

Fig. 1. Online educational technology tools used by the participant teachers

5 Discussion and Conclusions

The aim of this case study is to analyse the usage of BD and their Analytics in the Greek school education context. The findings revealed that the BD analytics are used to cover two different aspects of school life: the administration of education and the teaching-learning process. No particular focus emerged towards one of these two distinctively different uses. This is surprising, since a clearer focus could be expected on uses of BD analytics to support experimental and innovative forms of learning, due to the large number of relevant articles in the literature. This could be attributed to several factors, but more in-depth research is needed e.g. towards the topic of technology acceptance in relation to BD in school education. Another future research direction pinpoints to the development of appropriate BD Analytics for digital multimedia in school education, as well as to the development of relevant privacy frameworks, since it emerged that teachers are using digital multimedia that contain student-related data or school-related data.

Limitations of this work pertain to the fact that all participant teachers are living in Greece. The authors suggest conducting similar research in other countries as well. Cross-country comparisons on the use of BD Analytics could provide interesting insights both for the research community and the policymakers. The contribution of this work relates to the fact that there is lack of empirical evidence on the topic at stake in the context of K-12 education in the literature, while the usage of a new technology by the practitioners is a crucial parameter when designing a strategy for uptake at scale.

Also, the research implications of this work touch upon the recommendations for future research, while the practical implications upon the usage of BD Analytics in schools as a proxy for their readiness to effectively engage with this learning innovation. In turn, this insight can be useful in the design of teachers' professional development programs. For instance, it could be argued that no evidence was found herein with respect to using BD Analytics as a means of promoting high-order thinking skills among students, e.g. as a metacognitive tool; something which is recommended in the recent relevant literature [5]. Consequently, teachers' training programs on BD Analytics could try to address this gap. With respect to societal implications, the most frequently used BD Analytics among the participant teachers was students' grades and class attendance. The literature suggests that these two indicators combined have strong correlation with the identification of student at-risk of dropping out [10] which is in line with our findings. Finally, the need for updated privacy frameworks for multimodal BD Analytics has also emerged both herein and in the literature [14].

References

1. Advanced Electronic Scenarios Operating Platform (A.E.S.O.P.). http://aesop.iep.edu.gr. Accessed 9 June 2019
2. Cope, B., Kalantzis, M.: Sources of evidence-of-learning: learning and assessment in the era of big data. Open Rev. Educ. Res. **2**(1), 194–217 (2015)
3. e-learning service of GSN homepage. http://e-learning.sch.gr. Accessed 9 June 2019
4. Electronic Classroom service homepage. http://eclass.sch.gr. Accessed 9 June 2019
5. Gašević, D., Dawson, S., Siemens, G.: Let's not forget: learning analytics are about learning. TechTrends **59**(1), 64–71 (2015)
6. Greek School Network homepage. https://www.sch.gr/. Accessed 9 June 2019
7. Li, K.C., Lam, H.K., Lam, S.S.: A review of learning analytics in educational research. In: Lam, J., Ng, K.K., Cheung, S.K.S., Wong, T.L., Li, K.C., Wang, F.L. (eds.) ICTE 2015. CCIS, vol. 559, pp. 173–184. Springer, Heidelberg (2015). https://doi.org/10.1007/978-3-662-48978-9_17
8. Learning Activity Management System (LAMS) foundation homepage. https://www.lamsfoundation.org/. Accessed 9 June 2019
9. Learning Design system homepage. http://learning-design.sch.gr. Accessed 9 June 2019
10. Márquez-Vera, C., Cano, A., Romero, C., Noaman, A.Y.M., Mousa Fardoun, H., Ventura, S.: Early dropout prediction using data mining: a case study with high school students. Expert Syst. **33**(1), 107–124 (2016)
11. Megalou, E., Kaklamanis, C.: Photodentro LOR, the Greek national learning object repository. In: INTED2014 Proceedings, pp. 309–319 (2014)
12. "MySchool" homepage. https://myschool.sch.gr/. Accessed 9 June 2019
13. Nikolaou, S.M., Papa, M., Gogou, L.: Early school leaving in Greece and Europe and educational inequality: actions and policies against educational and social exclusion. Eur. J. Soc. Sci. Educ. Res. **5**(1), 212–220 (2018)
14. Pardo, A., Siemens, G.: Ethical and privacy principles for learning analytics. Br. J. Edu. Technol. **45**(3), 438–450 (2014)

15. "Photodentro" homepage. http://photodentro.edu.gr/. Accessed 9 June 2019
16. Reyes, J.A.: The skinny on big data in education: learning analytics simplified. TechTrends **59**(2), 75–80 (2015)
17. Sin, K., Muthu, L.: Application of big data in education data mining and learning analytics–a literature review. ICTACT J. Soft Comput. **5**(4) (2015)
18. Toetenel, L., Rienties, B.: Analysing 157 learning designs using learning analytic approaches as a means to evaluate the impact of pedagogical decision making. Br. J. Edu. Technol. **47**(5), 981–992 (2016)

Applying the Teach-Back Method and Mobile Technology to Support Elementary Students' Mathematics Problem-Solving Strategies

Chiung-ling Tung$^{(\boxtimes)}$, Chiou-hui Chou, Su-jiann Yang, and Chiu-pin Lin

National Tsing Hua University, Hsinchu, Taiwan
chiungtap@gmail.com

Abstract. A great amount of elementary students encounter failure to solve mathematical problems because they cannot understand the meanings of the problems. As indicated, problem-solving is the core of the mathematics curriculum. Thus, students need to develop reading comprehension ability to solve mathematics problems. The teach-back is a constructive method that can help students present the understanding of a certain topic through dialogues. This study investigated the effects of the teach-back approach, exploring elementary students' mathematics learning efficacy of problem-solving and attitudes towards an interactive learning platform, HiTeach. The participants in this study were sixgraders from a public school in Taiwan. There were twenty-four participants in the experimental group and twenty-four participants in the control group. The results indicated that students in the teach-back approach group performed better than those in the traditional collaborative group. Moreover, the teach-back approach helped students in comprehending the meaning of questions in problem-solving.

Keywords: The teach-back method · Mobile technology · Mathematics problem-solving strategiese

1 Introduction

Reading assessment and mathematics assessment have always been as the major subjects in Taiwan Assessment of Student Achievement (TASA) since 2004 as well as in the PISA (Programme for International Student Assessment) report. More important, reading comprehension cannot be just limited to the language field. It should be seen as an important skill in all the fields throughout the school years of the elementary school. When it comes to mathematics, many primary school students fail to solve mathematics problems, which is not because of their poor computing ability, but of their failure of understanding the problem, meaning that those students are unable to succeed in the first step of solving the problem (Huang 1996). As indicated, problem-solving is the core of mathematics curriculum. Thus, students need to develop reading comprehension ability to solve the mathematics problems.

© Springer Nature Switzerland AG 2020
E. Popescu et al. (Eds.): SETE 2019, LNCS 11984, pp. 10–20, 2020.
https://doi.org/10.1007/978-3-030-38778-5_2

In a traditional mathematics classroom in Taiwan, the math concept is often explained by the teacher standing in the front of the classroom, guiding students to the directions of how to solve the math problems. For those students with good logic abilities, they are able to learn and comprehend efficiently, while for those students with poor comprehension abilities, they might not be able to comprehend the meaning and they are usually stuck in the situation, waiting for the answers from the teachers or classmates instead of thinking. Being incapable of solving the math problem causes weak performance for these students. Cooperative learning is the instructional use of small groups so that students can work together to learn from solving problems. (Gillies 2016; Johnson et al. 2013; Slavin 2014).

Today, with the advancement of technology, the use of electronic whiteboards and tablets in the classroom has become prevalent. This study incorporated the teach-back method in cooperative learning, applying tablets and the HiTeach interactive learning platform, to investigate six graders mathematics learning efficacy. The purpose of this study is to explore the application of the feedback method, the teach-back approach, in the field of mathematics, hoping to help the sixth-grade students improve their effectiveness of and interests in learning how to solve problems in mathematics.

2   Literature Review

Mathematics Reading Comprehension and Problem-Solving Process
People rely on the ability of reading to get the information they need for the purpose of gaining knowledge. The mathematics reading comprehension mentioned in this study is, as Wakefield (2000) points outs, mathematics is a language; it is the tool and foundation of all sciences. Mathematics reading is a complete psychological process where students have to use language first to understand the problem. They then link to their prior knowledge and finally use their computation ability to solve the mathematics problem.

Problem-solving questions in mathematics are different from the general calculation questions. In solving the problem, learners must first comprehend the meaning of the problem and then calculate the figures. Polya (1945) in his book entitled, *How to Solve It: A new aspect of mathematical method*, points out that problem-solving is to achieve a goal—which is clearly understood but cannot be reached immediately. During the course of problem-solving, no method is told, but difficulty might be there waiting for learners to overcome. That is, learners need to bypass the obstacles to find a way to achieve this goal. In Polya's (1945) book, solving math problems is divided into four stages as follows:

(1) Understand the problem: The problem solver must understand the narrative of the problem and point out the main idea of the problem, meaning that the problem solver must characterize the problem.
(2) Devise a plan: The problem solver must find out the relationship between the known and the unknown, and set up the procedures to deal with the problem.
(3) Carry out the plan: The problem solver must perform various calculations and other necessary operations.

(4) Review/extend: The problem solver has to reexamine the process carefully, trying to see how this experience can help solve other problems.

In this study, the teacher applied the teach-back method, the students were paired (one high achievement student with one low achievement student). They introduce their understanding of the topic to each other. Then, tell each other the content of the study and question the content. If they have different opinions, intervention of teachers will occur. If they reach the consensus, the student will sum up.

The Teach-Back Method

In literature, the teach-back method is to confirm whether an individual understands the problem through a structured dialogue. In the past, doctors used the teach-back method to confirm whether patients knew how to use and manage medicine. Studies found that patients who learned through the teach-back method were more aware of how to use and manage medicine than those who did not. Although the teach-back method was not often seen in the teaching field, recently, Sharples et al. (2016) have found that students conducted science experiments using the teach-back method performed significantly higher achievements than those who did not.

In this study, the teacher applied the teach-back method to deliver knowledge, to give students opportunities to share and discuss ideas, and to maximize the effectiveness of cooperative learning. During the teach-back method stage, students were paired (one high achievement student with one low achievement student). The teaching steps are shown in Fig. 1.

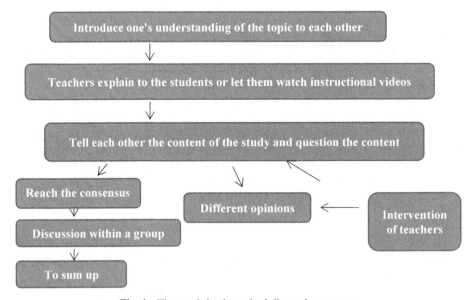

Fig. 1. The teach-back method discussion process

3 Method

The Subjects

The study was conducted in two grade-six classes in an elementary school in Taiwan; each class was composed of 24 students. The 48 students all have studied the basic concepts of numbers and quantities and algebra. The units discussed in this paper were selected from the students' mathematics textbook, including algebra topics mainly on calculating the numbers of chickens and rabbits in a same cage with the information of their feet. The two classes were randomly selected as the experimental group or the control group.

In the experimental group, four students were in a group. The heterogeneous grouping strategy, which means the group consists of low and high achievers was used. Each group was then again grouped into two pairs for the teach-back activity. The teach-back method was implemented for students to solve the math problem. After each group reached consensus, the group members used the tablet to show how to solve the math problem, using the HiTeach interactive learning platform to share their problem-solving steps.

In the control group: Four students were in a group. The heterogeneous grouping strategy was used for grouping. The group members used the tablet to show how to solve the math problem, also using the HiTeach interactive learning platform to share their problem-solving steps in the traditional cooperative learning method.

HighTeach Interactive Learning Platform

This study uses HiTeach interactive learning platform, developed by Taiwan Netcom Information Technology Co., Ltd.. The teacher used a desktop computer (see Fig. 2) and students used tablets to show their results on the platform (see Fig. 3).

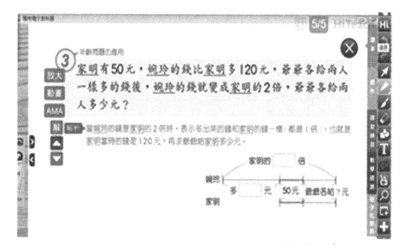

Fig. 2. HiTeach interactive learning platform: a screen showing the math problem

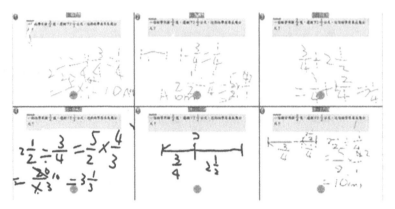

Fig. 3. A snapshot of the each group's discussion results

The Instruments

The research data came from students' test papers, a learning-attitude questionnaire, students' worksheets, and the data on the HiTeach interactive learning platform.

The math test papers of this study were designed by the teachers. The test papers were also validated by three senior math teachers and two math specialties. The expert validity as well as the content validity was achieved. The pre-test and post-test of student math performance were obtained from the test papers. The difficulty of the test paper is at 0.5, which is a mean value of the data contained in Table 1 for the level of difficulty. After the pilot test, the 18 official test items were selected. The difficulty distribution table of the test items is shown in Table 1.

Table 1. The allocation of test items

Levels of difficulty	>0.82	0.82–0.38	<0.38
Number of items	3	10	5
Proportional allocation	16%	56%	28%

The learning attitude questionnaire was designed to understand how learning attitudes could be influenced by the learning activities—including the teach-back method as well as the interactive teaching system. It was based on a five-point Likert scale, in which 5 indicates the strongest degree of agreement while 1 indicates the weakest degree of agreement. Ten items from the questionnaire were selected for the discussion in this paper. Items 1 to 5 were on the aspect of cooperative learning and items 6 to 10 were on the aspect of students' learning process

Data Collection

The study was carried out within four weeks. The pre-test was implemented in the first week. During the second and the third week, the implementation of teach-back method unit was carried out in the experiment group while in the control group the traditional discussion strategy was implemented. In the fourth week, the post-test and the attitude questionnaire were conducted. The teaching process of week 2 and week 3 is as follows:

(1) The whole class was taught: the teacher illustrated the example in the textbook.
(2) Understanding of the problem: The teacher wrote down similar questions, and the students wrote down their understanding of the questions and their process of solving the math problems. Students did not discuss what they wrote.
(3) Sharing understanding: The result of the second step was put into discussion. The experimental group members played the role of the commentator in turn, explaining the meaning of the question and the way to solve the math problem. If the methods of solving the problem from both parties were similar, the consensus was reached. In the control group, as four members were in each group, adopting a traditional group discussion strategy. If the answers within the group were similar, then the consensus was reached. If the answers were not the same, group members would continue discussing for the consensus answer.

Table 2. Comparison between the experimental group and the control group

Group	The experimental group (N=24)	The control group (N=24)
Platform	HiTeach interactive learning platform	
Teaching process and discussion methods	The whole class received instruction: The teacher illustrated examples. ↓ Problem understanding: teacher's present similar questions, and then everyone writes down their own understanding of what the questions mean and the process of solving the problems. What they write will not be discussed.	
	At the first stage, each group has four members. At the teach-back stage, each group was divided into two in a pair. The two in a pair took turns playing a role of a teacher, conducted dialogues, questioned each other and reached a consensus.	Four students in a group discussed the math problem-solving process.
	Sharing the discussion result of solving the math problem with each group ↓ Teacher summarized the result.	

(4) Sharing between groups: Each group uploaded a snapshot of their answers to the interactive teaching system, and the learners could refer to other groups' results and reviewed the answer all together.

(5) Summary: Finally, the teacher summarized and reviewed the main point of the math activity (Table 2).

4   Research Results

The Pre-test Results

In order to understand whether there are significant differences between the two classes of students in the concept of "how to solve the problem" before the experiment, the experiment group and the control group were tested by the pre-test, and the independent sample t-test was analyzed by SPSS statistics software for the purpose of understanding the difference between the two groups of students. The results are shown in Table 3:

Table 3. Independent sample T-tests results of the pre-test

	Group	Number of samples (n)	Average (M)	Standard deviation (SD)	F (F)	Pearson (P)	t (t)	Degree of freedom, (df).	Pearson (two-tailed) (P)
Pre-test score	EG	24	35.71	22.50	2.88	.096	−.928	45	.358
	CG	24	42.48	27.36					

*P < .05, **P < .01, ***P < .001

The average scores of the experiment group and the control group were 35.71 and 42.48, respectively. The Levene test of the homogeneity of the variance was of little significance ($F = 2.88$, $p = .096 > .05$), indicating there was no significant difference between the experimental group and the control group before the experiment, that is, the mathematics ability of the two classes before the experiment was equivalent.

The Post-test Results

The statistical analysis of the paired sample t-test is shown in Table 4. The test results of the experiment group are significant ($t(24) = −7.83$, $p = .000 < .05$) and the results of the control group are significant ($t(24) = −2.091$, $p = .048 < .05$). After the two groups of students went through different cooperative learning strategies, the two groups of students improved their math performance. From the post-test results, the scores of the experiment group are higher than those of the control group, and the progress score of the experiment group is also higher than that of the control group. It is found that the Teach-back method can make the two different groups summarize the meaning of the questions and can help students clarify the confusion happening during the discussion. In addition, HiTeach platform was used for students to show and share their discussion results. In doing so, students can apply different methods for solving questions and what they have done during the discussion sections can also be enhanced.

Table 4. Paired sample t-test of learning effectiveness

Group	Variable	Number of samples (n)	Average (M)	Standard deviation (SD)	t (t)	Degree of freedom (df)	Pearson (two-tailed) (P)
EG	Pre-test	24	35.71	22.50	−7.83	23	.000***
	Post-test	24	67.83	25.81			
CG	Pre-test	24	42.48	27.36	−2.091	23	.048*
	Post-test	24	55.46	34.17			

*p < .05, * *p < .01, ** *p < .001

Comparing Different Achievement Students' Learning Outcomes

In order to understand whether there are significant differences in the learning outcomes of high achievers and low achievers among the two groups, comparing the high-achievers from the experiment group with those from the control group showed no significant difference after the experiment (U = 67.5, p = .794 > .05). See Table 5. The result of comparing the low achievers from the experiment group with those from the control group was significant (U = 19.5, p = .002 < .01). The scores of experiment group was 16.88, higher than that of the control group, 8.13.

Table 5. Mann-Whitney test for post-test scores of high and low achievement students

Category	Group	Numbers of the sample (n)	The sum	The average	Mann-Whitney U test	Wilcoxon W test.	Z test	Pearson(two-tailed) (P)
High achievers	EG	12	154.5	12.88	67.5	145.5	−0.261	.794
	CG	12	145.5	12.13				
Low achievers	EG	12	202.5	16.88	19.5	97.5	−3.033	.002**
	CG	12	97.5	8.13				

*p < .05, ** p < .01, ***p < .001

After the implementation of the HiTeach interactive teaching platform with the teach-back method, the low-achieving students in the experimental group not only improved the average score, but also achieved significant differences in the learning outcomes, showing the low achievement students in the experimental group performed better than the low achievement students in the control group.

Cooperative Learning

The independent sample t-test was performed to test the influence of the treatment on the students' learning attitudes. In the cooperative learning phase, Items 1 to 5 were used to access students' behaviors and opinions during cooperative learning in the experiment group and the control group. The results are shown in Table 6.

Table 6. Cooperative learning results

Cooperative learning.	Experimental group		Control group		
	M	SD	M	SD	P
1. After listening to my classmates' explanations. I am willing to provide feedback to them for reference	4.54	0.66	3.71	0.91	.001**
2. I can accept the opinions or opinions of other students on me and constructively adopt the suggestions provided by you	4.63	0.65	4.21	0.83	.059*
3. I can publicly explain my thoughts to other classmates	4.08	0.83	3.79	1.10	.306
4. I will ask my classmates to explain more clearly their ideas I do not understand	4.71	0.46	4.25	0.74	.013**
5. The members of our group are able to work together to complete the tasks within the specified time	4.67	0.64	4.13	1.08	.039*

*p < .05, **p < .01, ***p < .001

The results of Item 1, 4, and 5 show that the experiment group students are significantly different from the control group. The researchers found that the feedback method made the students in the experiment group more willing to put forward their own opinions when faced with differences of opinions or when they had doubts about the other students' explanation. The degree of cooperation within the group was also better than that of the control group.

Thinking Process

Items 6 to 10 are used to access students' opinions regarding using the worksheet during the group discussion session. The results are shown in Table 7. It can be seen that students in the experiment group (using the Teach-back method) responded with better results than the students in the control group (the traditional cooperative learning). The reason is that the members of the Teach-back method group have more interactions within the group and also more interactions between the groups, which makes students have more opportunities to present their own thinking process, and when they listen to others' solutions, they can also recognize and overcome their weaknesses.

Table 7. Students' thinking process

Thinking process*	Experimental group		Control group		
	M	SD	M	SD	P
6. I feel that using the worksheet allows me to understand the content more	4.46	0.72	3.83	0.82	.007**
7. The learning task in the study is not simple, but this learning method is not difficult for me to understand	4.33	0.82	3.83	0.87	.046*
8. Compared with the previous learning method, using the worksheet makes me feel more challenging and interesting	4.46	0.83	3.79	0.88	.010*
9. Using a worksheet allows me to learn in a different way or in a different thinking style	4.54	0.72	3.96	0.62	.004**
10. After using the worksheet, I believe that I can get excellent results in this unit	4.08	0.83	3.58	0.72	.030*

*p < .05 , * *p < .01 , *** p < 001

5 Conclusion

The study explored elementary students' mathematics learning efficacy, using the teach-back method, and their attitudes, using the tablet and the HiTeach interactive learning platform. The results show that both the experiment group of "HiTeach interactive teaching platform integrated with the teach-back method" and the control group of "HiTeach interactive teaching platform integrated into traditional cooperative learning teaching" can effectively improve the effectiveness of students' ability of solving math problems. The learning achievement of the low-achieving students in the experiment group was significantly better than that of the low-achieving students in the control group. Moreover, students show much favor to the incorporation of technology into the teach-back method in a mathematics classroom, thinking that in this way, they can show their understanding of the meaning of questions by sharing their own ideas. Through the sharing of the HiTeach learning platform, they can also view the way other groups solve questions. As a result they can learn more different ways of thinking and, in the meantime, improve their motivation and interests in learning mathematics.

References

Gillies, R.M.: Cooperative learning: review of research and practice. Aust. J. Teach. Educ. **41** (2016). https://doi.org/10.14221/ajte.2016v41n3.3

Huang, Z.: Mathematical Teaching Method. Normal University Book Company, Taipei (1996)

Johnson, D.W., Johnson, R.T., Holubec, E.J.: Cooperation in the Classroom, 9th edn. Interaction Book Company, Edina (2013)

Polya, G.: How to Solve It: A New Aspect of Mathematical Method. Princeton University Press, Princeton (1945)

Sharples, M., et al.: Innovating Pedagogy 2016: Open University Innovation Report 5. The Open University, Milton Keynes (2016)

Slavin, R.E.: Cooperative learning and academic achievement: why does groupwork work? Anales de Psicología/Ann. Psychol. **30**, 785–791 (2014). https://doi.org/10.6018/analesps.30.3.201201

Wakefield, D.V.: Math as a second language. Educ. Forum **64**, 272–279 (2000)

Taiwan Achievement of Student Achievement (2004). https://www.naer.edu.tw/files/11-1000-1408-1.php?Lang=zh-tw

EFL Writing Assessment: Peer Assessment vs. Automated Essay Scoring

Meixiu Lu[1], Qing Deng[2], and Manzhen Yang[3(✉)]

[1] Eastern Language Processing Center, School of Information Science and Technology, School of Cyber Security, Guangdong University of Foreign Studies, Guangzhou, China
[2] Guangdong University of Technology, Guangzhou, China
[3] School of English and Education, Guangdong University of Foreign Studies, Guangzhou, China
63845636@qq.com

Abstract. This study aimed to explore problems and potentials of new technologies in English as foreign language (EFL) writing education. Forty-six students as a foreign language (EFL) learners in a Chinese university participated in this study. They submitted their draft to Pigai Network and Scholar Network separately and received automated essay scoring (AES) and peer assessment (PA) feedback. Results showed a moderate, positive partial correlation between PA and AES, controlling for performance level. The EFL learners in China preferred AES over PA. These findings raise several relevant issues in how to improve peer assessment feedback effectively, such as writing rubric in peer assessment, specialized peer assessment tool, technology assistant and peer feedback.

Keywords: Peer assessment · Automated essay scoring · English as foreign language

1 Introduction

In the past few decades, several forms of assessment have been used in English as a foreign language (EFL) classes, including teacher assessment, peer assessment (PA) and automated essay scoring (AES). According to the effectiveness of assessment, peer assessment and teacher feedback are widely used in writing classes [1, 2]. As technology advances, independent research on AES has only recently emerged [3–5] and has played an important role on writing teaching.

However, teacher assessment is regarded as the most authoritative way of assessment. Many teacher report that correction of student essays consumes the largest proportion of their time: about 40 min to comment on each individual essay times 3 essays per student tines 46 students per class yields 5, 5620 min or 92 h [6]. One alternative is having peers evaluate the quality or academic performance of each student (peer assessment, PA). Past studies show mixed results regarding the effectiveness of peer assessment for improving EFL, possibly because of its validity [7, 8] and the variability of assessment tasks [9]. For example, Chang et al. indicated that peer assessment based on web-based portfolio failed

E. Popescu et al. (Eds.): SETE 2019, LNCS 11984, pp. 21–29, 2020.
https://doi.org/10.1007/978-3-030-38778-5_3

to show students' performance and was not a reliable and valid assessment method [7]. Automated essay scoring (AES) might address both issues, and students' perceptions towards PA and AES has an important role in shaping students' views and behaviors in English writing, so both assessment methods are evaluated in this study.

Forty-six college students participated in this study. Two essays written by the students were submitted and implemented peer assessment and automated essay scoring. Quantitative and qualitative data were examined to yield findings, followed by a detailed discussion.

2   Related Work

2.1 Peer Assessment

Significant advantages of PA have been reported in the literature [10, 11]. Topping et al. reported that PA showed adequate reliability and validity in many kinds of applications, and the PA effects were as good as or better than teacher assessment effects [12]. Meek et al. also showed that higher participation in the peer review task correlated with higher performance [13]. However, some researchers found that PA scores and teacher assessment score differed significantly [14, 15] and suspected the validity of the PA.

In terms of perception towards PA, some students believe that they can gain benefit from PA [13]. However, some students found PA difficult, uncomfortable and time-consuming [16]. In spite of previous advantages and disadvantages of PA and mixed attitudes towards PA, there are also some potential limitations to be explored next. First of all, whether PA in EFL writing are the same as teacher assessment in China. Additionally, the effectiveness of PA adopted in writing assessment is remained more profound research as most of the related work focused on.

2.2 Automated Essay Scoring

Automated essay scoring (AES) can supplement writing assessment, but most studies of its validity show mixed findings. Fang showed that a majority of the students benefited from AES and that the automated feedback had a positive effect on writing skill development, particularly on the form rather than content [17]. Human raters and AES showed highly consistency and some evidence of validity supported AES [18].

However, how students perceived the effectiveness in EFL writing were mixed. Chen and Cheng found that students favoured using AES for early drafting and revising [19], and showed writing improvement with respect to accuracy and learner autonomy awareness [20]. However, another study showed that students' perceptions had minimal impact on their AES use to write and revise successfully, though some students continued to use it or would recommend it to friends [21].

2.3 Purpose of This Study

In summary, there is little evidence in the published literature on how to determine whether PA or AES is effective in EFL writing assessment. Lai found that EFL learners in Taiwan generally opted for PA over AES [22]. Inspired by previous ideas, the present study adopted both PA and AES to examine the difference between PA and AES, and explore the students' perceptions in EFL writing.

3   Research Design

This study explored the differences between PA and AES in an EFL writing learning environment and determined students' perceptions toward the two assessments methods. Quantitative data and qualitative questionnaire data were collected from 46 college students, along with 92 essays' PA score and AES score to ascertain the suitability of PA or AES as an assessment tools for EFL students. As explained in previous studies, the effectiveness of AES and PA heavily depends on how the assessment is conducted because the method can affect the validity of the feedback. Specifically, this study poses the following research questions:

(1) Do the EFL writing assessments of AES and PA differ?
(2) Does student's writing performance level affect this difference between PA and AES?
(3) What are the students' perceptions towards AES and PA?

3.1 Participants

46 college students in a comprehensive university in China participated this study. They were non-English major freshmen and did not have any PA or AES experience. They had 2 courses per week for a total of 18 weeks, and they had to submit 2 essays for PA and AES during the semester in 2018–2019. The researcher (first author) and two instructors (second and third author) attended this study. The researcher was responsible for experimental design and data analysis. The second author, 15 years of EFL teaching experience, is responsible for teacher practice and teacher intervention. And the third author, language testing expert, provides language teaching assessment theory support.

3.2 Instruments

Three network tools were adopted in this study in EFL writing assessment for PA and AES. Pigai Network is a Chinese AES network tool often used in EFL writing assessment in this university. Based on corpus and cloud computing technology, Pigai provides an automatic online correction service for English essays, along with scores and comments about the composition in real time. Scholar Network, an online academic information service platform, provides academic information management, academic exchange services, and a teaching curriculum platform to support an academic community. Questionnaire Star, a professional online questionnaire survey platform, provided an online questionnaires and analysis.

3.3 Procedure and Data Collection

This overall experiment included three phases: submit draft, PA and AES, revision and resubmit. Jones and Wheadon found that a comparative judgment approach can improve assessment validity during PA [23]. Based on this finding, the instructor organized the students in small groups of three to four students for PA.

During the draft submission phase, the instructor separately arranged the same writing task in Pigai Network and Scholar Network. Then, the participants completed two essays "Due Attention Should Be Given to Spelling" (30 min) and "The Importance of Good Manners" (at least 120 words within a week). Participants submitted their essays to Pigai Network and Scholar Network.

In the PA and AES phase, the instructor conducted PA in the lab and the Pigai Network provides instant scores and feedback. Conducting peer in a fixed time and place can help improve the quality of the assessment. Yu and Wu found that students who knew the names of their assessors tended to view them more favorably than those who remained anonymous or were identified with nicknames during PA [24]. So the instructor organized group discussions about the essay scores within each group in an anonymous form during PA. Then each individual anonymously submitted scores and reviews for each member of the same group through the Questionnaire Star platform. The PA scoring rubric included: (1) Expression of Ideas; (2) Organization; (3) Language Accuracy; (4) Language Fluency; (5) Language Complexity

At the revision phase, the participants should modify and re-submit the revised essay through Scholar Network one week later. After the first essay task, the instructor trained the students to conduct PA in writing, and the two essays repeated the same process.

The survey was originally designed to measure the students' attitudes toward two assessment methods. The questionnaire data was collected at the end of this semester, which was designed based on the related work [22] and had open-ended questions. The aim was to explore the students' attitudes towards PA and AES, and it included ten questions with the following choices (5-Strongly agree, 4-Agree, 3-Neither agree nor disagree, 2-Disagree, 1-Strongly disagree).

To explore whether the students' writing performance level affected the results, a paper-based test score was collected at the end of the period. It was based on College English Test (CET) 4, a large-scale high-stakes test in China, which included listening, grammar, reading and writing.

4 Data Analysis and Results

4.1 Difference Between PA and AES

A partial correlation indicated whether PA score and AES score were related, controlling for writing performance level. The variables were PA score (measured in the mean of peer within the same group) and AES score (measured in one hundred mark), the control variable was writing performance level (measured in paper-based test in one hundred mark).

The results (Table 1) indicated that the mean of the PA and Pigai scores were much higher than the paper-based test score given by the teacher (78.17 and 75.17 vs. 66.74;

78.07 and 80.61 vs. 66.74). Also, the standard deviations of PA (11.70 and 8.03) far exceeded those of AES (6.71 and 4.79) and the teacher (6.34 and 6.34). After teacher intervention for the second PA, the standard deviations of its scores fell from 11.70 to 8.03.

Table 1. Descriptive statistics between peer, Pigai and writing-performance.

Essay	Assessment	Mean	SD	N
First	Peer	78.17	11.70	46
	Pigai	75.17	6.71	46
	Wring-performance	66.74	6.34	46
Second	Peer	78.07	8.03	46
	Pigai	80.61	4.79	46
	Wring-performance	66.74	6.34	46

The results in Table 2 showed a moderate, significant positive partial correlation between PA and AES whilst controlling for performance level (first essay: $r(43) = 0.34$, $p = .02$; second essay: $r(43) = 0.47$, $p = .00$). Writing performance level had very little influence on the relationship between PA and AES.

Table 2. Correlations between peer and Pigai.

Essay	Type	Assessment	Pearson correlation	Sig.	Control variable	Pearson correlation	Sig.	R2
First	Peer	Pigai	0.34	0.02	Writing-performance	0.32	0.03	0.11
		Writing-performance	0.14	0.35				
	Pigai	Writing-performance	0.26	0.08				
Second	Peer	Pigai	0.47	0.00	Writing-performance	0.44	0.00	0.22
		Writing-performance	0.18	0.21				
	Pigai	Writing-performance	0.32	0.02				

Moreover, the results showed that there was no significant correlation between PA and student writing performance. But the teacher intervention can effectively improve the correlation coefficient between PA and writing performance. Also, the same results showed that there was moderate, positive partial correlation between AES and writing performance after teacher intervention ($r(43) = 0.26$, Sig. $= .08$ in the first essay, and r $(43) = 0.32$, Sig. $= .02$ in the second). In summary, teacher intervention can effectively improve the correlation coefficient of between PA and AES and writing performance.

4.2 Surveys About Students' Perceptions Towards PA and AES

Table 3 indicated that the students' attitudes toward PA and AES were often similar based on paired t-tests.

Table 3. Perceptions towards PA and AES.

Items	PA(AES)				
	Mean	SD	t-value	n	Sig.
RQ1	3.36 (3.96)	0.86 (0.74)	4.29	44	0
RQ2	3.36 (3.91)	0.86 (0.79)	4.43	44	0
RQ3	3.53 (3.89)	0.66 (0.71)	4.18	44	0
RQ4	3.56 (3.53)	0.76 (0.79)	−0.21	44	0.84
RQ5	3.70 (3.51)	0.70 (0.79)	−1.43	44	0.16
RQ6	3.42 (3.47)	0.66 (0.76)	0.42	44	0.67
RQ7	3.56 (3.62)	0.79 (0.65)	0.62	44	0.54
RQ8	3.38 (3.42)	0.61 (0.84)	0.4	44	0.69
RQ9	3.38 (3.58)	0.78 (0.75)	1.32	44	0.19
RQ10	3.58 (3.51)	0.75 (0.79)	−0.55	44	0.58

According to the first question "I regard Pigai (vs. my classmates) as the real audience", the results (Table 3) showed that the students showed more positive attitudes toward Pigai (Mean = 3.96, SD = 0.74) than PA (Mean = 3.36, SD = 0.86). Also, for questions "I highly value the comments from Pigai (vs. my classmates' comments) on my writing" and "I adopt comments from Pigai (vs. my classmates' comments) for revision," students valued Pigai comments more than from classmates' comments.

Student responses to three open-ended questions shed more light on these results. Responses to the first question "What are the factor influences the implementation of PA?" included emotional factors, writing rubric, performance level, peer relationships, PA tools, technology and the relationship between classmates.

The second question asked "Which tool is more suitable for PA?" Almost all the students believed that PA requires the support of online tools and one-third of students view a special-purpose online PA tool is necessary. Also, more than 90% of the students in the class take a view that instant feedback is more useful during essay revision

The third question asked "What are the advantages and disadvantages of implementing PA in classroom?" PA advantages included: "reduce the burden on teachers, provide instant feedback, improve learning and communication experience, share different writing ideas, help self-assessment and understand own shortcomings more comprehensively, and recognize some problems so that you can avoid writing your own text in the future." Disadvantages were: "lack of rating scale, unbalanced performance level, a bit long time and not timely enough, not know how to modify the essay and not confident to evaluate the classmates' essay".

5   Discussion and Limitations

5.1   Difference Between PA and AES

The results showed a statistically significant correlation between PA and AES, which can be used as an effective reference for assessment with appropriate teacher intervention, supporting the results of past studies [10, 11]. Human raters and AES were often consistent, though validity was greater for AES than human raters [18]. However, the peer process places the act of writing into the communicative realm and fosters a stronger sensitivity to audience for novice writers.

After the first essay, the teacher conducted PA training for the students, which improved both the mean and the standard deviation of the PA for the second essay. However, there was no significant correlation between PA and writing performance in this study, which differs from past studies [13]. But a strong rationale for PA is that giving peer reviews fosters improved writing.

Furthermore, the finding that college students in China prefer AES over PA also differs from past studies' results [22]. The qualitative data analysis results shed new light on PA in EFL writing context from several views, including writing rating scale, PA tools and feedback strategies. PA in this study is based on Scholar Network, not a specialized PA online tool, so it didn't provide instant peer review and no procedural management functions for PA.

Also qualitative analysis of student comments and questionnaire data analysis results indicated that student opinion on the effectiveness of the peer feedback was mixed, some strongly believed it benefited their learning, while others did not–similar to past studies [13].

5.2   Limitations

First, the sample size is small and the qualitative and quantitative data only reflects the learners who participated this study. Therefore, this study is more of a nature of experimental or exploratory research, and can't make strong statistical claims. Second, there were no specialized PA tools, and Scholar Network cannot provide instant peer feedback or manage the detailed PA process. And it can't provide high quality peer assessment conditions. Third, we did not explore the effectiveness of the two assessment methods regarding the content quality of the essay. Meanwhile, AES can provide immediate holistic and analytical feedback [25, 26].

Acknowledgements. The authors would like to express sincerely acknowledgements:

I am grateful to Professor Ming Ming Chiu for his constructive comments on drafting and revising this paper.

Funding.   This work was supported by [Teaching Quality and Teaching Reform Project in Guangdong Province] under Grant [number 236: No. 201, No. 218]; [Guangdong Provincial Philosophy and Social Sciences Project] under Grant [number GD18WXZ18]; and [The Ministry of Education's Higher Education Department, the second batch of industry-university collaborative education project] under Grant [number 201802083033]; [Guangdong University of Foreign Studies Postgraduate International Talents Training Innovation Project].

Appendix

Perceptions Toward Feedback

(A) Perceptions towards peer assessment from *Pigai*:
1. I regard *Pigai* as real audience.
2. I highly value the comments from *Pigai* on my writing.
3. I adopt comments from *Pigai* for revision.
4. I like writing with *Pigai*
5. I revise my writing more when I use *Pigai*.
6. Writing with *Pigai* has increased my confidence in my writing.
7. The essay scores *Pigai* gives are fair.
8. I feel *Pigai* won't avoid giving negative feedback for fear of hurting the writer.
9. I enjoy *Pigai* activities during this semester.
10. I hope my teacher in writing class will continue *Pigai* activities next semester.

(B) Perceptions towards Feedback from *Peer Evaluation*:
1. I regard my classmates as real audience.
2. I highly value my classmates' comments on my writing.
3. I adopt my classmates' comments for revision.
4. I like writing with my peer.
5. I revise my writing more when I have peer discussion.
6. Writing with my peer has increased my confidence in my writing.
7. The comments and suggestions my peer gives are fair.
8. I feel peer revision won't avoid giving negative feedback for fear of hurting the writer.
9. I enjoy peer revision activities during this semester.
10. I hope my teacher in writing class will continue peer revision activities next semester.

References

1. Berg, E.C.: The effects of trained peer response on ESL students' revision types and writing quality. J. Second Lang. Writ. **8**(3), 215–241 (1999)
2. Yang, M., Badger, R., Yu, Z.: A comparative study of peer and teacher feedback in a Chinese EFL writing class. J. Second Lang. Writ. **15**(3), 179–200 (2006)
3. Attali, Y., Burstein, J.: Automated essay scoring with e-rater®; V.2.0. J. Technol. Learn. Assess. **4**(2), i–21 (2006)
4. Dikli, S.: Automated essay scoring. Turk. Online J. Distance Educ. **7**(1), 735–738 (2006)
5. Deane, P.: On the relation between automated-essay scoring and modern views of the writing construct. Assessing Writ. **18**(1), 7–24 (2013)
6. Sommers, N.: Responding to student writing. Coll. Compos. Commun. **33**(2), 148–156 (1982)
7. Chang, C.-C., et al.: Reliability and validity of web-based portfolio peer assessment: a case study for a senior high school's students taking computer course.". Comput. Educ. **57**(1), 1306–1316 (2011)

8. Chang, C.-C., Yan, C.-F., Tseng, J.-S.: Perceived convenience in an extended technology acceptance model: mobile technology and English learning for college students. Australas. J. Educ. Technol. **28**(5), 809–826 (2012)
9. Topping, K.J.: Methodological quandaries in studying process and outcomes in peer assessment. Learn. Instr. **20**(4), 339–343 (2010)
10. Falchikov, N.: Product comparisons and process benefits of collaborative peer group and self-assessments. Assess. Eval. High. Educ, **11**(2), 146–166 (1986)
11. Falchikov, N., Goldfinch, J.: Student peer assessment in higher education: a meta-analysis comparing peer and teacher marks. Rev. Educ. Res. **70**(3), 287–322 (2000)
12. Topping, K.: Peer assessment between students in colleges and universities. Rev. Educ. Res. **68**(3), 249–276 (1998)
13. Meek, S.E.M., Blakemore, L., Marks, L.: Is peer review an appropriate form of assessment in a MOOC? Student participation and performance in formative peer review. Assess. Eval. High. Educ. **42**(6), 1000–1013 (2017)
14. Hovardas, T., Tsivitanidou, O.E., Zacharia, Z.C.: Peer versus expert feedback: an investigation of the quality of peer feedback among secondary school students. Comput. Educ. **71**, 133–152 (2014)
15. Tsai, C.-C., Lin, S.S.J., Yuan, S.-M.: Developing science activities through a networked peer assessment system. Comput. Educ. **38**(1–3), 241–252 (2002)
16. Hanrahan, S.J., Isaacs, G.: Assessing self-and peer-assessment: the students' views. High. Educ. Res. Dev. **20**(1), 53–70 (2001)
17. Fang, Y.: Perceptions of the computer-assisted writing program among EFL college learners. Educ. Technol. Soc. **13**(3), 246–256 (2010)
18. Enright, M.K., Quinlan, T.: Complementing human judgment of essays written by English language learners with e-rater® scoring. Lang. Test. **27**(3), 317–334 (2010)
19. Chen, C.-F.E., Cheng, W.-Y.E.C.: Beyond the design of automated writing evaluation: pedagogical practices and perceived learning effectiveness in EFL writing classes. Lang. Learn. Technol. **12**(2), 94–112 (2008)
20. Wang, Y.-J., Shang, H.-F., Briody, P.: Exploring the impact of using automated writing evaluation in English as a foreign language university students' writing. Comput. Assist. Lang. Learn. **26**(3), 234–257 (2013)
21. Roscoe, R.D., et al.: Presentation, expectations, and experience: Sources of student perceptions of automated writing evaluation. Comput. Hum. Behav. **70**, 207–221 (2017)
22. Lai, Y.-h.: Which do students prefer to evaluate their essays: peers or computer program. Br. J. Edu. Technol. **41**(3), 432–454 (2010)
23. Jones, I., Wheadon, C.: Peer assessment using comparative and absolute judgement. Stud. Educ. Eval. **47**, 93–101 (2015)
24. Yu, F.-Y., Wu, C.-P.: Different identity revelation modes in an online peer-assessment learning environment: effects on perceptions toward assessors, classroom climate and learning activities. Comput. Educ. **57**(3), 2167–2177 (2011)
25. Hoon, T.: Online automated essay assessment: potentials for writing development (2010). Accessed 9 August 2006
26. Yeh, Y.-L., Liou, H.-C., Yu, Y.-T.: The influence of automatic essay evaluation and bilingual concordancing on EFL students. English Teach. Learn. **31**(1), 117–160 (2007)

Dimensions of Learning Organization in Relation to Learning Time – Cross-Sectional Study at Secondary Schools from the Czech Republic

Vaclav Zubr[(✉)]

Faculty of Informatics and Management, University of Hradec Kralove, Rokitanskeho 62, 500 03 Hradec Kralove, Czech Republic
vaclav.zubr@uhk.cz

Abstract. The measurement of the learning organization with the Dimensions of Learning Organization Questionnaire (DLOQ) hasn't been dealt with very much in the Czech Republic. This study's aim was to conduct a questionnaire survey with DLOQ at secondary schools in the Czech Republic and to evaluate the time devoted to learning in these organizations. Respondents were approached via e-mail addresses obtained from the rehearsals of secondary schools in the Czech Republic. A total of 121 respondents the Czech Republic participated in the study. Most of them were employees aged 51–60 (47.11%), university graduates (95.04%) and managers (71.90%). When comparing the learning time, more than 40% of respondents spend 11–20 h per month with learning. Using t-test among the respondents with different learning time, a statistically significant difference (1–10 h per month versus 36 and more hours per month: p = 0.049, 21–35 h per month vs. more than 36 h per month: p = 0.012) was found.

Keywords: Learning organization · Secondary schools · Learning time

1 Introduction

In many organizations, we encounter the human resource development model, where education is a separate function. If we talk about a learning organization concept, learning in the organization is supported [1]. Employees in a learning organization are expected to learn, plan future skills, actions and risks and deal with issues, the learning organization concept is supported e.g. by teamwork, sharing information and learning communities [2, 3]. The core activity of the learning organization is organizational learning. Organizational learning can be characterized as a complicated, unplanned process that is alert and effective, interactive and dynamic, continuous and persistent, developing and growing and influenced by the knowledge base or cultural resources [4]. A part of organizational learning could be personalized and adaptive learning.

In the Czech Republic, there were 1,297 high schools providing day-to-day education in the school year 2017/2018, where 38,115 teachers were employed [5]. Schools

© Springer Nature Switzerland AG 2020
E. Popescu et al. (Eds.): SETE 2019, LNCS 11984, pp. 30–35, 2020.
https://doi.org/10.1007/978-3-030-38778-5_4

as a learning organization create a comprehensive teaching and learning environment, support initiatives and risk taking, provide opportunities for continuing professional development, enhance quality work, regularly review all aspects that affect schoolwork, and develop shared goals [6].

In the past, Watkins and Marsick defined 7 dimensions of learning organization, including: creating opportunities for systematic learning, supporting polling and dialogue, encouraging team learning and collaboration, creating systems for capturing and sharing learning, motivating people to a collective vision, system connecting and strategic leadership for learning. The Dimensions of learning organization questionnaire by Watkins and Marsick is often used to measure a learning organization's level, the questions focus on the above-mentioned dimensions [7]. This questionnaire can be used to evaluate an organization as a learning organization. The original version of the questionnaire is written in English, but it is possible to translate the questionnaire into other languages. In order to maintain the questionnaire's validity, return translation, expert review and the Cronbach alpha coefficient should be performed to ensure that the reliability of the dimensions is not significantly lower than the reliability of the current validation of the work [8].

In the Czech Republic, only one study with DLOQ has been conducted so far, focusing on small and medium-sized companies in the IT sector [9]. Following the study already conducted, this study's aim is to conduct a questionnaire survey with DLOQ at secondary schools in the Czech Republic. The research question is to evaluate the time spent learning in these organizations.

2 Methodology

A cross-sectional study was conducted in January 2019 via an electronic questionnaire survey. Altogether 1,304 secondary schools from all of the Czech Republic's 14 regions were approached. The individual schools were addressed via e-mail addresses obtained from the www.stredniskoly.cz secondary school database, where these addresses were listed as contact addresses. Therefore, the principals of schools and secretariat school staff were primarily addressed. The survey deliberately did not involve other staff from individual schools due to ambiguous data evaluation. From all respondents contacted, 91 emails were returned due to the absence of the given email address, 1 respondent directly refused to participate in the survey.

For the survey purposes, a shortened 21-question version of the DLOQ questionnaire was used. This questionnaire was translated into Czech and back into English by two independent translators to ensure the questionnaire's validity. At the same time, the Cronbach coefficient of reliability was calculated using IBM SPSS Statistics Version 24. The Alpha coefficient ranged from 0.620 to 0.854 for each dimension. Overall, the coefficient value was 0.941. The calculated values of the Cronbach coefficient appear to be satisfactory (a coefficient higher than 0.7 is "satisfactory") [10]. Individual dimensions were assessed by the respondents on the 6-point Likert scale.

The data obtained were analyzed using Microsoft Excel 2016 and IBM SPSS Statistics Version 24 using descriptive statistics, parametric and non-parametric assays at confidence levels $\alpha = 0.01$ and $\alpha = 0.05$.

3 Results

Altogether 1,304 secondary schools were addressed in the Czech Republic. In total 121 respondents participated in the study (9.28%).

The study was attended in total by 45 (37.19%) men and 76 (62.81%) women aged 25 to 70 years. A total of 115 respondents had university education, 4 respondents had secondary education, 1 respondent had higher vocational education and 1 respondent had primary education. Only 1 school represented an organization with more than 250 employees, the schools with fewer than 50 employees (a total of 73 schools) and schools employing up to 250 employees (47 schools) were represented the most. If we evaluate representation of schools by their type, secondary vocational schools (55.37%), grammar schools (36.36%) and secondary vocational practice schools (8.26%) were represented. Altogether, the study was attended by 87 (71.90%) executives and 34 (28.10%) tertiary staff. The majority were respondents who worked in the organization up to 10 years (39 respondents), followed by 11–20 years (33 respondents). On average, employees in organizations work 18.32 years, the shortest period of practice was 0.5 years, the longest was 49 years.

When comparing senior executives and executives, the senior executives are more involved in education in relation to employment. There is no statistically significant difference between common and senior employees ($p = 0.132$, $\alpha = 0.05$, t-test). If we compare employees from grammar schools and other secondary schools, there is no statistically significant difference ($p = 0.415$, $\alpha = 0.05$, t-test). At the same time, there is no statistically significant difference in the significance level 0.05 between employees of organizations with fewer than 50 employees and employees of organizations with 51 to 250 employees ($p = 0.495$). There is no statistically significant difference in relation to the time of education between employees who work in the organization for less than 10 years and employees who work in the organization for more than 10 years ($p = 0.326$) (Table 1).

Table 1. Comparison of respondents' responses with different intensity of education (own processing)

Hours a month	Average of D1	Average of D2	Average of D3	Average of D4	Average of D5	Average of D6	Average of D7
0	2.67	1.67	3.00	3.33	4.33	3.33	3.00
1–10	4.46	4.11	4.18	3.95	4.63	4.19	4.50
11–20	4.50	4.32	4.40	4.16	4.79	4.60	4.83
21–35	4.18	3.67	4.09	3.72	4.60	4.35	4.22
36 or more	4.83	4.50	4.50	4.28	4.50	4.72	4.44

If we compare the average dimensions assessment among respondents who do not learn at all and those who learn hour and more per a month, dimension assessment is usually higher with the time of learning. When performing a t-test, there is a statistically significant difference between the respondents who spend 1–10 h a month with learning and the respondents who learn for more than 36 h a month ($p = 0.049$) at the significance level of 0.05. At the same time, there was a statistically significant difference found via the t-test between respondents who learn for 21–35 h a month and respondents who learn for more than 36 h a month ($p = 0.012$).

4 Discussion

Many authors throughout the world [11–17] deal with introducing the learning organization concept in organizations of different types. In many cases, these authors use the DLOQ questionnaire to measure the concept of a learning organization [12–19]. Since no further studies with DLOQ were carried out in the Czech Republic, this study's aim was to conduct a questionnaire survey at secondary schools in the Czech Republic and evaluate the time devoted to learning in these organizations.

A total of 121 respondents from Czech Republic secondary schools were included in this study. Although the return on questionnaires was relatively low (9.28%), the number of respondents was comparable to other studies [15, 16]. Overall, 62.81% of women and 37.19% of men participated in the study. Percentage representation of women and men in the study in the Czech Republic corresponds directly to the general share of women and men in education, where according to the OECD the share of women in the secondary degree of education is 63% [20].

Most respondents were 51–60 years old (47.11%) and 41–50 years old (23.97%). This corresponds to the survey results of the Czech School Inspectorate of 2016, whereby almost 70% of the principals of the studied secondary schools are over 50 years of age and the average age of the teachers in the schools is 46.5 years [21].

The respondents who work in the organization for less than 10 years (32.23%) have the largest representation. One could expect that these respondents will be mainly young employees coming to work after school and those who are looking for a suitable job for them at a younger age. Looking closer at the data, it is interesting that these are respondents of different age groups (from the age of 25 to 70). This result may point to a possible large fluctuation in education staff.

Teachers are expected to devote more time to education than headteachers (due to a greater share of frontal teaching). It was found that most respondents (33.06%) devote 11–20 h to education per month. Through the t-test, a statistically significant difference was not found in relation to education at the significance level of 0.05 between the position in the job, the type of organization and the time of employment in the organization. The personalized and adaptive learning of teachers could be facilitated by using learning phone applications or through online webinars.

When assessing the dimensions of a learning organization in relation to the time spent on education, there is a statistically significant difference between respondents who spend 1–10 h a month or 21–35 h a month and respondents who learn for more than 36 h a month. Compared to the same study from the Czech Republic conducted in the IT sector, the results are higher in many dimensions [22].

A relatively small number of respondents who participated in the study may be considered as limiting the study. In the future, it would be appropriate to carry out the same study on a larger number of respondents.

5 Conclusion

This study focused mainly on the learning time analysis at secondary schools in the Czech Republic. The education results in relation to employment seem satisfactory in respondents in education in the Czech Republic. The interdependence between learning time and dimensions assessment of learning organization was demonstrated by t-test. In this way, it can be appreciated that the period of education has a positive impact on the assessment of the individual dimensions of the learning organization (and therefore the development of the organization as a learning organization).

Although the education of employees in secondary schools in the Czech Republic has been assessed as satisfactory, it would be beneficial to access new learning methods for supporting the learning of employees. Also, it is necessary to carry out similar studies in other sectors in the future to better compare the results and to design a more complex solution applicable to more than one discipline.

Acknowledgement. The paper was written with the support of the specific project 2019 grant "Determinants of Cognitive Processes Impacting the Work Performance" granted by the University of Hradec Kralove, Czech Republic and thanks to help of students František Hašek and Jan Petružálek.

References

1. Birdthistle, N.: Family Businesses and the Learning Organisation: A Guide to Transforming the Family Business into a Learning Organisation. VDM Verlag Dr. Müller Aktiengesellschaft & Co (2009)
2. Marquardt, M.J.: Building the Learning Organization. Davies-Black Publishing, Palo Alto (2002)
3. Zubr, V., Mohelska, H., Sokolova, M.: Factors with positive and negative impact on learning organization. In: Jedlicka, P., Maresova, P., Soukal, I. (eds.) Hradec Economic Days 2017, Double-Blind Peer-Reviewed Proceedings of the International Scientific Conference Hradec Economic Days 2017, vol. 7, no. 1, pp. 980–985. Gaudeamus, Hradec Kralove (2017)
4. Saadat, V., Saadat, Z.: Organizational learning as a key role of organizational success. Procedia Soc. Behav. Sci. **230**, 219–225 (2016)
5. Czech Statistical Office. https://www.czso.cz/documents/10180/61508174/2300421845.pdf/c5380c95-eb6d-4160-8ec3-920deaf76b00?version=1.2. Accessed 28 May 2019
6. Kools, M., Stoll, L.: What Makes a School a Learning Organisation? OECD Publishing, Paris (2016)
7. Watkins, K.E., Marsick, V.J.: Sculpting the Learning Organization: Lessons in the Art and Science of Systematic Change. Jossey-Bass, San Francisco (1993)
8. Watkins, K.E., O'Neil, J.: The dimensions of the learning organization questionnaire (the DLOQ): a nontechnical manual. Adv. Dev. Hum. Res. **15**(2), 133–147 (2013)
9. Zubr, V.: Dimension of a learning organisation in the IT sector in the Czech Republic – case study. In: Hao, T., Chen, W., Xie, H., Nadee, W., Lau, R. (eds.) SETE 2018. LNCS, vol. 11284, pp. 107–116. Springer, Cham (2018). https://doi.org/10.1007/978-3-030-03580-8_12
10. Institute for Digital Research and Education. https://stats.idre.ucla.edu/spss/faq/what-does-cronbachs-alpha-mean/. Accessed 1 June 2019

11. Marsick, V., Watkins, K.: Demonstrating the value of an organization's learning culture: the dimensions of the learning organization questionnaire. Adv. Dev. Hum. Res. **5**(2), 132–151 (2003)

12. Cierna, H., Sujova, E., Habek, P., Horska, E., Kapsdorferova, Z.: Learning organization at higher education institutions in the EU: proposal for implementing philosophy of learning organization – results from research. Qual. Quant. **51**, 1305–1320 (2017)

13. Reese, S.: Unlearning and the learning organization: revisited and expanded. Learn. Organ. **25**(3), 210–212 (2018)

14. Palos, R., Stancovici, V.V.: Learning in organization. Learn. Organ. **23**(1), 2–22 (2016)

15. Abo Al Ola, L.M.: The availability of Dimensions of Learning Organizations Questionnaire (DLOQ) in educational college at Taif University from the perspective of employees. J. Educ. Psychol. Sci. **18**(1), 447–487 (2017)

16. Nazari, K., Pihie, Z.: Assessing learning organization dimensions and demographic factors in technical and vocational colleges in Iran. Int. J. Bus. Soc. Sci. **3**(3), 210–219 (2012)

17. Voolaid, K., Ehrlich, Ü.: Organizational learning of higher education institutions: the case of Estonia. Learn. Organ. **24**(5), 340–354 (2017)

18. Mohamed Ali, M., Abdulhamed, K.R., Aljamoudi, S.S.: The dimensions of the learning organization in Omani school from employees point of view. Int. J. Sci. Technol. Res. **4**(11), 267–271 (2015)

19. Park, J.H.: Validation of Senge's learning organization model with teachers of vocational high schools at the Seoul Megalopolis. Asia Pac. Educ. Rev. **9**(3), 270–284 (2008)

20. OECD. https://www.oecd-ilibrary.org/docserver/54f0ef95-en.pdf?expires=1560189519& id=id&accname=guest&checksum=7D33376875CDF7E59C3EE6B48B05A4CE. Accessed 29 May 2019

21. Czech School Inspection. http://www.csicr.cz/html/VZCSI2015_2016/html5/index.html?& locale=CSY. Accessed 3 June 2019

22. Zubr, V., Mohelska, H.: Learning time analysis – case study in the IT sector in the Czech Republic. In: Al-Sharhan, A., et al. (eds.) I3E: Conference on e-Business, e-Services and e-Society 2018, LNCS, vol. 11195, pp. 21–29. Springer, Heidelberg (2018). https://doi.org/10.1007/978-3-030-02131-3_3

How Much Is Online Community Engaged in Learning Content? Case of World Top Universities' Facebook

Pavel Bachmann$^{(\boxtimes)}$

University of Hradec Kralove, Rokitanskeho 62, 50003 Hradec Kralove, Czech Republic
pavel.bachmann@uhk.cz

Abstract. Social media (SM) has become a part of everyday life, including higher education and its learning environment. Therefore, this study aims on understanding of content published on SM, its learning impact, as well as on identification of relevant level of community engagement. Research sample used official Facebook sites of six world top universities, specifically posts (N = 120) communicated during November 2018 were investigated in detail. A new scale, specifically designed for this study, was designed to capture a learning potential of content communicated on the SM. An analysis oriented on main characteristics of engagement: its responsiveness measured by number of "likes" and other available symbols, its involvement measured by number of comments, its virality, measured by number of sharings, and finally its total engagement expressed as the sum of preceding characteristics. Several interesting results are provided in the study: the research is the most frequent topic communicated by top universities; different content strategies are taken by universities to engage their communities; and different engagement levels exist according to the university as well as according to the content published on its Facebook site.

Keywords: Online community · Higher education · Educational content · Social Media · Facebook

1 Introduction

Social media are not only technical tools [1]; they are rather collections of online communities, people and human interactions. Communities that are ready to be engaged, ready to discuss, and ready to learn and to be educated. There are numerous studies on use of Social Media (SM) in higher education environment [2–5].

Despite of rather general acceptance of SM tools in academic environment and even its implementation in learning processes [3, 6–9] some negative or more complex comments on SM use in the field are discussed also. Manca and Ranieri [4, 10] in their recent studies documented that there are still several barriers for use of SM in academic environment as cultural resistance, pedagogical issues, or institutional constraints. Application of SM in this learning environment depends mainly on a field of discipline and the personality of teacher. Moreover, in 2015 Alt [11] introduced a scale reflecting psychological behavior of undergraduate students including SM engagement, fear of missing

© Springer Nature Switzerland AG 2020
E. Popescu et al. (Eds.): SETE 2019, LNCS 11984, pp. 36–45, 2020.
https://doi.org/10.1007/978-3-030-38778-5_5

out, and academic motivation. Sharma, Joshi, and Sharma [12] predicted determinants that affect students' intention towards academic use of Facebook. Results showed that resource sharing is the most influential determinant in the decision to use Facebook in higher education, followed by perceived usefulness, perceived enjoyment, collaboration and social influence.

Nowadays, various research studies confirm a positive impact of SM use on the learning processes of higher education [8, 9, 13]. Sobaih, Moustafa, Ghandforoush, et al. [8] stress out that SM could be an innovative and effective tool for teaching and learning. Moreover, Neier and Zayer [5] demonstrated in their study an openness for use SM in higher education and interactive and information motivation on the side of students. Similarly, Bozanta and Mardikyan [6] underline that perceived ease of use is a predictor of perceived usefulness which implies SM tools can be successfully used for educational purposes. SM improves peer interaction and course engagement of students and also students' interaction with faculty members. Also, peer interaction and course engagement have positive significant effect on collaborative learning. Megele [13] in her paper examined ways how to enhance students' engagement and learning through embedding social media technologies into the academic curriculum as a learning and assessment strategy and showed that such based action learning model expands the interrelational dimensions of students' learning; mainly increased the students' engagement and the depth and breadth of their learning.

Even with numerous quantities of research on investigation SM and learning, the lack of studies aiming on the description of current level of student' engagement with existing SM used by universities, was found. As a research gap was identified and from the context mentioned above, to identify an engagement of university community in online collaborative learning, the following research questions are investigated:

1. What learning content and how much of this content is offered on Facebook sites of universities?
2. Does Facebook community (a) responsiveness, or (b) involvement, or (c) virality, and (d) total engagement differ in top world universities?
3. Does Facebook community (a) responsiveness, or (b) involvement, or (c) virality, and (d) total engagement differ according to educational/non-educational content type of posts?

2 Materials and Methods

2.1 Sample

Facebook sites and specifically published posts of top six universities according to Times Higher Education World University Ranking 2018 were subject for detailed analysis. Since these universities are solely American or British a similar learning conditions and backgrounds can be expected. Twenty posts published from Nov 30, 2018 backwards on each university official Facebook site were studied in relation to its content, responsiveness (reactions), involvement (comments), and virality (sharings). The month of November was selected as the academic terms are in progress in the all universities investigated. Universities published these twenty posts during the period of 15 days, in average. The quantity of posts was limited due to the high time-consuming coding of the content.

The sampled universities characteristics varied in the number of full-time students enrolled (the biggest Harvard with over 22,000 students vs the smallest Caltech with over 2,000 of students), but namely in size of fan' and follower' base, where the differences are even bigger (Harvard with 5 mio of fans vs Caltech with 380,000 students). Therefore, later, the size of fan base is taken into account, when presenting the results. The list of universities with more detailed characteristics is available in Table 1.

Table 1. Facebook sites of top universities: engagement, fan', and follower' bases

Rank	Name	Number of students	Ownership	Fan' base	Follower' base
1	Univ. of Oxford	20,631	Public	3,610,779	3,607,384
2	Univ. of Cambridge	19,203	Public	2,124,811	2,128,944
3	Caltech[a]	2,239	Private	378,555	377,920
3	Stanford Univ.	16,135	Private	1,273,421	1,265,202
5	MIT[b]	11,145	Private	1,134,207	1,138,346
6	Harvard Univ.	22,727	Private	5,320,978	5,284,886

[a]California Institute of Technology, [b]Massachusetts Institute of Technology

In addition, the intentions of using Facebook site by the university were studied. All sampled universities have placed a Facebook site link on their main webpage, three of them (Oxford, Cambridge and Caltech) with "connect with us" challenge. Two universities stated their intention of site existence in the "about" section: Caltech institute considers its site to be "a place to encourage curious, thoughtful dialogue about topics related to scientific discovery and the Caltech experience", Oxford site intent is to publish news, events, and admissions. The other universities used this section for presenting an ethical code of conduct for visitors.

2.2 Method

Content analysis of published Facebook posts was chosen as the main research method of the study. This kind of investigation is a part of Internet-mediated research defined by Hewson [14]. Only one coder was used for collection of the data to avoid distortion of results thanks to different way of coding. Moreover, a new construct for measuring the nature of content published was developed. The construct design reflected both, the marketing needs of higher institutions on one side, and the educational and learning mission, on the other side. Classification of content types of posts is depicted in Fig. 1.

More precise explanation of construct details and definition of individual categories and examples of posts is formulated and available in Table 2.

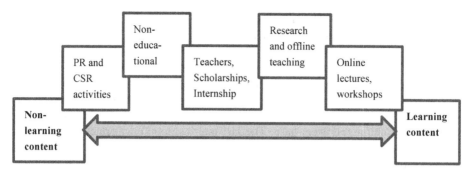

Fig. 1. A continuum of content communicated by higher education institutions

Table 2. Responsiveness, involvement, and virality of world top universities

Impact scale	Post content	Examples of posts
1 – the weakest impact	Public relations and social responsibility activities, informational and fun messages	Information on admissions. Position in higher education rankings. Appeal for alumni' financial donation, New/renovated facilities or buildings, Happy Thanksgiving
2 – moderate impact	Events supporting academia/students teamwork (without learning events)	Graduation/matriculation ceremonies, anniversaries, celebrations. Exhibitions, concerts, balls, sport events. Clubs and associations events
3 – average impact	Information on teachers, students, fellowships, scholarships and internships. New published research outputs	Rhodes scholarship. Teachers' testimonies/ Presentation of new/guest lecturers. New books/research publication
4 – significant impact	Research findings presentation, information on teaching events (offline). Student projects	Research findings as palm oil use issue, Mars mission participation and many others. First film in Babylonian language. New toys development by students
5 – the strongest impact	Online educational events (live broadcasting, etc.)	Lectures (live broadcasting), participation in research

Measuring level of engagement online communities on SM is a complex activity, which requires introduction of several specific metrics. For the purpose of this study, a set of metrics used by Bachmann [15] was taken to measure an engagement impact and modified for the needs of education. The first metrics - responsiveness (also called popularity in other studies) – can bring a better reflection of students' engagement than only base of Facebook fans or followers. In 2016, the five new reactions as "love", "haha", "wow", "sad", and "angry" were introduced besides the original "like". New responses on the post published enable us to better recognize the views and needs of the users. The second metrics - involvement is expressed by the number of comments. Writing a comment requires much higher participation, consideration and thinking of students (or other users) than a simple one-click reaction. Virality, expressed through the number of posts shared, is a metrics with a high impact on the expansion of communication across the other sites. In this way, the communication can affect much broader auditorium than just page fans and/or followers base. The last metrics, total engagement rate is than sum of preceding three metrics. Although, in practice the weight of latter two metrics is multiplied at least three times, due to its much higher real engagement, in this study and for better understanding of results, the metrics will be only a single sum of the metrics mentioned.

The statistical significance of differences in engagement characteristics according to the university as well as the content communicated to the public was analyzed with the use of MS Excel and one-way analysis of variance.

3 Results

3.1 Universities and Engagement

Responsiveness, Involvement, and Virality of University Facebook Posts
The highest responsiveness per one post was found in Harvard which reached nearly 1,500 reactions per post. The more precise metric is provided after including the size of relevant online community. Thus, relative highest engagement of community was recorded in MIT and Stanford (over 400), followed by Harvard and Caltech (over 250).

Surprisingly, an involvement rate differed from the previous type of engagement. Absolutely, the highest involvement was recorded in two universities: Harvard and Oxford (with nearly 50 comments per post). Interestingly, the rest of universities reached maximally 20 comments per post. However, in relation to online community, the highest involvement reached Stanford with nearly 16 comments; then other two universities (Oxford and MIT) reached over 10 comments.

Similarly, the differences among institutions were found in relation to virality of posts published. The highest percentage of posts shared was found in Harvard which is probably mainly determined by its largest fan' base. In relation to the fan base the posts are shared the most by MIT' (77 sharings) and Stanford' community (54 sharings).

The results analysis confirmed statistically significant differences among universities in all measured variables. Very strong differences exist in total engagement (p-value < 0.001), number of reactions as likes and other symbols (p-value < 0.001), and virality (p-value < 0.001). Detailed results are available in Table 3.

Total Engagement of University Facebook Posts
Overall, the posts published by Harvard have the highest reach, where one post gets an attention of at least 2,000 of users. However, an actual engagement can be determined by the size of Harvard fan base. Since the fan base was developed during the years and to avoid distortion of results, we should relate an engagement to the fan base size. After this,

Table 3. Responsiveness, involvement, and virality of world top universities (N = 120)

(Ranking) University Name	Likes etc. per post		Comments per post		Sharings per post	
	Abs.	Fans[a]	Abs.	Fans[a]	Abs.	Fans[a]
(1) Univ. of Oxford	513	142	47	13	58	16
(2) Univ. of Cambridge	291	137	13	6	48	23
(3) Caltech	98	259	3	8	13	34
(3) Stanford Univ.	530	416	20	16	69	54
(5) MIT	509	449	13	12	87	77
(6) Harvard Univ.	1,496	281	50	9	172	32

[a]per 1 mio of fans

the highest total engagement was found in MIT (702 engaged users per post) and Stanford (610). The medium engagement exists in Harvard and Caltech (nearly 400 users). The lowest level of engagement was found in communities of British Oxford and Cambridge. The results analysis confirmed statistically significant differences among universities in both total engagement per post (p-value < 0.001) as well as total engagement per fan base (p-value = 0.0009). Detailed results are available in Table 4.

Table 4. Facebook sites of top universities: engagement, fan', and follower' bases (N = 120)

(Ranking) Name	Total engagement per post	Total engagement per fan base[a]
(1) Univ. of Oxford	781	216
(2) Univ. of Cambridge	461	217
(3) Caltech	143	378
(3) Stanford Univ.	777	610
(5) MIT	796	702
(6) Harvard Univ.	2,112	397

[a]In mio of fans

3.2 Engagement and Content of Posts

Content Communicated by Universities

Content analysis of posts showed that there are two universities publishing rather learning content; the University of Oxford and Caltech (avg. impact score around 3.5 pts. on 1 to 5 scale). Conversely, a Harvard University can be marked as rather publishing marketing content towards their online community on Facebook. Interestingly, more than half of published posts (51.7%) contained presentation of research findings. These posts included various research insights and were frequently commented, also. Content communicated by universities is summarized in Table 5.

Table 5. Content of posts published by universities (in %) (N = 120)

Content of posts	Oxford	Cambridge	Caltech	Stanford	MIT	Harvard	% of total
1- PR and information messages	15	35	10	30	40	50	30.0
2- Events (without learning ones)	0	10	10	0	0	5	4.2
3- Instructors, Fellowship, Scholarship	10	15	5	20	10	15	12.5
4- Research findings, students' projects	65	40	75	50	50	30	51.7
5- Online teaching	10	0	0	0	0	0	1.7

Content Type and Engagement

The highest responsiveness was found in not educational events with the moderate learning impact; the post of this content type was assigned a "like" or other symbol by more almost 900 community reactions in average. Very high responsiveness rate was identified for PR and informational messages (787 symbols) and online teaching activities (712).

Online teaching was also the content type of posts with highest involvement with over one hundred (110) comments per post. However, as there were only two posts oriented on online teaching, no conclusions should be made on this basis. Excluding online teaching, the results rather showed that community comments more marketing content than the learning one. University events with not educational orientation can be considered as the most viral content type of posts (136 sharings per post).

The results analysis confirmed statistically significant differences according to content of posts only for number of likes and other reactions (p-value = 0.030); an engagement expressed by comments and sharings was not found as statistically significant. Detailed results of engagement characteristics related to content type are summarized in Table 6.

Table 6. Content type and its responsiveness, involvement, and virality (N = 120)

Content of the post	Likes, etc.		Comments		Sharings	
	Abs.	Per post	Abs.	Per post	Abs.	Per post
1- PR and information messages	28,324	786.8	1,038	28.8	2,856	79.3
2- Events (without learning ones)	4,474	894.8	202	40.4	680	136
3- Instructors, Fellow- & Scholarship	9,436	629.1	266	17.7	789	52.6
4- Research findings, Stud. projects	25,101	404.9	1,318	21.3	4,341	70.0
5- Online teaching	1,423	711.5	220	110.0	246	123
In total	68,758	573.0	3,044	25.4	8,912	74.3

Total Engagement

The level of total engagement complies with the levels already found for previous engagement characteristics. The results analysis confirmed only weak statistical difference significant on 0.1 level in total engagement according to the content of posts (p-value = 0.094). All the details are available in Table 7.

Table 7. Structure of content in relation to its learning potential (N = 120)

Content of posts	Number of posts	Total engagement	Total engagement per post
1- PR and information messages	35	32,218	895
2- Events (without learning ones)	6	5,356	1,071
3- Instructors, Fellowship, Scholarship	15	10,491	699
4- Research findings, students' projects	62	30,760	496
5- Online teaching	2	1,889	945
In total	120	68,758	573

4 Discussion and Conclusions

The presented study brings several inspiring findings, especially the following:

1. Research oriented content is the most frequently communicated topic of examined universities; over 50% of all posts were related to research progress or presentation of research findings. Despite of this, the different publishing content strategies exist among universities. For example, three quarters of Oxford University posts are associated either with research, thus content with significant learning impact. On the other hand, Harvard University posts are mainly oriented on public relations and informational messages and only less than one third of posts have stronger learning impact.
2. The highest relative engagement (per fan base) was recorded in American universities MIT and Stanford, while the lowest in two British universities Oxford and Cambridge. MIT reached more than 3-times higher relative engagement level than it was found for Cambridge.
3. Significant differences in engagement exist among universities included in the sample; it is obvious in both: an absolute number of people attracted by the posts published as well as a relative percentage of the Facebook community engaged. Harvard university works with community of over 5 mio fans and followers, which is 14-times higher than Caltech online community. However, an engagement rate of both universities is about the same (5% higher in favour of Harvard) referring to part of community engaged.
4. The highest overall engagement and the level of its partial characteristics as responsiveness, involvement, and virality was recorded for events related posts communicated on the Facebook site. An engagement of research related posts is not much different with public relations messages. Importantly and comparing to other contents, the research topics are more tend to be commented and shared, than only liking.

Obviously, there are some limitations of the study, which should be discussed. At first, although the number of posts is enough for collection of some findings in the field, its increase would make given values more trustworthy as well as allow more conclusions, mainly in relation to online teaching. At second, including top universities exclusively enable reaching insightful data and enough area to examine engagement in all its aspects. However, and as was already mentioned, a real student' engagement in marketing/learning content could be distorted by wider social roles of the universities.

Nowadays, the world top universities play much broader social role than only providing a service to their actual students. As these institutions are offline and online research leaders, their community is much wider, including students and alumni relatives and friends, private and public research and development agencies, researchers and many other interested groups. Some implications for these communities and institution communication strategies can be mentioned. As the highest engagement was found in universities where half of their communication were posts related to research and student project, thus this topic should be included in the university's communication strategy. Simultaneously, an online teaching reached very high level of comments and sharings, so we recommend to work with this theme as well.

The next research should expand the sample in both, an extent of posts published as well as the number of sampled universities. As SM are becoming omnipresent communication platform, including learning, the higher attention should be paid to investigation of relationships among individual engagement characteristics and the type of content communicated.

References

1. King, P.: Social networks: getting your organization working for them! In: Geier Jr., P.H., Greenfield, J.M., Hart, T., MacLaughlin, S. (eds.) Internet Management for Nonprofits: Strategies, Tools and Trade Secrets, p. XIII. Wiley, Hoboken (2010)
2. Cerna, M., Svobodova, L.: Current social media landscape. In: Conference Proceedings on Efficiency and Responsibility in Education 2013, Prague, Czech Republic (2013)
3. Lam, J.-H., Ma, W.W.K.: When and how does learning satisfy? Working collaboratively online with a clear purpose. Int. J. Innov. Learn. **23**(4), 400–415 (2018)
4. Manca, S., Ranieri, M.: "Yes for sharing, no for teaching!": social media in academic practices. Internet High. Educ. **29**, 63–74 (2016)
5. Neier, S., Zayer, L.T.: Students' perceptions and experiences of social media in higher education. J. Mark. Educ. **37**(3), 133–143 (2015)
6. Bozanta, A., Mardikyan, S.: The effects of social media use on collaborative learning: a case of Turkey. Turk. Online J. Distance Educ. **18**(1), 96–110 (2017)
7. Choo, E.K., Ranney, M.L., Chan, T.M., et al.: Twitter as a tool for communication and knowledge exchange in academic medicine: a guide for sceptics and novices. Med. Teach. **37**(5), 411–416 (2015)
8. Sobaih, A.E., Moustafa, M.A., Ghandforoush, P., Khan, M.: To use or not to use? Social media in higher education in developing countries. Comput. Hum. Behav. **58**, 296–305 (2016)
9. Zheng, B.B., Niiya, M., Warschauer, M.: Wikis and collaborative learning in higher education. Technol. Pedagog. Educ. **24**(3), 357–374 (2015)
10. Manca, S., Ranieri, M.: Facebook and the others. Potentials and obstacles of social media for teaching in higher education. Comput. Educ. **95**, 216–230 (2016)
11. Alt, D.: College students' academic motivation, media engagement and fear of missing out. Comput. Hum. Behav. **49**, 111–119 (2015)
12. Sharma, S.K., Joshi, A., Sharma, H.: A multi-analytical approach to predict the Facebook usage in higher education. Comput. Hum. Behav. **55**, 340–353 (2016). Part A

13. Megele, C.: eABLE: embedding social media in academic curriculum as a learning and assessment strategy to enhance students learning and e-professionalism. Innov. Educ. Teach. Int. **52**(4), 414–425 (2015)
14. Hewson, C.: Gathering data on the Internet. Qualitative approaches and possibilities for mixed methods research. In: The Oxford Handbook of Internet Psychology. Oxford University Press, Oxford (2007)
15. Bachmann, P.: Citizens' engagement on regional governments' Facebook sites. Empirical research from Central Europe. In: Conference Proceedings of Hradec Economic Days 2019, vol. 1, pp. 6–14. University of Hradec Kralove (2019)

HandLeVR: Action-Oriented Learning in a VR Painting Simulator

Raphael Zender[1]([✉]), Pia Sander[2], Matthias Weise[1], Miriam Mulders[2], Ulrike Lucke[1], and Michael Kerres[2]

[1] University of Potsdam, August-Bebel-Str. 89, 14482 Potsdam, Germany
{raphael.zender,matthias.weise,ulrike.lucke}@uni-potsdam.de
[2] Universität Duisburg-Essen, Universitätsstr. 2, 45117 Essen, Germany
{pia.sander,miriam.mulders,michael.kerres}@uni-due.de

Abstract. The development of vocational competence has so far been inefficiently implemented in some trades, as for example in the training of vehicle painters. The HandLeVR project therefore underscores the use of Virtual Reality to promote action-oriented learning of techniques for carrying out vehicle painting work. This article describes both the instructional and technological aspects of a VR Painting Simulator developed in the project and presents intermediate results.

Keywords: Virtual Reality · Simulation · Vocational training

1 Motivation

A competence–oriented approach in vocational education and training requires comprehensive, action-oriented learning units with learning progress checks. By observing actions in authentic learning and exercise situations, it must be possible to become insight into the underlying competencies, both through reflection (by the trainee) and evaluation (by the trainer). Problems with the consistent implementation of this requirement are common, for example, in the training of vehicle painters. Here, various techniques for applying individual layers of paint to workpieces must be trained. Adequate, frequent and action-oriented training, however, is hampered by economic, physical, and social factors.

With Virtual Reality (VR), psychomotor coordination and skills can be trained as discussed in explorative learning approaches. VR technology enables a high degree of immersion and authenticity of the learning situation, allowing learners to immerse themselves in a learning world where they can control their learning process to a high degree and learn by exploring the digital artifacts. In addition, painting is predestined for VR use. For example, no haptic feedback from the 3D workpieces is required (apart from the paint spray gun), as these are not touched during paint application.

The aim of the HandLeVR project is to develop and evaluate an effective training system with a central VR learning application - the VR Painting Simulator. The system will be used for training and following evaluation of paint applications on 3D workpieces. It consists of an authoring tool for trainers as well as the VR learning application and

© Springer Nature Switzerland AG 2020
E. Popescu et al. (Eds.): SETE 2019, LNCS 11984, pp. 46–51, 2020.
https://doi.org/10.1007/978-3-030-38778-5_6

a reflection application for trainees. The instructional and technical conceptions as well as intermediate results are presented in the following sections.

2   VR Painting Simulator

This section describes the design of a VR training application, which is developed within the HandLeVR[1] project. The research questions ask weather VR technology can contribute to effective training of action-oriented learning in vocational education and how instructional design principles can be applied in this technology to ensure appropriate learning success.

2.1   Instructional Concept

While emerging technologies have fostered the development of technologically advanced VR learning applications, these solutions often lack a thorough instructional approach [1–3]. Consequently, some of these VR learning applications contribute little to the acquisition of competences and clearly stay behind their potential.

VR learning applications have proven to support both the training of simple psychomotor tasks and the development of complex competences including knowledge, skills and attitudes. These more complex competencies, however, need elaborated instructional concepts, which are based on findings in the field of learning psychology. Those concepts can be used to design appropriate VR applications to efficiently help learning and the acquisition of theses competences.

It becomes clear that digital technology by itself will not improve learning sufficiently and enduringly [4]. It is open to what extent available concepts for the instructional design of educational media will be applicable to the instructional use of VR technology [5, 6]. Although many VR applications try to address an educational problem, the lack of empirical studies on the instructional design of VR in the field of training, has been criticized [7, 8]. Therefore, the usefulness of already existing and new instructional design models for VR learning applications has to be studied and validated in the field.

The present aim is to apply a highly validated instructional design model, namely the 4C/ID model [9], in the earlier described VR training application to facilitate the development of skills and action-oriented learning in the vocational training of vehicle painters. The model was developed to train complex cognitive skills and provide instructional principles to design effective training programs. It focusses on the development of skills rather than knowledge by providing authentic whole-task practice and frequent part-task practice.

An additional aim of the current project is to study two instructional approaches in the current context, namely an exploratory approach versus a more systematic approach. Previous studies have shown that an exploratory approach often results in learning strategies on a trial and error basis. It remains questionable whether this is effective for the development of action-oriented competences [10, 11] as needed by vehicle painters. In addition, the often heterogeneous group of trainees found in the training for vehicle

---

[1] https://handlevr.de.

painters ask for more individual learning paths that can be customized according to trainees' proficiency level. Therefore, both approaches will be compared:

A. Explorative approach: Learners have access to all VR learning tasks. They can freely navigate through the learning application and independently decide which learning task they perform.
B. Systematic approach: The trainer or educational institution gives a pre-defined learning path that the trainees have to work through. However, the learning path may be customized according to the proficiency level of an individual trainee.

The presented instructional design results in two concrete technical requirements of the VR learning application. First, to allow a systematic instructional approach, a well-constructed authoring tool is needed that allows the trainer to define customized learning paths according to the proficiency and needs of the trainee. Second, to foster the development of action-oriented competences (plan, execute, check, if necessary correct and lastly evaluate actions) a reflection application is needed that will present performance feedback to the trainee (e.g. thickness of the coat) and reports individual stages of learning and support self-reflection.

2.2 Technical Concept

The central instrument for investigating the usefulness of the instructional design models for VR learning applications is a multi-component learning system, the VR Painting Simulator. The core of this system is the training and quality control of paint applications on 3D workpieces. On the technical side, there are particular challenges in simulating the physics of paint applications (e.g. paint particle density) and the reproduction of the paint spray gun both in VR and as a comprehensible, sensor-equipped input device.

As visualized in Fig. 1, the use of the system is subdivided into 3 phases, which are based on the instructional requirements. In the preparation phase (1), a web-based authoring tool is used by the trainer or the training institution to concretize the general scenario (application of color layers). The tool supports the integration of finished templates for specific learning units and 3D models as well as the creation of new learning units and their interconnection in terms of learning paths.

In the next phase, the trainees perform their learning actions (2) in the VR learning application within the context of the previously defined specific learning scenarios. They use a typical HMD which immerses them into the virtual world. With a physical controller in the form of the familiar paint spray gun and its virtual counterpart visible in the VR, virtually displayed 3D workpieces can be painted by the trainee in authentic actions. The detailed results of these actions are transferred into a trainee profile.

In the last phase, this profile can be imported into the web-based reflection application to assess the learning performance with fellow trainees or the trainer (3).

2.3 Intermediate Results

Regarding the instructional concept a training analysis was conducted which included interviews and field observations at two different sites. First, interviews at the painting

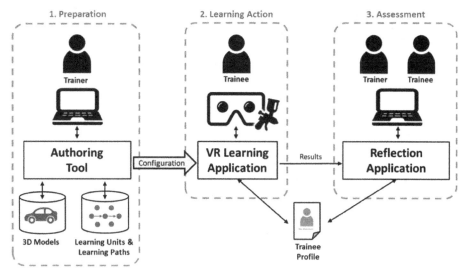

Fig. 1. Architectural sketch of the overall learning system.

shop of a German automobile manufacturer were carried out with (1) the trainer for car painting, (2) three trainees and (3) two former trainees now working on the production site. In addition, a typical training session in the painting shop was observed. The 4C/ID model served as a basis to design the interview scheme and the observation guidelines. The collected data provided the input to design a first concept for the training of vehicle painters in VR. In the second phase of the training analysis the developed concept was validated with a group of trainers for vehicle painters working at a center for cross-regional education for vehicle painters. The results of this second phase are currently analyzed.

Independent from the instructional concept, a basic realistic representation of paint jobs, the working environment and the tools used is required. Therefore, the early technical developments focused on both, an authentic VR setting in terms of a multifunctional painting booth and paint gun as well as an accurate simulation of the basic painting process. Figure 2 shows the current version of the painting booth including an exemplary engine hood and the user interface (left image). The 3D models of the painting booth and our highly authentic paint gun (right image) where created on basis of their real counterparts. The user interface in the form of a monitor on the wall gives access to the current functionalities of the application. Besides an engine hood, several parts of a car were modelled in detail and integrated into the application.

The aim of the current prototype was realistic representation and behavior of the spray cone and the paint job on the workpiece. To help the user find the correct distance to the work-piece, a ray can be activated that turns green when the correct distance is reached. Additional first in-process evaluation possibilities were integrated, allowing to determine the quantity and costs of the paint used and how much of the paint has been wasted. If too much paint is applied the paint runs down the workpiece. This is one of the

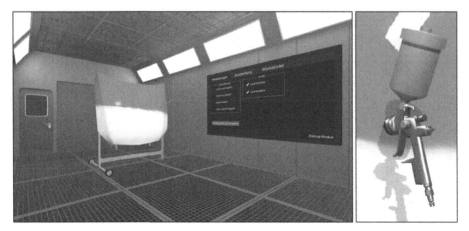

Fig. 2. Paint booth with a blank car part and the user interface on the wall (left image) and the current version of our highly authentic paint gun (right)

error types which have to be implemented. Furthermore, a measurement mode allows the highlighting of areas where too much or too less paint has been applied.

3   Conclusion and Future Work

The VR Painting Simulator described in this article focuses on the promotion of action-oriented learning of techniques for performing automotive painting work through virtual reality. First, it is investigated which contribution VR technologies offer to enable action-oriented learning in vocational education and training and how instructional design principles can be applied in these technologies to ensure appropriate learning success. The findings from this study will be transferred into a VR-supported training (the VR Painting Simulator). This learning framework consists of an authoring tool for trainers as well as a VR learning application and a reflection application for trainees.

Concerning the instructional design, the developed concept will be revised and validated repeatedly. Therefore, a close collaboration with trainers and trainees in the field of car painting as well as with computer scientists to transfer the instructional concept into VR is needed. The resulting VR Painting Simulator and its prototypes are evaluated continuously during the project as well as in dedicated field tests.

In addition to vehicle painters, the transferability of the results to other trades with related learning activities (e.g. classical painters, welders) will be examined during the project. The project team will transfer the project results to the vocational training centers of the chambers of skilled trades located throughout Germany and provide appropriate advice to accompany the practical application. In addition, the sustainability of the project will be promoted by the final publication of the project results under an open source license and as an open educational resource.

References

1. Zender, R., Weise, M., von der Heyde, M., Söbke, H.: Lehren und Lernen mit VR und AR - Was wird erwartet? Was funktioniert? In: Proceedings of DeLFI Workshops 2018 Co-located with 16th e-Learning Conference of the German Computer Society, CEUR Workshop Proceedings (2018)
2. Mikropoulos, T.A., Natsis, A.: Educational virtual environments. A ten-year review of empirical research (1999–2009). Comput. Educ. **56**(3), 769–780 (2011)
3. Fowler, C.: Virtual reality and learning: where is the pedagogy? Br. J. Educ. Technol. **46**(2), 412–422 (2015)
4. Kerres, M.: Wirkungen und Wirksamkeit neuer Medien in der Bildung. In: Education Quality Forum. Wirkungen und Wirksamkeit neuer Medien, pp. 31–44. Waxmann, Münster (2003)
5. Hochberg, J., Vogel, C., Bastiaens, T.: Gestaltung und Erforschung eines Mixed-Reality-Lernsystems. MedienPädagogik: Zeitschrift für Theorie und Praxis der Medienbildung **28**, 140–146 (2017). Tagungsband: Bildung gemeinsam verändern: Diskussionsbeiträge und Impulse aus Forschung und Praxis
6. Cheng, K.-H., Tsai, C.-C.: Affordances of augmented reality in science learning: suggestions for future research. J. Sci. Educ. Technol. **22**(4), 449–462 (2013)
7. Elliott, J.B., Gardner, M., Alrashidi, M.: Towards a framework for the design of mixed reality immersive education spaces. In: 2nd European Immersive Education Summit-E-iED, pp. 63–76 (2012)
8. Chen, P., Liu, X., Cheng, W., Huang, R.: A review of using Augmented Reality in Education from 2011 to 2016. In: Popescu, E., et al. (eds.) Innovations in Smart Learning. LNET, pp. 13–18. Springer, Singapore (2017). https://doi.org/10.1007/978-981-10-2419-1_2
9. van Merriënboer, J.J.G., Clark, R.E., de Croock, M.B.M.: Blueprints for complex learning: the 4C/ID-model. Education Tech. Research Dev. **50**, 39–61 (2002)
10. Hetemank, A., Mok, S.Y., CHU Research Group: Ist Lernsoftware wirklich effektiver, wenn SchülerInnen den Lernprozess selbst in die Hand nehmen? (Kurzreview No. 8). Clearing House Unterricht - TUM School of Education (2014). https://www.clearinghouse.edu.tum.de/wp-content/uploads/2017/07/CHU_KR_8_Karich_2014_Lernersteuerung-Software.pdf. Accessed 17 May 2019
11. Kerres, M.: Mediendidaktik. Konzeption und Entwicklung digitaler Lernangebote, 5th edn. De Gruyter, Oldenburg (2018)

Reflection of HCI in Foreign Language Teaching

Sarka Hubackova[✉]

Department of Applied Linguistics, Faculty of Informatics and Management,
University of Hradec Kralove, Hradec Kralove, Czech Republic
sarka.hubackova@uhk.cz

Abstract. The present time is significantly influenced by the development of information and communication technology, that allows us to access a huge amount of information and widen our possibilities. Using advanced digital technology has become an essential tool of advancement in every branch. Students consider ICT as a commonplace, as an integral part of their lives. The organization of the study is influenced by this fact, for example, consultations are agreed through email correspondence, submitting of assignments also works on an online basis.

The biggest focus of Human-computer interaction (HCI) as a multidomain discipline is put on a user interface. The interconnection with IT science world shall be obvious. We even today in times of modern technologies, even better computers and cell phones know, or at least suspect, that there is always something remaining for improving. We aim to mediate the communication between human and computer in such a way, that it would be as most intuitive and natural.

Students consider ICT as a commonplace, as an integral part of their lives. The organization of the study is influenced by this fact, for example, consultations are agreed through email correspondence, submitting of assignments also works on an online basis. We tried to explore the current state of the use of multimedia in teaching and learning with research. We focused primarily on what devices students use most frequently. To identify the relationship of students to ICT and to determine students' views on teaching supported by ICT, we used the method of a questionnaire in such a process. The paper brings a short reference to another grasp of the problematic nature of effectiveness in an educational process. The final part of the paper deals with the possible effectiveness of eLearning which may – under certain circumstances - be a bit higher than the effectiveness of face to face teaching.

Keywords: Human-computer interaction · Evaluation · Reflection · eLearning · Education · Teaching · Foreign languages · Teaching methods

1 Introduction

The biggest focus of Human-computer interaction (HCI) as a multidomain discipline is put on a user interface. The interconnection with IT science world shall be obvious. We even today in times of modern technologies, even better computers and cell phones know, or at least suspect, that there is always something remaining for improving. We

© Springer Nature Switzerland AG 2020
E. Popescu et al. (Eds.): SETE 2019, LNCS 11984, pp. 52–59, 2020.
https://doi.org/10.1007/978-3-030-38778-5_7

aim to mediate the communication between human and computer in such a way, that it would be as most intuitive and natural.

The very beginning of HCI is often meant 1857 with the first mention on ergonomics. With the development of industrialization, scientists examined unfriendly working conditions of workers operating the machines. At the beginning of the 20th century first studies appeared focused on safety and health protection during work with various types of machines.

The first document to be considered a direct ancestor of today's HCI comes from Russia from 1930. It is dealing with human factor analysis within the airplane cockpit. In the fifties of the 20th century, human factors and ergonomics became key domains worldwide. With growing automatization of working processes, a new milestone for HCI occurred in the sixties – standardization and international certification, which are until today considered an important component of industrial production and quality management. Until the second half of the seventies, the only people to come in contact with computers were IT professionals or enthusiasts. This was totally changed with the development of personal computers followed by personal software (as productive applications, interactive games) and platforms (hardware, programming languages, operation systems). Extended opportunities made a potential user of IT of almost anyone.

HCI is a very broad and multi-disciplinary domain. It is often very tightly bounded to another domain, where it solves different domain-specific tasks. In informatics, for instance, it may deal with application or user interface design, while in connection with psychology it analyses user behavior.

Today we already cannot imagine life without media, the Internet and especially mobile phones and applications. All these technologies bring us a brief information overview, facilitated data processing, and last but not least fun. Multimedia technologies have become an integral part of the present time and through their properties have begun to influence and change the whole society. Information technology and Internet management allow us to overcome distances in communication, transfer and share information incredibly fast, faster than any other available technology. They give us new opportunities and their rapid development opens up new ways constantly.

Multimedia supported teaching is nowadays connected mainly with a computer. Teaching materials are created with a computer and presented also.

Students consider ICT as a commonplace, as an integral part of their lives. The organisation of the study is influenced by this fact, for example, consultations are agreed through email correspondence, submitting of assignments also works on an online basis.

The creation of a multimedia application puts higher demands on the creator, then common application. Involving different types of data means to contemporary master several professions at once. Whether it is a presentation or tutorial, it is always necessary to prepare quality drawings or pictures. So the creator becomes an artist or photographer. Good sound of the program requires knowledge of a sound man, whether technical or music, not to mention the difficulty of creating quality animation [1].

The interactive multimedia is a phrase, that defines a new wave of computer software, that primarily deals with information provision. The multimedia component is characterized by the presence of text, image, audio, animation, and video, that are organized into an intelligible program. The part "interactive" relates to the process of empowering the user to control the environment with a computer [2].

2 Methods

To identify the relationship of students to ICT and to determine students' views on teaching supported by ICT, we used the method of a questionnaire. All questions were closed and offered a choice of several options. The research was initiated in the year 2017/18 and had two phases.

3 Findings

The process of remembering is dependent on external and internal influences and also on how the current information is being received and processed. How much people can remember is shown by Dale's cone of learning [3, 4]. On the model we can see, that by a simple reading of study (or other) material one can remember only 10% of information. With the cooperation of sight and hearing the successfulness of learning increases substantially. This all highlights the advantages of multimedia supported teaching (Fig. 1).

Fig. 1. Dale's cone of learning

Learning with multimedia support has gradually become a global trend. Smartphones and tablets open up almost limitless possibilities for teachers. Educational applications may serve as didactical tools to explanation or practice of curriculum.

The use of multimedia applications may be very broad. An especially important property that multimedia offer is its interactivity. Students can individually set their pace in learning, the difficulty, the number of repetitions, etc. They can also choose different procedures or leave some less important parts behind.

Although the importance of multimedia is being emphasized, in the process of learning the mere multi medialization of study materials still does not provide the desired effect. Important is the correct use and combination of the individual media in the context of the presented content.

When creating multimedia files we follow several important rules:

- Video has to be short, clear and understandable. Important information has to be repeated.
- The file must be focused on one main topic, the theory may be followed by examples.
- It is necessary to estimate the right amount of new information, not to glut students with redundant information.
- It is appropriate to include video files into teaching regularly, but not to an excessive degree.

It is appropriate to use animation and music background reasonably.

Nowadays the m-learning is being increasingly widespread, the teaching and learning supported with smartphones. Also, in this case, the teaching is based on multimedia. Smartphones have become easily available and often used.

From the advantages of m-learning we can emphasize:

- Simplicity
- Accessibility - varied content is available in many ways.
- Immediacy and ubiquity - the student is able to find desired information wherever.
- Cooperation - mobile devices simplify group education.
- Interactivity - contact, and cooperation of professionals, teachers or colleagues in synchronous or asynchronous communication.
- Situation - education can be integrated into everyday life, to places where we face authentic problems.
- Context - is produced by students through interaction with the surrounding world.
- Convenience - m-learning is the paperless, transportable and interactive educational environment.

In our lessons, we use multimedia and multimedia features quite commonly. Multimedia online courses we create ourselves, form a part of German-language teaching already many years. These courses usually serve as a supplement to face-to-face teaching and are therefore blended learning. In our courses, we use already prepared multimedia materials we draw from original German-language sources - eg. Deutsche Welle [5, 6]. The most proving show the audio texts, which offer besides audio texts also text files and listening exercises. Very suitable are also video files, which are supplemented by texts and exercises created by us. To the courses, we include also many of the students PPT presentations [7, 8].

We tried to explore the current state of the use of multimedia in teaching and learning with research. We focused primarily on what devices students use most frequently. It turned out, that while on secondary schools tablets are the most used, at university students use laptops in combination with smartphones [9, 10]. This can be probably explained by the intensity of study when tablets are no longer sufficient and simultaneously the availability and constant presence of smartphones is well usable (Figs. 2 and 3).

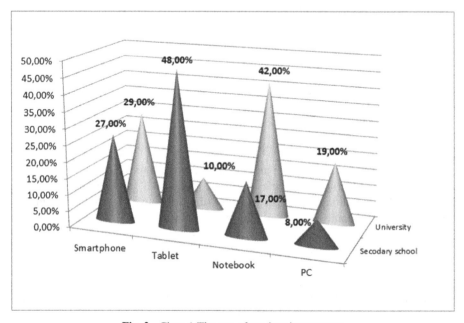

Fig. 2. Chart 1 The use of modern instruments

Chart 3 - During the self-study I use most often:

Dictaphone   1%
TV   4%
DVD/video   4%
Textbook   15%
Smartphone   18%
Internet   27%
Multimedia courses 31% (Fig. 4).

The next question was: More suitable for you is contact learning or teaching supported by the multimedia courses, that is blended learning? The method of blended learning pivoted in both groups in a single-minded way.

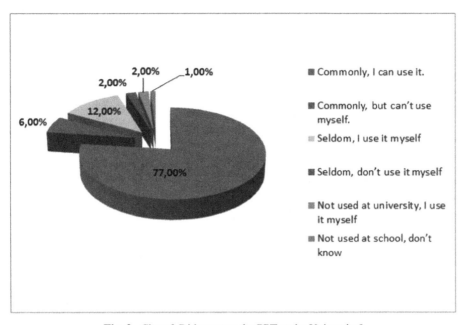

Fig. 3. Chart 2 Did you use the PPT at the University?

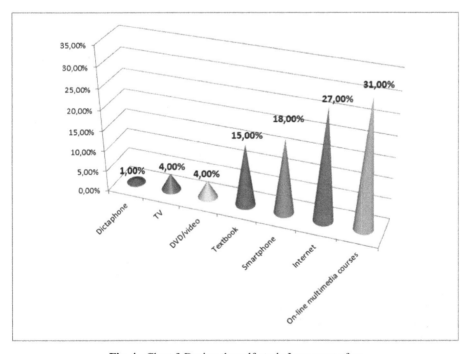

Fig. 4. Chart 3 During the self-study I use most often

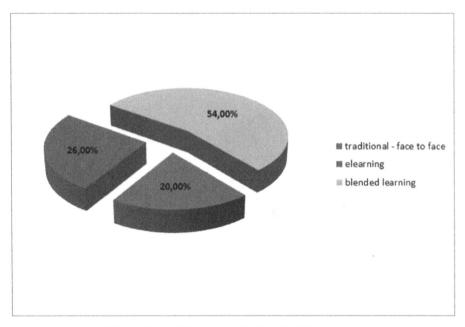

Fig. 5. Chart 4 The more suitable method for students

4   Discussion

Our survey has shown that modern methods are popular both with full-time students and distance students and that the entire educational process depends mainly on the teacher's approach to teaching and his usage of methods in its implementation.

eLearning will probably never entirely replace the face-to-face form of education, especially in areas, where personal contact between teacher and student is essential. In spite of this fact, it became a very important part of the education process. There are particularly various ways of using eLearning in the scope of further education. Contemporary, mobile technologies are on a huge rise. They are faster, technologically more sophisticated and they deal with almost the same abilities and tools like notebooks and PCs. But they are smaller, therefore more utilizable on the go.

5   Conclusion

The multimedia courses are a very good motivation tool. They surely support all education, foreign language teaching inclusive. The blended learning method is very popular among the students. We constantly complete the current materials from the foreign web pages. We have prepared the language multimedia courses for beginners or advanced students of German. We can offer the courses of ordinary, business, and banking languages. Based on our praxis we consider the form of combined education as a very suitable one and we count on its further extension to other fields.

Acknowledgment. This study is supported by the IGS project 2019, run at the Faculty of Informatics and Management, University of Hradec Kralove, Czech Republic.

References

1. Sokolowsky, P., Šedivá, Z.: Multimédia: Současnost budoucnosti. Grada, Praha (1994). 204 s.
2. Sanjaya, M., Ramesh, S.C.: Interactive Multimedia in Education and Training. Group Publishing, Hershey (2005). 421 s.
3. Anderson, H.M.: Edgar Dales Cone of Experience (2016)
4. Dales Cone of Experience. http://www.mywallpaper.top/edgar-dales-cone-of-learning.html
5. Čáp, J.: Psychologie pro učitele, Praha (2001)
6. Frydrychova Klimova, B.: Blended learning, in Research, Reflections and Innovations in Integrating ICT in Education, Lisboa (2009)
7. Pikhart, M.: New horizons of intercultural communication: applied linguistics approach. Procedia Soc. Behav. Sci. **152**, 954–957 (2014)
8. Pikhart, M.: Multilingual and intercultural competence for ICT: accessing and assessing electronic information in the global world. In: Choroś, K., Kopel, M., Kukla, E., Siemiński, A. (eds.) MISSI 2018. AISC, vol. 833, pp. 273–278. Springer, Cham (2019). https://doi.org/10.1007/978-3-319-98678-4_28
9. Pikhart, M.: Communication based models of information transfer in modern management – the use of mobile technologies in company communication. In: Innovation Management and Education Excellence through Vision 2020, IBIMA 2018, pp. 447–450 (2018)
10. Hubackova, S.: Foreign language teaching with WebCT support. Procedia Soc. Behav. Sci. **3**(2010), 112–115 (2010)
11. Khan, B.H., Granato, L.A.: Program Evaluation in eLearning. http://asianvu.com/digitallibrary/elearning/elearning_program_evaluation_by_khan_and_Granato.pdf. Accessed 23 Sept 2017

Expert-Oriented Digitalization of University Processes

Raine Kauppinen[(✉)], Altti Lagstedt, and Juha P. Lindstedt

Haaga-Helia University of Applied Sciences, Helsinki, Finland
`raine.kauppinen@haaga-helia.fi`

Abstract. Digitalization challenges the way business processes are seen. The potential for enhancement is recognized even in business areas that traditionally have little to do with IT. Even though universities have long traditions of how work is organized, they have not been eager to adopt digitalized processes. Because core processes of universities rely on highly skilled experts, digitalizing processes is not as straightforward as in more mechanical work. We developed an expert-oriented digitalization model (EXOD) for university processes' digitalization and tested it using a case study. After digitalizing a core process, we interviewed the experts involved. The results show the usefulness and adaptability of the model. Based on the results, we recommend future studies be done to refine and test the model more comprehensively. Also, based on the adaptability of the model, we recommended it as a baseline for university process digitalization projects in general.

Keywords: Digitalization · University · Expert · Process · Model · Thesis

1 Introduction

Due to digitalization, the importance of information systems (IS) has grown in business areas that are not normally considered to be IT-oriented [1]. Universities are no exception, even though some university processes have a long and rather changeless tradition, inherited from as far back as the 15th century. Long traditions could be seen as an obstacle for digitalizing university processes, but there are also other obstacles. The core education processes of universities rely heavily on expert work; the amount of mechanical work is rather small. Experts with strong opinions and expertise combined with high autonomy have to be taken into account in university digitalization projects.

In this study, we selected one of the core processes of every university: the thesis process. Even though the thesis process is critical for universities, it is not usually considered as a systematic process, but more as the repetition of unique handicraft done with the supervisors' best skills and will.

The challenges of the thesis process have been recognized, and some related work has been done in the areas of both quality improvement and ICT system support [2–4]. One of the tested thesis process support systems is SciPro [5], which has been studied from the viewpoints of the student and supervisor interaction and the effective implementation of the process [3, 6]. Scaling the process for a larger scale implementation has also been studied from a quality [7] and resource management viewpoint [5].

© Springer Nature Switzerland AG 2020
E. Popescu et al. (Eds.): SETE 2019, LNCS 11984, pp. 60–69, 2020.
https://doi.org/10.1007/978-3-030-38778-5_8

However, in addition to the quality and resource aspects, the issues in scaling the process include integrations with other (core) processes and both manual and ICT systems. Existing work identifies the thesis process as a core activity in universities [5], but the process and systems integration at the organizational level has not been discussed in detail. These have a considerable impact on, for example, the level of automation as well as information availability and quality of the organizational level. In addition, it seems that prior literature considers the thesis process only as a research process [see, e.g., 3], which is not the reality in all universities. Other types of theses are also used [see, e.g., 4], and in different disciplines, different aspects are emphasized within the same type of thesis. Furthermore, if Davenport's [8] knowledge work classification is applied, thesis supervising can be classified as an expert model of knowledge work, where experts organize their work individually and are not ready to consent to a mechanical, "cookbook" approach [8]. The thesis process and the supporting IS have to be flexible enough to allow efficient supervision of different types of theses.

Since prior literature considers the process–system integration on a limited organizational and individual level, we developed an expert-oriented digitalization model (EXOD) for digitalizing universities' learning supporting processes.

To test the developed model, we formulated the following research questions:

RQ1: What are the experiences of the expert-oriented digitalization model?
RQ2: How was the user involvement realized in the digitalization project?

To answer these research questions, we studied a thesis process digitalization project at Haaga-Helia University of Applied Sciences, conducted in 2016–2019.

2 Theoretical Background

2.1 Business Process Development

If digitalization is done just by automating processes as they are, the existing problems are fixed with IS, and the potential of IS is not exploited. In addition, as Argyris [9] points out, people seldomly do exactly what they claim to do, and automating the assumed process brings out this discrepancy: the new IS may follow the known process model exactly but is not suitable for use [10]. Thus, automating the processes could be one part of functional stupidity [11], but as Venkatraman [12] points out, in some cases, it could be the rational choice of an organization to avoid radical changes in processes. An organization may choose to automatize existing practices only, instead of attempting big re-engineering projects. According to Venkatraman [12], IT-enabled business transformation can be classified roughly into two categories: evolutionary levels and revolutionary levels, where the former needs minimal changes to business processes, and the latter requires fundamental changes to existing processes. Venkatraman claimed that with the revolutionary approach, organizations could benefit more, but the costs (efforts) of the change would be higher as well. So, there is no right or wrong or optimal level of business transformation; the cost and potential benefits, as well as the enablers and inhibitors of the organization, should be taken into account, and each case should be discussed separately [12].

Davenport and Short [13] present a five-step model for process redesign. In their model, the first step is to develop a business vision and process objectives. This is a rather general level step and should be done as a part of strategic planning. The second step of the Davenport and Short [13] model is to select a suitable process(es) to be redesigned. They point out that it is not necessary to go through all processes of organization exhaustively; it is enough to identify the most important or most problematic process to be developed. The third step is understand and measure the selected process(es) to find out current problems and set a baseline for improvements. The fourth step of the Davenport and Short [13] model is to identify IT levers, i.e. how IS can enhance the current process or enable totally new kinds of approaches. The last step is to design and build a prototype of the process by implementing the new process on a pilot basis and modifying as necessary [13].

In process development, it is not enough to consider the organizational level: individual levels have to be taken into account, especially in knowledge work [8]. When Taylor composed his principles of scientific management, the assumptions about humans were rather mechanistic: replaceable components doing simple, repeatable tasks, and by optimizing the tasks, the maximum efficiency is achieved [14]. This, however, is shown to be an oversimplification, and later process-development models, such as business process management (BPM), emphasize the role of people and culture [15]. People are more complex than just parts of a machine; they are not fully rational [11, 16], nor are they are always reliable. According to Argyris [9], there is a difference between what people say they do and what they really do. This kind of cover-up culture, or inhibiting loops of organizational learning, as Argyris [9] calls them, hides the real causes of the problems [9].

As Davenport [8] points out, knowledge work is difficult to structure and seldom seen as a process. In addition, knowledge workers easily resist instructions and models given outside and view a formal process approach as a bureaucratic, procedural annoyance [8]. Even though knowledge workers resist change, there are examples in which knowledge work is significantly improved through process management [8].

Davenport [8] formulated a model of four approaches to knowledge work to clarify different knowledge work situations (see Fig. 1).

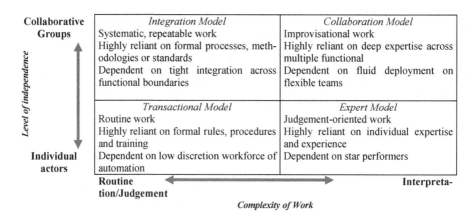

Fig. 1. Four approaches to knowledge work [8]

As thesis supervising, like many other university processes, is clearly more about judgement and interpretation done alone, we place thesis supervising in the "expert model" category. According to Davenport [8], expert work can be improved with processes, but workers themselves easily resist the change and strict, cookbook-type process models. So, instead, expert model processes should consist of higher level guidelines, giving expert workers enough flexibility to decide how to do the actual work [8]. To overcome the expert workers' resistance and to structure their work, Davenport [8] recommends finding a way to embed a computer in the middle of the work process. However, IS should not be an obstacle for experts to reach their full potential [17].

2.2 Information Systems Development

From a control point of view, IS development methods can be classified roughly into two categories: plan-driven and change-driven methods [18]. Plan-driven IS development models (ISDMs) dominated selections at the end of the 20th century, whereas the popularity of change-driven ISDMs has grown during the last two decades and appears to be a current mainstream [19]. In plan-driven IS development, planning and development are divided into separate phases. The assumption is that every aspect of development work—objectives and their required metrics, tasks, money, and resources—can be planned thoroughly in advance. Development starts immediately after the planning phase is completed.

The plan-driven methods, such as the waterfall method, are a straightforward way to develop software, but there are many known problems, e.g., early mistakes are found late and are difficult (and costly) to solve. The assumption is that no changes happen during software development, i.e., what is defined in the beginning will be implemented in the later phases. Even if all the definitions are done correctly, this does not guarantee success in IS development since circumstances might have changed [20].

In change-driven development, such as agile methods, the idea is that the whole information system is not planned at once, but planning and development are done in small steps. After each step, the situation is re-evaluated, and necessary changes are made to the objectives. Each development step results in a new IS release after each cycle. Despite the good success rate of projects done with agile methods, 61% of agile projects are still not considered to be successful [21]; an agile ISDMs do not guarantee success for ISD projects [22].

One alternative is to use a hybrid approach, where parts of plan-driven and change-driven development are combined [19]. Since no method fits all cases, it is important to discuss (and select) a method on a case-by-case basis [23].

2.3 Change Management

The role of individuals in process change is remarkable, especially in knowledge work. One part of the change is change management. It is natural for humans to resist change, and if the change is not managed well, a new process and the IS supporting it may not be used, no matter how efficient the new systems are. Some change management models are rather mechanical, where organizations are seen more or less as machines [24]. Some see organizations as evolving organisms and believe different social aspects should be considered. A rather famous example of the latter belief is Kotter's eight-step model [25], in which the change sticks only when "new behaviors are rooted in social norms and shared values" [25]. In Kotter's eight-step model, the idea is that the change process goes through change steps, and skipping steps creates problems. The steps of the model are 1. establishing a sense of urgency, 2. forming a powerful guiding coalition, 3. creating a vision, 4. communicating the vision, 5. empowering others to act on the vision, 6. planning for and creating short-term wins, 7. consolidating improvements and producing still more change, and 8. institutionalizing new approaches [25].

As process change often manifests itself as a new IS, the success of the new IS represents the success of the process change. It is, therefore, natural to consider how new IS are taken in use. There are related theories, for example, technology acceptance model (TAM), which can be applied as well. According to TAM, the perceived usefulness and perceived ease of use affect the behavioural intention to use a system [26]. So, to get users to use a new system, a user has to be made to see that the system increases work performance and can be used without additional effort.

As mentioned, not all problems in process change are easily seen [11] or recognized [9]. Thus, it is not possible to deal with them early, and Kotter's eight-step model is hard to apply as such. Cooper and Zmud [27] proposed an IT implementation process, where diffusion of IT does not happen all at once, but as a gradual process. We claim that Cooper and Zmud model is useful when actual process change (and the supporting IS) is implemented, whereas Kotter's model is effective when the change is communicated to users, keeping the objectives of TAM (usefulness and ease of use) in mind.

2.4 Expert-Oriented Digitalization Model

Based on the theories of business process and IS development and change management, we formulated an expert-oriented digitalization model (EXOD) for knowledge work, especially for university processes. EXOD has four main steps:

1. **Initiation**. Process identification and exploring development opportunities. Find the potential benefits of the digitalization of the selected process and communicate these to the users (experts) involved. Form an effective development group with experts in IS, process development, and the process in question [8, 13, 25, 27].
2. **Process re-engineering emphasis.** Major, high level changes to the process and main requirements for the IS. Select a suitable IS development method for the case. Develop a new process with users (experts), and implement it as far as possible without a new IS. Communicate the potentials usefulness of the IS, and empower the experts to act on the vision [8, 12, 13, 23, 25, 26].
3. **IS development emphasis.** Develop a process-supporting IS based on requirements, in cooperation with the experts. Perform iterative development with pilot projects and make changes to the process when needed. Experts' work flexibility should be kept in mind and communicated to all parties [8, 13, 19, 25].
4. **Stabilization.** Induce the experts to commit the digitalized process as a normal activity. Make minor refinements to the IS [8, 19, 25, 27].

3 Methodology

3.1 Research Method

In the case study research, we followed the recommendations of Yin [28]. We used four data collection sources extensively that Yin [28] recommends, namely documentation, archival records, participant-observation, and interviews. In the analysis, the main emphasis was on the interviews; the other sources were considered complementary.

Since one of the researchers was responsible for the thesis process development and another for the development of IS (Konto) supporting it, we had access to the thesis process development, as well as all of Konto's development documentation (process models, notes, product backlogs, version history, plans, e-mails, guidelines). We also utilized Konto's logs and registers as supporting data to understand the actual usage of the IS. In addition, as supervisors and thesis coordinators, we also used and guided the use of the digitalized process and made participant observations during the process.

The interviews were done by applying an interview method protocol developed by Dahlberg, Hokkanen, and Newman [29]. During an interview, questions were presented on screen either face-to-face or via a video call to the interviewee. The interviewer recorded and presented the responses immediately before moving to the next question. Recording the responses gave interviewees the ability to validate the typed answers immediately. The interviews can be described as expert interviews [30].

The interview had two parts; 27 participants were interviewed. Nearly half, 13 responded to the first and, almost all, 25 to the second part. The interviewees were chosen based on their above average activity around Konto. In this study, data from the first part, covering the process of digitalization, is analyzed. The second part, focusing on the resulting process and tool will be analyzed in our future work.

Of the 13 interviewees, 10 performed a single role, two performed two roles, and one performed three roles. The fields of expertise covered administration (4), degree program management (2), thesis coordination (5), and thesis supervision (6).

The digitalization part of the interview consisted of identifying the role of the interviewee and responding to six open-ended questions, as well as an opportunity to provide open comments. The answers were coded based on the theory presented in Sect. 2 (process development, IS development, and change management) and on RQ1 and RQ2 (expectations, experiences, and realization of involvement). One code (service promise) emerged based on the answers.

3.2 Case: Thesis Process

A thesis process as a core activity [5] is often considered relatively simple: the supervisor as the expert advices, and the student writes the thesis [3]. In practice, the process is more complicated [2, 6]. For example, in our case study, the process at the Haaga-Helia University of Applied Sciences (HH) included other experts, such as the thesis coordinator (organizes information sessions, checks students' thesis ideas, and assigns supervisors), degree program management (oversees supervisors' and coordinators' workload), and the administration (publishes the resulting thesis and records the grade).

This process was digitalized using the EXOD model. In initiation (before 2014), HH described its core processes, revealing that the thesis process was the most complicated. The benefits of digitalization were apparent, so work started with experts on the process and IS development with a process re-engineering emphasis (2014–2017). The resulting process has six phases. The main requirements for the IS were integration with data sources, automatic data transfer and being a modern platform supporting mobile use.

A hybrid approach [19] that supported the expert involvement was selected, and the Konto tool was developed in the IS development emphasis (2016–2019) based on the requirements. Changes to the process were implemented and communicated. After the fall 2018 test period, the Konto tool was launched for full use with thesis projects starting from January 2019, resulting in stabilization (from 2019) where the digitalized process is being committed as a normal activity. Refinements are done as needed.

4   Results

Regarding the experiences (RQ1), the majority of interviewees (10 out of 13) had formed expectations early, after being involved in the digitalization. From administrative, management, and coordination viewpoints, as expressed in interviews (*translated to English*), process visibility (*on every level of the organization*), process automation (*automating parts of the process*), and statistics recording (*getting rid of manually keeping track of supervisors and their resources*) were considered especially important. The supervisors and coordinators emphasized the change in communication and the usefulness of the single platform (*fewer e-mails when the communication and materials are in the same place*), and the transparency (*the supervision is visible*).

Of the interviewees, four out of 13 identified only positive experiences, eight identified both positive and negative, and one identified only negative. The experiences were higher in number and more detailed for coordination and supervision, while experiences of the administration and management were fewer and more general. The positive experiences were related to the model (*extremely useful, agile model that utilizes in-house competencies well and is generalizable to similar, well-scoped development efforts*), the involvement (*it has been valuable, being able to participate and try out, which also helps in commitment to the result*), and influencing the result (*the needs of the users have been taken into account*).

The negative experiences were doubts about the coverage of the involvement (*the piloting phase could have been longer, and more people could have been involved*), and coping with incompleteness (*some may have felt insecure due to the changes*). It is worth noting that the interviewee stating only negative experiences still felt the participation itself positive and considered related work on the service promise to be helpful. Another interviewee also mentioned the service promise as supporting the involvement.

The realization of involvement (RQ2) was difficult to pinpoint. While eight out of 13 interviewees acknowledged having development ideas, most comments were general and did not name concrete examples. Instead, they were showing trust in taking the ideas into account (*there may be something that I also have pointed out, but it is hard to specify a single one*). Only a few could name a concrete and implemented idea (*it was not possible to send a message in a certain situation, but now it is*).

However, involvement also meant interviewees were participants in change management since 10 out of 13 interviewees took an active role by communicating process- or tool-related changes (*answered the questions and provided instructions to the supervisors*). The communication was two-directional as information and guidance were provided to users and feedback from users was relayed back to developers (*informed developers about the comments from the supervisors and the coordinator team*).

Studying the available documentation and observations showed that there were some difficulties with terminology and combining old practices related to the process and IS development; some of these only came out during IS implementation. But, based on the Konto log files, the digitalized process has been taken into use comprehensively. Moreover, Konto is considered to be visually clear (perceived ease of use in [26]), and the thesis process improved (perceived usefulness in [26]). As stated earlier, more detailed analysis of Konto and the digitalized process is a topic for further study.

5   Discussion and Conclusions

The interview data, Konto logs, documentation, and observations all confirmed that the EXOD model performed well in digitalizing the expert-driven thesis process. The findings met the goals set for the EXOD model: the experts felt that they had been listened [8, 25], the developed IS decreased the workload of experts [8], it was easy to use [26], and it ensured that the process was followed [8]. The level of process development was meaningful [12, 13] and gave a good basis for the development of the IS. The selected IS development method [23], the hybrid approach [19], was suitable in this case.

The best results were achieved in change management. Thesis supervision is considered to be personal expert work [8], and external interventions, such as process enforcing and automation, are often considered undesirable. However, in this case, the experts felt they could affect the outcome [25] and automation, for example, was seen useful as it reduced mechanical work and clarified information handling [8, 13, 25, 26].

However, there is still room for improvement. Some experts perceive continuously changing IS to be confusing, so, plan-driven development could be emphasized. In addition, some felt that pilots were short, so feedback could be collected over a longer period and from a larger user group. Also, in some cases, users claim to follow the process but implementing the IS revealed that they actually do not [9]. While this cannot be fully avoided, it should be considered in EXOD model steps 2 and 3 by engaging experts to pursue objectives. In addition, some supervisors emphasize their expertise in supervising, while others see it more as routine work, so compromises need to be made.

Interestingly, the EXOD model seems to produce committed change agents [24], even though it was not an explicitly pursued objective. This effect should be studied and further developed to make it more robust. Overall, we recommend future studies be done to refine and test the EXOD model more comprehensively. Also, based on the suitability for processes with high actor expertise and autonomy, we recommended it be used as a baseline for university process digitalization projects in general.

References

1. Borg, M., Olsson, T., Franke, U., Assar, S.: Digitalization of swedish government agencies — a perspective through the lens of a software development census. In: International Conference on Software Engineering (2018)
2. Aghaee, N.: Finding potential problems in the thesis process in higher education: analysis of e-mails to develop a support system. Educ. Inf. Technol. **20**, 21–36 (2015). https://doi.org/10.1007/s10639-013-9262-z
3. Karunaratne, T.: Blended supervision for thesis projects in higher education: a case study. Electron J. e-Learn. **16**, 79–90 (2018)
4. Lagstedt, A.: Diary thesis as a tool for professional growth and for co-operation between universities and business. In: Proceedings of the 2015 UIIN Conference, June 2015, Berlin, Germany (2015)
5. Hansson, H.: How to produce quality theses at universities in a large scale: SciPro IT system - Supporting the Scientific Process. In: Proceedings - Frontiers in Education Conference, FIE (2014)
6. Hansen, P., Hansson, H.: Optimizing student and supervisor interaction during the SciPro thesis process – concepts and design. In: Li, F.W.B., Klamma, R., Laanpere, M., Zhang, J., Manjón, B.F., Lau, R.W.H. (eds.) ICWL 2015. LNCS, vol. 9412, pp. 245–250. Springer, Cham (2015). https://doi.org/10.1007/978-3-319-25515-6_23
7. Larsson, K., Hansson, H.: The challenge for supervision: mass individualisation of the thesis writing process with less recourses. In: Online Educa Berlin 2011-17th International Conference on Technology Supported Learning & Training, pp. 2007–2009 (2011)
8. Davenport, T.H.: Process management for knowledge work. In: vom Brocke, J., Rosemann, M. (eds.) Handbook on Business Process Management 1. IHIS, 2nd edn, pp. 17–35. Springer, Heidelberg (2015). https://doi.org/10.1007/978-3-642-45100-3_2
9. Argyris, C.: Organizational learning and management information systems. Acc. Organ. Soc. **2**, 113–123 (1977)
10. Lagstedt, A., Dahlberg, T.: Requirements engineering as a part of business process and information system development. In: Proceedings of the Seventh International Conference on Well-Being in the Information Society: Fighting Inequalities (WIS 2018), pp. 35–39 (2018)
11. Alvesson, M., Spicer, A.: A stupidity-based theory of organizations. J. Manag. Stud. **49**, 1194–1220 (2012). https://doi.org/10.1111/j.1467-6486.2012.01072.x
12. Venkatraman, N.: IT-enabled business transformation: from automation to business scope redefinition. Sloan Manage. Rev. **35**, 73–87 (1994)
13. Davenport, T.H., Short, J.E.: The new industrial engineering: information technology and business process redesign. Sloan Manage. Rev. **31**, 11–27 (1990)
14. Taylor, F.W.: The Principles of Scientific Management. Harper & Brothers Publishers, New York (1913)
15. Brocke, J., Sinnl, T.: Culture in business process management: a literature review. Bus. Process. Manag. J. **17**, 357–377 (2011). https://doi.org/10.1108/14637151111122383
16. Simon, H.A.: Administrative Behavior, 4th edn. The Free Press, New York (1997)
17. Wenger, E.C., Snyder, W.M.: Communities of practice: the organizational frontier. Harv. Bus. Rev. **78**(1), 139–145 (2000)
18. Moe, N.B., Aurum, A., Dybå, T.: Challenges of shared decision-making: a multiple case study of agile software development. Inf. Softw. Technol. **54**, 853–865 (2012). https://doi.org/10.1016/j.infsof.2011.11.006
19. Theocharis, G., Kuhrmann, M., Münch, J., Diebold, P.: Is *Water-Scrum-Fall* reality? On the use of agile and traditional development practices. In: Abrahamsson, P., Corral, L., Oivo, M., Russo, B. (eds.) PROFES 2015. LNCS, vol. 9459, pp. 149–166. Springer, Cham (2015). https://doi.org/10.1007/978-3-319-26844-6_11

20. Hansen, S., Lyytinen, K.: Challenges in contemporary requirements practice. In: Proceedings of the Annual Hawaii International Conference on System Sciences, pp. 1–11 (2010). https://doi.org/10.1109/HICSS.2010.98

21. Hastie, S., Wojewoda, S.: Standish group 2015 chaos report - Q&A with Jennifer Lynch. In: InfoQ, blog (2015). https://www.infoq.com/articles/standish-chaos-2015. Accessed 22 Feb 2018

22. Dahlberg, T., Lagstedt, A.: There is still no " Fit for All" IS development method : business development context and IS development characteristics need to match. In: Proceedings of the 51st Hawaii International Conference on System Sciences (2018)

23. Lagstedt, A., Dahlberg, T.: A contingency theory motivated framework to select information system development methods. In: Pacific Asia Conference on Information Systems, pp. 1–14 (2018)

24. Cameron, E., Green, M.: Making Sense of Change Management, 2nd edn. Kogan Page Ltd., London (2009)

25. Kotter, J.P.: Leading change: why transformation efforts fail. Harv. Bus. Rev., 59–67 (1995)

26. Davis, F.D., Bagozzi, R.P., Warshaw, P.R.: User acceptance of computer technology: a comparison of two theoretical models. Manage. Sci. **35**, 982–1003 (1989). https://doi.org/10.1287/mnsc.35.8.982

27. Cooper, R.B., Zmud, R.W.: Information technology implementation research: a technological diffusion approach. Manage. Sci. **36**, 123–139 (1990). https://doi.org/10.1287/mnsc.36.2.123

28. Yin, R.K.: Case Study Research: Design and Methods, 4th edn. Sage Publications, Thousand Oaks (2009)

29. Dahlberg, T., Hokkanen, P., Newman, M.: How business strategy and changes to business strategy impact the role and the tasks of CIOs: an evolutionary model. In: Proceedings of the Annual Hawaii International Conference on System Sciences, pp. 4910–4919 (2016)

30. Bogner, A., Littig, B., Menz, W.: Introduction: expert interviews – an introduction to a new methodological debate. In: Bogner, A., Littig, B., Menz, W. (eds.) Interviewing Experts, pp. 17–42. Palgrave Macmillan, New York (2009)

Itinerant Virtual Museum: An Innovate Technique to Learn Ancient History

Luz Díaz Granados$^{(\boxtimes)}$ ⓘ

Universidad Nacional de Costa Rica, Heredia, Costa Rica
ludiga25@gmail.com

Abstract. The aim of this study is to consolidate specific knowledges about ancient history in high school students, mediated using the itinerant virtual museum and virtual lenses, due to difficulties to learn history in Social Studies subject students have shown. This research presents a series of authors who support the use of virtual museums as a strategy in history contents and education. The methodology in this study is the co-design and it presents phases to co-create the itinerant virtual museums with the users to learn ancient history according to the Costa Rica curriculum. The data recollect was analyzed with different methods.

Keywords: Virtual Museum · Itinerant Virtual Museum · Ancient civilization · Difficulties in history · Co-design · Participative design

1 Introduction

The ancient civilizations of the world (Sumerian, Egyptian, Greek and Roman), constitute one of the most complex topics of the Costa Rican Social Studies curriculum. The history contents related to these civilizations are relevant because of their legacy to humanity, in fields like the cultural, architectural, social, political, economic and geographical. However, the learning such contents and history in general present a series of difficulties in some places in the world such as Costa Rica.

The Social Studies subject is taught trough a behavioristic lecture and does not allow to develop to critical skills or 21st century skills in the students. This causes a negative perception towards the learning process, and more specifically towards learning about history. Some additional consequences are memorization [7–16, 19], the episodic narrative, magistral class [6, 12], the lack of historical understanding [7–16], it is anachronistic [6, 13], it is boring [16, 18], it is useless [16] and teachers' methodology [15, 16]. The previous difficulties seek to be solved with different methods by teachers and researchers, who understand that contextualization to digital natives to learn is the key approach to understanding learning of history in Social Studies.

In this research an innovate technique is proposed to learn history in a contextualized style of the current society and allows learning through experiences, this method is the use of virtual museums with virtual lenses. In this study, this new type of museum with virtual lenses will be called Itinerant Virtual Museum (IVM). The reason of the name is due to the museum that can be mobilized (itinerant means that it travels from one

© Springer Nature Switzerland AG 2020
E. Popescu et al. (Eds.): SETE 2019, LNCS 11984, pp. 70–75, 2020.
https://doi.org/10.1007/978-3-030-38778-5_9

place to another) to any kind of school or place inside or outside of the country, to learn about specific historical topics. In some Costa Rican museum *valijas didácticas* (teaching bags) are used, which have some museum elements to learn history and they can be taken around the country to some schools or institutions that do not have financial resources or the time. That is how the idea to create an IVM that can travel to communities was born, it is not only to use the platform where the museum is, but the use of the lenses and a device with Wi-Fi in case internet is needed in the community (Fig. 1).

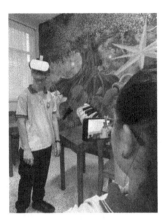

Fig. 1. Workshop 1

The purpose to use Virtual Museum is to benefit education and history teaching, like the approach to this area knowledge [5], motivational space and attractiveness [5, 17], promoting cultural legacies and learning experiences [5, 11], developing skills as creativity, critical thinking, autonomy, digital competences among others [1, 11], observing events or phenomenon that are difficult to understand [8, 20], saving time and money [17]. In brief, the IVM could become and innovate tool to learn ancient history and it could solve some problems when someone is learning history in Social Studies.

2   Methodology

The nature of the research is qualitative and it uses a methodology called participative design, also known co-design. This methodology seeks to solve a problem in an innovative way with the contribution of the users (in this research they will be students). This methodology is Scandinavian, and it applies to different areas [9] such as the education, where to evaluate an educational need by a prototype is essential to approach an educational innovation [3] with the cooperation of the users, which is imperative [2–4, 14]. The co-design phases applied in this research [3] are Preparation (determine the research problem), Exploration (seek to have greater clarity regarding the research problem), Vision (users and teachers explain how they could solve the problem), Operationalization (researcher and users create IVM prototypes) and Evaluation (assessment of experiences and project is improved and re-evaluated).

2.1 Study Group

The first group is a sample of seven students (three men and four women) from a high school in Santo Domingo de Heredia. They are thirteen and fourteen years old and belongs to middle socioeconomic class. It is important to mention the students in the research will be named users. One of the reasons why the sample is so small, is due to the administrative permissions in the high school (for the loss classes time in other subjects and the schedule provided by the principal), the use of virtual lenses (the school only has four devices) and lack of space. The application to small sample allows a manageable task when the researcher applies methods like interview or the observations [10]. The second group is formed for a team of Social Studies teachers who will evaluate the IVM in the workshop number four, to value the ancient history learning. The third group are the experts, who will evaluate the technical part of the product in the fields as content, design and navigation of the IVM. In this group are three professionals like a graphic designer, an historian and a virtual specialist.

2.2 Data Collection and Analysis

The qualitative techniques to data collect applies in the study are five focus group with users, teachers and experts (the first one asked for history, difficulties, solutions, tools and the next ones ask for navigate, content, design, experiences, preferences of the IVM). Four participant observations and four participative workshops to users, teachers and experts. These workshops test the IVM prototypes and each Workshop has methods to collect data (Thinking loud or do small assignment in the IVM). Data has been transcripted, classified, reviewed and compared several times to obtain a reliable result. There are two important moments missing to finish the study, these moments are the last test of prototype with users (third workshop) and the evaluation from the experts (fourth workshop).

2.3 Results

The results obtained so far were achieved implementing the last two co-design phases, however, we are presenting results in advance with techniques and analysis of data collect to this point.

1. Alternative tools to learning history: The users-students in the first focus group and the second workshop applied, mentioned that teachers must use different methodologies and tools to teach history in Social Studies. The seven students said that they like the subject, but six of them get bored in class and when they study for the exam, they consider the contents or topics very broad and boring. All the students agree that is necessary to apply new tools in class. The examples provided for the students after a web research of strategies or tools to help the learning history are: videos, civilizations o culture play, virtual walks, google earth, 360 grades pictures and Spanish information, because most the information found is in English and the information in Spanish is small and is not interesting.

2. Use of visual information: The focus group in the workshop one and two, provide information about how the students and users don't like the textual information, let alone if the information is vast. In both workshops applied, the students look for information in small videos, summary and specific images, places and information with a lot of colors and the information in videos or images is inside of the IVM, because in the first prototype some information was in a website outside of the IVM; they preferred to stay only in the IVM and could access all the information there.

3. Immersion research: In the first focus group and second workshop, four of six users indicate the preference to move inside the IVM, the words used by two of them were *"Poder caminar"* (be able to walk). Moreover, the users would like play inside of IVM something related with the civilization when they selected some element in the museum, and they would like to visit places of each ancient civilization.

4. More guidance: In the first workshop, for many of the users it was complicated to use the virtual lenses, the pointer and to search information in the IVM. Four users of six consider it complex the use of the pointer and one user suggest that a guide was necessary to learn how to learn used it. Even though in the second workshop, the use of the pointers and virtual lenses were more natural and simpler, one user still said it was difficult to navigate inside of the IVM and to use the pointer. Most of the users consider important to have a guide inside of the museum, in physical appearance, audio or information.

5. Viable as a learning tool: Mostly of the users consider technology as a tool to help in the learning process like the IVM can support the history learning. Because the lesson and the learning became a dynamic, interactive and interesting space and process, this motivation allows to learn history, because is not boring. In the third focus group, one question was about learn history mediated by IVM, and one of the users said *"Entonces al ser menos aburrida no nos va a costar tanto aprender"* (So, being less boring, it is not going to be difficult to learn).

3   Conclusion

The research is in the final phases and the information presented is the first clue to understand how the application of new learning tools can approach positive results. The use of IVM can incite motivation to learn ancient history or history in general and change the negative perception of some students about Social Studies. This learning tool can work the difficulties to understand learning about history, because there is a closer approach to history, development of empathy, interest, pleasure, contextualization to actual society and innovation. This research is expected to became in a learning tool for ancient history or others subjects. The research done so far is a platform with information of four ancient civilization so far away from Costa Rica (one of the reasons to explain the difficulty to learn this topic) with the most user's suggestions, opinions, preferences and elements that they like or dislike. Although the study has been satisfactory, some improvements must still be made, apply the last two workshops and analyze the data obtained again, because is the only way to support the idea that IVM is a learning tool to understand ancient history.

4   Limitations

Among some limitations so far in this research after to apply the mostly phases are: Few technological devices such as lens (only for), the high school's internet has blocked a lot of websites, there is no a stimulating place to apply the IVM prototypes with the users, problems continue with the use of the pointer, limitations in the platform used to create the IVM (sound, levels of navigation, small areas to visualize information, cannot export); difficulties to find places to take 360° pictures to IVM, and difficulties to find and manuals to add in the IVM, because this information is in other languages.

5   Suggestions and Next Steps

The next suggestions are written based on the data collect and analyzed until this moment: apply the IVM to a seventh grade in the same high school where the study was applied and another high school far away from the first one, validate the design, content and navigation with the experts and look for another type of platform to elaborate the IVM.

References

1. Ahmed Ismaeel, D., Al-Abdullatif, A.: The impact of an interactive virtual museum on students' attitudes toward cultural heritage education in the region of Al Hassa, Saudi Arabia. iJET **11**, 32–39 (2016). https://doi.org/10.3991/ijet.v11i04.5300
2. BakirlioğLu, Y., OğUr, D., DoğAn, C., Turhan, S.: An initial model for generative design research: bringing together generative focus group (GFG) and experience reflection modelling (ERM). Des. Technol. Educ. Int. J. **21**(1), 40–50 (2016)
3. Barbera, E., García, I., Fuertes-Alpiste, M.: A co-design process microanalysis: stages and facilitators of an inquiry-based and technology-enhanced learning scenario. Int. Rev. Res. Open Distrib. Learn. **18**(6) (2017). https://doi.org/10.19173/irrodl.v18i6.2805
4. Burkett, I.: Co-designing for social good: the role of citizens in designing and delivering social services. In: Burkett, I. (ed.) An Introduction to Co-Desing, pp. 3–11. Knode. https://www.yacwa.org.au/wp-content/uploads/2016/09/An-Introduction-to-Co-Design-by-Ingrid-Burkett.pdf. Accessed 2018
5. Elisondo, R., Melgar, M.: Museos y la Internet: contextos para la innovación. Innovación educativa **15**(68), 17–32 (2015)
6. Folgueira Lombardeo, P.: Dualidad de la Historia en el mundo 2.0. Tiempo y sociedad **18**, 133–143 (2015)
7. Gloria Zúñiga, C.: ¿Cómo se ha enseñado historia en Chile? Análisis de programas de estudio para enseñanza secundaria. Pensamiento educativo. Revista de investigación educacional latinoamericana, 119–135 (2015). https://doi.org/10.7764/pel.52.1.2015.9
8. Gonzalez Yebra, O., Aguilar, M., Aguilar, F., Lucas, M.: Co-design of a 3D virtual campus for synchronous distance teaching based on student satisfaction: experience at the University of Almería (Spain). Educ. Sci., 1–16 (2019). https://doi.org/10.3390/educsci9010021
9. Gros, B., Zhang-Yu, C., Ayuste, A., Escofet, A.: La apropiación de los dispositivos móviles en ciudadanos inmigrantes: el segundo nivel de división digital. Athenea Digit. **18**(3), e2175 (2018). https://doi.org/10.5565/rev/athenea.2175
10. Hernández Sampieri, R., Fernández Collado, C., Baptista Lucio, M.: Metodología de la Investigación, vol. 6. McGraw-Hill, México (2014)

11. Islek, D., Asiksoy, G.: The studies conducted regarding virtual museum area: a content analysis research. World J. Educ. Technol. Current Issues **11**(1), 087–093 (2019). https://doi.org/10.18844/wjet.v11i1.4012
12. Ledezma, I.: Aprendizaje significativo en la enseñanza de la historia. Sede Rodrigo Facio, Tesis de licenciatura en la enseñanza de los estudios sociales y la cívica de la Universidad de Costa Rica (2007)
13. Lombardi, A.: La enseñanza de la historia: consideraciones generales. Teoría y didáctica de las ciencias sociales, 9–23 (2000). ISSN 1316-9505. http://www.redalyc.org/articulo.oa?id=652/65200502. Accessed 2018
14. Maina, M., Pérez Mateo, M., Guardia, L., Sangrà, A.: Diseño de un curso de formación docente como práctica educativa abierta. Revista CIDUI, 1–15 (2015). https://doi.org/10.1016/j.sbspro.2015.07.021
15. Pleguezuelos Castillo, E.: Problemas para aprender ciencias sociales. Tesis de Master Profesorado de Educación Secundaria y Bachillerato, Formación Profesional y Enseñanza de Idiomas en la Universidad de Almería (2012). http://repositorio.ual.es/bitstream/handle/10835/2816/Trabajo.pdf?sequence=1. Accessed 2018
16. Prats, J.: Retos y dificultades para la enseñanza de la historia. In: Sanz Camañes, P., Molero García, J., Rodríguez González, D. (eds.) La historia en el aula Innovación docente y enseñanza de la historia en la educación secundaria, pp. 15–32. Editorial Milenio, Leiida (2017)
17. Sabbatini, M.: Centros de ciencia y museos científicos virtuales: teoría y practica. Teoría de la educación: educación y cultura en la sociedad de la información, vol. 4. Obtenido de Centros de ciencia y museos científicos virtuales: teoría y práctica (2003)
18. Tok, B.: Learning problems in History subject among the Secondary School-Students of Papum-pare district of Arunachal Pradesh. IRA-Int. J. Educ. Multidiscip. Stud. **2**, 133–139 (2016). https://doi.org/10.21013/jems.v5.n2.p9
19. Valverde, J.: Aprendizaje de la Historia y Simulación Educativa. Tejuelo, 83–99 (2010)
20. Yildirim, G., Elban, M., Yildirim, S.: Analysis of use of virtual reality technologies in history education: a case study. Asian J. Educ. Train. **4**(2), 62–69 (2018). https://doi.org/10.20448/journal.522.2018.42.62.69

Influence of the Type of Organizations on Their Readiness for Implementing Industry 4.0

Majid Ziaei Nafchi[✉] and Hana Mohelská

University of Hradec Králové, Rokitanského 62, 500 03 Hradec Králové, Czech Republic
{majid.ziaeinafchi,hana.mohelska}@uhk.cz

Abstract. Many studies have been conducted about Industry 4.0 and also about readiness and maturity models. The available studies are mostly from the technological point of view. Nonetheless, the organizational culture dimension of Industry 4.0 has some importance and requires more attention. The goal of this paper is to find out if the type of an organization impacts the innovative culture and subsequently the readiness of the organization for implementing industry 4.0. Results confirm that in fact the innovative organizational culture according to the index of organizational culture does depend on the type of an organization, and therefore type of the organization affects the readiness of the organization for implementing Industry 4.0.

Keywords: Industry 4.0 · Organizational culture · Type of organization

1 Introduction

The essence of the fourth Industrial revolution is considered and known as Industry 4.0, and manufacturing sector has been using it lately by utilizing cyber-physical systems (CPS) in order to grasp high levels of automation (Ziaei Nafchi and Mohelská 2018). The Cyber-Physical System (CPS) is the basis for smart factories and it makes it possible to interconnect sensors, machines and IT systems within the value chain throughout the boundaries of the enterprise (Kopp and Basl 2017).

Many studies have been conducted about Industry 4.0 and also about readiness and maturity models. The available studies are mostly from the technological point of view. Nonetheless, the organizational culture dimension of Industry 4.0 has some importance and requires more attention.

There are three types of organizational culture introduced by Wallach (1983), among them the innovative culture is believed to be as the type of culture that is enhances the implementation of Industry 4.0. In other words, Organizations with higher level of innovative culture are more ready and will have a smoother transition when it comes to implementing Industry 4.0.

Based on this assumption, the main objective of this study is to find out if the innovative culture, which is believed to be an important pre-condition for implementing Industry 4.0, differs in organizations of different types.

© Springer Nature Switzerland AG 2020
E. Popescu et al. (Eds.): SETE 2019, LNCS 11984, pp. 76–82, 2020.
https://doi.org/10.1007/978-3-030-38778-5_10

2 Theoretical Background

2.1 Organizational Culture

Armstrong (2006) defines organizational culture as: "Organizational or corporate culture is the pattern of values, norms, beliefs, attitudes and assumptions that may not have been articulated but that shape the ways in which people in organizations behave and things get done. It can be expressed through the medium of a prevailing management style in the organization."

Organizational culture is the shared beliefs, principles, standards, and assumptions that form behavior by making commitment, offering direction, engendering a collective identity, and building a community. An organizational culture is thought to be effective when it is in the same orientation with the organization's environment, resources, values, and goals (Okatan and Alankus 2017).

Verdu-Jover et al. (2018) believe that organizational culture is defined and used generally as a accurately steady set of values, beliefs, assumptions, and symbols distributed in the organization and according to this foundation, scholars have developed studies regarding the relationship between several types of cultures and innovation results.

According to Rahman et al. (2018) Organizational culture is considered as a foremost enabler in constructing a positive knowledge transfer environment; and additional researches about this subject came to the conclusions that organizational cultural elements like trust, communication, reward system, and organizational structure can have some influence on knowledge sharing in organizations in a positive way.

Companies that seeking excellence in the open innovation paradigm, need to enable their inspiring leaders to endorse a learning culture (Naqshbandi and Tabche 2018).

2.2 Wallach's Model

Ellen J. Wallach characterized organizational culture into three dimensions: bureaucratic, supportive, and innovative. Bureaucratic culture is understood to be a prominent hierarchical organization that is vastly organized on the basis of a clear definition of authority.

The attention of the supportive culture is on interpersonal relationships and it is originated on mutual trust, encouragement and co-operation. Innovative culture instead is dynamic and it supports creative work, takes on new challenges and motivates risky behavior (Wallach 1983).

Wallach's Questionnaire (1983), similarly known as The Organizational Culture Index (OCI), is universally recognized. This questionnaire is designed in a way in order to analyze the organizational culture level and due to the fact that individual questions of the questionnaire are very simple, social and technological developments have little to no major effects on it.

Due to the simplicity of Wallach´s Questionnaire and since it allows for the results to be compared internationally, scholars are still finding this method to be useful today. Reviewing of scientific sources like "Scopus" and "Web of Science" proves the validation of this model, as it is evident in impact factor journals that researchers are still using this method.

2.3 Industry 4.0

Kopp and Basl (2017) state "Industry 4.0 concept can be characterized as a transformation of production as separate automated factories into fully automated and optimized manufacturing environments. Production processes are linked vertically and horizontally within enterprise systems".

Thanks to Industry 4.0, manufacturing unique products in terms of excellent quality has become possible and with a price that is matching the price of mass-produced products (Nowotarski and Paslawski 2017).

Implementing Industry 4.0 and digital transformation concepts in theory is gradually significant for manufacturing businesses that are performing in such markets that are dynamic and competitive. Though in practice, there are a few challenges for organizations while implementing such concepts since Industry 4.0 is considered to be more as a concept rather than a ready-to-implement solution; Furthermore, the complex nature of Industry 4.0 triggers delays to the successful implementation of Industry 4.0 systems in such a way that they combine all organizational features and levels accurately (Issa et al. 2018).

Suitable resources, accomplished and competent employees and well-organized processes, that are appropriately flexible and innovative, are believed to be necessities while implementing the Smart concept (Odważny et al. 2018).

Lak and Rezaeenour (2018) state "Maturity models can be considered as a structured collection of elements in which certain aspects of the capability maturity in an organization are described." Maturity models are normally used as a tool to conceptualize and measure maturity of an organization or as a process concerning certain target state (Schumacher et al. 2016).

The following three implementation phases are suggested by Odważny et al. (2018) to be distinguished within company: Aspiration phase, Maturity phase, and Smart factory.

Basl and Doucek (2018) state that at the "micro" level, the readiness of the organization is essentially an evaluation or assessment of the maturity degree of the organization, thus the readiness models (maturity models) prevail.

Colli et al. (2018) state "The transformation of the manufacturing sector towards Industry 4.0 is setting the scene for a major industrial change. Currently, the need for assisting companies in this transformation is covered by a number of maturity models that assess their digital maturity and provide indications accordingly."

To accomplish success in an environment that is as uncertain as Industry 4.0, learning, training, and innovation capability play substantial roles. Organizational training, learning, and innovations are intensely dependent on the role employees in the organization and therefore, organizations need to arrange their strategies in accordance with to what they expect from their employees (Shamim et al. 2017).

Transparency is another important parameter to be considered as it plays an important role in rationality, decent governance, and better progress (Ziaei Nafchi et al. 2018).

3   Methodology and Objectives

The main objective of this study is to find out if the innovative culture, which is believed to be an important pre-condition for implementing Industry 4.0, differs in organizations of different types. Thus the hypothesis was formulated as following:

H0: The innovative organizational culture according to the index of organizational culture depends on the type of an organization (domestic (Czech in this case), international, state).

The Organizational Culture Index (OCI) questionnaire was used as the main method for the purpose of this study as well as methods of analysis and synthesis, induction and deduction, abstraction and concretization were used.

Data was collected from 1500 copies of the Wallach's questionnaire (translated to Czech language) that were printed and distributed among part-time students of university of Hradec Kralove in the years 2013, 2015, and 2017.

To test and analyze the obtained data, ANOVA, Kruskal-Wallis, Brown-Forsythe, and Cronbach's alpha were used.

4   Results and Analysis

Results of statistical analysis show that for the whole period 2013–2017, there are noticeable differences among different types of companies in all different types of cultures. The least differences are evident in the supportive culture, where it has a significant difference only between Czech and state organizations (Table 1) Ziaei Nafchi (2019).

Table 1. Results of Statistical analyses of dependence of the culture indexes on the type of company (C-Czech, I-international, S-state organization)

	Bureaucratic	Innovative	Supporting
ANOVA	<0.001	<0.001*	0.029*
Kruskal-Wallis	<0.001	<0.001	0.003
Differences	C-I, C-S	C-I, C-S, I-S	C-S

* Brown-Forsythe test used for non-homogeneity of scattering.

The innovative culture is the highest in international organizations, and then Czech organizations are slightly lagging behind. Finally the state organizations with a large distance from the other two types have the least amount of innovative culture, which completely makes sense.

Figure 1 clearly shows the differences mentioned before between the different types of organizations, it is evident that the state organizations have the least innovative culture and the international organizations have the most bureaucratic culture.

Cronbach's alpha was calculated for Wallach's questionnaire based on the dimensions they were associated with in order to check the internal consistency of the questionnaire. The internal consistency of the bureaucratic culture and the innovative culture are considered to be acceptable and the internal consistency of the supportive culture is good.

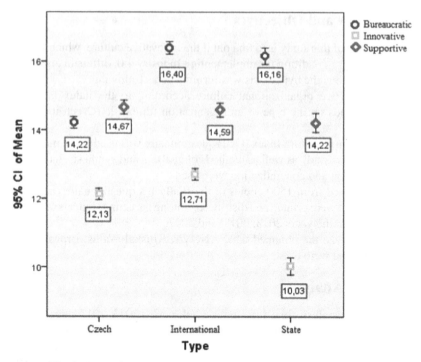

Fig. 1. Dependence on the type of the organization. **Source: Author.**

5   Discussion and Conclusions

Generally international organizations had the highest innovative culture in the evaluation and not far behind are Czech organizations, and with huge distance from them the state organizations. To explain the reason behind these differences we have to go back to the 24 parameters of the Organizational Culture Index; below the individual parameters are organized in front of the type of culture they are generally associated with:

- Bureaucratic culture: hierarchical, procedural, hierarchical structured, the Order rules here, activities are managed and regulated here, established/solid, careful, aimed at holding power.
- Innovative culture: risking, results-oriented, creative, overpressure/explosive, stimulating, posing challenges, entrepreneurial, full of new ideas.
- Supportive culture: based on cooperation, relationship-oriented, supporting, friendly, and allowing for personal freedom, fair, safe, trusting their employees.

Based on these parameters it is possible to explain why state owned organizations are less innovative; normally state organizations have a hierarchical structure and people who have power manage them with rules and procedures. These people prefer to stay in power so they do not endorse creative work, they don't let anyone to pose any threats or challenges to them and so on.

It is possible to argue why the supportive culture gets weaker the larger the organization gets in a similar fashion; supportive culture is established on cooperation and it is relationship-oriented with greater levels of trust, clearly it is more challenging to establish such values with others in an environment where there are more people.

Based on the findings there is sufficient evidence to conclude that the innovative organizational culture according to the index of organizational culture depends on the type of an organization. Hence, the null hypothesis H0 is NOT rejected.

Therefore, it can be said that the type of organization has an impact on the readiness of it for the implementation of industry 4.0.

Acknowledgement. The paper was written with the support of the specific project 2106/2019 grant "Determinants of Cognitive Processes Impacting the Work Performance" granted by the University of Hradec Králové, Czech Republic.

References

Armstrong, M.: Armstrong's Handbook of Management and Leadership: A Guide to Managing for Results, 2nd edn. Kogan Page, London (2006)

Basl, J., Doucek, P.: Metamodel of indexes and maturity models for Industry 4.0 readiness in enterprises. In: Doucek, P., Chroust, G., Oškrdal, V. (eds.) IDIMT 2018: Strategic Modelling in Management, Economy and Society - 26th Interdisciplinary Information Management Talks Kutná Hora, Czech Republic, 5–7 September 2018, pp 33–40 (2018). ISBN 978-3-99062-339-8

Colli, M., Madsen, O., Berger, U., Møller, C., Wæhrens, B.V., Bockholt, M.: Contextualizing the outcome of a maturity assessment for industry 4.0. In: IFAC Papersonline, 16th IFAC Symposium on Information Control Problems in Manufacturing INCOM 2018, vol. 51, pp. 1347–1352 (2018). https://doi.org/10.1016/j.ifacol.2018.08.34

Issa, A., Hatiboglu, B., Bildstein, A., Bauernhansl, T.: Industrie 4.0 roadmap: framework for digital transformation based on the concepts of capability maturity and alignment. In: Procedia CIRP, 51st CIRP Conference on Manufacturing Systems, vol. 72, pp. 973–978 (2018). https://doi.org/10.1016/j.procir.2018.03.151

Kopp, J., Basl, J.: Study of the readiness of czech companies to the industry 4.0. J. Syst. Integr. (1804-2724) **8**(3), 40 (2017). https://doi.org/10.20470/jsi.v8i2.313

Lak, B., Rezaeenour, J.: Maturity assessment of social customer knowledge management (SCKM) using fuzzy expert system. J. Bus. Econ. Manag. **19**(1), 192–212 (2018). https://doi.org/10.3846/16111699.2018.1427620

Naqshbandi, M.M., Tabche, I.: The interplay of leadership, absorptive capacity, and organizational learning culture in open innovation: testing a moderated mediation model. Technol. Forecast. Soc. Change **133**, 156–167 (2018). https://doi.org/10.1016/j.techfore.2018.03.017

Nowotarski, P., Paslawski, J.: Industry 4.0 concept introduction into construction SMEs. IOP Conf. Ser. Mater. Sci. Eng. **245**(5), 1 (2017). https://doi.org/10.1088/1757-899x/245/5/052043

Odważny, F., Szymańska, O., Cyplik, P.: Smart factory: the requirements for implementation of the industry 4.0 solutions in FMCG environment - case study. Logforum **14**(2), 257 (2018). https://doi.org/10.17270/j.log.2018.253

Okatan, K., Alankuş, O.B.: Effect of organizational culture on internal innovation capacity. J. Organ. Stud. Innov. **4**(3), 18 (2017)

Rahman, M.H., Moonesar, I.A., Hossain, M.M., Islam, M.Z.: Influence of organizational culture on knowledge transfer: evidence from the Government of Dubai. J. Public Aff. **18**(1) (2018). https://doi.org/10.1002/pa.1696

Schumacher, A., Erol, S., Sihn, W.: A maturity model for assessing industry 4.0 readiness and maturity of manufacturing enterprises. In: Procedia CIRP, The Sixth International Conference on Changeable, Agile, Reconfigurable and Virtual Production (CARV 2016), vol. 52, pp. 161–166 (2016). https://doi.org/10.1016/j.procir.2016.07.040

Shamim, S., Shuang, C., Hongnian, Y., Yun, L.: Examining the feasibilities of industry 4.0 for the hospitality sector with the lens of management practice. Energies (19961073), **10**(4), 1 (2017). https://doi.org/10.3390/en10040499

Verdu-Jover, A.J., Alos-Simo, L., Gomez-Gras, J.: Adaptive culture and product/service innovation outcomes. Eur. Manag. J. **36**, 330–340 (2018). https://doi.org/10.1016/j.emj.2017.07.004

Wallach, E.: Individuals and organization: the cultural match. Training Dev. J. **37**, 28–36 (1983)

Ziaei Nafchi, M., Mohelská, H.: Effects of industry 4.0 on the labor markets of Iran and Japan. Economies **6**(3), 39 (2018). https://doi.org/10.3390/economies6030039

Ziaei Nafchi, M., Mohelská, H., Marešová, P., Sokolová, M.: E-governance: digital trancparency and the model of interaction within Czech municipalities. In: Doucek, P., Chroust, G., Oškrdal, V. (eds.) IDIMT 2018: Strategic Modelling in Management, Economy and Society - 26th Interdisciplinary Information Management Talks, Kutná Hora, Czech Republic, 5–7 September 2018, pp. 41–48 (2018). ISBN 978-3-99062-339-8

Ziaei Nafchi, M.: Industry 4.0 and preparing companies for implementing it. Doctoral dissertation, University of Hradec Kralove, 2019. Hradec Kralove, Czech Republic: Faculty of Informatics and Management (2019)

Semantic Competency Directory
for Constructive Alignment in Digital Learning
Designs and Systems

Ilona Buchem[✉] and Johannes Konert

Beuth University of Applied Sciences, Luxemburger Str. 10, 13351 Berlin, Germany
{buchem,konert}@beuth-hochschule.de

Abstract. The paper describes the semantic competency directory as a technology which can be used to support constructive alignment in digital learning designs and systems. This article describes the competency directory developed in the Open Virtual Mobility project which can be used to align competencies (learning objectives) with learning activities, e-assessment and digital credentials (Open Badges). We describe technical considerations, requirements and the implementation of the competency directory with three components, i.e. Node.js-based backend with REST API, Neo4j graph database and a web-based user interface which fetches information from the REST-API backend. The paper demonstrates the value of the competency directory for support of constructive alignment in learning designs and systems especially in context of competency alignment in digital credentials.

Keywords: Competency alignment · Constructive alignment · Competency directory · Semantic alignment · Learning design · Digital credentials · Virtual mobility

1 Introduction

The model of Constructive Alignment by Biggs [1] proposes the systemic alignment of three elements of learning design, i.e. learning outcomes, learning activities and assessment of learning focused on demonstrating the achievement of the learning outcomes. The model has been widely used to guide impactful learning design both in context of traditional teaching and learning practices as well as in technology-enhanced learning, including Open Educational Practices [2] and Massive Open Online Courses [3]. In competency-based learning approaches, learning outcomes are defined as skills or competencies, e.g. in form of statements which describe what and how well learners will able to do after completing a course [4]. Defining learning outcomes as competencies and the constructive alignment approach have led to improving clarity and transparency in education [5]. However, some of the practical challenges in the application of constructive alignment model remain the development of learning activities and assessment tasks which are aligned to the learning outcomes [3]. Constructive alignment has been also discussed in relation to digital micro-credentials, e.g. Open Badges, which can be constructively aligned with learning outcomes and can serve as evidence that a learning

© Springer Nature Switzerland AG 2020
E. Popescu et al. (Eds.): SETE 2019, LNCS 11984, pp. 83–88, 2020.
https://doi.org/10.1007/978-3-030-38778-5_11

outcome has been achieved [6]. The problem of alignment of competencies in context of Open Badges has been the ambiguity of competency descriptions and the lack of semantic metadata of competency frameworks [7]. One of the approaches to this problem are semantic description of competencies and tools which allow for improved constructive alignment.

In this paper we describe the semantic competency directory and demonstrate its value for competency alignment in digital learning designs and systems following the principles of constructive alignment. We present the competency directory as a technology part of the semantic alignment of competencies and describe an application example from the Open Virtual Mobility project to reference a set of skills in Open Badges. The paper ends with conclusions and recommendations for future work.

2   Background and Related Work

The first prototype of the semantic competency directory was developed in the Open Badge Network project (OBN, Erasmus+, 2014–2017) as a service for the decentralized search and cross-referencing of linked-data descriptions of competencies [7]. The next iteration of the competency directory is goal of the Open Virtual Mobility project (OpenVM, Erasmus+, 2017–2020). Open Virtual Mobility is a strategic partnership for innovation and the exchange of good practices and aims at enhancing the uptake of virtual mobility in higher education by improving virtual mobility skills. To achieve this, the Open Virtual Mobility Learning Hub was developed as a learning environment for achievement, assessment and recognition of virtual mobility skills [8]. The OpenVM Learning Hub hosts altogether eight different miniMOOCs each dedicated to a specific virtual mobility skill area. The eight skill areas were identified through a Group Concept Mapping study [9]. The research results were used to define the skill set with eight main skill areas and respective sub-skills at three levels, i.e. foundation, intermediate and advanced [9].

The OpenVM skill set has served as a foundation for constructive alignment in the design of the set of OpenVM miniMOOCs [15]. The OpenVM skill set includes semantic definitions of competencies and their cross-references, e.g. "is part of". The competency directory provides unique URL access to altogether 33 OpenVM competency definitions [7]. Each miniMOOC addresses one of the eight OpenVM skill areas as learning outcomes and aligns learning activities and e-assessment to support the achievement of these learning outcomes. The alignment of learning outcomes, learning activities and e-assessment has been supported by semantic competency definitions referenced in the competency directory. Upon successful completion of each miniMOOC at one of the three levels, a digital micro-credential (Open Badge) can be claimed by the learner to recognise the specific competency. Digital micro-credentials serve as evidence for achievement of learning outcomes. The following section describes the current version of the semantic Competency Directory and its possible uses for Constructive Alignment in digital learning designs and systems.

3   Competency Directory for Semantic Referencing of Skills

3.1   Technical Considerations

The decentralized semantic web allows to create new competency directories by cross-referencing the definitions by IRIs. If humans access IRIs, a directory will provide an HTML website with the competency definition, existing cross-references and a search interface to navigate the content. If an algorithm fetches IRIs, a directory will answer with a more suitable format for automatic interpretation like JavaScript Object Notation Linked Data (JSON-LD) [10]. Alternatively, the answer to a request could always be a HTML website with embedded semantic data using Rich Structured Data Markup for Web Documents (RDFa) [11]. Since Open Badge Standard version 1.1 encourages to use JSON-LD, this format is implemented in the OpenVM project [12]. The vocabulary, which is important for expressing the semantic meaning of competences and their cross-references, is the set of noun terms for nodes and relationship terms for edges, which are used to express the competence definitions and their structure in a graph. To enable a decentralised network of competence frameworks referencing each other, the ESCO dataset and vocabulary is used in the OpenVM project. ESCO, the European Skills Competencies and Occupations Framework, includes vocabulary definitions to express competences and their relation to each other. ESCO competency directory provides a web-interface for humans to search and a REST-API that delivers RDF or JSON-LD data. ESCO enables the expression of semantic relationships within ESCO and to other competence frameworks [13].

3.2   Requirements

The competency directory project serves as a provider for machine-readable semantic competency definitions. Thus, the elements of the learning pathway, i.e. learning outcomes, learning activities, e-assessment and micro-credentials, can be constructively aligned by referencing the appropriate competency definitions. By using IRIs it is easier for algorithms that parse such parts of the learner pathway to calculate similarities due to overlapping or identical competency references. Additionally, it is useful to have a web-interface for humans to access the available information via HTML pages. To elicit the requirements, an online survey was conducted in 2018 involving nine technology-enhanced learning experts [7]. The following 13 key requirements were extracted: (1) list of all competencies of the OpenVM framework, (2) search by keywords; (3) unique IRIs for individual competences, (4) multi-language support (user interface), (5) direct access via ID (to competences), (6) competency descriptions, (7) cross-referencing competences (e.g. similarity, inclusion), (9) search by existing translation (language), (10) low latency in responses (<200 ms), (11) encrypted communication via HTTPS, (12) REST level 2 compliant HTTP API, (13) JSON-LD format for input/output, (14) multi-language support (for competency definitions) [7]. All requirements except for 4, 8 and 10 have been implemented. HTTPS communication will be added by using LetsEncrypt technology, which provides free-of-charge SSL-certificates HTTPS. A multi-language interface will be added, e.g. for Open Badge issuing.

3.3 Implementation

The implementation includes three loosely coupled components, all running in stan-dalone containers using Docker Runtime. The first component is a Node.js-based back-end with a REST API (Level 2), which provides the competence entries via unique IRIs in the JSON-LD format using ESCO vocabulary (Listing 1). It uses the second component, which is a Neo4j graph database that contains the competency entries as nodes and the references between them as directed edges. Both, nodes and edges are tagged with attributes like node-type, reference-type, and available languages. ESCO was used as vocabulary for node and reference types as far as data allows. The third component is a web-based user interface created with the React.js framework as a single page application which fetches information from the REST-API backend (Fig. 1).

```
[{
  "http://www.w3.org/2004/02/skos/core#altLabel": [],
  "http://purl.org/dc/terms/description": [{
    "@language": "en",
    "@value": "Learning in an open digital context"
  }],
  "@id": "http://localhost:6060/entries/15",
  "http://localhost:6060/context/isEssentialPartOf": [],
  "http://localhost:6060/context/isOptionalPartOf": [],
  "http://localhost:6060/context/isSameAs": [],
  "http://localhost:6060/context/isSimilarTo": [],
  "http://localhost:6060/context/needsAsPrerequisite": [],
  "http://www.w3.org/2004/02/skos/core#prefLabel": [{
    "@language": "en",
    "@value": "Demonstrating independent learning"
  }],
  "http://data.europa.eu/esco/model#skillReuseLevel": [{
    "@value": "1 Transversal"
  }],
  "http://data.europa.eu/esco/model#skillType": [{
    "@value": "Skill or Competence"
  }]
}]
```

Listing 1. REST-API response example for competency entry ID 15 as extended dataset in JSON-LD format, IRI http://localhost:6060/entires/15?format=extended

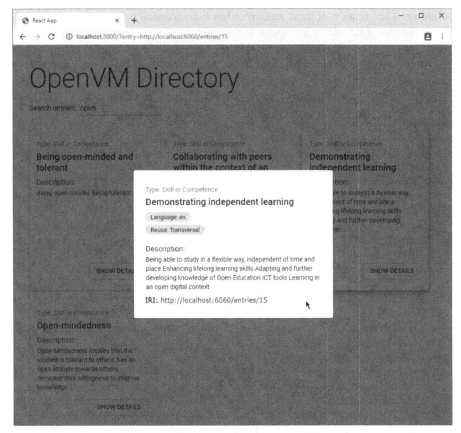

Fig. 1. Screenshot of the frontend for human search with a single-view overlay (entry ID 15) providing IRIs to be used for deep-linking, e.g. in Open Badge specifications.

4   Conclusions and Future Work

The benefits of using the competency directory and adding metadata to the elements of the learning pathway, e.g. learning outcomes, activities, e-assessment, digital credentials, can be reached by using the algorithmic ability to recommend suitable resources for identified skills, adapt learning pathways and define criteria for issuing digital credentials after passing the e-assessment [8]. Especially in view of the Open Badge Specification 2.0, which allows the use of extended URLs as IRIs, the competency directory may be used to avoid ambiguities in referencing the same competency in different digital credentials [15]. The positive effects on better constructive alignment of the learning design and on improved achievement of the skills by learners need to be evaluated in user studies in the future. Until end of 2020 the applicability for Open Badge alignment is planned to be evaluated within the OpenVM project as an expert interview after integration in the project infrastructure.

Disclaimer: The creation of these resources has been (partially) funded by the ERAS-MUS+ grant program of the European Union under grant no. 2017-1-DE01-KA203-003494. Neither the European Commission nor the project's national funding agency DAAD are responsible for the content or liable for any losses or damage resulting of the use of these resources.

References

1. Biggs, J.: Enhancing teaching through constructive alignment. High. Educ. **32**(3), 347–364 (1996)
2. Paskevicius, M.: Conceptualizing open educational practices through the lens of constructive alignment. Open Prax. **9**(2), 125–140 (2017). International Council for Open and Distance Education. https://www.learntechlib.org/p/181424. Accessed 20 June 2019
3. Karunanayaka, S., Naidu, S., Rajendra, J.C.N., Ariadurai, S.A.: Designing continuing professional development MOOCs to promote the adoption of OER and OEP. Open Prax. **10**(2), 179–190 (2018). International Council for Open and Distance Education https://www.learntechlib.org/p/183584. Accessed 20 June 2019
4. Boyd, S.: Learning outcomes and opportunities in property education through constructive alignment. In: Proceedings of the 21st Pacific-Rim Real Estate Society Conference, pp. 1–18 (2015)
5. Remneland Wikhamn, B.: Challenges of adopting constructive alignment in action learning education. Action Learn. Res. Pract. **14**(1), 18–28 (2016)
6. Cross, S., Galley, R.: MOOC Badging and the Learning Arc. OLDS MOOC Blog Post. The Open University's repository of research publications and other research outputs (2012). http://oro.open.ac.uk/42038/7/OLDS%20MOOC.pdf. Accessed 20 June 2019
7. Konert, J., Buchem, I., Lewis, L., Hamilton, G., Riches, T.: Competency alignment of open badges. In: Stracke, C.M., Shanks, M., Tveiten, O. (eds.) Smart Universities Education's Digital Future. Kristiansand, Official Proceedings of the International WLS and LINQ Conference 2017, Logos Verlag Berlin, pp. 30–36 (2017)
8. Buchem, I., et al.: Designing a collaborative learning hub for virtual mobility skills - insights from the European project *Open Virtual Mobility*. In: Zaphiris, P., Ioannou, A. (eds.) LCT 2018. LNCS, vol. 10924, pp. 350–375. Springer, Cham (2018). https://doi.org/10.1007/978-3-319-91743-6_27
9. Firssova, O., Rajagopal, K.: Open VM Competence Framework (2018). https://www.openvirtualmobility.eu/topics/outputs. Accessed 18 June 2019
10. W3C JSON-LD Working Group: JSON-LD - JSON for Linking Data. https://json-ld.org. Accessed 19 June 2019
11. The RDF Web Apps Working Group: RDFa. http://rdfa.info. Accessed 20 June 2019
12. IMS Global Learning Consortium: Open Badges v2.0 IMS Final Release. http://www.imsglobal.org/sites/default/files/Badges/OBv2p0Final/index.html. Accessed 18 June 2019
13. European Commission ESCO handbook. European Skills, Competences, Qualifications and Occupations (2019). https://ec.europa.eu/esco/portal/document/en/0a89839c-098d-4e34-846c-54cbd5684d24. Accessed 18 June 2019
14. Konert, J.: O3-A1.2/A1.3 Competency Directory requirements and functional prototype (accepted for publication). Open Virtual Mobility Erasmus+ (2019). https://www.openvirtualmobility.eu/topics/outputs. Accessed 16–18 June 2019

Education Needs in Context of Migration and Industry 4.0 in Selected EU Countries

Libuše Svobodová[1]([⊠]), Martina Hedvicakova[1], and Alfiya Kuznetsova[2]

[1] University of Hradec Kralove, Rokitanskeho 62, 50003 Hradec Kralove, Czech Republic
{libuse.svobodova,martina.hedvicakova}@uhk.cz
[2] Bashkir State Agrarian University, Street of the 50th Anniversary of the Octobrya,
450001 Ufa, Russia
alfia_2009@mail.ru

Abstract. Migration is a phenomenon of the 21st century. A lot of countries are looking for an effective solution to solve it. The use of information and communication technologies (ICT), which plays a key role during the fourth industrial revolution is one of the options. ICT have a crucial role in societal and technological progress. If domestic countries use ICT and modern technologies that are encouraged, their people will be able to use advanced technologies more than in countries where they are not used to such an extent. For this reason, the Digital Adoption Index (DAI) results for selected countries were evaluated in the article. The DAI is a worldwide index that measures countries' digital adoption across three dimensions of the economy: people, government and business. The aim of the article is to compare all countries from Visegrad group and from Germany. Migrants in the Czech Republic and in Germany were connected with Digital Adoption Index and DAI People sub-index from countries of their origin were evaluated into deeper evaluation.

Keywords: Migration · Industry 4.0 · Digital Adoption Index · ICT · Labor market · Education

1 Introduction

The globalization of migration processes at its best has a positive effect on the economic development of host countries: it contributes to the growth of gross domestic product, compensation for a shortage of labor resources, growth and creation of new knowledge, active development of innovations and others. On the other hand, migration processes increase the level of competition in local labor markets, reduce the cost of labor and lead to an increase in unemployment. The study of domestic and foreign experience of studies devoted to the study of the influence of international labor migration on the development of labor markets in recipient countries shows that there are many-sided directions for scientific research. Consistency of regulatory measures is necessary to ensure the safety and orderliness of migration processes. To reduce or accelerate migration flows, maximize economic and social preferences while minimizing the costs of migrants and host

© Springer Nature Switzerland AG 2020
E. Popescu et al. (Eds.): SETE 2019, LNCS 11984, pp. 89–98, 2020.
https://doi.org/10.1007/978-3-030-38778-5_12

communities, you need to know exactly how migration transformations affect economic policy in the European Union.

Migration has become a key area of the 21st century. National governments are making great efforts and financial resources to address this problem. The use of ICT in education is a key role in migration issues. Simultaneously, information and communication technologies (ICT) have a crucial role in societal progress [1, 2]. The application of digital technologies in sectors such as governments, nongovernmental organizations and organic social movements has the potential to improve participation, transparency and accountability [1, 3].

Several existing studies indicate that other dimensions of education are also helping to shape return migration. First, studying in a foreign country is a quickly growing phenomenon around the world (Appave 2010; Boyle et al. 1998; Globerman and Shapiro 2008). The education obtained abroad helps migrants to establish themselves in the labour market of the host country, but it may be highly valued in the origin country as well, facilitating return migration. For example, the study by Bijwaard (2010) shows that most foreign students return to their homeland upon graduating from host country universities. Second, previous research has established that many immigrants do not find a job to match their level of education (Hardy 2010), which potentially increases their willingness to return. Analogous behaviour may be observed when many immigrants focus on earning the best possible income instead of finding a job that corresponds to their qualification (Drinkwater et al. 2009; Trevena 2011) [17].

2 Methodology and Goals

This paper discusses the issue of education migrants and the development of computer literacy in Czech Republic in context Industry 4.0. Habits of future education and use of new technology in education are analyzed. Data from Strategic framework for employment policy by 2030 in the Czech Republic and digital Czech Republic are presented. Data from Eurostat about migration and education are presented.

The aim of this paper is to analyze the impact of migration processes on the labor market in the context of Industry 4.0. The impacts of the level of education of individual migrants from selected countries will be analyzed. Emphasis will be placed on market requirements within the current fourth industrial revolution and the need for ICT knowledge and skills. The aim of the article is comparison all countries from Visegrad group and Germany that is the most important country in the export for the Czech economy. Into deeper evaluation was focused on the main groups of migrants in the Czech Republic, in Germany connected with Digital Adoption Index and DAI People Sub-index from countries of their origin.

Literature review encompasses following areas: definitions to key expressions relevant to the scope of the paper like migrants, Industry 4.0, Digital Adoption Index, ICT and technology enhancing ageing experience.

The article is based on secondary sources. The secondary sources provide information about Digital Adoption Index and education, professional literature, information collected from professional press, web sites, discussions and previous participation at professional seminars and international conferences related to the chosen subject. It was then necessary to select, classify and update accessible relevant information from the numerous published materials that provide the basic knowledge about the selected topic. The DAI is a worldwide index that measures countries' digital adoption across three dimensions of the economy: people, government, and business. The index covers 180 countries on a 0–1 scale and emphasizes the "supply-side" of digital adoption to maximize coverage and simplify theoretical linkages. The overall DAI is the simple average of three sub-indexes. Each sub-index comprises technologies necessary for the respective agent to promote development in the digital era: increasing productivity and accelerating broad-based growth for business, expanding opportunities and improving welfare for people, and increasing the efficiency and accountability of service delivery for government [30].

3   Literature Review

International labor migration is an integral part of the global labor market. Being formed under the influence of the processes of globalization and regionalization, in the conditions of technical and technological development in countries and regions of the world, modern labor migration is characterized by an unprecedented increasing scale and complexity. With an increase in the population's spatial mobility, international migration flows increasingly affect various socio-economic development aspects of host territories — economic, social, demographic, and other characteristics. On the one hand, the influx of migrant workers increases the number of labor resources in the territory, and therefore its economic potential. On the contrary, the competition that arises on the local labor market, in the absence of large investment projects, stimulates unemployment growth and reduces wages in industries most dependent on foreign labor. Analysis of the accumulated domestic and foreign experience in studying the impact of international labor migration on the development of labor markets in the host territory showed the breadth and diversity of existing research directions. Given the complex nature of the labor migration impact on all aspects of territories socio-economic life, there is a need to develop an integrated economic approach using an index analysis method.

Hedvičáková and Svobodova published papers aimed at labor market and unemployment [4–8], sustainable development [9], Consequences of Industry 4.0 in Business and Economics [10], indicators focused on well-being, welfare etc. [11] and the education of people in the connection with use of advanced technologies [12]. Volejníková's published paper, Influence of migration on the labor market in the Czech Republic [13] and is also focused on unemployment and labor market [14, 15]. Janderová focused on immigration and asylum policies in the EU [16]. ICT has certainly had a major impact on the whole process of mobility and migration [19, 20]. In his conceptual study, Kellerman (2011) concludes that all current mobilities are based on and dependent on ICT. Whence the emerging research on ICT and it is recognized that ICT have had a major impact on migration trends by considerably diversifying and increasing migration opportunities [19, 20]. ICT also directly influence employment; both by creating new jobs and by acting as a tool that empowers workers to manipulate data and innovate [21, 22]. Telecommunications infrastructure generates employment across a wide range of sectors and within a variety of professions by aiding in the creation and maintenance of networks of communication [23]. Employment, according to Andrianaivo and Kpodar [23] is also generated through the use of ICT to establish new retailing networks. Further, when taken as tools, ICT empower workers by making labor markets "more transparent, innovative, and inclusive" [21].

3.1 Strategic Framework for Employment Policy by 2030 in the Czech Republic

It appears that the modern labor market requires a more complex approach for some groups of disadvantaged people, which is not applicable in the current system to the necessary extent. One of them is further education and retraining. The main problem with retraining remains, in particular, their ability to respond to labor market demands, especially in the situations of dynamically changing skill needs. However, employers and workers are not satisfied with retraining and their process. Therefore, document action plan of work 4.0 in the Czech Republic was done. Being aware of these new trends, and the Industry 4.0 Initiative, the Ministry of Labor and Social Affairs in 2016 develop a research study, Work Initiatives 4.0 ("Work 4.0"). The main effort of the Ministry of Labor and Social Affairs in this area is to analyze the current situation and future labor market trends related to the 4th Industrial Revolution and to prepare scenarios and measures to respond adequately to these changes. Addressing the impact of the 4th Industrial Revolution, digitization of state administration and the economy on society is a complex issue and, by its very nature, multiresort with regard to the spheres of social and economic life that interferes. For this reason, on the basis of Government Resolution No. 629/2018, program Digital Czech Republic was created, which is an umbrella strategic cross-sectional document. The process of setting up and implementing the program is coordinated by the Government Council for the Information Society. The Digital Czech Program consists of three basic pillars: Czech Republic in Digital Europe, Information Concept of the Czech Republic and The Digital Economy and Society. No less important role, such as the actual impacts of technological change, will be the demand for some services and the public sector's response to it in the future market.

The upcoming topic in the coming decade will be, in particular, to promote the adaptability of workers and their employers to new conditions and to significantly enhance the role of lifelong learning, including the employment of substantial further education. Further education will not be influenced only in terms of content or meaning in terms of acquiring skills and competencies for remaining or retention on the labor market, but the role of its actors will change as a result of changes in the organization of work.

We can expect to strengthen the role of competences, especially key transferable, and the emphasis on higher education and skills flexibility and the ability to work with ICT technologies and related digital literacy [24].

4   Digital Adoption Index – the Czech Republic, Germany and Domestic Country of Their Migrants and Countries from Visegrad Group

The country of origin of migrants may also have an impact on the country's market and economy. The biggest impacts will be on the labor market and thus on GDP. Currently, with the advent of the Fourth Industrial Revolution, which is referred to as Industry 4.0 and associated with high use of ICT, labor market conditions vary significantly. It will also be necessary to educate migrants, when it is again appropriate to use modern methods of education using ICT. It can be expected that if ICT is used in the home country and modern technologies are supported, residents will be able to use advanced technologies more than in countries where they are not used to such a great extent. For this reason, the 2016 Digital Adoption Index (DAI) was investigated with a second survey of this indicator. The first was carried out in 2014. Since 2016, newer data have not been published.

Into comparison were involved firstly all countries from Visegrad group and Germany. Into deeper evaluation was focused on the main groups of migrants in the Czech Republic, in Germany connected with Digital Adoption Index and DAI People Sub-index from countries of their origin.

Germany achieved the best results in both Index and Sub-index. The Czech Republic has achieved similar values with the DAI Business Sub-index as Germany. In the Digital Adoption Index, the Czech Republic achieved the best result from Visegrad four. The DAI People's Sub-Index and DAI Government Sub-Index were similar in the Vise grad countries but lower than in Germany (Fig. 1).

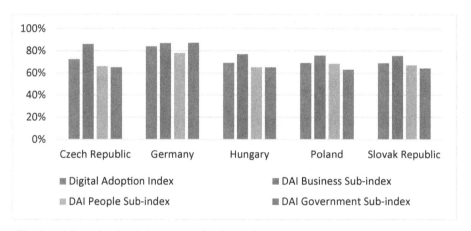

Fig. 1. Digital adoption index – countries from Visegrad Group and Germany [based on 25]

Based on results of the Digital Adoption Index and DAI People Sub-index from countries of origin it is necessary to focus on the composition of individual citizenship in selected states (see Table 1). The Czech Republic and Germany were selected for comparison. The Czech Republic and Germany are neighboring states [26].

These are economically different countries that differ in size and population too. The population of the Czech Republic is 10,65 million people and population of Germany is 82,67 million people.

The table above shows that both countries have different migrants with different nationalities and different percentages. In the Czech Republic, Ukrainians and Slovaks are the most represented. Until 1993, the Czech Republic was part of Czechoslovakia.

Table 1. Main country of citizenship and birth of the foreign/ foreign-born population, 1 January 2018 [based on 27]

Czech Republic			Germany		
Citizens of	Thousand	%	Citizens of	Thousand	%
Ukraine	114,2	22.2	Turkey	1330,8	13.7
Slovakia	11,8	21.7	Poland	758,4	7.8
Vietnam	54,9	11.5	Syria	655,2	6.8
Russia	34,6	6.7	Romania	586,6	6.1
Germany	21,3	4.1	Italy	577,5	6
Other	174,1	33.8	Other	5770,4	59.6

For this reason, the proportion of Slovaks is so high. In contrast, in Germany, the Turks are the most represented, followed by Poles, Syrians and Romanians.

This composition of people with different citizenship will have an impact on the labor market and the ability to learn new ICT skills and knowledge needed for Industry 4.0. Germany responded to the needs of skilled work according to the new immigration law, skilled labor from abroad with the adequate training and education will face fewer restrictions when they attempt to get a job in Germany. Any non-EU citizen will now be permitted to work in Germany if they have the qualified vocational training or degree course and an employment contract [28].

5   ICT, Education and Integration of Migrants

Destination countries are increasingly adopting selective immigration policies. These can effectively increase migrants' average education even if one allows for endogenous schooling decisions and education policies at origin. Still, more selective immigration policies can reduce social welfare at origin [29].

The integration of migrants, including refugees, in many Member States of the European Union and Associated Countries remains a challenge for both public authorities and local communities. ICT-enabled solutions and toolkits for the implementation of inclusion policies by public administrations may facilitate the management of the integration of migrants, improve autonomy and inclusion and therefore the lives of migrants. Such tools may help alleviate the tasks of public administrations and local authorities. They may also analyses available data and provide migrants with information on and easy access to relevant public services specific to their needs or support policy-makers and public administration at all levels in planning and taking decisions on migration-related issues through data analytics and simulation tools. The specific cultural features, including possible gender differences, the skills and capacities of migrants to express their needs as well as the equity of access to ICT may be considered in this regard.

Horizon 2020 Work Programme 2018–2020 13 is solving project Europe in a changing world – Inclusive, innovative and reflective societies. This Work Programme covers

2018, 2019 and 2020. Scope of the research is an efficient management of migrant integration requires clear understanding of migrants' personal and family situation, including their legal status, origin, cultural background, skills, language skills, medical records, etc. Once such information is available to public authorities, it can improve societal outcomes to the benefit of both host countries and migrants.

Expected Impact are new or enhanced ICT solutions and tools will facilitate the efforts of public administrations at EU, national and local levels to manage the integration of migrants. They will allow for developing and deploying the necessary processes and services in the view of the efficient identification and inclusion of migrants. They will also facilitate communication with migrants and their access to services such as community language teaching, education, training, employment, welfare and healthcare systems within the host communities [30]. The need for continuous training and retraining will become increasingly important in the years to come. The more national governments are able to use modern ICT in this area thus gain greater competitiveness and will reduce the costs associated with rising levels of unemployment.

Interesting is the experience with teaching migrants and inclusive education from Sweden. This relates to special education, as attainment is central to the definition of the need for special educational support in Sweden. Similar to international patterns, pupils with lower socio-economic background and with migrant-backgrounds are overrepresented among SEN-pupils in Sweden (Giota and Lundborg 2007; Berhanu 2008; Dyson and Berhanu 2012; Dyson and Berhanu 2012; Cook and Kiru 2018; Cook and Kiru 2018), groups that exercise choice to a lower degree (Bunar 2010; Daun 2003). Pupils from different socio-economic backgrounds are thus likely to experience different choice situations and to experience different outcomes from their choices (Vamstad 2014) [31]. Docquier et al. (2012) investigate the relationship between remittances and migrants' education both theoretically and empirically, using original bilateral remittance data. At a theoretical level they lay out a model of remittances interacting migrants' human capital with two dimensions of immigration policy: restrictiveness, and selectivity. The model predicts that the relationship between remittances and migrants' education is ambiguous and depends on the immigration policy conducted at destination. The effect of education is more likely to be positive when the immigration policy is more restrictive and less skill-selective [18].

6 Conclusion and Discussion

The European Migration Crisis culminated in 2015. Currently, individual states are addressing the influx of migrants and their economic impacts. A key element for the inclusion of national grants is their level of knowledge and skills. Nowadays, when the 4th Industrial Revolution, also called Industry 4.0, is underway, ICT knowledge is key. There is a need for a coherent concept of integrating and training individual citizens of countries with lower ICT skills and knowledge. In some countries, where there is a high influx of people with primary or lower education, there is also a change in the law that would make it easier for foreigners to integrate and be able to find employment.

It can be expected that if ICT is used in the home country and modern technologies are supported, residents will be able to use advanced technologies more than in countries where they are not used to such a great extent. It will also be possible to better educate them with modern education methods (e.g. blended learning or eLearning, etc.) For this reason, Digital Adoption Index and DAI People Sub-index from countries of origin were used in the article after comparing digital progress.

Highly skilled workers are key drivers in the contemporary knowledge-based economy with destination countries making increasing efforts to attract immigrants from this group, while emigration countries are equally attempting to encourage them to move back home (Beine et al. 2001; De Haas 2010; Jakoby 2011; Stark et al. 1997; Thaut 2009). Perhaps the most easily accessible variable, describing "skills", is education. Previous research on the relationship between the level of education and return migration has presented mixed evidence. Based on Swedish data, Nekby (2006) found that returning emigrants have higher levels of education compared to those who stay, i.e. the initial "brain drain" could become a "brain gain" for the source country. Jensen and Pedersen (2007) obtained a similar result for all immigrants leaving Denmark, but their findings were less straightforward by source country groups. In contrast, Dustmann (1996; 2003) found that there was a negative effect of years of schooling on the intention of immigrants living in Germany to return to their home countries. These ambiguous results call for a more comprehensive treatment of education together with an analysis on the association between skills and return migration behavior [17].

In further research we will deal with the economic impact of migration on the Czech economy. Work 4.0 was developed for the ongoing Industry 4.0 initiative, which specifies the market needs for Industry 4.0. However, when examining the effects of migration on the economy, two key aspects of the component need to be taken into account: the Czech Republic has the lowest unemployment rate across the EU (2% in June 2019) and an aging population. On the Czech labor market there is an excess of demand and supply of labor and companies are not able to execute all the orders they have, which results in a slower GDP growth (2.7% in the second quarter of 2019). The second area to be examined will be the calculation of the number of migrants needed annually to ensure the stability of the social and pension system due to the aging of the Czech population.

Acknowledgement. The paper is supported by the project SPEV 2019 at the Faculty of Informatics and Management of the University of Hradec Kralove, Czech Republic. In addition, the authors thank Anna Borkovcova for her help with the project.

References

1. Altenburg, F., Faustmann, A., Pfeffer, T., Skrivanek, I.: Migration und Globalisierung in Zeiten des Umbruchs. Festschrift für Gudrun Biffl. Krems (Edition Donau-Universität Krems), pp. 417–434 (2017)
2. Majchrzak, A., Markus, M.L., Warcham, J.: Designing for digital transformation: lessons for information systems research from the study of ICT and societal challenges. MIS Q. **40**(2), 267–277 (2016)
3. Majchrzak, A., Markus, M.L., Warcham, J.: Call for papers. MISQ special issue on ICT and Societal Challenges (2012)

4. Hedvicakova, M., Svobodova, L.: Impact of low unemployment on the labour market in the context of the Industry 4.0. In: Vision 2020: Sustainable Economic Development, Innovation Management, and Global Growth, vol. I–IX, pp. 5450–5455. Madrid (2017) (2017)

5. Hedvicakova, M., Svobodova, L.: The labour market of the Czech Republic in the context Industry 4.0. In: 20th International Colloquium on Regional Sciences Location. Kurdejov, pp. 303–310 (2017)

6. Hedvicakova, M., Svobodova, L.: Unemployment in the European Union with the emphasis on the Visegrad Four. In: Vision 2020: Sustainable Economic Development, Innovation Management, and Global Growth, vol. I–VII. Seville, pp. 4217–4221 (2016)

7. Hedvicakova, M., Sokolova, M., Mohelska, H.: The impact of economic growth on wages and the supply of employee benefits in the Czech Republic. Transform. Bus. Econ. **17**(3), 140–154 (2018)

8. Hedvicakova, M.: Unemployment and effects of the first work experience of university graduates on their idea of a job. Appl. Econ. **50**(31), 3357–3363 (2018)

9. Bednarska-Olejniczak, D., Olejniczak, J., Svobodova, L.: Towards a smart and sustainable city with the involvement of public participation-the case of Wroclaw. Sustainability **11**(2), 332 (2019)

10. Maresova, P., et al.: Consequences of Industry 4.0 in business and economics. Economies **6**(3), 46 (2018)

11. Svobodová, L., Černá, M., Hruša, P.: Selected simple indicators in the field of advanced technologies as a support of SMART cities and their impact on tourism. In: Kar, A., et al. (eds.) Digital Nations – Smart Cities, Innovation, and Sustainability. I3E 2017. Lecture Notes in Computer Science, vol. 10595, pp. 172–182. Springer, Cham https://doi.org/10.1007/978-3-319-68557-1_16

12. Svobodova, L., Hedvicakova, M.: Use of smart technologies for hybrid learning as a way to educate people became full smart cities residents. In: Nguyen, N., Pimenidis, E., Khan, Z., Trawiński, B. (eds.) Computational Collective Intelligence. ICCCI 2018. LNCS, vol. 11056, pp. 419–428. Springer, Cham (2018). https://doi.org/10.1007/978-3-319-98446-9_39

13. Volejnikova, J., Knezackova, R.: Influence of migration on the labour market in the Czech Republic. In: 12th International Scientific Conference on Economic Policy in the European Union Member Countries, Ostravice, pp. 892–900 (2015)

14. Volejníková, J.: Structural unemployment in the Czech Republic. In: 13th International Scientific Conference on Hradec Economic Days, Hradec Králové, pp. 343–349 (2015)

15. Knezackova, R., Volejnikova, J.: The labour market in the Czech Republic after accession to the European Union. In: 8th International Days of Statistics and Economics, Praha, pp. 687–697 (2014)

16. Janderova, J., Gyamfi, S.: Common European asylum system evolution and its perspectives. In: 5th International Multidisciplinary Scientific Conference on Social Sciences and Arts SGEM 2018, Vídeň, pp. 235–244 (2018)

17. Pungas, E., Toomet, O., Tammaru, T., Anniste, K.: Are better educated migrants returning? Evidence from multi-dimensional education data, Norface migration discussion paper no. 2012–18 (2019). http://ww.w.norface-migration.org/publ_uploads/ndp_18_12.pdf

18. Docquier, F., Rappoport, H., Salomone, S.: Remittances, migrants' education and immigration policy: theory and evidence from bilateral data. Reg. Sci. Urban Econ. **42**(5), 817–828 (2012)

19. Codagnone, C., Kluzer, S.: ICT for the Social and Economic Integration of Migrants into Europe. Luxembourg: Office for Official Publications of the European Communities (2011)

20. Collin, S., Karsenti, T.: ICT and migration: a conceptual framework of ICT use by migrants. In: Conference: World Conference on Educational Multimedia, Hypermedia and Telecommunications At: Denver, Colorado, USA, vol. 2012, pp. 1492–1497 (2012)

21. Raja, S., Imaizumi, S., Kelly, T., Marimatsu, J., Paradi-Guilford, C.: Connecting to Work: How information and communication technologies could help expand employment opportunities. (Report – ICT Sector Unit, The World Bank) (2013)
22. Datta, A., Agarwal, S.S.: Telecommunications and economic growth: a panel date approach. Appl. Econ. **36**(15), 1649–1654 (2004)
23. Andrianaivo, M., Kpodar, K.R.: ICT Financial Inclusion and Growth: Evidence from African Coutries (IMF Working Paper WP/11/73, International Monetary Fund) (2011)
24. Strategic framework for employment policy by 2030 in the Czech Republic
25. World Bank, Digital Adoption Index. http://www.worldbank.org/en/publication/wdr2016/Digital-Adoption-Index
26. Svobodova, L., Hedvicakova, M.: Technological readiness of the Czech Republic and the use of technology. In: Themistocleous, M., Morabito, V. (eds.) Information Systems. EMCIS 2017. Lecture Notes in Business Information Processing, vol. 299 (2017). Springer, Cham. https://doi.org/10.1007/978-3-319-65930-5_53
27. Eurostat, Main countries of citizenship and birth of the foreign foreign born. https://ec.europa.eu/eurostat/statistics-ex-plained/images/f/f6/Main_countries_of_citizenship_and_birth_of_the_foreign_foreign-born_population%2C_1_January_2018_%28in_absolute_numbers_and_as_a_percentage_of_the_total_foreign_foreign-born_population%29.png
28. Germany Visa. Germany's new immigration laws open door for skilled labor. www.germany-visa.org/germanys-new-immigration-laws-open-door-for-skilled-labor/
29. Bertoli, S. Brücker, H.: Selective immigration policies, migrants' education and welfare at origin. Econ. Lett. **113**(1), 19–22 (2011)
30. European Commission, Horizon (2020). https://ec.europa.eu/info/funding-tenders/opportunities/portal/screen/opportunities/topic-details/dt-migration-06-2018-2019
31. Magnússon, G.: Inclusive education and school choice lessons from Sweden. Eur. J. Spec. Needs Educ. **35**(1), 25–39 (2019). https://doi.org/10.1080/08856257.2019.1603601

Students' Language Needs Analysis
as a Motivation Mover - Czech and Taiwanese
Case Study

Miloslava Cerna[1]([✉]) [iD] and Chi-Jen Lin[2] [iD]

[1] Faculty of Informatics and Management, University of Hradec Kralove, Rokitanskeho 62, Hradec Kralove, Czech Republic
miloslava.cerna@uhk.cz
[2] College of Liberal Arts and Social Sciences, National Taiwan University of Science and Technology, 43, Section 4, Keelung Rd., Taipei 106, Taiwan
cjlin@mail.ntust.edu.tw

Abstract. The paper discusses a proved pedagogical scenario on active involvement of students into the learning process by formulating their needs and expectations and sharing experience on individual subjects at the introductory lesson at the beginning of semester. This study investigates students' language learning behaviour, their approach and motivation in Czech and Taiwanese university environment. The paper focuses on students' experience in utilization of online study material and correlation between their needs in practising individual language competences and their level of language competence.

A mixed qualitative-quantitative research was conducted. Data collection consisted of the survey based on the key tool, which was a questionnaire on Students' language needs and a follow up-discussion on students' experience, expectations and perceived potential benefits of on-line sources as well as traditional teaching/learning approaches.

The output of the study brought the following conclusions. The case study has shown that students' learning background, experience and behaviour was different in several analysed areas in two compared environments but highly inspiring and leading to the fruitful discussion enlarged with an intercultural dimension. The tutors' interest in students' needs proved to be a motivating factor enabling students to think of their language needs, formulate them and discuss them so that they could adapt and widen their language learning habits.

Keywords: Needs analysis · Case-study · Language · Web 2.0 · Motivation · Education · Survey

1 Introduction

The paper discusses a proved pedagogical scenario. Students' needs analysis is commonly used as a starting point for the teaching/learning process especially in the university environment [1]. Affective learning dominates in this scenario with its affective objectives like attitudes, feelings and motivation [2]. Currently technology enhanced

© Springer Nature Switzerland AG 2020
E. Popescu et al. (Eds.): SETE 2019, LNCS 11984, pp. 99–108, 2020.
https://doi.org/10.1007/978-3-030-38778-5_13

environment is characterized by involvement of social media and other Web 2.0 tools into the process of education, into creation, adaptation and sharing of study content material together with evaluation of students' performance within blended learning concept [3–6].

The authors approached the case study from students' perspective; gained findings belong to the category of pedagogical experience with e-learning. The paper contributes to blended instruction of online and traditional approaches based on students' experience and needs.

This study investigates students' language learning behavior, their approach and motivation in Czech and Taiwanese university environment. The paper focuses on students' experience in utilization of online study material and correlation between their needs in practicing individual language competences and preferable form of study material and running of the teaching/learning process in mastering the English language as a second language.

A mixed qualitative-quantitative research was conducted. Data collection consisted of the survey based on the key research tool, which was a questionnaire on Students' language needs and a follow up-discussion on students' experience, expectations and perceived potential benefits of on-line sources as well as traditional approaches.

The output of the study brought the following *conclusions.* The case study has shown that students' learning background, experience and behavior was different in several analyzed areas in two compared environments but highly inspiring and leading to the fruitful discussion enlarged with an *intercultural dimension.* There were statistically significant differences between not only the two samples but between male and female students, as well. *The tutors' interest in students' needs proved to be a motivating factor enabling students to think of their language needs, formulate them and discuss them so that they could adapt and widen their language learning habits.* The awareness of students' needs and students' behavior in utilizing virtual space, including social applications, websites, films, videos or podcasts has a great potential to provide fruitful learning environment [5].

2   Methodological Frame

This chapter provides readers with literature review, state of art, goals and individual stages of the research, research tool and sample.

2.1   Literature Review

Integration of technical innovations and their utilization have an undisputable drive in young people. Students perceive these innovations as natural. Valtonen et al. used the term net generation when they conducted the research on social software in the process of education from the perspective of students [7]. These developing trendy technical tools should be designed and planned thoughtfully reflecting learning context, learners' knowledge and needs, and aims of the course or study programme [8].

Utilization of the Web 2.0 offer, e.g., educational web sites with a wide range of services, social applications and current possibilities of virtual learning space in teaching/learning languages in university setting is highlighted in this case study research.

E-learning has become a standard inseparable part of the process of education at all levels of the educational system. It got embedded in individual subjects as well as in development and mastering of various skills in students. Lin in her study discusses an on-line peer assessment approach supporting mind-mapping flipped classrooms [9]. Smart and Cappel added an attribute 'smart' to the learning system already 13 years ago in their comparative study on perception of online learning. They defined the term 'Smart learning system' as learning services which included concept of the awareness of user behaviour and capability of handling multimedia resources efficiently [10].

The research presented in this paper was conducted in the university setting that is why selection of sources refers predominantly to tertiary education. Relevant literature review on utilization of Web 2.0 technologies in higher education was made by Greener [3]. She approached the phenomenon of Web 2.0 technologies from the perspective of students as well as academics. Another literature review on utilization of social applications in university setting gave Tess [11]. Schroeder et al. made an analysis on utilization of Web 2.0 technologies in tertiary education [12]. Cheung focused on affective part of learning in university students learning behaviour [13].

2.2   State of Art

Web 2.0 and incorporation of its tools into the process of education at the Faculty of Informatics and Management, University of Hradec Kralove has been part of its policy since its establishment 25 years ago. Utilization of the Internet and eLearning experience on the wide scale of all students entering the Faculty of Informatics and Management has been systematically monitored for more than two decades, see more in the longitudinal study [14]. The academics approach the research on the Internet use from various perspectives. As for language teaching/learning, Kostolanyova and Simonova explored development of language competences and designed an adaptive model of e-Learning where learner's sensory characteristics were reflected [15]. Cerna focused on the power of motivation, she applied in her research on the development of language competences a psychodidactic approach, and designed a modified expectancy model [1].

In this study, we focus on students' learning behavior, their approach to learning English language as a second language, their experience with utilization of virtual space as well as traditional ways of learning. The survey itself has a decade long history; it has been repeatedly run at the beginning of academic year with both full-time and part-time students of Information Management, Financial Management and Applied Informatics within the frame of bachelor study programmes at the University of Hradec Kralove (UHK) [5]. In May 2019 the survey was newly conducted during Erasmus+Mobility Programme at the National Taiwan University of Science and Technology in Taipei, Graduate Institute of Digital Learning and Education with students attending classes of Language learning with digital technology and classes of Motivation and Learning.

2.3   The Goal and Sub-goals of the Paper

The goal of the paper is to present findings relating to current language needs of students, their learning behavior and their experience in studying languages with focus on utilization of Web 2.0 tools in two university settings.

- The first sub-goal is to compare selected findings and highlight similarities and differences between students from different language and cultural backgrounds.
- The other sub-goal refers to students' language competences measured according to CEFR scale. The sub-goal is to put into context reached levels of students' language competences with students' requirements on desirable improvement of their language skills.

2.4   Procedure, Research Tool and Sample

A mixed qualitative-quantitative research was conducted. A mixed approach to data collection and processing seemed to be the most suitable approach in the case study with a limited research sample [16]. Data collection consisted of the survey based on the questionnaire on Students' language needs, and a follow up-discussion on students' experience and expectations. The study is based on a relatively small sample where two compared groups differ in cultural background, other parameters like age, level of reached education, studied subject which is English as a second language are similar. Due to this specific characteristics of the small sample, instead of standard statistical analyses, the following research methods which mingled in individual sections of the research were applied: primarily comparison and secondly analysis, induction and synthesis and in suitable cases also classification (e.g. subchapter 3.4).

The procedure consisted of three steps: distribution of the questionnaire, presentation of findings from previous surveys, discussion and in case of University of Hradec Kralove, modifications in the e-course accompanying the subject were made. The procedure was the same at University of Hradec Kralove (UHK) as well as in National Taiwan University of Science and Technology (NTUST). Only time of conducting the survey differed. UHK students start their semester in the Professional English subject with 'Students Language Needs analysis'. They are shown the questionnaire during face-to-face classes, after that, they can download the form from their e-course, answer the questions without any hurry and submit back to the e-course. During following F2F classes the issue on needs, expectations, experience with studying languages, perception of online sources is discussed and findings from previous years presented. As for conducting the survey in NTUST university in Taipei the procedure had to be slightly adapted. Students were distributed questionnaires in a hard copy form, then the questionnaire was placed also in the e-course supporting their classes on Language learning with digital technology. Students filled in the forms, then a lecture on utilization of social software application together with findings from Students' language Needs analysis from University of Hradec Kralove were given. Final stage was a follow-up discussion with NTUST students.

The analyzed questions were following: Q1 – Do you study 'on the Internet'? Q2 – What language educational websites have you used for practicing languages? Q3 – Which of these websites would you recommend and why? Q4 – Which functionalities should the language educational web-site have to fit your requirements? Q5 – What would you like to practice most during 'our' language classes? Q6 – What is the biggest trouble: Listening, reading, writing, grammar or just speaking? Q7 – What level of English are you at A1 – C2? Q8 – What fits you when you are studying languages? – Internet website, language e-course, F2F classes, textbook, films, taking notes or keeping a log.

There were 45 students in each group in UHK and NTUST sample of students, who submitted the questionnaire. All participants studied English language as their second language. Their language competence was comparable as can be seen in the subchapter Findings 3.4. The UHK sample consisted of Czech students attending bachelor study programme at the Faculty of Informatics and Management, their age span was 20 to 24. The NTUST sample consisted of students from Taiwan, Malaysia, Vietnam, Thailand, two students were from Kenya and two students were from Ethiopia. Students attended Graduate Institute of Digital Learning and Education. Their age span was also 20 to 24, four students were over 30, those were students from Ph.D. programme.

3   Findings

3.1   Q1 - Do You Study on the Internet?

Only 7% of students from the NTUST sample don't use the Internet for language study purposes. In UHK sample there are astonishing 25% of students who claim that they do not use the Internet for studying English language. There are big differences between men and women in the Internet use in the discussed issue: 91% of men to 76% of women at NTUST, 59% of men to 75% of women at UHK. From the follow up discussion we learned that women in the UHK sample prepare more regularly for classes, e.g., they do the tasks in Blackboard and use other on-line sources like BBC learning English. High percentage of male students start using on-line sources at the end of semester when they have to sit for listening and reading tests which are based on sources from language portals.

3.2   Q2 - What Language Educational Websites Have You Used for Practising Languages?

The second question was focused on students' experience with language websites and applications. Findings are illustrated in the Fig. 1.

Website *'Help for English'* dominates in the UHK student sample; nearly half of students knows and uses this language educational portal. *Popularity of the language portal is especially based on the fact that it is a Czech portal,* it means students are given explanations in Czech, more over students know it from secondary school.

As for the sample from Taiwan-tech, there was no similar portal mentioned, no one used any language educational portal at the secondary school.

The most often mentioned sites in Taiwan-tech student sample *is YouTube* reaching 30%. 'YouTube' used to be the most favorite social application in former surveys [5]. But in the latest survey it was mentioned only 4 times out of 45 UHK students.

BBC is a highly represented web in both samples. *BBC Learning English* is globally well-established language web portal with abundant functionalities and links to main social nets reflecting IT and social development, changes and demands. But the ratio of current UHK users is getting lower. BBC learning English websites are used by a quarter of Taiwan-tech.

Wide popularity still holds the *'Duolingo' application* in UHK student sample, in previous years those were mostly part-time students who used this application. Only one student from Taiwan-tech University uses this application. During a follow-up discussion, this application had success; students may enrich their used language sources with this app.

A new player entered the scene of utilized educational language web sites by UHK student sample, which is a portal *Perfect English Grammar*. Taiwan-tech students noted down 3 times 'Grammarly.com' sites 3 times.

20% of Taiwan-tech students use *VoiceTube* sites, which are unknown to UHK students. Another unknown site which is popular in Taiwan-tech students is *'Ted Talks'*.

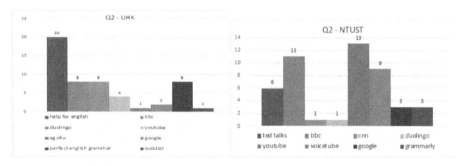

Fig. 1. Comparison of used language websites and applications

3.3   Q5 and Q6 - What Would You like to Practice Most During Language Classes? What Is the Biggest Trouble: Listening, Reading, Writing, Grammar or just Speaking?

Due to the place limitation findings relating required functionalities of websites are not presented in this paper. Results from Q5 and Q6 are visualized in one graph and compared as illustrated in Fig. 2. The blue bar represents: what students would like to practice most and the orange one what causes them the biggest troubles.

In both samples practising of language speaking skill dominates. Comparable results refer to practising *speaking*.

UHK sample shows slightly more balanced results in practising skills and individual segments of language.

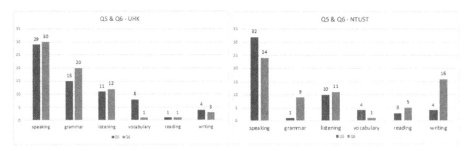

Fig. 2. What do the students want and need to practice most? (Color figure online)

More than 70% NTUST students want to practice speaking during classes and over a half of them realizes or feels that they have problem with this skill.

Nearly half of the UHK respondents feels that they have troubles with grammar and would like to learn it during classes as well as in the e-course. There can be seen big difference between two samples in their approach to grammar. In the NTUST sample only every fifth student realizes that grammar might be a problem but they do not require grammar issue to be incorporated into language classes.

Grammar and Writing skill represent key differences between two samples and shows one of few differences caused by students' background.

Next findings come from the follow-up discussion with students. Czech students insist more on particulars, they focus on prepositions, articles and somehow it makes a problem for many of them to grasp the whole unit – e.g. write an essay or take the minutes. Moreover, they believe that 'Mr. Google' will do their job in sense of writing and checking their written tasks. The NTUST students realize the importance of good level of writing skills. At NTUST University, they have to submit a great deal of written assignments. One third of them realizes that they have problem with this skill but only four of them would like to incorporate development of this skill into the classes.

3.4 Level of Language Competence and Students Requirements to Practice Individual Language Segments

Q7 in the questionnaire is 'What is your level of language competence?' Findings show *that samples from both universities are in this case comparable*, see Fig. 3. In both samples B2 level dominates.

Based on the findings researchers put into context the students' level of language competence and their requirements to practice individual language segments. See the findings in the Fig. 4.

It is not possible to make firm conclusions, firstly the samples are small and secondly not purely cognitive part of the learning process is analyzed; beside reached language competence level measured on the introduced scale, students' feelings on potential problems or limitations in language competences are discussed. However, there are findings worth highlighting; they are quite inspiring for opening the discussion with students. NTSUT students with the lowest level of language competences enumerated many language segments to be practiced. Nicely visualized is already mentioned need to develop

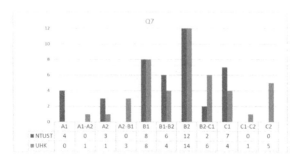

Fig. 3. Comparison of students' language competence according to CEFR

writing skills in NTSUT students, especially of those with the higher and highest level of competences feel writing skill as a problem. On the other side in UHK students grammar and speaking dominate. Students of lower language competence focus on speaking, listening so that they could be able to understand and start communicate. Students reaching higher levels of language competence include grammar category more frequently to be practiced. They do not have problems with understanding, they can focus on mastering the language, where use of proper grammar is desired.

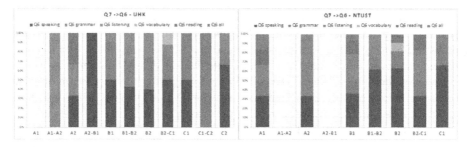

Fig. 4. Reached language competence and students requirements on practicing skills

3.5   Q8 - What Fits When You Are Studying Languages?

Last chapter on findings deals with preferred ways of studying language. The dominating activity is watching films in both samples. This chapter brings an insight into backgrounds of research sample from two universities. Strong influencing factor is that the UHK sample consisted purely from Czech students attending compulsory subject Professional English without any foreigner. That is why, they find *speaking with foreigner* special and beneficial and mentioned this activity in their responses. On the other side NTUST students take talking to foreigners as a common activity not worth mentioning as we found out during the follow-up discussion. When books are mentioned, respondents in both groups mean *English-language textbooks*. They are much less popular in the UHK sample; with 20% to 50% in favor of the NTUST sample. On the other hand, *UHK respondents are much more playful, they like songs, vides and games and like F2F* classes where they believe 'everything' can be explained without their effort. This conclusion is based on findings from both questionnaire as well as the follow-up discussion. None from Taiwan-Tech respondents mentioned games or songs in classes during the discussion.

Rather surprising fact is that UHK participants favored language websites so little. In spite of the fact that they gained some experience with websites from previous years but they prefer more entertaining way of language study. As for language websites, students from Kenya made an interesting note. They said: "we don't need to speak perfect and study systematically from websites, we are from multilingual environment. We need to speak, we need to communicate, we don't need to be perfect." UHK sample is strongly influenced by Czech environment where shyness to speak plays an important role. Fear of making mistakes greatly limits communication.

4   Conclusions

The goal and sub-goals of the paper were reached. The comparative study brought an updated view of the current use of sources supporting practicing language in Czech and Taiwanese university settings. The study shows difference in priorities in utilization of study materials which reflects different language approaches stemming from different cultural background of the compared groups.

As a conclusion, it can be stated that conducting language needs analysis with a follow up discussion and consequently with worked out electronic presentation of findings presented and shared on the virtual learning platform is a proven pedagogical scenario applicable in various setting; bringing updated, beneficial and inspiring ideas to all 'stakeholders'. In this scenario both teachers and students profiteer: teachers can adapt study materials to current situation based on formulated requirements, experience and expectations and students get motivated as they can see that their needs are discussed, taken into consideration in further planning, respected and shared. Intercultural dimension represents precious added value.

Acknowledgements. The paper is supported by the project SPEV 2019 at the Faculty of Informatics and Management of the University of Hradec Kralove, Czech Republic. In addition, the authors thank Anna Borkovcova for her help with the project.

References

1. Cerna, M.: Psychodidactic approach in the development of language competences in university students within blended learning. Open Learn. J. Open Distance e-Learn. **33**(2), 142–154 (2018). https://doi.org/10.1080/02680513.2018.1454834
2. Mohanty, A.: Cognition, Affection and Conation: Implications for Pedagogical Issues in Higher Education (2010). pedagogy.iitkgp.ernet.in/downloads/Cognition_Pedagogy.doc
3. Greener, S.: How are web 2.0 technologies affecting the academic roles in higher education? A view from the literature. In: 11th European Conference on e-Learning, ECEL 2012, Groningen, pp. 124–132 (2012)
4. Klimova, B., Poulova, P.: Pedagogical principles of the implementation of social networks at schools. In: Gong, Z., Chiu, D.K.W., Zou, D. (eds.) ICWL 2015. LNCS, vol. 9584, pp. 23–30. Springer, Cham (2016). https://doi.org/10.1007/978-3-319-32865-2_3

5. Cerna, M., Borkovcova, A.: Enhancing students' involvement in the process of education through social applications. In: Uskov, V.L., Howlett, R.J., Jain, L.C., Vlacic, L. (eds.) KES SEEL-18 2018. SIST, vol. 99, pp. 185–193. Springer, Cham (2019). https://doi.org/10.1007/978-3-319-92363-5_17

6. Popescu, E., Kubincová, Z., Homola, M.: Blogging activities in higher education: comparing learning scenarios in multiple course experiences. In: Li, F.W.B., Klamma, R., Laanpere, M., Zhang, J., Manjón, B.F., Lau, R.W.H. (eds.) ICWL 2015. LNCS, vol. 9412, pp. 197–207. Springer, Cham (2015). https://doi.org/10.1007/978-3-319-25515-6_18

7. Valtonen, T., et al.: Net generation at social software: challenging assumptions, clarifying relationships and raising implications for learning. Int. J. Educ. Res. **49**, 210–219 (2010)

8. Cerna, M., Poulova, P.: Social software applications and their role in the process of education from the perspective of university students. In: Proceedings of the 11th European Conference on e-Learning, pp. 87–96. Academic Publishing, Groningen, Reading (2012)

9. Lin, Ch. J.: An online peer assessment approach to supporting mind-mapping flipped learning activities for college English writing courses. J. Comput. Educ. Springer, Heidelberg (2019). https://doi.org/10.1007/s40692-019-00144-6

10. Smart, K.L., Cappel, J.J.: Students' perceptions of online learning: a comparative study. J. Inf. Technol. Educ. **5**, 201–219 (2006)

11. Tess, P.A.: The role of social media in higher education classes (real and virtual) – a literature review. Comput. Hum. Behav. **29**, A60–A68 (2013)

12. Schroeder, A., Minocha, S., Schneider, C.: The strengths, weaknesses, opportunities and threats of using social software in higher and further education teaching and learning. J. Comput. Assist. Learn. **26**, 159–174 (2010)

13. Cheung, S.K.S.: Distance-learning students' perception on the usefulness of open educational resources. In: Cheung, S.K.S., Kwok, L., Ma, W.W.K., Lee, L.-K., Yang, H. (eds.) ICBL 2017. LNCS, vol. 10309, pp. 389–399. Springer, Cham (2017). https://doi.org/10.1007/978-3-319-59360-9_34

14. Poulova, P., Cerna, M.: Utilization of the internet and eLearning experience in students entering university-a longitudinal study. Adv. Sci. Lett. **24**(4), 2573–2577 (2018). https://doi.org/10.1166/asl.2018.11008

15. Kostolanyova, K., Simonova, I.: Learning English through the adaptive model of e-learning reflecting learner's sensory characteristics. In: Cheung, S.K.S., Kwok, L., Kubota, K., Lee, L.-K., Tokito, J. (eds.) ICBL 2018. LNCS, vol. 10949, pp. 57–68. Springer, Cham (2018). https://doi.org/10.1007/978-3-319-94505-7_4

16. Brannen, J.: Mixing Methods: Qualitative and Quantitative Research. Routledge, London (1992). https://doi.org/10.4324/9781315248813

Uncovering the Potential of the Google Search Engine for L2 Learning and L2 Translator Training

David Mraček[(✉)]

University of Hradec Králové, Rokitanského 62/26, 500 03 Hradec Králové, Czech Republic
`david.mracek@uhk.cz`

Abstract. The paper presents a study investigating the use of the Google Search Engine in L2 translation and L2 learning. A group of undergraduate students in Tourism Management was introduced to three tips for effective Google search as part of their optional course in the basics of translation. A week later, half of the students attended a session devoted to further practice of the tips. Later, both groups were asked to translate a short text from Czech, their native language, into English with the assistance of the Google Search Engine. Drawing on the participants' translations, written protocols and search histories, the study analyses their online behavior during L2 text production, providing examples of successful applications of search strategies and explaining cases where online search techniques failed to connect effectively with the user's language skills and reflection.

Keywords: Google Search Engine · Translation · L2 translation · Language teaching · Translation in language teaching

1 Introduction

The Google Search Engine (GSE) has become a permanent presence in people's daily lives and the default option that people refer to if they have a query about a certain topic, evidenced by the fact that it processes an average of around 40,000 search queries per second [1]. However, its benefits for language learning and translation are much less known and researched.

The present paper explores several of many ways in which the GSE can be exploited by users of a foreign language (here referred to as L2), be it learners, translators, or in fact any text producers. It presents the methodology and results of a study which was a follow-up on an earlier investigation into the opportunities that the GSE offers to L2 translation teaching [2]. And while the previous study suggested that the tool can, in general, improve the quality of written language and enrich the learning experience, some questions were left unanswered and several limitations were identified in the methodology. The aim of the present study was, therefore, to place more emphasis on the search process itself in an attempt to shed more light on the possibilities and limitations of the GSE in respect to its use during L2 text production.

© Springer Nature Switzerland AG 2020
E. Popescu et al. (Eds.): SETE 2019, LNCS 11984, pp. 109–121, 2020.
https://doi.org/10.1007/978-3-030-38778-5_14

2 Methodology

As the present study is intended as a contribution to the author's long-term research into the possibilities of the GSE in L2 learning and translator training, its methodology is inspired by his previous investigation [2]. The aim is to explore how the tool can assist the language user in producing better L2 material, specifically more acceptable grammar and lexicon. The focus is on the following three basic search strategies (the examples are taken from [2]):

(1) enclosing the query (a string of words) in quotes makes the GSE return results with those exact words in that exact order; this operator is a sine qua non of effective Google search and will be referred to as the quotes operator throughout the present text; e.g. phrases "According to a recent study" or "it will benefit the elderly" all yield a high number of hits;
(2) doing a wildcard search by using an asterisk (*) in the middle of a string of words (which is itself enclosed in quotes), with the asterisk acting as a placeholder for one or more words; the mechanism will be referred to as the asterisk operator; e.g. the query "countries have * measures to" produces results including the verbs taken, adopted and introduced;
(3) restricting the search (of a phrase enclosed in quotes) to a specific domain by using the site operator; e.g. the phrase "suffer unwanted side effects" can be restricted to US institutions of higher education by adding site:edu or to British websites by typing site:uk into the search box after the query enclosed in quotes (with one space between them).

At the same time, three of the limitations identified in the previous study were taken into consideration in the methodology design. Firstly, as the previous experiment included only one in-class demonstration of what appears to be a largely new set of skills, the question emerged whether exposing the students to a further demonstration and practice session might help them better understand the possibilities offered to them by the GSE. Secondly, the time period between the in-class demonstration and the submission of the home assignment was reduced substantially compared to the previous experiment to ensure that the know-how demonstrated to the students is not forgotten by the time they can utilize it in the home assignment. Thirdly, to cast more light on the actual role of the GSE in the process of L2 production, the data collection has been made more nuanced so that the GSE can be isolated from other tools and strategies used by the user or, alternatively, its interaction with these other tools and strategies can be better explained. Therefore, a combination of data collection methods more conducive to a detailed qualitative analysis was selected for the present study; similarly, the small number of participants in the present study enabled more thorough investigation.

The study involved four students enrolled in their second year of a bachelor's degree program in Tourism Management at the University of Hradec Králové, Czech Republic, with their English language skills between levels B2 and C1 of the Common European Framework of Reference for Languages. The optional course in translation, of which the experiment was part, aims at developing, *inter alia*, students' L2 writing competence and research skills, making the GSE an ideal educational solution.

The experiment consisted of two stages, described in detail in the subsections below: (1) two in-class Google Search Engine demonstrations, (2) home assignment comprising the translation of a short text and the completion of a verbal protocol.

2.1 In-Class Google Search Engine Demonstrations

One of the translation seminars in April 2019 was devoted to introducing the students to three of the numerous tips for effective use of the GSE, namely (1) the quotes operator, (2) the asterisk operator, and (3) the site operator. The present author believes these three tips to be well applicable to translation and foreign-language learning.

During the demonstration, the teacher (i.e. the present author) explained the three tips and conducted a number of GSE searches, using his own examples, on the classroom computer, with everything projected onto a screen at the front of the room. To promote active learning, the students were encouraged to follow the teacher step by step using their own laptops, which they had been asked to bring.

As the previous study [2] has shown, these tips are rather unknown even among students in their early twenties, who are otherwise known to be conversant with the latest technology and accustomed to using the GSE for private and educational purposes on a regular basis. Therefore, a second demonstration was held to help the students better internalize the tips that had been explained to them. As a preparatory exercise, the students were asked to translate a short text from Czech into English at home and bring their translations to the class the following week. The text, an extract of 75 words from a newspaper article on the overuse of medication by elderly Czechs, was of similar length and difficulty and contained a similar range of linguistic issues to the one the students were to translate in the next stage of the experiment (see Sect. 2.2).

The second demonstration, which was only attended by two students, revolved around the translation assigned for home practice. The teacher and the students discussed the text phrase by phrase, sentence by sentence, commenting on the three GSE search tips – and various combinations thereof – and how they could assist the user in producing a good English translation text. Collectively, various search scenarios were tested, using the classroom projector and the students' own laptops. Although the primary, narrow focus was on the correct use of articles, prepositions and collocations, the more general objective was to enable the students to better understand the complexity of the translation process as well as the possibilities and limitations of the GSE in L2 text production; most importantly, as Mráček [2] says, students need to learn to accept and appreciate that "items that can be entered into the search box go well beyond isolated words, and can include entire clauses or even sentences."

2.2 Home Translation with Verbal Protocol

In the next stage, the participants were asked to translate, at home, a short text from Czech, their native language, into English; no time limit was imposed. They were free to make use of any resources, paper or electronic; however, they were particularly encouraged to use the GSE search tips to which they had been introduced. They were only given general instructions regarding the translation: they were to translate the text into English as best as they could; they were told that their translations would be used in a study on the GSE but would not affect their overall course assessment.

The source text was a short extract (with some minor editing) from a news item on the rising use of prescription drugs among the elderly published in a Czech daily. Although the text is composed of several complex sentences, it is easy to understand for non-professionals and contains general vocabulary, being an efficient instrument for testing students' grasp of grammar rules (e.g. word order, articles, countability of nouns, verb tenses) and use of English in general (collocations, prepositions).

The following is the text in Czech:

Počet lidí, kteří denně spolknou multivitaminovou tabletku, se zvýšil ve Spojených státech za posledních dvacet let o deset procent. Spojené státy jsou ve spotřebě doplňků stravy na prvním místě na světě. Zkušenosti lékařů ukazují, že i Češi se vydávají stejnou cestou. Podle vědců spočívá problém v tom, že si mnoho lidí myslí, že jim nemohou ublížit. Pokud se však těchto doplňků stravy v těle nahromadí moc, mohou vést i k úmrtí. Odborníci se shodují na jednom: kdyby byly tyto doplňky na předpis, riziko jejich nadužívání by se snížilo.

What follows is an English version produced by a native speaker:

The number of people in the United States who take a multivitamin pill every day has gone up by ten percent over the last twenty years, and the US is now the world leader in the consumption of diet supplements. Doctors' experience suggests that the Czechs are going down the same path. The problem, scientists say, is that people believe they cannot do them any harm. But if too many of these supplements accumulate in the body they can be fatal. The experts all agree on one thing: if diet supplements were only available on prescription, it would reduce the risk of people overusing them.

Besides producing the translation in MS Word document format, the participants were asked to copy the complete history of their Google searches to the same file below the translation. To enable the participants to 'think aloud' and reflect on their strategies and solutions, a verbal protocol in the form of an Excel spreadsheet was administered to be filled in during the actual translation. As they translated, the participants underlined and numbered the segment in the English translation (a word, phrase, part of a sentence or an entire sentence) that they verified via the GSE. In the protocol, they were instructed to comment on each segment by (1) indicating why they researched that particular segment (e.g. to compare the number of hits with two similar phrases) and whether dictionaries were used (print or online, monolingual or bilingual), (2) specifying the operator(s) used and (3) expressing their degree of satisfaction with the search result and, if need be, describing what they did to arrive at a more satisfactory result.

Finally, the translations (including the search history) and protocols were submitted to the present author via email for analysis, and the results are presented in Sect. 3. Within a week of submission, the students received individualized feedback, which highlighted examples of successful and unsuccessful strategies and identified possible causes of failure to encourage the students to integrate the know-how received throughout the experiment into their learning processes.

2.3 Research Questions

The translations, search histories and verbal protocols were analyzed to answer several questions related to the principal objective of the present study. Of particular interest were the number of searches made throughout the translation process, the type of searches, including the extent to which combinations of two or more operators were used, and the length and structure of queries. This type of data was made available primarily by the translations and search histories. For their part, verbal protocols are generally effective in accessing the respondent's intentions and motivations as well as the emotional impact, and therefore these aspects were analyzed as well. As the previous study suggested that multiple expositions to demonstrations might lead to more efficient and effective search strategies, a comparative aspect was included. The sample consisted of four participants, two of whom had attended one GSE demonstration before producing their translations and protocols, the other two had attended two such demonstrations. The analysis and discussion thus partially focused on how these two pairs of participants differed with regard to their search behavior.

3 Data Analysis

The following section contains the analysis of the data obtained through the three methods described above. Each subsection deals with one participant, describing his/her GSE behavior and how it relates to the quality of the translation. Each participant's translation is followed by a quantitative summary of the search process (stating the total number of queries, proportion of searches involving one of the three operators) and a discussion of selected searches, with special focus on the length and structure of the query and how effective it was in assisting the user to reach an acceptable solution; examples in the translations are numbered using superscript. The intention is not to conduct a thorough assessment of the translations in terms of language quality or translation procedures used. Rather, the objective of the analysis is to attempt at identifying the profile of each participant with regard to his/her behavior on the GSE and how it may be affected by whether he/she took part in two GSE sessions (participants 1 and 2) or only one (participants 3 and 4).

3.1 Participant No. 1

The following is the participant's translation:

The number of people in the United States[2] who swallow[3] a multivitamin pill every single day has grown by ten percent[4] in the last twenty years[5]. The United States is[1] a leader in world supplement consumption. Doctor's experience show[7] that Czech people are headed in a simmilar[8] direction. The problem is, according to scientists, that many people think supplements can cause them no harm. However[12] supplement overdose can in some cases resault[9] in death. The experts agree on one thing[6]: If the supplements were a precription[10] drug, the thread[11] of overuse would become lower.

The translator did a total of 13 searches, 12 of which using quotes; of these, 1 query combined quotes and the asterisk, and 10 combined quotes with the site operator; no combination of all three operators was used.

The one search which contained no operator (*the united states is or are*, Ex. 1) helped the translator access an article on whether the name of the country should be treated as singular or plural, ultimately leading her to the correct conclusion.

A total of eight commentaries were made in the verbal protocol and all reflect good search strategies which allow the translator to produce acceptable English. Besides Ex. 1, examples of other effective searches include the following:

Ex. 2: *"people in the United States" site:edu* vs. *"people in United States" site:edu*
Ex. 3: *"people who swallow" site:uk* vs. *"people which swallow" site:uk*
Ex. 4: *"grown by 10%" site:uk* to check the preposition which normally follows the verb (moreover, a noun phrase was included in what is a laudable attempt to verify an entire part of a sentence)
Ex. 5: *"in the last twenty years" site:uk* vs. *"in last twenty years" site:uk*. When looking at the number of hits returned for either version, the translator correctly concluded that the former (with the definite article) is to be preferred.

As the examples above show, the translator was not afraid to make multi-word queries involving entire parts of sentences (complex adverbials etc.), frequently using the combination of quotes and the site operator to ensure the excerpts returned came from British and US sites only (increasing native-speaker authenticity), with queries mostly aimed at comparing two versions offered to the user by her intuition (nouns with/without an article, two alternative verb forms etc.).

However, except for Ex. 6 (where an asterisk was used as a placeholder for the preposition *"experts agree * one thing"*), the searches were confined to the first two sentences. It can be argued that if the translator had applied the above strategies throughout the entire translation process, she could have avoided a number of infelicities found in the rest of the text. For instance, the phrase *doctor's experience show* (Ex. 7) contains two mistakes (*doctors'* and *experience shows* are correct); a more critical approach to the translator's own knowledge of grammar (which she did manifest when verifying such basic issues as *people who/which*, see Ex. 3) could have led her to review this particular formulation. Similarly, spelling or typographic errors such as those in Examples 8, 9, 10, 11 can be avoided, with the GSE drawing the user's attention to them; punctuation rules (Ex. 12: *however* is normally followed by a comma when placed initially) can be inferred by the user from the excerpts returned by the GSE providing the word is part of a longer query (e.g. *"however, the number" site:edu*).

In sum, participant No. 1, who attended both GSE demonstrations, manifested a solid grasp of the know-how presented to her, which enabled her to be in better control of grammar issues such as articles, pronouns, prepositions and verb forms. She failed, however, to maintain the same level of rigor till the end of the exercise, which may have been due to lack of time or other factors unknown to the author.

3.2 Participant No. 2

The following is the participant's translation:

In the United States,[6] a number of people who[7] take[1] a multivitamin pill daily have[4] increased by[2] 10% in the last twenty years. The United States are in the first place worldwide in[3] using food supplements. Doctors' experience show, that even Czech people follow the same way. According to scientists the problem is that many people think food supplements can't cause any damages. But if there's too much[5] food supplements in the body, they can cause even death. Professionals agree on one thing: if the food supplements were on prescription, the risk of their overuse would decrease.

The translator did a total of 83 searches, 82 of which using quotes (the one search where no quotes were used was immediately followed by a repeated query with quotes as the translator realized that quotes were needed for a meaningful result); of these, 20 queries combined quotes and the asterisk, and 23 combined quotes with the site operator; 6 instances were noted in which all three operators were combined in one query.

In general, this translator spent a considerable amount of time and effort on her language research, often trying different operators or replacing some components of queries with possible alternatives when verifying a single item. This tendency is apparent from the following examples:

Ex. 1. When comparing two different collocations, *"take a pill"* vs. *"swallow a pill"*, the translator used not only a combination of the quotes and site operators but she later also changed the infinitive form of both verbs to an –ing form in order to see the items searched in more than one syntactic function.

Ex. 2. In order to verify her hypothesis that the preposition normally accompanying the verb *increase* is *by*, the translator created a complex query, combining all three operators: *"increase * 10% in the last" site:uk*. She then tried several modifications: changing the verb form to *increased*, omitting the figure 10 and expanding the site operator to *site:bbc.co.uk*. And although she found that sometimes the preposition is omitted (failing to notice that this is normally only done in newspaper headlines), she preferred to use *by* found in the majority of the hits.

Ex. 3. In an attempt to find an idiomatic formulation concerning the US being the top consumer of dietary supplements, the translator tried multiple variations by changing the name of the country and the numeral, and by deleting and adding words: moving from *"the US * the first place in"* to *"the UK * the first place in using"* and *"the US take the * place in"*, she later found that the query *"first place worldwide"* returned a large number of hits; she inspected the results carefully, noticing that a definite article and two prepositions *in* are needed for the phrase to be usable in a sentence.

Nevertheless, two examples illustrate that good search techniques do not guarantee success on their own. In Ex. 4, the comparison of *"a number of people have"* vs. *"a number of people has"*, using the quotes and, later, *site:uk*, led the user to choose the former as it appears in many more results than the latter. And although the phrase is correct in terms of grammar, it is wrong in the context at hand as it carries a completely different sense than the correct *the number of people*, which requires the singular *has*.

Ex. 5. In another attempt to confirm her intuition, she compared a phrase she considered correct, *"too many food supplements"*, with the much less acceptable *"too much food supplements"*. Finding that the latter had many more hits, she opted for it, although – as she pointed out in the protocol – this was contrary to her belief. In this instance, the student failed to exercise her usual critical judgment, for it is evident on closer inspection that many of the results returned for *"too much food supplements"* reflect a different linguistic context to that investigated by the translator. Typically, one part of the query belongs to a different sentence than the rest of the query; it is apparent that *much* is a modifier of the uncountable *food* not the countable *supplements*, cf. *"So, do not eat too much food. Supplements also provide…"*.

Finally, two examples are worth a closer look as they illustrate the user's meticulous approach to the text production task at hand, the object of verification being punctuation. In Ex. 6, the translator compared *"In the United States, a number of"* vs. *"In the United States a number of"*. With the GSE being punctuation insensitive, it makes no difference whether a comma is used or not. Still, the user was able to notice in the examples returned that when placed initially, adverbials such as *in the United States* are separated by a comma from the rest of the sentence. Similarly, a quick glance at the results returned for the queries *"a number of people, who"* and *"a number of people who"* enabled her to opt for the correct version without a comma in Ex. 7.

In sum, participant No. 2, who attended both GSE demonstrations, did systematic and well-considered research, using multiple queries which involved whole phrases and clauses (and even paying attention to punctuation, an issue ignored by the other three translators), often combining different operators and manifesting no small degree of creativity in a laudable effort to gain access to authentic linguistic material. Unlike participant No. 1, she was consistently rigorous throughout the exercise, although some of the queries led her to revise what had originally been a correct formulation.

3.3 Participant No. 3

The following is the participant's translation:

The number of people in the United states who take multivitamins on the daily basis[1] has increased by 10% in the last 20 years. The United States occupy the first place in the world in consumption of dietary supplements. The experiences of many doctors illustrate[5] that the Czech are following the same path. According to scientists, the problem lies in people thinking that the dietary supplements cannot hurt them. If too many of these supplements pile up in the human body[3] though, they can lead to one's death. Experts agree on one thing[4]: if these supplements were to be sold on a prescription[2], the risk of overconsumption[6] would decrease.

The translator did a total of 24 searches, 23 of which using quotes (the one search where no quotes were used was immediately followed by a repeated query with quotes as the translator realized that quotes were needed for a meaningful result); of these, 7 queries combined quotes and the asterisk, and 3 combined quotes with the site operator; no combination of all three operators was used.

The fact that the 24 searches dealt with no more than 5 segments may lead to the conclusion that the translator decided to rely on her command of English which is reasonably good. There are whole segments which are grammatically correct and idiomatic although no verifying was reported in the protocol, e.g. *The number of people in the United states who take multivitamins* (except for the misspelling in *states*, which the translator could have noticed if she had seen the segment in whole sentences returned by the GSE); *has increased by 10% in the last 20 years; According to scientists, the problem lies in people thinking that…*).

On the other hand, a few minor infelicities could have been corrected had the translator made consistent use of the GSE. For instance, the use of articles in fixed phrases can be verified efficiently via the GSE: the search "multivitamins on the daily basis" (Ex. 1) returns no hits compared to almost 2,000 hits for "multivitamins on a daily basis". Similar results are achieved with other words which can reasonably be expected in the syntactic position before the fixed phrase, e.g. "taken on a daily basis" vs. "taken on the daily basis". Therefore, the key idea that learners need to internalize is that while queries need to be long enough to return authentic linguistic material, individual words which are less directly relevant to the issue being verified can be replaced with items that are more likely to occur in that position. The phrase "on a prescription" (Ex. 2, where "on prescription" is correct) is another example of a mistake avoidable through rigorous use of the GSE.

In the few queries made, the translator sometimes reported relying on, or being assisted by, her language instinct:

Ex. 3. She first made a total of 5 queries with the asterisk operator to explore the possible verbs linking the words *medicine, minerals, supplements* and *human body* (e.g. *"medicine * in human body", "supplements * in a human body"*). Having found no solution acceptable to her, she tried substituting the asterisk with two verbs she thought might be used. The comparison of *"minerals congest in human body", "minerals pile up in human body", "medicine piles up in human body"* and *"medicine piled up in human body"* brought no convincing results and so the translator followed her intuition (while adding, correctly, the definite article), producing a relatively acceptable version.

Ex. 4. By comparing *"experts agree on one thing"* vs. *"experts agree on one point"* she came to the conclusion that both versions are acceptable but the former is used more frequently – and sounds better to her – than the latter.

Ex. 5. The translator decided to verify the phrase *"experience of doctors show"*, using the *site:uk* operator to narrow the results down to British websites. She found no results, failing to realize that this was caused by her mistake in subject-verb concord (singular noun vs. plural verb). She then modified the query to *"experiences of many doctors show"* and, using the quotes operator only, found no results again; this is probably to do with the fact that unlike its direct Czech equivalent, the English word *experience* is normally used in the singular when referring to the collection of knowledge acquired over a long period of time. The translator then shortened the query to *"experiences of many doctors"*; the GSE returned 9 instances, which the translator believed to be a satisfactory result. She then finalized the segment by using her language knowledge and/or intuition, adding, correctly, the definite article and a new verb, *illustrate*, although her initial choice, *show*, would have been a much more natural collocate.

Ex. 6. After finding very few occurrences of the collocation *"overconsumption of medicine"*, the user shifted her focus onto the word *overconsumption* on its own, first using the quotes only, later adding *site:uk*. That brought her to what she calls "a satisfactory number of results (including the Guardian)". On the one hand, her ability to assess the reliability of the source offered (based on the renown of the British daily) is commendable; on the other hand, had she attempted different modifications of collocations involving the word, e.g. *"the overconsumption of dietary supplements"*, her solution could have been informed more by hard data than her instinct.

In sum, participant No. 3, who attended only one GSE session, used the asterisk and site operators in addition to the basic quotes operator, demonstrating, in more than one instance, a willingness to modify the query for more convincing results. It can be argued, however, that a more systematic use of the GSE, based on less intuition and more reflection on the possibilities of grammar, as well as a generally higher number of queries and segments verified would have resulted in a more acceptable English text.

3.4 Participant No. 4

The following is the participant's translation:

Number of people,[4] who swallow vitamin tablets[1] daily, has increased by 10 percent[2] in the United States in the last[3] 20 years. United States are on top of the list in dietary supplement usage. Experienced doctors say, that Czechs will go down the same path[5]. According to the scientists, the problem is, that many people think, that it can't harm them. If too many of these supplements accumulate in human body, they can even lead to death[6]. Experts agree on one thing: If these supplements were under prescription, the risk of overuse[7] would reduce.

The translator did a total of 36 searches, 32 of which using quotes; of these, 2 queries combined quotes and the asterisk, and 17 combined quotes with the site operator; no combination of all three operators was used.

Three of the four searches which involved no operator were made to elicit the meaning of a phrase by adding the word *meaning* into the search box, in which case quotes are unnecessary (e.g. *on top of the world meaning*). The remaining one search without quotes was immediately followed by a repeated query with quotes.

The translator was generally willing to verify his solutions and make regular use of the site operator. However, his queries were typically rather short, and although some led him to a successful version, it can be argued that in a number of cases, a more sophisticated query would have yielded more convincing results as to how the item is used in contexts similar to that in the translation. The following are several examples:

Ex. 1. *"vitamin pills" site:uk* vs. *"vitamin tablets" site:uk*. Possible expanded versions include *"vitamin tablets daily" site:uk* or *"who * vitamin pills" site:uk*, both of which offer a few results that contain the verb *to take*; thus the user could have realized that *take* is a much more appropriate choice than *swallow*.

Ex. 2. *"10%"* or *"10 percent"*. Finding that both queries yield enough hits, the user decided for the latter based on his own preference. However, a query with much more value for his task and for his long-term learning could look like this: *"has increased by 10 percent" site:bbc.co.uk* vs. *"has increased by 10%" site:bbc.co.uk*. In this way, the item is searched in a wider co-text involving the verb phrase which it normally accompanies; moreover, the site operator is used to narrow the results further down to the website of a particular organization to see results in contexts stylistically equivalent to the source text (apart from the BBC example above, compare for instance *site:guardian.co.uk* or *site:washingtonpost.com*).

Ex. 3. Similarly to Ex. 2, the queries *"in the last" site:uk* and *"in last" site:uk* can arguably be called unstrategic. Combining these items with that immediately following in the sentence would yield more convincing results again, e.g. *"in the last 20 years" site:uk* vs. *"in last 20 years" site:uk*. Alternatively, the word *years* can be replaced with *months* or *weeks* and the site operator can be made more specific (e.g. *site:bbc.co.uk*). As they were, the queries were so general that the user was left to decide solely based on the total number of hits shown for each, instead of considering at least some contextual information.

The fact that the immediate context of the item searched is crucial (perhaps even more so than the overall number of results) can be illustrated with Ex. 4. The user verified the phrase *"number of people"*, using the quotes operator only. Seeing a huge number of results (including in an Oxford dictionary, a trustworthy source), he used the phrase without thinking too much about grammar rules. Had he paid more attention to how the item was used in entire sentences (looking carefully at the first two or three pages of the results returned by the GSE would have sufficed), he would probably have noticed that (1) the definite article is a constant component of the phrase and (2) the *-who*-sentence which follows the phrase is normally *not* preceded by a comma, being a defining clause. The three wrongly placed commas before *that* are the result of the same interference of his native language, which, too, could have been avoided if careful reading of the results had been part of the search strategy.

On the other hand, in at least two cases, the translator searched entire phrases. For instance, *go down the same path* was checked for naturalness, although an incorrect verb form was used (Ex. 5; *are going* would be more precise than *will*). As for *can even lead to death* (Ex. 6), the phrase was compared with *can end up with death* and the former was chosen on the basis of frequency. In one instance (Ex. 7), a word offered by a dictionary, *overuse*, was first searched with the quotes only, then *site:uk* was added, and later the query was expanded to cover an entire collocation: *"medication overuse" site:uk,* followed by *"supplements overuse" site:uk* and *"supplement overuse" site:uk*; as the latter two yielded very few results, the former query was repeated and the user, seeing enough hits, decided that *overuse* can indeed be used in the context of medicine.

In sum, participant No. 4, who attended only one GSE session, did no small number of searches but they were rarely strategic: either they contained too few words or were deemed successful even though the immediate context was not taken into consideration.

4 Discussion and Conclusion

The aim of the present paper was to shed more light on the role that the Google Search Engine can play in producing better-quality language, be it by a foreign-language learner or a translation trainee, with students assuming both these roles in some educational contexts. Rather than attempting a detailed quality assessment, the analysis focused on the different strategies that learners adopt when confronted with the realities of, on the one hand, L2 text production and, on the other, an online search engine.

The analysis of the data gleaned from the respondents' translations, search histories and verbal protocols revealed, first and foremost, a considerable amount of variation among participants of the experiment as to the number of queries made in relation to the same task, which consisted in the translation of a short Czech text into English, the participants' L2. The lowest (13) and highest (83) number of queries was made by the two respondents who attended two sessions dedicated to GSE, while those who only attended one made an average of 30 searches. The use of combinations of two operators (quotes plus site, quotes plus asterisk) was comparable in both groups, although only one participant (having attended both sessions) was prepared to make a regular use of a combination of all three operators. In general, queries served to verify frequent issues pertaining to English grammar and vocabulary, with articles, pronouns, prepositions and collocations leading the list. Occasionally, punctuation was the object of verification and in some instances, the GSE provided access to background materials (such as online dictionaries and articles on points of grammar).

The aspects of GSE research in which the two pairs were found to differ most were the length and structure of queries, where those students who had attended two sessions made longer queries which comprised entire complex phrases and clauses rather than single words and simple phrases. Moreover, one of the more advanced students demonstrated a willingness to invest time and cognitive effort to the search process, making numerous modifications to her queries in order to explore as best as she could the way in which the item is used in authentic language. Without making strong claims about the representativeness of the sample, it could be argued that every additional demonstration or controlled practice session may enhance the learner's command of GSE search strategies and, even more importantly, her understanding of how these strategies need to complement her use of existing and developing language knowledge.

Indeed, it appears reasonable to suppose that the need to verify items of language depends to a large extent on the learner's or translator's current level of target language skills, and there was undoubtedly a degree of heterogeneity among the participants with respect to language skills. No less importantly, the level of language knowledge impacts, in turn, on the learner's online search dexterity. This leads Fujii to say that the GSE "has strong potential for advanced learners, who are resourceful enough to generate a higher number of syntactic/lexical combinations" [3]. With less advanced learners of a foreign language, a text production exercise involving the use of a search engine would be considerably more time-consuming.

However, another factor may be at play here, one that has less to do with language knowledge. As the analysis made obvious, the four participants differed with regard to their personalities, some exhibiting, to a larger degree than others, reflection, healthy skepticism, attention to detail and other qualities conducive to successful research.

While the study only relied on a modest sample of four participants, it has pointed to the potential that the GSE has for improving the quality of a translator's or learner's written output in L2. As they work on their text production task, language users (including native speakers of that language) can complement their language skills and intuition with systematic search procedures involving simple words and, more effectively, complex lexical and syntactic structures, thereby increasing their control of the language material they produce.

On a more general educational level, the integration of search engines into the learning process is in line with transformationist approaches as such activities work with what the student already knows (grammar rules and the use of search engines in real life situations), transforming this knowledge into higher-level skills where language and technology combine to assist in the production of better-quality L2 communication.

The teacher here acts in her capacity of facilitator, pointing students to more effective strategies for online search and, more generally, language learning.

At the same time, the GSE can contribute to learner autonomy: when provided the basic know-how by the teacher (during a face-to-face tutorial where a demonstration of search tips is given together with instructions for home practice), learners can uncover the potential of the tool for their own learning process, exploring for themselves and self-regulating on the basis of individualized feedback as long as it includes an assessment of the quality of the search process in addition to the quality of language.

At the methodological level, it appears that gaining a meaningful insight into the thought and search processes can only be made possible by triangulation. As Ericsson and Simon [4, cited in 5] stressed, think-aloud data from working memory will always be incomplete and exclude a number of thought processes which are not held in working memory long enough to be expressed verbally. It has, therefore, become a common practice to supplement think-aloud data with other data-collection strategies. In the present study, the use of search history turned out to be effective in providing more details where verbalizations were incomplete or even inaccurate in the protocols.

Future investigations into the use of search engines in L2 translation and FL learning may attempt to establish a firmer link between the quality of language output, the student's level of language skills and online search skills. To that end, a more robust and interdisciplinary research framework may be needed, possibly involving different data collection methods such as observation, video recording, and interviews.

References

1. Nasser, L.: Exploring the benefits of Google trends. The Next Ad, online (2018). https://www.thenextad.com/blog/exploring-the-benefits-of-google-trends/. Accessed 23 June 2019
2. Mraček, D.: The Google search engine: a blended-learning tool for student empowerment. In: Proceedings of the International Symposium on Educational Technology (ISET 2019), pp. 224–229. IEEE, Piscataway (2019). https://doi.org/10.1109/iset.2019.00054
3. Fujii, Y.: Making the most of search engines for Japanese to English translation: benefits and challenges. Asian EFL J. **23**, 41–77 (2007). http://www.asian-efl-journal.com/pta_Oct_07_yf.pdf. Accessed 12 June 2019
4. Ericsson, K.A., Simon, H.A.: Verbal reports as data. Psychol. Rev. **87**(3), 215–251 (1980)
5. Charters, E.: The use of think-aloud methods in qualitative research: an introduction to think-aloud methods. Brock Educ. **12**(2), 68–82 (2003)

The Effect of Gamification in User Satisfaction, the Approval Rate and Academic Performance

Gabriela Martínez[1,3], Silvia Baldiris[2,3]([☒]), and Daniel Salas[4]

[1] Centro de Educación Continua, Escuela Politécnica Nacional, Ladrón de Guevara E11-253, Quito, Ecuador
gmartinez@cec-epn.edu.ec
[2] Fundación Universitaria Tecnológico Comfenalco, Sede a Barrio España
Cr 44 D No 30A – 91, Cartagena, Colombia
sbaldiris@tecnologicocomfenalco.edu.co, silvia.baldiris@unir.net
[3] Universidad Internacional de La Rioja, Rectorado – Avda. de La Paz, 137, Logroño, Spain
[4] Universidad de Córdoba, Carrera 6 no. 77- 106 Montería - Córdoba, Córdoba, Colombia
danielsalas@correo.unicordoba.edu.co

Abstract. Continuous Education Centre from the National Polytechnic School of Ecuador (CEC-EPN) develops online education courses under a constructivist academic approach, following the ADDIE instructional approach, reaching more than 10,000 students per year. These courses implementation suffers common problems related to low student participation, low academic performance, low approval rate and low student satisfaction. The current trends of virtual education are influenced by new strategies such as the use of gamification in the design of virtual content; this is due to the good results it has had on motivation, academic performance and student participation. This document describes the implementation of a strategy of gamification based on role-play in a MOOC course on Prevention of Child Sexual Abuse in the CEC-EPN. The strategy was validated through an experimental design involving a control group (receiving a traditional course) and an experimental group (receiving the gamified course). The evaluation focuses on the analysis of the following variables: User Satisfaction, Approval Rate and Academic Performance. The results show the implemented strategy contributes to the improvement of the aforementioned variables.

Keywords: Virtual education · Gamification · Playful strategies · MOOC courses

1 Introduction

In Ecuador, the numbers of allegations of sexual abuse are dispersed and incomplete but as well they are worrying. The data of the Office of Criminal Policy of the Prosecutor's Office, between 2014 and 2017 indicated the existence of 13,671 complaints of sexual abuse [11]. In this sense, UNICEF and the Ecuador Government are carrying out different campaign such as "Open your Eyes", with the purpose of informing and sensitizing families and society about this critical problem.

© Springer Nature Switzerland AG 2020
E. Popescu et al. (Eds.): SETE 2019, LNCS 11984, pp. 122–132, 2020.
https://doi.org/10.1007/978-3-030-38778-5_15

The CEC-EPN aware of this situation, consistent with the UNICEF Ecuador campaign, and in cooperation with several inter-institutional organizations such as the Association for Children and the Family, intend to support the abuse prevention through the generation of free training strategies, among them Massive Online Open Courses (MOOC). However, it was identified the courses offered by the CEC-EPN suffers common problems related to low student participation, low academic performance, low approval rate and low student satisfaction, being necessary to explore strategies to improve the participants experience in the offered courses.

Currently, the concept of Gamification is being used in different contexts: business, education, health, government and even in daily tasks [1]. This is due to the benefits of applying different elements from games in non-play contexts, especially considering the influence it has on people's behavior, through stimulating motivation.

According with Rodriguez and Santiago: "Gamification is a process by which mechanics and game design techniques are applied, to seduce and motivate the audience in the granting of certain objectives" [2].

In educational settings, Gamification has reported benefits in the learning process. Mateo [6] in his thesis concludes, at a theoretical level, that gamification brings important advantages to the dynamization of the work climate through motivating and awakening the interest of the student. Sánchez [7] describes the implementation of a mobile application implementing gamification in a secondary school with the aim of achieving greater motivation and adherence to healthy oral habits. Their results showed that 100% of the students in the control group showed interest in the gamified strategy and 47% consider that educational gamification is more interesting than the master class. The gamification strategy, the contents, the procedures and activities were widely accepted. There was also an increase of 27% of students who improved their oral health habits. On the other hand, the mixed study conducted by Vélez [8, 12] carried out through an experimental design demonstrated that the students of the gamified group showed higher attention spans than the students of the master class group. In addition, the students of the gamified group showed greater motivation to participate in the class and greater interaction both in student-student and teacher-student relationships. This result supports the thesis of the present project in which it is stated that a gamification strategy affects the level of user interaction. In the same line, the studies of Jorge-Soteras [9] or INSERVER [9] also show gamification can improve the results obtained by the students in educational processes.

On the base of the literature, the present the study describes the use of a gamification strategy based on role-play, applied to the MOOC of Preventive Strategies for Child Sexual Abuse offered by the CEC-EPN, aimed at parents, family and teachers, as a contribution to support the awareness of the Ecuadorian population on the issue of prevention of child sexual abuse. The validations was oriented to measure the measures user satisfaction, the approval rate and academic performance of the participants to compare the participants' behaviors in both, a traditional course and a gamified course.

The paper is divided into fourth sections. The first section correspond to the introduction that introduce the problem and supported literature. The second section describes the design of the gamification strategy. The third section describes the methodology applied in order to assess the level of impact of the gamification strategy, and finally, the fourth section presents the conclusions obtained and the future work that the obtained results could lead to.

2   Gamification as a Strategy to Support the Creation of a MOOC Virtual Course for the Prevention of Child Sexual Abuse

Several methodologies and models have been defined to support the design of a gamified system [2, 3, 5]. In the present study we have used the proposal of formal design frameworks by Marczewski [2–4, 10] because it fix the requirements of our context and strategy. The model consists of two loops:

(1) First Loop, Definition and Design. The following elements are defined:

- Definition of the Problem: includes the definition of what we want to improve with the gamification strategy.
- Definition of Users: allows defining the type of user of the course with its general characteristics and the type of player that will participate in the game.
- Definition of Success: which involves defining what will be the success of the gamification strategy and the success of the game for the user.

(2) Second Loop, Construction of the Solution. The second loop is designing the user's journey, which will be the basis of the mechanics, motivations and behaviors that will be used in the gamification. The user's journey consists of four stages:

- Discovery: It is the mechanism used for the user in order to discover how to perform the gamification strategy.
- On Board: It is the tutorial that allows the user to understand how the game will develop.
- Immersion: It is the longest phase in which the user interacts with the mechanics of available games.
- Master: It is the stage in which the user has reached the maximum level.
- Repetition: It is the stage in which it is decided if it makes sense for the user to play again.

There is a diversity of classifications between genres and subgenres of game design, each of which promotes different pedagogical aspects. In this project the strategy of role-play was implemented, which means that the player assumes the role of a character in a fictitious world that adequately combines elements such as the perception of progress, setting and narrative. The reason to select the role-play was the intention of the strategy, the Prevention of Child Sexual Abuse. We consider the best way to involve the people in this problem is to permit them play a role of a main actor in a particular situation.

In the next sub-section we explain each loop, detailing each element presented before.

2.1 First Loop

As mentioned the main purpose of the gamification strategy designed in this study was support the prevention of child sexual abuse, but also improve the participants experience in the course offered by the CEC-EPN.

The definition of the type of user was made through an initial survey that allows defining the general characteristics of the user, and in this way identify the type of player using Marczewski's classification [4] defining 6 types of players: Disruptors, Free Spirit (Explorers), Achievers, Players, Socializing and Philanthropists.

The users definition was carried out through the application of a short test similar to that of Bartle Play Time Test[1] to potential participants. The results show a greater percentage of potential players of the Explorer type (32.3%) and Achiever (26.9%), as shown in Fig. 1. This definition was useful for gamification mechanics.

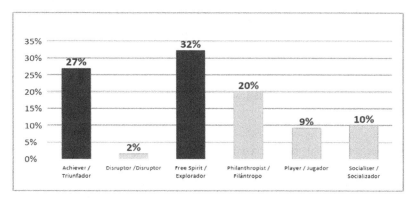

Fig. 1. Results of the application of the test for player type analysis (Designed by the authors)

Regarding the definition of success, it was conceived on three levels:

- The success of the gamification strategy that means to achieve improvement in user satisfaction, approval rate and academic performance has been verified in the evaluation of the strategy presented in this paper.
- The players' success happens when the participants rescue children and families who are at risk of abuse.
- The academic success is achieved when the participants successfully learn about prevention strategies.

The participants advance through the levels of progressive difficulty, solving a challenge for each level.

The user will have reached the master level when he has completed the safety route, solving the challenges of the four levels.

---

[1] Available at: https://gamified.uk/UserTypeTest2016/user-type-test.php?q=l&lang=en#.XMron TBKiUl.

The repetition or "Replay" is placed in each level of game, when the user loses their three lives, the game will be restarted.

2.2 Second Loop

The *User's Journey* according with Arnedo and Riera [10] consists of the following stages:

- Discovery: when the user enters the gamified content, he is invited to assume the role of Great Psychologist and complete the safety route by rescuing the children victims of abuse. The condition to access the game will be to read the material corresponding to the lessons. The material is in a downloadable format, so that it can be consulted at any time.
- On Board: once the user confirms the beginning of the gamified content, the user receives the challenge or conflict and the rules of the gamification. Each level has its own challenges and rules. The user must express the understanding of them before starting.
- Immersion: in the immersion phase, the "Great Psychologist" will enter the educational scenario in which the challenge will be carried out; in it he/she will find the gamification mechanics associated with the different types of player according with Table 1.

Table 1. Mechanics and dynamics according to the type of player (Designed by the authors)

Player type	Recommended gamification mechanics and dynamics	Gamification mechanics and dynamics implemented in the course
Disruptors	Innovative platforms Voting mechanisms Development Tools Creativity tools Competition Challenges Anarchy	Mechanisms voting Competition Challenges
Free spirit (Explorers)	Exploratory tasks Nonlinear games Easter eggs Unlockable content Creative tools Learning Challenges Personalization	Exploratory tasks Unlockable content Learning challenges

(*continued*)

Table 1. (*continued*)

Player type	Recommended gamification mechanics and dynamics	Gamification mechanics and dynamics implemented in the course
Achievers	Challenges Certificates Searches Learning new skills Badges Missions Levels Anonymity Progression	Challenges Certificates Searches Learning new skills badges Missions Levels Progression
Players	Points Rewards Leaderboards badges Virtual Economy Levels Lottery or gambling	Points Rewards Tables classification Badges levels
Socializing	Guilds social Networks Status Pressure Social discovery	Networks Status Pressure Discovery
Philanthropes	Collecting and trade Donation Knowledge exchange Administrative functions	Knowledge exchange

In addition to these mechanics, some game elements were used in order to create a fun environment. These elements are presented in Table 2.

Table 2. Elements of the game (Designed by the authors)

Elements	Description
Fantasy and Theme	An educational scenario in which the main character, "Great Psychologist" is hired by Ana, the director, to solve the challenges, was designed. The narrative emerges as a dialogue between the two personals within which the challenges of the game are silvered
Progress/Feedback	A progress bar known as "Completion Status" is integrated into the virtual platform, in such a way as to allow the user to verify the progress he has within the course

(*continued*)

Table 2. (*continued*)

Elements	Description
Aversion to loss	A system of gain and loss of points and lives was designed. The loss of points originates when the user makes an incorrect selection of the presented options; When the point marker reaches 0 the user loses a life. If you lose both lives the game restarts. If the user use one of the clues to solve the challenge, he/she lose one point for each track used
Rules	Although each of the challenges has its rules, the following basic rules were defined:
	• To select the correct answer, you must click on the option that you believe is correct
	• Each option has two tracks, by using the tracks you will subtract one point per track
	• The user starts the gamified strategy with two lives, each life gives him 10 points
	• If you choose the correct option you will receive 10 points, if you choose the wrong option you will lose 10 points
	• Each time the score reaches 0 you will lose a life
	• If he loses all lives he will have to start the gamified strategy again
	• The user will go to the next level when he has successfully resolved the challenge

2.3 Moodle Instance to Display the Learning Object

The created learning object was displayed in a Moodle instance, being necessary to configure and add the blocks presented in Table 3. For the execution of gamification elements, rankings, badges, states of completion and validation of levels that favored a more playful learning experience were implemented in the virtual platform.

Table 3. Blocks in the Moodle platform according to the Traditional and Gamified courses

Moodle Block	Description	Traditional course	Gamified course
Completed state	Bar that allows to track the progress of the user and the fulfillment of their activities	x	x
Ranking	Lateral block that allows to visualize the points obtained by the users in the course is independent of the qualifications and operates with the activities selected by the administrator		x

(*continued*)

Table 3. (*continued*)

Moodle Block	Description	Traditional course	Gamified course
Badges	These are rewards that are awarded to the user who completes a level or course	1 per course	1 per level (4) and 1 per course
Recent badges	Displays the badges recently awarded to course users		x
Badges ranking	Displays the total badges won by users, and can be viewed by the course administrator		x
Level up	Grants points for the experience in the course, to do so follows rules independent of the grades The system was programmed with 10 levels of experience with different points		x

3 Evaluation

3.1 Description

To evaluate the gamification strategy, a research was conducted under a quasi-experimental quantitative study that allowed us to describe the effect of the gamification strategy on user satisfaction, the approval rate and academic performance.

The users of the courses were education professionals and parents between 25 and 35 years old from different cities of Ecuador. In the experiment we worked with a total population of 502 enrolled users who were divided into two groups randomly: 251 in the control group and 251 in the experimental group. The general characteristics of the users were:

- Users are mostly women between 21 and 35 years old.
- Academic training of mostly third level. Teachers and university students.
- Mostly workers from public or unemployed institutions.
- The majority of users are residents of Ecuador, from the province of Pichincha.
- Most users access the course for professional improvement or as a requirement for study, and have had experience in virtual courses. They are able to dedicate 7 h per week to the course.
- The users have basic knowledge of Moodle and intermediate level on office automation.

The control intervention was carried out in the context of a web-based traditional course implemented under ADDIE model without gamification.

The experimental intervention was carried out in the context of the MOOC implemented using the gamification strategy defined in Sect. 2.

At the end of the course an analysis of the results obtained was carried out doing several comparisons: Comparison of the level of user satisfaction, Comparison of the Approval Rate, Comparison of academic performance and Comparison of academic performance.

3.2 Description

The results found in the Satisfaction of the User category show in Fig. 2, do not reflect a significant level of impact of the strategy of gamification on satisfaction considering both the control group and the experimental group are in the Fully Satisfied category, with a minimum difference of percentages: 94.9% for the control group and 93.7% for the experimental group.

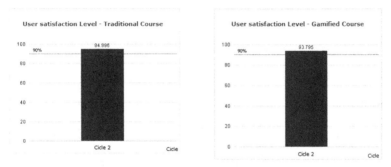

Fig. 2. Comparison of user satisfaction

The elements that make up user satisfaction are: the Methodology, Evaluation and Administrative Technical Management. When evaluating these items, it is possible to observe that users of the gamified course show greater satisfaction with the methodology of the course (95.6%) in relation to the control group (95.6%); However, the difference is not significant either.

When analyzing the approval rate results, the difference between the groups is significant. As shown in Fig. 3, the control group obtained an approval rate of 42% while the experimental group a rate of 56%. Therefore, considering this variable, the impact of the gamification strategy on the approval of the course is certainly higher.

Regarding the academic performance, the users of the control group obtained an average of 41.31 points out of 100 in performance, while the experimental group obtains an average of 58.30. The comparison of the distribution of users by academic performance reflects that there are more users of the experimental group at the high level (Experimental Group 44% vs. Control Group 33%). At the same time, when the averages distributed by groups are compared, the ratings' average of the experimental group are higher than those of the control group in all cases, as shown in Fig. 4.

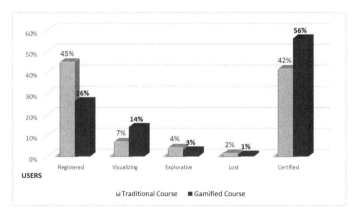

Fig. 3. Comparison of percentages of users distributed in behavior groups (Designed by the authors)

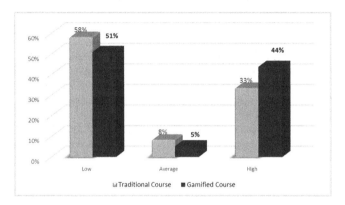

Fig. 4. Comparison of the academic performance by groups (Designed by the authors)

4 Conclusions and Future Work

Based on the results presented by other authors and on the theoretical foundation of gamified systems design, a strategy of gamification based on role play has been implemented in a MOOC on Prevention of Child Sexual Abuse offered by CEC-EPN.

Our research shows for a particular case, the power of gamification in educational contexts, offering positive findings about its benefits on academic performance and the approval rate. One of the limitations of this study is that its application has been reduced to the implementation of the strategy in a MOOC course with a specific topic. However, starting with the results obtained, this can be replicated in other courses.

The strategy has been built applying a particular model of formal design, in this sense it is limited to the elements and the procedure established by Marczewski. However, our interest for future work is to apply other design models.

References

1. INSERVER: Gamification against bullying (2018)
2. Jorge-Soteras, M.: Application of gamification for the improvement of a didactic unit in higher vocational training. International University of La Rioja (2017)
3. Mateo, C.: Application of the methodology of the gamification through TIC in 3° of ESO. Universidad Internacional de la Rioja (2016)
4. Marczewski, A.C.: Even Ninja Monkeys Like to Play. CreateSpace Independent Publishing Platform (2015)
5. Mora, A., Riera, D., Gonzalez, C., Arnedo-Moreno, J.: A literature review of gamification design frameworks. In: 7th International Conference on Games and Virtual Worlds for Serious Applications (VS-Games), pp. 1–8. Skovde (2015)
6. Park, S., Kim, S.: An optimized number of game mechanics and PLEX fun factors for the gamification development. J. Digital Contents Soc. **19**, 2009 (2018)
7. Rodriguez, F., Santiago, R.: Gamification: how to motivate your student and improve the climate in the classroom. Editorial CEANO S.L.U, Barcelona (2015)
8. Sánchez, N.: Gamificación educativa a través de aplicaciones móviles en 1o ESO. Universidad Internacional de la Rioja (2018)
9. The Marczewski framework. https://www.youtube.com/watch?v=506cWlmhghE&feature=youtu.be. Accessed 01 Jul 2019
10. Tondello, G.F., Wehbe, R.R., Diamond, L., Busch, M., Marczewski, A., Nacke, L.E.: The gamification user types hexad scale. In: Proceedings of the 2016 Annual Symposium on Computer-Human Interaction in Play, pp. 229–243. New York, NY, USA (2016)
11. Vanégas, A: Cifras y denuncias sustentan la pregunta en la consulta sobre abuso de niños. EL UNIVERSO. https://www.eluniverso.com/noticias/2017/10/24/nota/6447337/cifras-denuncias-sustentan-pregunta-sobre-abuso-ninos. Accessed 01 Jul 2019
12. Vélez, I.: The gamification in the learning of the university students. Traces Faces **18**, 1–12 (2016)

Topic Detection for Online Course Feedback Using LDA

Sayan Unankard$^{(\boxtimes)}$ (ID) and Wanvimol Nadee (ID)

Information Technology Division, Faculty of Science, Maejo University,
Chiang Mai, Thailand
sayan@gmaejo.mju.ac.th, wanvimon@mju.ac.th

Abstract. In an online course, student feedback is used widely in order to enhance the quality of teaching and learning process by improving the teacher-student relationship. If a lecturer wants to get a summary of these comments, the lecturer has to manually read and summarize all these comments. However, dealing with a very large number of comments is difficult. In this paper, we proposed an approach for topic detection for online course feedback by adopting Latent Dirichlet Allocation (LDA). The course feedback from the website of Coursera (i.e., Machine Learning course) is used to demonstrate the effectiveness of our approach.

Keywords: Course feedback · Online learning · Topic detection · LDA

1 Introduction

Online learning has been on the rise in recent years. Students can fit them around their existing responsibilities and commitments, and can engage with multimedia content and learning materials at whatever time is most convenient to them. Online courses are easily accessible on much smaller budgets. In addition to the convenience and the cost, a large number of students are turning to online learning courses because they have become a better way to learn [30,34]. Those students who are serious about improving their understanding, learning new skills and gaining valuable qualifications are keen to enroll in the type of course that will be the most effective.

In an online courses, students may deliver various feedback to evaluate everything they experience online. They share learning feelings about online courses, which provides many opportunities to discover students' emotional states. However, the unstructured textual data may pose a difficulty for teachers who want to understand the feedback. Therefore a system to summarize all student feedback and giving an overall summary will be very useful for teachers, lecturers, schools, universities, and all education systems to attend to the student feedback and to improve the education system [5,19,23].

With the large amount of feedback, it is difficult for people to comprehend a large number of comments in a chronological order and monitor student comments manually. Several approaches are proposed to summary student course

© Springer Nature Switzerland AG 2020
E. Popescu et al. (Eds.): SETE 2019, LNCS 11984, pp. 133–142, 2020.
https://doi.org/10.1007/978-3-030-38778-5_16

feedback based on text summarization techniques [1,13,15,35]. For example, In [11,20,21] Luo et al. and Fan et al. used phrase extraction and natural language processing (NLP) to address the lexical diversity from student response. In this paper, we developed a Topic Detection for Online Course Feedback system. We adopted a Latent Dirichlet Allocation (LDA) for detecting feedback topics and group all similar comments into the same topic. We used this system to detect topics from student feedback that can help teachers, lecturers, schools, universities, and all education systems for course improvement.

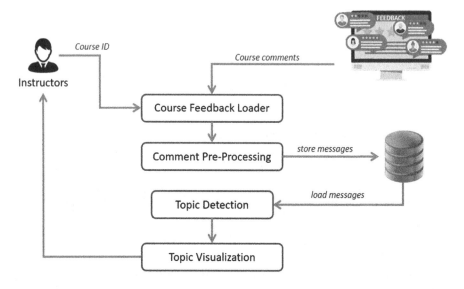

Fig. 1. The architecture of our system.

Our approach has three stages. Firstly, the pre-processing is performed to improve quality of the dataset. Secondly, we propose a topic detection approach to automatically group the messages into topics. Finally, we develop a visualization model for representing feedback topics. The experiments are conducted to demonstrate the effectiveness of our approach. The architecture of our system can be seen in Fig. 1.

The rest of the paper is organized as follows. First, we describe the related work in Sect. 2. Second, the proposed approach is presented in Sect. 3. Third, we present the experimental setup and results in Sect. 4. Finally, the conclusions are given in Sect. 5.

2   Related Works

Education research has studied in various areas in order to improve the design and delivery of the academic programme. Student course feedback provides important information on their learning experience includes teaching and learning problem that can be used to inform course design and development. To create more effective teaching and learning experiences, different approaches are developed and used to explore students' opinions and perspectives of the student evaluation of teaching. Basically, the students' feedback is evaluated by a human judge or teaching evaluation center. This method may not analyze complex feedback and in a costly manner.

Recent year, some studies focus on using automatic text summarization techniques to collect and generate the automatic summarization of student course feedback for instructors and students, e.g., multi-document summarization, keyword and phrase frequency, key phrases extraction, and topic modeling approaches [1,13,15,35]. Traditionally, the approaches to summary annotation have been based on either sentence extraction or document abstraction [24,28,36,39].

Since students tend to use different word expressions to communicate the same or similar meaning in feedback. Luo et al. [20] and Fan et al. [11] proposed to summarize student responses based on phrase extraction and a natural language processing (NLP) by extracting noun phrases from student response. They display student responses in a mobile application named CourseMIRROR. However, there lacks a comprehensive evaluation of the results. Later, In [22], Luo et al. introduced a phrase summarization framework to improve the annotation scheme. They explore a phrase-based highlighting scheme in both the human summary and student responses that assigns a specific color to a similar topic. The result showed that the new phrase extraction model provides a better result than using the noun phrase only. Luo et al. [23] proposed the extractive methods to summarizing student course feedback at a sentence level using the integer linear programming (ILP), phrase-based approach, clustering, and ranking approaches. They focus on the co-occurrence statistics and alleviates sparsity issue.

In other works related to student feedback, In [31] Steyn et al. used content analysis to analyze the qualitative feedback from students for course development. To address the ambiguity and noise in annotation student feedback, Chathuranga et al. [7] used opinion target extraction to investigate student course feedback based on their opinion. They proposed a simple annotation scheme with clarity to annotate general feedback for sentiment analysis. Sung et al. [32] used Latent Semantic Analysis (LSA) technique to develop an automatic summary assessment and feedback system. They use concept maps and concept words to find relevance feedback. Welch et al. [38] used the students' comments from a Facebook group to identify their positive or negative expression.

Topic models are applied in various fields including medical sciences [17,40], software engineering [18,33], geography [9,10], political science [8,12], and etc. A significant amount of research has previously been conducted on topic detection on social networks [2,6,14,25].

Topic modeling is the one approach which is taken into consideration since the use of content and topic of documents play a significant role in the topic detection process. Topic modeling is gaining increasingly concern in different text mining communities. The model provides the algorithms to capture the topic patterns and we can track how the topic has changed over time. *Latent Dirichlet Allocation* (LDA) is a statistical model of document collection and is an unsupervised machine learning technique. It becomes a standard tool in topic modeling. LDA is a generative probabilistic model which is used to discover the text patterns over topics in large document collections [4]. The approach is based on a bag of words, which treats each document as a vector of word counts. Each document is represented as a probability distribution over topics and each topic is represented as a probability distribution over a number of words [3,16]. With the powerful tool to identify latent text patterns in the content [16], many promising approaches have been used and applied LDA in topic detection and tracking process [26,27,29,37] but it is not for online course feedbacks summarization.

3   Proposed Approach

3.1   Pre-processing

In order to improve the quality of our dataset and the performance of the subsequent steps, the pre-processing was designed to ignore common words that carry less important meaning than keywords and remove irrelevant data. The comments are converted into lower case and are removed by a single character word. The stop words are removed and all words are converted into a seed word (stemming word) by using Lucene 3.1.0 Java API[1]. All comments after pre-processing are stored in the database.

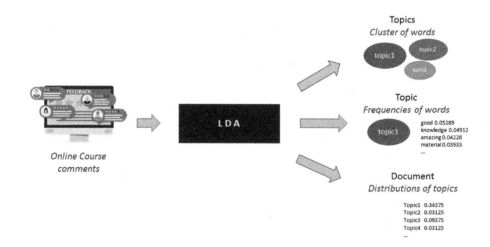

Fig. 2. Understanding of LDA.

---

[1] http://lucene.apache.org.

3.2   Topic Detection

In this stage, we aim to automatically group comments into the same topic. We adopt Latent Dirichlet Allocation (LDA) proposed in [4] to cluster comments in an online course into different topics. In LDA, each comment may be viewed as a mixture of various topics where each comment is considered to have a set of topics that are assigned to it via LDA. Finally, we can obtain the topic distribution in each comment and the word distribution in each topic. Based on our observation, 10 is the best number of topics for each course. The concept of LDA can be seen in Fig. 2.

LDA model is a probability sample process which describes how to generate document words based on potential topic. The model of LDA can be seen in Fig. 3. A summary of LDA variables is presented in Table 1.

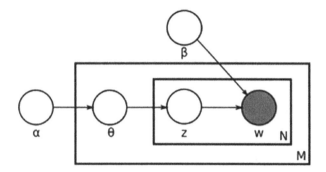

Fig. 3. LDA Model.

Table 1. A summary of variables used in LDA.

Variable	Description
M	Number of comments
N	Number of unique words (vocabulary)
α	Dirichlet prior for Θ
β	Dirichlet prior for Φ
Θ_m	Topic distribution in comments
Φ_k	Word distribution in topics
z	Topic Assignment of Words
w	Words in documents

LDA is a generative model, which assumes each comment is a mixture of a set of topics and words in the comment are generated given their topics. Unlike other data clustering methods, LDA does not assume that each comment can only be assigned to one topic. Therefore, a many-to-many relationship between comment and topic is possible.

3.3   Topic Visualization

For a given topic, it can be shown in Fig. 4. Wordcloud is a novelty visual representation of text data, typically used to depict keyword metadata (tags) on websites, or to visualize free form text. Tags are usually single words, and the importance of each tag is shown with font size. For each topic, the size of word indicates the probability distribution of words in topics.

Fig. 4. Example of Wordcloud for each topic.

4   Experiments and Demonstration Scenario

4.1   Dataset

A collection of online feedback comments are collected from the website of Coursera[2]. We use the dataset crawled by Jan Charles Maghirang Adona which is available online at the Kaggle website[3].

The dataset that will be used in this study contains three colums. Firstly, *CourseId* - this is in the URL of the course in the Coursera website. For example, in this URL, machine-learning would be the *CourseId*. Secondly, *Review* - a review in a specific course. Finally, *Label*, the rating of the course review. An example of *Course feedback* data is shown in Table 2.

Table 2. An example of *Course feedback* data.

CourseId	Review	Label
accounting-analytics	Very boring	1
accounting-analytics	Easiest accounting common sense. If you ever took acct, this will be a wasting of time	1
addiction-and-the-brain	VERY simple	2

---

[2] https://www.coursera.org/.
[3] https://www.kaggle.com/septa97/100k-courseras-course-reviews-dataset.

Table 2. (*continued*)

CourseId	Review	Label
addiction-and-the-brain	Unable to even start it... Click on videos of week 1 and nothing happens	
machine-learning	Very thorough and motivating instructor, showing good examples. I would recommend having linear algebra knowledge as a pre-requisite for the course	5
machine-learning	Low quality video and audio	2
machine-learning	It is a good beginner course with lots of detail	3
machine-learning	One of the best and valuable courses you can take	5
machine-learning	It was quiet mathematical for a beginner like me	3
machine-learning	It's a good introduction to ML	2
machine-learning	It's so low that I can do nothing now after learning with every work in this course done	3

4.2   Demonstration Scenario

For demonstration, a collection of feedbacks from Machine-learning course with 8,109 comments is used. We decided to choose this course because it has large number of comments. We also try to find out how many topics (k) to obtain the best performance. The number of topics (k) is assigned to LDA Model by 10, 20 and 50 topics. The number of topics might be different for each course. For our experiment, 10 is the best number of topics. Figure 5 shows the example of topics detected by LDA Algorithm.

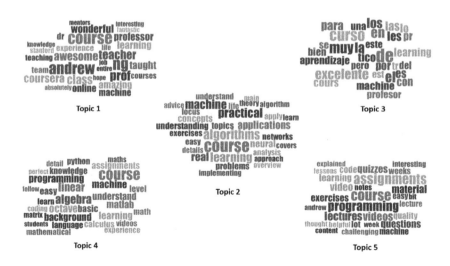

Fig. 5. Example of topics detected by LDA algorithm.

However, there are some limitations for LDA. The number of topics is fixed and must be known ahead of time and no evolution of topics over time. Despite its limitations, LDA is still central to topic modeling and has really revolutionized the field.

5   Conclusions

In this paper, we proposed an approach for topic detection of online course feedback by utilizing Latent Dirichlet Allocation (LDA). We describes our demonstration system for detecting feedback topics over online course system. Our system is able to summarize topics and present to instructors via Wordcloud. The course feedback related to Machine Learning course from the website of Coursera is used to demonstrate the effectiveness of our approach. For future work, the further performance evaluation will be performed and opinion analysis for student course feedback will be studied to discover students' emotions. Moreover, student learning behavior patterns will be studied.

References

1. Allahyari, M., et al.: Text summarization techniques: a brief survey. arXiv preprint arXiv:1707.02268 (2017)
2. Alvanaki, F., Michel, S., Ramamritham, K., Weikum, G.: See what's enblogue: real-time emergent topic identification in social media. In: Proceedings of 15th International Conference on Extending Database Technology, EDBT 2012, Berlin, Germany, 27–30 March 2012, pp. 336–347 (2012)
3. Blei, D.M.: Probabilistic topic models. Commun. ACM **55**(4), 77–84 (2012). https://doi.org/10.1145/2133806.2133826
4. Blei, D.M., Ng, A.Y., Jordan, M.I.: Latent dirichlet allocation. J. Mach. Learn. Res. **3**(1), 993–1022 (2003)
5. Bonnel, W.: Improving feedback to students in online courses. Nurs. Educ. Perspect. **29**(5), 290–294 (2008)
6. Cataldi, M., Caro, L.D., Schifanella, C.: Emerging topic detection on twitter based on temporal and social terms evaluation. In: Proceedings of the Tenth International Workshop on Multimedia Data Mining, pp. 4:1–4:10 (2010)
7. Chathuranga, J., Ediriweera, S., Hasantha, R., Munasinghe, P., Ranathunga, S.: Annotating opinions and opinion targets in student course feedback. In: Proceedings of the Eleventh International Conference on Language Resources and Evaluation (LREC-2018) (2018)
8. Cohen, R., Ruths, D.: Classifying political orientation on twitter: it's not easy!. In: Proceedings of the 7th International Conference on Weblogs and Social Media, ICWSM 2013, pp. 91–99, January 2013
9. Cristani, M., Perina, A., Castellani, U., Murino, V.: Geo-located image analysis using latent representations. In: 2008 IEEE Conference on Computer Vision and Pattern Recognition, pp. 1–8, June 2008
10. Eisenstein, J., O'Connor, B., Smith, N.A., Xing, E.P.: A latent variable model for geographic lexical variation. In: Proceedings of the 2010 Conference on Empirical Methods in Natural Language Processing, pp. 1277–1287. EMNLP 2010. Association for Computational Linguistics, Stroudsburg (2010). http://dl.acm.org/citation.cfm?id=1870658.1870782

11. Fan, X., Luo, W., Menekse, M., Litman, D., Wang, J.: Coursemirror: enhancing large classroom instructor-student interactions via mobile interfaces and natural language processing. In: Proceedings of the 33rd Annual ACM Conference Extended Abstracts on Human Factors in Computing Systems, pp. 1473–1478. ACM (2015)
12. Fang, Y., Si, L., Somasundaram, N., Yu, Z.: Mining contrastive opinions on political texts using cross-perspective topic model. In: Proceedings of the Fifth ACM International Conference on Web Search and Data Mining, pp. 63–72. WSDM 2012. ACM, New York (2012). http://doi.acm.org/10.1145/2124295.2124306
13. García-Hernández, R.A., Montiel, R., Ledeneva, Y., Rendón, E., Gelbukh, A., Cruz, R.: Text summarization by sentence extraction using unsupervised learning. In: Gelbukh, A., Morales, E.F. (eds.) MICAI 2008. LNCS (LNAI), vol. 5317, pp. 133–143. Springer, Heidelberg (2008). https://doi.org/10.1007/978-3-540-88636-5_12
14. Goorha, S., Ungar, L.H.: Discovery of significant emerging trends. In: Proceedings of the 16th ACM SIGKDD International Conference on Knowledge Discovery and Data Mining, Washington, DC, USA, 25–28 July 2010, pp. 57–64 (2010)
15. Hasan, K.S., Ng, V.: Automatic keyphrase extraction: a survey of the state of the art. In: Proceedings of the 52nd Annual Meeting of the Association for Computational Linguistics, vol. 1: Long Papers. pp. 1262–1273 (2014)
16. Hong, L., Davison, B.D.: Empirical study of topic modeling in Twitter. In: Proceedings of the First Workshop on Social Media Analytics. SOMA 2010, pp. 80–88. ACM, New York (2010). http://doi.acm.org/10.1145/1964858.1964870
17. Paul, M.J., Dredze, M.: You are what your tweet: analyzing twitter for public health. Artif. Intell. **38**, 265–272 (2011)
18. Linstead, E., Rigor, P., Bajracharya, S., Lopes, C., Baldi, P.: Mining concepts from code with probabilistic topic models. In: Proceedings of the Twenty-second IEEE/ACM International Conference on Automated Software Engineering. ASE 2007, pp. 461–464. ACM, New York (2007). http://doi.acm.org/10.1145/1321631.1321709
19. Lumpkin, A., Achen, R.M., Dodd, R.K.: Student perceptions of active learning. Coll. Stud. J. **49**(1), 121–133 (2015)
20. Luo, W., Fan, X., Menekse, M., Wang, J., Litman, D.: Enhancing instructor-student and student-student interactions with mobile interfaces and summarization. In: Proceedings of the 2015 Conference of the North American Chapter of the Association for Computational Linguistics: Demonstrations, pp. 16–20 (2015)
21. Luo, W., Litman, D.: Summarizing student responses to reflection prompts. In: Proceedings of the 2015 Conference on Empirical Methods in Natural Language Processing, pp. 1955–1960 (2015)
22. Luo, W., Liu, F., Litman, D.: An improved phrase-based approach to annotating and summarizing student course responses. arXiv preprint arXiv:1805.10396 (2018)
23. Luo, W., Liu, F., Liu, Z., Litman, D.: Automatic summarization of student course feedback. arXiv preprint arXiv:1805.10395 (2018)
24. Martins, A.F., Smith, N.A.: Summarization with a joint model for sentence extraction and compression. In: Proceedings of the Workshop on Integer Linear Programming for Natural Language Processing, pp. 1–9. Association for Computational Linguistics (2009)
25. Mathioudakis, M., Koudas, N.: Twittermonitor: trend detection over the twitter stream. In: Proceedings of the ACM SIGMOD International Conference on Management of Data, SIGMOD 2010, Indianapolis, Indiana, USA, 6–10 June 2010, pp. 1155–1158 (2010)

26. Mehrotra, R., Sanner, S., Buntine, W., Xie, L.: Improving LDA topic models for microblogs via tweet pooling and automatic labeling. In: Proceedings of the 36th International ACM SIGIR Conference on Research and Development in Information Retrieval, pp. 889–892. ACM (2013)
27. Ramage, D., Dumais, S., Liebling, D.: Characterizing microblogs with topic models. In: Fourth International AAAI Conference on Weblogs and Social Media (2010)
28. Rush, A.M., Chopra, S., Weston, J.: A neural attention model for abstractive sentence summarization. arXiv preprint arXiv:1509.00685 (2015)
29. Schinas, M., Papadopoulos, S., Kompatsiaris, Y., Mitkas, P.A.: Visual event summarization on social media using topic modelling and graph-based ranking algorithms. In: Proceedings of the 5th ACM on International Conference on Multimedia Retrieval, pp. 203–210. ACM (2015)
30. Shapiro, H.B., Lee, C.H., Roth, N.E.W., Li, K., Rundel, M.Ç., Canelas, D.A.: Understanding the massive open online course (MOOC) student experience: an examination of attitudes motivations and barriers. Comput. Educ. **110**, 35–50 (2017)
31. Steyn, C., Davies, C., Sambo, A.: Eliciting student feedback for course development: the application of a qualitative course evaluation tool among business research students. Assess. Eval. High. Educ. **44**(1), 11–24 (2019)
32. Sung, Y.T., Liao, C.N., Chang, T.H., Chen, C.L., Chang, K.E.: The effect of online summary assessment and feedback system on the summary writing on 6th graders: The LSA-based technique. Compu. Educ. **95**, 1–18 (2016)
33. Thomas, S.W.: Mining software repositories using topic models. In: 2011 33rd International Conference on Software Engineering (ICSE), pp. 1138–1139, May 2011
34. Toven-Lindsey, B., Rhoads, R.A., Lozano, J.B.: Virtually unlimited classrooms: pedagogical practices in massive open online courses. Internet High. Educ. **24**, 1–12 (2015)
35. Wan, X., Yang, J.: Multi-document summarization using cluster-based link analysis. In: Proceedings of the 31st Annual International ACM SIGIR Conference on Research and Development in Information Retrieval, pp. 299–306. ACM (2008)
36. Wang, L., Ling, W.: Neural network-based abstract generation for opinions and arguments. arXiv preprint arXiv:1606.02785 (2016)
37. Wang, Y., Agichtein, E., Benzi, M.: TM-LDA: efficient online modeling of latent topic transitions in social media. In: Proceedings of the 18th ACM SIGKDD International Conference on Knowledge Discovery and Data Mining, pp. 123–131. ACM (2012)
38. Welch, C., Mihalcea, R.: Targeted sentiment to understand student comments. In: Proceedings of COLING 2016, the 26th International Conference on Computational Linguistics: Technical Papers, pp. 2471–2481 (2016)
39. Xiong, W., Litman, D.: Empirical analysis of exploiting review helpfulness for extractive summarization of online reviews. In: Proceedings of coling 2014, the 25th International Conference on Computational Linguistics: Technical Papers, pp. 1985–1995 (2014)
40. Zhang, Y., Chen, M., Huang, D., Wu, D., Li, Y.: iDoctor: personalized and professionalized medical recommendations based on hybrid matrix factorization. Future Gener. Comput. Syst. **66**, 30–35 (2017)

SPeL (Social and Personal Computing for Web-Supported Learning Communities)

An Educational Model for Integrating Game-Based and Problem-Based Learning in Data-Driven Flipped Classrooms

Muriel Algayres⬡ and Evangelia Triantafyllou(⊠)⬡

Aalborg University, Copenhagen, Denmark
evt@create.aau.dk

Abstract. Active learning has been employed in higher education, as a way to engage students more efficiently and encourage the development of 21st century skills. The flipped classroom (FC) in particular has known a remarkable development. The FC is defined as a teaching method where "events that have traditionally taken place inside the classroom now take place outside and vice versa". The FC takes place into three stages: pre-class, in-class and post-class, all of which have used various technological tools and online environments. There is still, however, some lacks in research and development around the FC. Research into combining the FC with other active learning methods such as Problem-Based Learning (PBL) or Game-Based Learning (GBL) is a recent field of study. Furthermore, any endeavor into combining the FC and other methodologies or expanding the FC has been limited to one of its three stages, usually either for pre-class preparation or for in-class activities. Similarly, use of technology and learning analytics had so far been mostly limited to out-of-class periods. Therefore, we consider that there is potential in building a new theoretical model to enhance the FC methodology by incorporating problem-based learning and learning analytics in the full learning process, and to develop the new FC model as an adaptive, data-driven, personalized experience. This paper will therefore present the new pedagogical model, its structure, and the technological tools that will support its development.

Keywords: Flipped classroom · Problem-based learning · Learning analytics · Game-based learning

1 Introduction

The past decades have seen a transformation in the way educators and course designers approach education. The development of technology-enhanced learning appears as a response to the needs of a new society and a major change in education [1]. Technological developments herald a necessary change in learning paradigms and forms of traditional schooling. Conventional education focused mostly on transmission of knowledge. Recent developments in educational technology focus on learning, i.e. the acquisition of new mental schemes, knowledge, abilities, and skills that can be used to solve problems successfully [2]. This resulted in an increased appreciation for active learning. According to Lee in [3], active learning "shifts the focus of learning from passively receiving

© Springer Nature Switzerland AG 2020
E. Popescu et al. (Eds.): SETE 2019, LNCS 11984, pp. 145–154, 2020.
https://doi.org/10.1007/978-3-030-38778-5_17

content information to diligently participating in learning activities", and allow students to develop and nurture important skills such as "critical thinking, creativity, communication, and collaboration" while promoting "social interactions, allowing students to work collaboratively with their peers and teachers". Literature has already discussed innovative learning strategies, such as learning-by-doing, the Flipped Classroom (FC), Problem-Based Learning (PBL), Game-Based Learning (GBL), collaborative learning, and Learning Analytics (LA) [4]. However, efforts put into combining two or more of these methods together are still a recent approach. This paper therefore proposes an educational model based on the FC structure incorporating PBL elements and using LA and GBL to in order to better structure out-of-class and in-class activities, increase student engagement and motivation, and better monitor student progress in FCs.

2   Background

2.1   The Flipped Classroom (FC)

The FC is "a set of pedagogical approaches that (1) move most information-transmission teaching out of class, (2) use class time for learning activities that are active and social and (3) require students to complete pre- and/or post-class activities to fully benefit from in-class work" [5, p. 6]. The FC model offers a change of paradigm in education, relying on various educational theories that encourage active engagement among students [4, 6]. For our educational model, we employed the FC Model proposed by Gernstein [8], shown in Fig. 1.

According to this model, the FC process begins with concept exploration. The "concept exploration" stage is an educator-led part of the process that introduces learners to learning material. This is traditionally the presentation part of a course outside the classroom (by e.g. video lectures). After concept exploration, students make meaning out of the information they have been exposed to by engaging in various assessment or reflection activities. The "meaning-making" stage is also situated outside the classroom. The "experiential engagement" stage occurs when the learner and instructor interact in a FC. It may occur before the concept exploration stage, when educators engage students in activities with the aim to pique their interest in a topic (e.g. play a game). It may also occur after the meaning-making stage, where students have to apply what they have learned (e.g. practice a skill, work on a project, etc.). At this stage, the educator has a chance to support students in applying their knowledge. The "demonstration and application" stage is the last of the FC Model. During this stage, students analyze, evaluate and create, while educators can evaluate for mastery and offer additional support where needed.

For the purpose of this educational model, we endeavored to combine first this FC model with PBL elements, in order to better frame the learning activities in FCs.

2.2   Problem-Based Learning

PBL is a student-centered pedagogy in which learners learn through the experience of problem solving [9, 10]. In PBL, learning starts with an ill-defined problem. Students must study the initial problem formulation in order to formulate a concrete problem they can solve. Then, they analyze the problem by gaining knowledge on the topics related to it, and finally design, implement and evaluate a solution to it. Research has shown that the flipped classroom combined with the problem-solving strategy was more effective than e-learning, or learning through isolated problem-solving sequences [11]. Lai and Hwang similarly emphasized that a self-regulated flipped classroom approach can improve students' learning performance. Moreover, the problem-solving and personalized interaction, which takes place face-to-face, sets these classes apart, making them more effective than MOOCs [12].

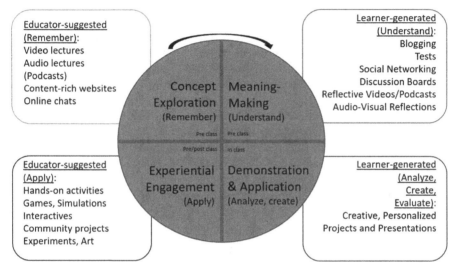

Fig. 1. The Flipped Classroom Model adapted from [8].

2.3 Learning Analytics (LA)

Based on the most commonly cited definition, "LA is the measurement, collection, analysis and reporting of data about learners and their contexts, for purposes of understanding and optimizing learning and the environments in which it occurs." [13]. LA can provide useful information to instructors by combining and analyzing students' historical data during the course. Intervention also plays a major role in LA; instructors can choose to intervene after identifying students' needs and issues through LA, and can use LA to improve the learning design of the curriculum (e.g. [14]). Doko and Bexheti [15] thus consider that the introduction of the FC and the rapid development of data science enable the exploitation of Educational Data Mining (EDM) and LA to optimize the learning process. Their study of 122 papers revealed that LA and EDM help discover hidden patterns and respond to educational questions and problems, and that most studies should use more that one data mining technique. It is therefore evident that LA can play a major role in learning design and implementation, while there are many approaches to exploiting and analyzing educational data.

2.4   Game-Based Learning (GBL) and Gamification

Research into educational games is long established, with recent developments along the fields of serious games [16], digital GBL [17], and gamification, the last defined as "the use of video game elements to improve user experience and user engagement in non-game services and applications" [18]. Games embody well-established principles of active learning and allow replacing the learning activity into a meaningful context [19].

Research in combining the FC and GBL is also a recent approach, which has gained traction in recent years. Several studies highlighted how GBL and gamification could improve the FC model, both for support in the pre-class process [20] or through gamified activities in the classroom [21].

Furthermore, research into LA applied to GBL and gamification shows that there is great potential in using these methodologies with EDM in the FC. For example, Klemke et al. [7] proposed the model of the flipped MOOC to prepare the students for class, using LA and gamification to track the students' engagement with the learning material during pre-class preparation. Other studies underline the fact that using these methods in so-called smart classrooms could support adaptive learning, allowing students and educators to tailor the learning process to individual needs [4]. For example, Yang [22] developed the master learning theory to present a model supporting GBL and LA, where gaming elements and personalized feedback reinforce the learning process in students. Similarly, Busch et al. [23] presented the development of a learning mobile game model, where LA were used in evaluating the success and fail rates of players with the aim to support the learning experience.

3   The Proposed Educational Model

The proposed educational model is based on the stipulation that learners should be able to gain control and reflect on their learning process. Following the learning cycle in the FC Model established by Gernstein [8], the learning sequence should allow students to analyze, apply, and create based on knowledge that they have accessed, with opportunities to understand and remember it. Finally, learners should be able to evaluate their own progression to support their self-directed learning. With these objectives in mind, we have devised a three-tier model that supports learning in FCs (Fig. 2).

3.1   Learning Activities Layer

The first layer of the model describes the learning activities that take place in the FC. These activities are organized following the FC cycle of pre-class, in-class and post-class. They are supported by the Learning Design methodology, whose successful application in the FC has already been studied in [24]. Learning design "...is defined as the description of the teaching-learning process that takes place in a unit of learning (e.g., a course, a lesson or any other designed learning event)" [25, p. 13]. The key principle in Learning Design is that it represents "the learning activities and the support activities that are performed by different persons (learners, teachers) in the context of a unit of learning" [25].

The most common framework for Learning Design is defined in the Larnaca Declaration on Learning Design [26]. This declaration defines the core concepts of Learning Design (guidance, representation, sharing), and the development of a Learning Design activity by three steps: planning activity, design core-learning concepts, and implement activity.

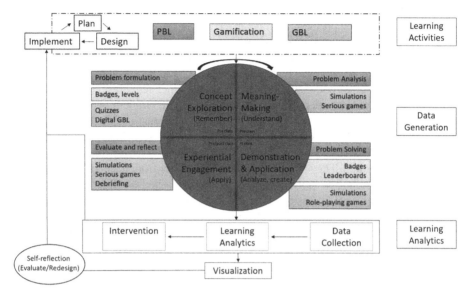

Fig. 2. The proposed three-tier educational model

This approach allows embedding layers of PBL elements, gamification, and GBL in the learning activity. While it would be impossible to provide an extensive list of the learning activities on the design level, previous research provides us with examples of combining such methodologies with the FC:

– *Gamification*: the use of gamification in the FC appears the most common, as elements like badges and leaderboards are a common feature of Virtual Learning Environments (VLEs) such as MOOCs. Klemke et al. [7] suggested the model of the flipped MOOC to combine online preparation for class with gamification and Tsay et al. [27] similarly tested a model of FC supported by gamification (with goals, variable difficulties, badges and leaderboards), and tested it as more efficient than traditional learning in terms of learning outcomes.
– *GBL*: educational games are flexible and diverse and appear both in pre-class preparation [28] and as an in-class activity. In-class games can help students to practice notions [21], and they can also be used as simulations of real-life situations [29].
– *PBL*: research exploiting active use of PBL in the FC is still rare. Song et al. [30] presented the FC as a means to exploit the classroom time for appropriately designed interactive learning activities such as collaborative and PBL activities. Çakiroglu and Özturk [31] carried PBL activities in FCs to promote self-regulation among undergraduate students with positive results. They concluded that this method resulted in

higher levels of goal setting, planning and task strategies, and promoted self-regulation skills among the students.

In our framework, learning activities are inspired by the PBL approach and are distributed along the FC cycle (Fig. 2). If the experiential engagement FC stage is employed for introduction to the next FC cycle, learning activities aiming at introducing students to an ill-defined problem can take place during this stage. Such activities could include watching videos, listening to podcasts, or reading. During the concept exploration FC stage, students can be invited to understand and analyse the ill-defined problem. Problem analysis can be achieved by following video or audio tutorials, reading material on websites or textbooks, or consulting experts, among other activities. For the meaning-making FC stage, students are called to formulate a specific problem, which stems from the ill-defined one, and that they will solve during the next stages of the FC. During this process, students may discuss or brainstorm with their peers or their teachers through discussion boards or blogs, and they may produce written material for arguing on the selection of the problem. They may also get feedback either from peers or from teachers on the problem formulation. Moreover, students may be invited to reflect on the problem formulation or they may be assessed on the knowledge they gained so far, in order to assure that they come to the in-class session prepared. Learning activities such as audio-visual reflections, reflective videos/podcasts, and tests/quizzes can be employed for this matter. For the demonstration and application FC stage, the students can work in class on designing and implementing a solution to the selected problem. During this stage, students can work in groups, while the teachers will support students on problem-solving. Finally, during experiential engagement (when implemented as the final stage of the FC), students can evaluate and reflect on the implemented solution by running out-of-class experiments, surveys, or tests/simulations and producing reports on the evaluation results. The aforementioned PBL/FC cycle does not presupposes that students have to work with different problems in every cycle. Students may select a problem that will be solved in several iterations. In every iteration, students may solve parts of the problem or may re-define the problem.

In our framework, learning activities will also take opportunities to exploit GBL and gamification to support the educational model. The whole of the FC is supported by a gamification system that uses common features such as badges, levels and leaderboards to help students track their own progress, visualize their progress and manage their own learning paths. Furthermore, GBL can be used at each step of the educational model to support engagement in the learning activity. During the concept exploration process, quizzes and digital GBL can be used to check that students have engaged with the learning material. In the meaning-making stage, specific serious games can be used for students to practice the new concepts that they have learned. In the demonstration and application stage, both gamification and GBL can be implemented, especially during in-class sessions. Levels, badges and leaderboards can be used to monitor students' progression and help them visualise the different steps of the learning process. Similarly, various forms of serious games can be used as tools for application. In the last stage, experiential engagement, the debriefing process of a serious game can be used as a means to engage the students in self-reflection regarding the learning process and what they learned.

3.2 Data Generation Layer

The second level of the model relies on the data generated in the FC. Using LA in the FC implies to collect data related to the online activity of students, the use of the online resources provided before the class sessions, and the results of the exercises solved (before, during and after the class session) to infer the amount of work done by students, and the results of this work [32]. Due to the unreliable nature of self-reported data, collection of data traces from VLEs appears as a source of choice for data collection. Jovanovic et al. [33] provided a common example of trace data, which consisted of a quadruple containing: event id, type of action, anonymized student id, and timestamp. Such trace data was recorded in continuous learning sequences, where events occurred within a 30-minute period.

In-class activities, however, generated thus far less data for EDM, owing to the fact that such activities are often student- or instructor-led, which do not always require use of a VLE [34]. Therefore, our model aims to gather data through all the steps of the FC, and not be limited to off-class data. The post-class process, mostly neglected in recent studies in the FC, should also be a point of specific interest. Some studies previously used data for evaluating students' performance through completion rates and success rate in the course [35, 36], self-regulation in learning [37], and interactions with peers or teachers in a MOOC platform [38]. However, no system so far has tried to combine all these different sources of data.

3.3 Learning Analytics Layer

Finally, the final layer of the proposed model will rely on learning analytics to provide to students a fully personalized adaptive learning experience. Learning analytics occurs in three steps: data collection, learning analytics, and intervention. Specific LA techniques and tools to process data are available, such as network analysis, user modelling or knowledge domain modelling. The prime objective of LA is to monitor individual learners' progress and behavior continuously in order to explore factors that may influence learning efficiency and effectiveness [1]. To that end, data visualization must support learners and educators as a means to evaluate, transform and adjust the learning process. Such indicators and visualizations can include learner activity (time spent on videos and reading material), learner engagement level (access to the platform and participation to written exchanges), scores and common mistakes [32]. This data in the long term allows for the introduction of corrective feedback to encourage the students to learn through trial and error [22], competence-based assessment [1], and peer-based learning and evaluation [39]. Therefore, the proposed educational framework aims at developing an online environment that will support active learning through the integration of PBL elements and GBL, and will enable data generation and LA to support the FC process by encouraging self-regulated learning in students and an adaptive learning experience.

4 Conclusion

In conclusion, our educational model aims at providing a new expanded model based on the FC methodology, which can improve and get beyond the standard, and sometimes limited, pre-class/in-class/post-class traditional system. We used the model of the FC as a "wheel" of conceptual stages and reinforced them through the implantation of PBL elements, and support from GBL and gamification tools. In this model, data generation and the use of LA is crucial to support the learning experience, both for students and educators. With this educational model, we aim at developing a FC that can engage students at a higher level, support educators to adjust the course as the students need it, and finally provide a fully adaptive and personalized learning experience.

Acknowledgement. This research was conducted in the context of the FLIP2G project. This project has been funded with the support of the Erasmus+programme of the European Union. This paper reflects the views only of the authors, and the Commission cannot be held responsible for any use which may be made of the information contained therein.

References

1. Chen, N.S., Cheng, I.L., Chew, S.W.: Evolution is not enough: revolutionizing current learning environments to smart learning environments. Int. J. Artif. Intell. Educ. **26**(2), 561–581 (2016)
2. Alonso, F., López, G., Manrique, D., Viñes, J.M.: An instructional model for web-based e-learning education with a blended learning process approach. Br. J. Edu. Technol. **36**(2), 217–235 (2005)
3. Frey, B.: The SAGE Encyclopaedia of Educational Research, Measurement, and Evaluation, pp. 39–40. SAGE Publications, Thousand Oaks (2018)
4. Uskov, V.L., Bakken, J.P., Penumatsa, A., Heinemann, C., Rachakonda, R.: Smart pedagogy for smart universities. In: Uskov, V.L., Howlett, R.J., Jain, L.C. (eds.) SEEL 2017. SIST, vol. 75, pp. 3–16. Springer, Cham (2018). https://doi.org/10.1007/978-3-319-59451-4_1
5. Abeysekera, L., Dawson, P.: Motivation and cognitive load in the flipped classroom: definition, rationale and a call for research. High. Educ. Res. Dev. **34**(1), 1–14 (2015)
6. Nechodomu, T., Falldin, M., Hoover, S.: CEHD Flipped Learning Guide (2016)
7. Klemke, R., Eradze, M., Antonaci, A.: The flipped MOOC: using gamification and learning analytics in MOOC design—a conceptual approach. Educ. Sci. **8**(1), 25 (2018)
8. Gerstein, J.: The flipped classroom: a full picture, User Generated Education (2011). http://usergeneratededuction.wordpress.com/2011/06/13/the-flipped-classroom-model-afull-picture/
9. Neville, A.J.: Problem-based learning and medical education forty years on. Med. Principles Pract. **18**(1), 1–9 (2009)
10. Barge. S.: Principles of Problem and Project Learning, the Aalborg PBL Model. Aalborg University, Aalborg (2010). http://www.aau.dk/digitalAssets/62/62747_pbl_aalborg_modellen.pdf
11. Chiang, T.H.C.: Analysis of learning behavior in a flipped programing classroom adopting problem-solving strategies. Interact. Learn. Environ. **25**(2), 189–202 (2017)
12. Lai, C.L., Hwang, G.J.: A self-regulated flipped classroom approach to improving students' learning performance in a mathematics course. Comput. Educ. **100**, 126–140 (2016)
13. Long, P., Siemens, G.: Penetrating the fog: analytics in learning and education. Educause Rev. Online **46**(5), 31–40 (2011)
14. Lu, O.H., Huang, J.C., Huang, A.Y., Yang, S.J.: Applying learning analytics for improving students' engagement and learning outcomes in an MOOCs enabled collaborative programming course. Interact. Learn. Environ. **25**(2), 220–234 (2017)

15. Doko, E., Bexheti, L.A.: A systematic mapping study of educational technologies based on educational data mining and learning analytics. In: 2018 7th Mediterranean Conference on Embedded Computing (MECO), pp. 1–4. IEEE (2018)
16. Michael, D.R., Chen, S.L.: Serious Games: Games That Educate, Train, and Inform. Muska & Lipman/Premier-Trade, Boston (2005). Thomson Course Technology
17. Prensky, M.: Digital game-based learning. Comput. Entertainment (CIE) **1**(1), 21 (2003)
18. Deterding, S., Sicart, M., Nacke, L., O'Hara, K., Dixon, D.: Gamification. using game-design elements in non-gaming contexts. In: CHI 2011 Extended Abstracts on Human Factors in Computing Systems, pp. 2425–2428. ACM (2011)
19. Van Eck, R.: Digital game-based learning: it's not just the digital natives who are restless. Educause Rev. **41**(2), 16 (2006)
20. Jo, J., Jun, H., Lim, H.: A comparative study on gamification of the flipped classroom in engineering education to enhance the effects of learning. Comput. Appl. Eng. Educ. **26**(5), 1626–1640 (2018)
21. Hung, H.T.: Gamifying the flipped classroom using game-based learning materials. ELT J. **72**(3), 296–308 (2018)
22. Yang, K.H.: Learning behavior and achievement analysis of a digital game-based learning approach integrating mastery learning theory and different feedback models. Interact. Learn. Environ. **25**(2), 235–248 (2017)
23. Busch, C., Claßnitz, S., Selmanagic, A., Steinicke, M.: Developing and testing a mobile learning games framework. Electron. J. e-Learning **13**(3), 151–166 (2015)
24. Triantafyllou, E., Kofoed, L.B., Purwins, H., Timcenko, O.: Applying a learning design methodology in the flipped classroom approach–empowering teachers to reflect and design for learning. Tidsskriftet Læring og Medier (LOM), **9**(15) (2016)
25. Koper, R.: Current research in learning design. J. Educ. Technol. Soc. **9**(1), 13–22 (2006)
26. Dalziel, J., et al.: The Larnaca declaration on learning design (2013). http://www.larnacadeclaration.org/
27. Tsay, C.H.H., Kofinas, A., Luo, J.: Enhancing student learning experience with technology-mediated gamification: an empirical study. Comput. Educ. **121**, 1–17 (2018)
28. Ling, L.T.Y.: Meaningful gamification and students' motivation: a strategy for scaffolding reading material. Online Learn. **22**(2), 141–155 (2018)
29. Bye, R.T.: A flipped classroom approach for teaching a master's course on artificial intelligence. In: Escudeiro, P., Costagliola, G., Zvacek, S., Uhomoibhi, J., McLaren, B.M. (eds.) CSEDU 2017. CCIS, vol. 865, pp. 246–276. Springer, Cham (2018). https://doi.org/10.1007/978-3-319-94640-5_13
30. Song, Y., Jong, M.S.Y., Chang, M., Chen, W.: Guest editorial: "HOW" to design, implement and evaluate the flipped classroom? – a synthesis. Educ. Technol. Soc. **20**(1), 180–183 (2017)
31. Çakiroglu, Ü., Öztürk, M.: Flipped classroom with problem based activities: exploring self-regulated learning in a programming language course. J. Educ. Technol. Soc. **20**(1), 337 (2017)
32. Fernández, A.R., Merino, P.J.M., Kloos, C.D.: Scenarios for the application of learning analytics and the flipped classroom. In: 2018 IEEE Global Engineering Education Conference (EDUCON), pp. 1619–1628. IEEE (2018)
33. Jovanovic, J., Gaševic, D., Dawson, S., Pardo, A., Mirriahi, N.: Learning analytics to unveil learning strategies in a flipped classroom. Internet High. Educ. **33**, 74–85 (2017). https://doi.org/10.1016/j.iheduc.2017.02.001
34. Blau, I., Shamir-Inbal, T.: Re-designed flipped learning model in an academic course: the role of co-creation and co-regulation. Comput. Educ. **115**, 69–81 (2017)
35. Kaw, A., Clark, R., Delgado, E., Abate, N.: Analyzing the use of adaptive learning in a flipped classroom for preclass learning. Comput. Appl. Eng. Educ. **27**(3), 663–678 (2019)

36. Yang, Y., Wu, H., Cao, J.: Smartlearn: predicting learning performance and discovering smart learning strategies in flipped classroom. In: 2016 International Conference on Orange Technologies (ICOT), pp. 92–95. IEEE (2016)
37. Hwang, G.J., Chen, P.Y.: Effects of a collective problem-solving promotion-based flipped classroom on students' learning performances and interactive patterns. Interact. Learn. Environ. 1–16 (2019). https://doi.org/10.1080/10494820.2019.1568263
38. Ji, Y., Han, Y.: Monitoring indicators of the flipped classroom learning process based on data mining-taking the course of "virtual reality technology" as an example. Int. J. Emerg. Technol. Learn. **14**(3), 166–177 (2019)
39. Valdez, M.T., Ferreira, C.M., Barbosa, F.M.: Implementation of methodological strategies, attitudes and instruments as a PBL resource. In: 2018 17th International Conference on Information Technology Based Higher Education and Training (ITHET), pp. 1–4. IEEE (2018)

Distributed Student Team Work in Challenge-Based Innovation and Entrepreneurship (I&E) Course

Galena Pisoni[1]([✉]) [iD], Javier Segovia[2], Milena Stoycheva[1], and Maurizio Marchese[1]

[1] Department of Information Engineering and Computer Science, University of Trento, via Sommarive 9, 38122 Trento, Italy
{galena.pisoni,milena.stoycheva@unitn.it,maurizio.marchese}@unitn.it
[2] Universidad Politecnica de Madrid, 28660 Boadilla del Monte, Madrid, Spain
javier.segovia@upm.es

Abstract. Challenge-based learning is proposed as an alternative to traditional learning in training engineering graduates with the skills for the future. It puts equal emphasis on academic learning and on competences that students need more for their jobs. Challenge-based leaning is the learning in which students learn through understanding and resolution of a real-world challenge. In this paper we show how such challenge-based course can be implemented in a cross-university setting in which students work on challenges provided by companies: the Universities that implemented the course are University of Trento, UNITN, Italy and Universidad Politécnica de Madrid, UPM, Spain and in it students form and work in teams composed of students coming from both of the locations. Both of the locations delivered the course at the same time. The positive feedback from the students shows the importance of such new multi method to train students adequately for remote team-work and training them with skills for 21st century, especially in the era of digital transformation. In addition, our paper draws important leanings on how to set such cross-university teams as well as important future research directions.

Keywords: I&E Education · Remote learning · Challenge-based learning · Collaborative learning · Team work

1 Introduction

Challenge-based education is alternative to traditional education in training engineering graduates to become independent learners, critical thinkers, problems solvers, life long learners as well as team payers [16]. This educational model is relatively (dates from around 2011), it is built on problem-based learning, and it represents the next step forward. It does not require only to have a problem at the center of the learning process, it requires the problem proposer to be

E. Popescu et al. (Eds.): SETE 2019, LNCS 11984, pp. 155–163, 2020.
https://doi.org/10.1007/978-3-030-38778-5_18

involved as a stakeholder and to intensively cooperate with the students and mentor them while they are working on the project, like this students to develop practical competences thought resolution of a real business case [9].

Since the introduction of challenge-based learning, its role has been to improve education by increasing the degree of students' satisfaction, retention factor, and enrollment, as well as developing students' skills and competences apart from the theoretical knowledge gained during traditional lessons [16]. In real world students when they go out of university need to work in teams, and in challenge-based learning, by design students to work in small groups towards achieving the learning outcomes. It facilitates cooperative team working and enables the students to develop communication and group skills, encourage peer thinking, incorporate feedbacks, and support self and peer assessments on ongoing basis [3,14,15].

Recently, also entrepreneurship education is growing on popularity and universities use it as a way to try to link education to labour market. Universities aim to train specialists that meet the real-life market needs. Entrepreneurship education is important as competitiveness, innovation and economic growth depend on being able to produce future leaders with the skills and attitudes to be entrepreneurial in their professional lives, whether by creating their own companies or innovating in larger organisations [17].

Specifically tailored courses joining entrepreneurship education and challenge-based learning are starting to appear, with prominent examples for design of such courses that that start to pop up [7,8,12]. Still, besides all the advantages of the challenge-based learning, there are actually little in our universities that implement it.

In challenge-based learning researchers and teachers participate as mentors and are important part of it. They are in charge of the knowledge formation process and monitor the development of skills and competences. In such a context, the instructors constantly monitor the level of knowledge the learners assimilate during the study process and in the same time make the stakeholders collaborate with each other during the learning, applications, hands on workshops and long term projects. It is important to continuously adapt the methods of teaching/training as well as the contents and tasks, according to the goals achieved by the students.

The use of technology to foster team work and collaboration can make teaching and learning processes more efficient [10], and can improve collaboration in settings where faculty members from university and instructors from industry are involved [4]. Computer Supported Collaborative Learning (CSCL) research has shown that technology can support successfully practical collaborative activities [1,2,6]. One example of this is online learning communities, but similarly, these require to be careful designed to tackle all the different aspects of challenge-based learning, like for instance how to handle tracing of the skills and competences development, as well as how to trace knowledge assimilated during hands on workshops. Practices and applications can vary in each local context and the goals defined by the teacher responsible for the course influence the final design of the course.

In our paper we present one such challenge-based course and investigate how students physically located at distant Universities can collaborate and work in team between each other in it. We present how we designed the course and the results we obtained from questionnaires delivered after the course asking them questions on which aspects of the experience they appreciated the most and why, which aspects students appreciated less and why, if they liked the experience and if they found it useful. The cross-university collaboration that we describe in this paper took place between University of Trento, UNITN, Italy and Universidad Politécnica de Madrid, UPM, Spain over the course Innovation and Entrepreneurship Study delivered in both of the places at the same time.

This paper is structured as follows: Sect. 2 presents the educational context, the course structure, and the methods we used to conduct this study, Sect. 3 presents the results from the evaluation with the students and the impact of the course on their learning, in Sect. 4 we discuss the leanings from the deployment and in Sect. 5 we outline our next steps.

2 Course "Innovation and Entrepreneurship Studies"

2.1 Context

Both of the Universities are part of the European Institute of Innovation and Technology (EIT) and more specifically of EIT Digital network of Universities. The EIT Digital Master School is a joint initiative by the leading technical universities and business schools in Europe with the aim to train IT graduates at Masters levels, with strong innovation and entrepreneurial competences. Our partner network of High Educational Institutions works together to provide cutting-edge ICT education in combination with innovation and entrepreneurship (I&E) blended education [5,11,13]. Each partner university in the EIT Digital network implements an Innovation and Entrepreneurship (I&E) minor, for which the Universities need to implement three harmonized I&E courses: I&E Basics, Business Development Lab, I&E study and one elective course. The two Universities collaborated on the course of I&E study.

2.2 Course Design

The I&E Study pivots around a case which is a challenge/question proposed and provided by a company that may be related to considering alternative business models or go-to-market scenarios in relation with the innovation or entrepreneurial case, fed by exploration in some specific areas: business environment, competition, suppliers, partners, environmental, sustainability issues, etc. Prior to solving that challenge/question the students acquire concepts and tools pertaining to the assessment of the impact of a technology on an industry, market and/or organization, and business research. We observed that the I&E Study case is a perfect playground to develop the skills necessary to work in international teams located in different countries but working on the same project so we decided to design an I&E Study model course with teams of students from the two Universities working on the I&E Study case together.

2.3   Method

We had in total 21 students at University of Trento and 23 students at UPM. At both Universities there are local groups, that is groups composed only of local students working on the delivery on a challenge from the local ecosystem of the respective University, while there were three groups, composed of 2 members coming from University of Trento and 2 members coming from UPM, working on an shared challenge (see Table 1). The shared challenges were provided by companies located in Madrid: Comunica A+, Graffter and Minsait - Indra. The group members of all the teams need to work together to deliver the case and like this improve their abilities to work in teams. The whole process was monitored by three teachers involved in the course.

The feedback collection was done with a survey, composed of 5 likert scale and 2 open-ended questions. With the survey we try to understand if the cross-university pilot a useful learning experience for the students (on a scale from 1 to 5), if it increased their sense of belonging to the EIT Digital community (on a scale from 1 to 5), if the pilot increased ability to work in distributed teams (on a scale from 1 to 5), how engaged in learning the students were (on a scale from 1 to 5), how supportive technology was in the pilot (on a scale from 1 to 5), what were the aspects of this cross-university collaboration they appreciated the most and why, and what were the aspects they appreciated least and why. For each likert scale question we left the possibility for the students to explain why they gave the rating as they did in more detail.

Table 1. The distribution of students to teams.

Condition	Number of students	Number of teams
UNITN and UPM	6	3
UNITN	15	4
UPM	17	5

After completion of the course the students part in the mixed groups undertook questionnaire evaluation. All the six students participants in the mixed teams responded.

Below a short description on the challenges that the mixed teams worked on:

Challenge on Stand-alone Voice Assistants (provided by Comunica A+): From the perspective of an advertising agency and marketing company such as Comunica + A, and the technology of Voice Assistants, the company is interested to understand: how will the customers' relationship and sale models change? What value-added services can an agency provide using this technology? How will be the monetization model for the technology providers? Will a unique technology/provider monopolize the market? And where should the company start from and where to aim?

Challenge on IoT Sensorization in Industrial and ATEX Environments (provided by Minsait - Indra): Minsait - Indra promotes transformation of business and society through innovative solutions and services based on sensorisation and IoT technologies. In this case the students are asked to provide market analysis of companies with IoT sensor devices (wireless, long battery life, connectivity with IoT platform, cybersecurity, reduced cost....), to provide examples of solutions they provide, and to develop a proposal/comprehensive implementation business plan for the company for the specific case of ATEX Environments detailing elements like: pricing model, implementation schedule, etc.

Challenge on Graffter-User Engagement using Blockchain (provided by Graffter): In this challenge the company asked the students to understand and define mechanisms to engage end users in a cultural and tourism scenarios sponsored (in some cases) by brands and define strategies how they can achieve the great user engagement. The company looked for reward programmes solutions based on the blockchain.

3   Learning Impact and Discussion

In general, students responded positively on all the likert questions, with only the question on how helpful was technology in this pilot receiving an average mark of 3 (Fig. 1).

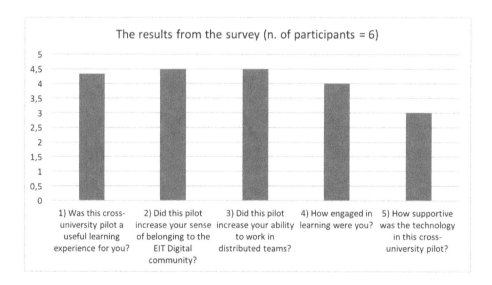

Fig. 1. The results from the survey.

Students Considered the Pilot a Useful Learning Experience. Some of them commented that it was nice to work with different cultures over long distance, and that it is something that will most likely be a part of the working life later on. One students commented: "The team work was challenging having to coordinate remotely but at the same time it was a fun experience doing all the brainstorming sessions over Skype meetings and developing over our work".

Another student commented that it was great to learn how to manage group projects remotely, and that the only minor downside was not directly meeting the company representative. Indeed this is an aspect which we need to improve in our future design and think thoroughly how to provide the same "access" to the challenge provider to all the students in the teams.

In this respect, and how to improve communication with the distributed challenge provider, one of our students suggested: "I think there could be one or two personal meet ups organized between team members and the industry so that the team members away from the country of the industry location also get a chance of exposure to what they are actually dealing with".

Students Considered That the Pilot Increased Their Sense to the Community. One of them commented: "Get to know (or know better) people that are part of the community but have chosen a different university path". Another student shared that it was interesting to learn how it hear the experience on how it is to study at the other university where this participant did not studied yet.

Students Felt That the Pilot Increased Their Ability to Work in Distributed Teams. The general comments were that the fact that the team members were not physically close to them made them more responsible in the process of planning the video calls and were more sensitive for the availability of the other team members. One student commented: "Scattered chances of meeting meant learning how to properly manage those kind of workload", while another student shared that "Collaborating over Skype is a different skill than discussing things in person, and I feel that this skill has been improved".

Students Were Engaged in Learning. One students commented that in the beginning the engagement was low due to the distance with the company, however as the assignment was getting more clear, the engagement level significantly improved: "Not a lot at the beginning since the request from the company was fuzzy, but greatly increased going on".

Technology Support Was Average and Could be Further Improved. Students both, acknowledged and criticized the support the technology was providing in their team work. One student for instance commented: "Couldn't have done it without video conference, screen sharing and editing tools like Google docs (specially for the revision system)", while other said that "We had a terrible wifi connection at home, so we could not use video and the phone call would break up a lot of times. Moreover, we did not have time slots free during the week so we had to Skype during the night, on which times the wifi was worse than during the day". The common problems reported were mainly of a technological nature and problems with finding adequate technology to do video calls in front of audiences present in two different location.

The Aspects of Pilot That the Students Appreciated the Most and Why

Overall, the students found the experience fun and felt that the collaboration went well. One student commented positively on the challenge-based learning approach: "We got to know how dynamic it is to work for a real industry as compared to a coursework business solution. Especially, I have the fact that we had to manage it across two different locations with coordinated collaboration with our teammates gave us a great deal of learning experience". Another student commented: "The overall experience of working with students from different country was amazing, working remotely was an experience that was needed for the real world working environment too".

The Aspects of Pilot That the Students Appreciated the Least and Why

One of the students in Madrid commented that they had a lot more work to do since they had to update the company every week for which they also need to prepare each time. The other university could not contribute to this greatly and therefore they felt that the balance was not there and that the students from Madrid worked harder on the project.

Students also complained on the difficulty to find adequate time to communicate between them selves: "We had to work after 9 pm because our classes always ended late and their classes always started early".

Some students felt that in general, the cross-country collaboration cost a lot more effort and time than the normal projects. They feel that they have learned a lot, but also that it was not compensated for it (also because they felt that it was much harder to collaborate through Skype and bad connections than being able to collaborate when meeting in person)".

4   Conclusions

Our aim with this paper was to develop innovative teaching format for students to get deeply involved with company provided cases using a participative and collaborative approach connecting the two Universities involved. The multi-method teaching approach based on group projects increased student's ICT skills as well as their ability to work in heterogeneous groups.

The experiment was successful in terms of operation and in terms of satisfaction of the students and the companies. We also observed that the students in the mixed teams, despite the difficulties of the physical separation, were more motivated to work and that they had expanded their network of contacts within the EIT community.

On the other side, the experiments forced the faculty of both universities to coordinate and share practices, enriching the original version of their own I&E Study course. In the experiment we also noticed that the I&E Study case, with all the interaction with the company provider and the final exposition of results before it, would be a perfect scenario to develop and practice communication and entrepreneurship skills and this is what we aim at in out next steps.

5 Next Steps

In future we want to repeat and extend the concept of the experiment in 2019. We will include in 2019 students from University of Aalto, with the aim of including other universities from the EIT Digital network in 2020. Based on our experience from this year, the organisers founding the experience too burdensome to coordinate distributively, we will try a model in which there is only one university organizing the course and the others are just users. Learning also from the experience that the coordination and collaboration in teams for the students was not easy in distributed settings as ours, and with the aim to even further study collaborative learning dynamics, so we will incorporate in the teams' dynamics the use of tools to make their coordination and communication easier: Slack for communication and Trello for planning and coordination of tasks. Finally, developing of communication and entrepreneurship skills require not only learning from experts but also from peers, so we will include in the final pitching a peer-evaluation phase made by all students using a voting tool such as Voxvote. The course will be developed as follows: (1) UPM will play the role of Organizer. The organizer will be in charge of supervising each case, mentoring the teams. UNITN and AALTO will play the role of User, with their students remotely supervised by the organizer. (2) Organizer and Users will synchronize lectures, online modules and assignments (3) The students from the three universities will be assigned to cases, in teams composed by at least one member from each university. (4) In any team the students from the country of origin of the case will be in charge of communication with the company provider. (5) The students will plan and develop the case using professional tools, mentored by the organizer. (6) There will be a final "entrepreneur pitching" evaluated by the "investors committee" (teachers and company), and peers.

Acknowledgment. The authors would like to acknowledge and thank the companies (Graffter, Comunica A+, Minsait - Indra) for their participation and all the students who took part in this 'cross-university' pilots initiative. The pilots were supported financially by EIT Digital under the Innovation and Entrepreneurship Improvements Education projects.

References

1. Abrami, P.C., Bernard, R.M., Bures, E.M., Borokhovski, E., Tamim, R.M.: Interaction in distance education and online learning: using evidence and theory to improve practice. J. Comput. High. Edu. **23**(2–3), 82–103 (2011)
2. Boling, E.C., Hough, M., Krinsky, H., Saleem, H., Stevens, M.: Cutting the distance in distance education: perspectives on what promotes positive, online learning experiences. Internet High. Edu. **15**(2), 118–126 (2012)

3. Charosky, G., Leveratto, L., Hassi, L., Papageorgiou, K., Ramos-Castro, J., Bragós, R.: Challenge based education: an approach to innovation through multidisciplinary teams of students using design thinking. In: 2018 XIII Technologies Applied to Electronics Teaching Conference (TAEE), pp. 1–8. IEEE (2018)
4. Crepon, R.: Closing the university-business gap: model of blended learning for the collaborative design of learning resources
5. Dion, G., Dalle, J., Renouard, F., et al.: Change management: blended learning adoption in a large network of European universities. In: International Conference on e-Learning, pp. 77–83. Academic Conferences International Limited (2018)
6. Faltin, N., Böhne, A., Tuttas, J., Wagner, B.: Distributed team learning in an internet-assisted laboratory. In: International Conference on Engineering Education, pp. 18–22, Manchester (2002)
7. Pisoni, G., Hegyi, B., Marchese, M., Renouard, F.: Portfolio of innovative online courses in a Pan-European network of universities. In: INTED (2019)
8. Kirch, J., Eisenbart, B.: Teaching entrepreneurship, digitalization, leadership, and gender at the same time: how a new learning approach integrates all four perspectives. In: ICERI (2018)
9. Malmqvist, J., Rådberg, K.K., Lundqvist, U.: Comparative analysis of challenge-based learning experiences. In: Proceedings of the 11th International CDIO Conference, Chengdu University of Information Technology, Chengdu, Sichuan, PR China (2015)
10. Oztok, M., Zingaro, D., Brett, C., Hewitt, J.: Exploring asynchronous and synchronous tool use in online courses. Comput. Edu. 60(1), 87–94 (2013)
11. Pisoni, G., et al.: Towards blended learning implementation of innovation and entrepreneurship (I&E) education within eit digital: the models and lessons learnt. In: EDULEARN18 Proceedings of 10th International Conference on Education and New Learning Technologies, IATED, pp. 10496–10502, 2–4 July 2018. https://doi.org/10.21125/edulearn.2018.2553
12. Pisoni, G., Marchese, M., Renouard, F.: Benefits and challenges of distributed student activities in online education settings: cross-university collaborations on a Pan-European level. In: 2019 IEEE Global Engineering Education Conference (EDUCON), pp. 1017–1021 (2019)
13. Pisoni, G.: Strategies for pan-european implementation of blended learning for innovation and entrepreneurship (I&E) education. Edu. Sci. 9(2), 124 (2019)
14. Ramirez-Mendoza, R.A., et al.: Towards a disruptive active learning engineering education. In: 2018 IEEE Global Engineering Education Conference (EDUCON), pp. 1251–1258. IEEE (2018)
15. Serçe, F.C., Swigger, K., Alpaslan, F.N., Brazile, R., Dafoulas, G., Lopez, V.: Online collaboration: collaborative behavior patterns and factors affecting globally distributed team performance. Comput. Hum. Behav. 27(1), 490–503 (2011)
16. Willis, S., Byrd, G., Johnson, B.D.: Challenge-based learning. Computer 50(7), 13–16 (2017)
17. Yoo, Y., Boland Jr., R.J., Lyytinen, K., Majchrzak, A.: Organizing for innovation in the digitized world. Organ. Sci. 23(5), 1398–1408 (2012)

Semantic Recommendations and Topic Modeling Based on the Chronology of Romanian Literary Life

Laurentiu-Marian Neagu[1], Teodor-Mihai Cotet[1], Mihai Dascalu[1(✉)],
Stefan Trausan-Matu[1], Lucian Chisu[2], and Eugen Simion[2]

[1] University Politehnica of Bucharest, 313 Splaiul Independentei, Bucharest, Romania
laurentiu.neagu@cti.pub.ro, teodor_mihai.cotet@stud.acs.upb.ro,
{mihai.dascalu,stefan.trausan}@cs.pub.ro
[2] The "G. Călinescu" Institute of Literary History and Theory, Romanian Academy,
Calea 13 Septembrie, Bucharest, Romania
lucianchisu@gmail.com, eugen.ioan.simion@gmail.com

Abstract. As part of the Romanian Academy's effort aimed at underlining the importance of events centered on national authors and writings across time, the Chronology of Romanian Literary Life (also referred to as CVLR) is a centralized text repository which contains all important literature-related events that occurred after World War II. The current work presents an approach to capture topics' evolution across time and helps learners by recommending events from the chronology on a given topic, based on a subset of 24 years of the CVLR. Our method combines techniques from information retrieval, topic modeling using LDA (Latent Dirichlet Allocation), and recommender systems to improve e-learning centered on Romanian literature. The most frequent topics in each year are ranked in order to identify and visualize the main interests in literature across time periods. Recommendations are performed in order to facilitate the exploration of the chronology, as it is currently indexed only by event dates.

Keywords: Analysis of the chronology of Romanian literary life · Information retrieval · Topic modeling · Latent Dirichlet Allocation

1 Introduction

In the context of understanding the importance of Romanian authors and writings across time, one of the most important on-going projects of the "G. Călinescu" Institute of Literary History and Theory is the Chronology of Romanian Literary Life (commonly referred to as CVLR). CVLR is aimed to register chronologically all the important literature-related events which happened nationwide after World War II.

Two important periods are mapped from the historical perspective, namely communism (years between 1949 and 1989) and post-communism (years between 1990 and 2000; year 2000 being the last one which is covered in the current version of CVLR).

© Springer Nature Switzerland AG 2020
E. Popescu et al. (Eds.): SETE 2019, LNCS 11984, pp. 164–174, 2020.
https://doi.org/10.1007/978-3-030-38778-5_19

The total number of years to be documented by the chronology is 56, whereas the current analysis considers only 24 years, the remaining ones being work in progress or not having a proper format for parsing and indexing.

Our aim is to capture the evolution of topics across time and to recommend literary events from the CVLR considering searches on keywords mapped to specific topics. Our work relies on Natural Language Processing (NLP) and Information Retrieval (IR) techniques tailored for our aim [1]. Moreover, one of the main areas of interest in the domain of AI in Education is related to providing recommendations of learning objects and adaptive learning support [2], which is currently a challenging task. Even though the range in which recommender systems are used is widen (from which products to buy, to which music to listen, or which information to learn from) [3], the end goal is the same: to help users or learners to take decisions easier.

The proposed solution aims to provide relevant recommendations of historical literary events to the learner, which are based on previously discovered topics of interest. To our knowledge, this is the first work which analyzes, summarizes, and presents the topics of interest, their evolution in the history of the Romanian literary life. and is able to make recommendations of historical events which can be used by the learning communities interested in Romanian literary.

Chapter two describes similar work conducted in the Information Retrieval field, the usage of semantic models, and discusses how similar recommender systems were implemented and used in education. The method chapter presents the used corpus, how the data was pre-processed, details on topic modeling and determining the topic coherence score, as well as recommender system was developed. The paper continues with results obtained and it is followed by conclusions and possible future work directions.

2   State of the Art

2.1   Semantic Models

Topic modeling considers NLP techniques used to detect the latent topics of a document. Latent Dirichlet Allocation (LDA) [4] is a probabilistic graphical model used to automatically find the latent topics. In this model, both the distribution of topics and the distribution of words over a topic are assumed to have a sparse Dirichlet prior distribution, meaning that each document is assumed to be composed only of a small number of topics, and each topic is assumed to be formed mainly on a limited number of words.

2.2   Recommender Systems

In the development of recommender systems there is a multi-disciplinary effort, which involves various fields such as Artificial Intelligence, Human-Computer Interaction, Data Mining, Statistics, Information Technology, Adaptive User Interfaces, as well as Marketing or Customer Behavior [5]. A recommender system is defined as a software tool which incorporates techniques to provide suggestions to be used by the end-user.

However, in order to provide proper recommendations, the system needs to be capable to represent user behaviors (through a user profile or user model) and the items which are recommended. There are several techniques used to create a user profile and to gather information, such as questionnaires, users' item ratings through time (which are called explicit techniques), or learning based on the users' activities through time (which are the implicit techniques).

Thus, a recommender system is part of one of the three categories listed below based on the methods used for gathering information [2]:

- Content-based recommender system – using items similar to those previously preferred by the user;
- Collaborative recommender system – using items that other people who have similar preferences and marked them as interesting in the past;
- Hybrid recommender system – using a mixed approach between content-based and collaborative recommender systems.

Even though the recommender systems were initially used and are popular in other fields, such as in recommending movies, news or e-commerce, there are more and more scenarios in which such systems are used in education, more specifically in the e-learning environments.

There are still some issues, which are specific for e-learning recommender systems, and those are [6]: (a) items which are marked of interest for learners might not be pedagogically appropriate for them; (b) customization should not only be made about the choice of learning items, but also about their delivery; and (c) learners are not expected to read too many documents/information.

Several approaches on e-learning recommender systems were conducted, out of which some were aimed to recommend online learning activities or shortcuts in a web course based on learners history using web mining [7]. Dagadita et al. [3] recommended articles based on content-based filtering and collaborative filtering, whereas Klasnja-Milicevica [8] personalized programming curricula for learning using hybrid recommendation strategy.

3   Method

Our proposed solution is a content-based recommender system, storing a user profile based on the items user has searched and marked them of interest in the past. The data queried is the Chronology of the Romanian Literary Life and each event in the chronology is associated to a set of topics. An item in the recommender system is a particular event and, based on user preferences of items, system can map topics which user likes and is able to make recommendations of similar events.

Figure 1. depicts the processing pipeline, where CVLR corpus was initially indexed in Elasticsearch and data was afterwards pre-processed. After the pre-processing step, LDA is applied in order to identify trending topics. The last step in the processing pipeline consists of presenting possible use-cases of our method in real scenarios, where learners can search for literary events using keywords and the system is able to recommend further events based on their profile.

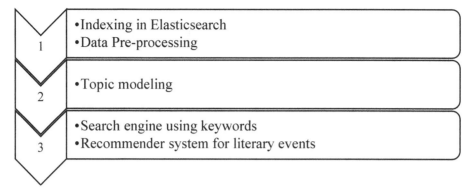

Fig. 1. Processing pipeline.

3.1 Corpus

The corpus consists of events indexed chronologically by day. Each event generally describes a publication of an author, some of them containing a short description of the impact of the publication in the literature field. As previously mentioned, not all years are covered in our analysis, because some of them were not yet written or could not be properly parsed. Thus, 24 years are covered: 1949–1959, 1964–1967 and 1990–2000, with the exception of years 1957 and 1999. Each event is considered a separate document in the following analyses; the current work relies on 1962 indexed entries.

3.2 Data Pre-processing

Stop words were filtered for each document, together with words which contained non-alphabetic characters and words with a high frequency (i.e., words appearing in more than 10% of the documents), or words with an absolute frequency lower than 4. For each remaining word, only the lowercase version was considered. There was also a process of grouping neighboring words within the same named entity category as these words are referring to the same entity. The NER (named entity recognition) was trained on RONEC corpus[1] with a standard spacy model for NER[2].

3.3 Topic Modeling

After the subsequent pre-processing operations are performed, LDA is applied. Moreover, specific methods which approximate LDA parameters must be applied because the exact inference of the parameters is considered intractable. The genism LDA model[3] was used which implements an online variational Bayes algorithm [9]. LDA cannot infer the number of topics; therefore, multiple LDA models were trained with different number of topics and the coherence score was computed for each of them, followed by the selection

---

[1] https://github.com/dumitrescustefan/ronec.

[2] https://spacy.io/usage/training.

[3] https://radimrehurek.com/gensim/models/ldamodel.html.

of the number of topics that maximizes coherence (in our case 20 topics). The coherence score is computed using the genism[4] which implements the algorithm introduced by Röder, Both and Hinneburg [10]. The cohesion values depending on incremental topic numbers is depicted in Fig. 2.

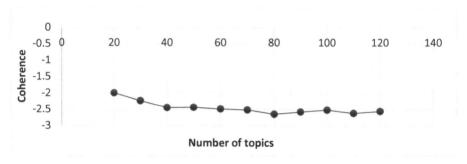

Fig. 2. Coherence per number of topics.

3.4 Search Engine

This phase implies building a search engine for literary events using a list of keywords, based on the list of previously computed topics. Each user is able to input an array of keywords, which are then filtered using ReaderBench Python library. Only content words are kept, removing stop words and also merging named entities. Filtered keywords are afterwards passed to each topic and the probability of each word is determined. The weight of each topic is computed by using the probability of all keywords in a topic.

Afterwards, topics are ordered descendent by weight and each topic receives a ratio/proportion in determining the final results. A number of representative events for each particular topic is selected based on this ratio. For example, if topic 3 has a ratio of 50%, topic 7 has a ratio of 30% and topic 4 has a ratio of 20%, the search engine returns a paged response with the following first page entries: 5 events with highest weight from topic 3, 3 events with highest weight from topic 7, and the 2 events with the highest importance from topic 4. The second page of results could contain: the next 5 events from topic 3, the next 3 events from topic 7, and the next 2 events from topic 4. The weight of each topic in an event is already calculated in the previous section; thus, determining the best events for a topic implies only their re-ordering. This can be done for the full period (all years from CVLR corpus), or for specific years (if search would need to be performed only for some of the years).

3.5 Recommender System for Literary Events

The list returned after performing a search is paged, each page containing 10 events (event ID and corresponding description) while events are ordered based on their topic

---

[4] https://radimrehurek.com/gensim/models/coherencemodel.html.

importance. After reading an event in particular, based on its ID, users are able to mark it of interest and store it in their preferences.

The storing mechanism relies on an XML file whose root node has children containing user IDs. For each child, there is a list of other children which are the event ids. On when showing interest for a specific event, a new entry is appended in the XML file to that specific user ID parent. Within the reversed process, that entry is removed from the file, if it exists.

A simple user profile/learner model is built by using the preferred events by each specific user. In a typical e-learning task recommender system [7], the recommendations are based on the tasks already done by the learner and the measure of their success, but also on tasks made by "similar" learners. Common techniques used for providing recommendations in the technology enhanced learning field consider [11]:

- "out-of-the-box", while user is browsing through items;
- explicitly suggested items;
- initial user exploration or in testing phase;
- particularly new or novel items;
- suggested items (around a topic of interest);
- other relevant interests pertaining to similar people.

As the current system stores the user preferences, it is possible to provide recommendations based on their topics of interest. In order to achieve this, the system checks if the current user has any preferred events and, if not, it recommends the events with the highest value for each topic. If users have previously stored into their profile a list of events, the system maps their events of interest with corresponding topics and new events are recommend based on those topic scores.

4 Results

Elasticsearch was used to store the CVLR corpus, whereas LDA modeling, search engine and recommendations functionalities were developed in Python, with no GUI yet linked to the backend functionalities. The obtained results are interesting. The first subsection introduces the trending topics of the Romanian literary life after World War II and their evolution, year by year. In the second part, the search engine is described, including topic modeling results and the recommender system, following a simple use-case with corresponding step-by-step results.

4.1 Trending Topics

After performing the topic modeling, the list of 20 top topics in the corpus, with their associated words and weight was obtained. Topics, numbered from 1 to 20, together with their top 7 words and corresponding theme are presented in Table 1. In some cases, the same word appears in the same topic in different forms (e.g., "socialist" and "socialism" in topic 2) due to automated lemmatization errors. Another problem is the appearance of different words describing the same entity (e.g., "Paul Goma" and "Goma" in topic with ID 1). Although named entities were merged, the authors are not mentioned in the same manner all the time; therefore, all versions may still be assigned high probabilities by the LDA.

The reason behind having different words naming the same concept is generated by the manner in which CVLR was written, namely by the usage of artistic literary language which is different than standard Romanian language. Within artistic literary language, authors use personalized stylistic methods for creating their texts.

Table 1. Top words per topic

Topic ID	Top 7 words per topic	Theme
1	Marin Preda, Eugen Simion, Paul Goma, Preda, Nicolae Breban, Nicolae Manolescu, Goma	Major personalities
2	Muncitor, Socialist, Clasă, Realism, Socialism, Erou, Sovietică	Socialism
3	Evreu, Antisemitism, Eseu, Democrație, Sistem, Europa, Fenomen	Anti-semitism
4	Pământ, Patrie, Inimă, Munci, Sat, Zi, Muncă	Work
5	Ion, Nicolae, Mircea, Alexandru, George, Gheorghe, Constantin	Common Names
6	Ed, București, Jurnal, Eseu, Exil, Editură, Ediție	Writings in exile
7	Nichita Stănescu, Nichita, Călinescu, Arghezi, Crohmălniceanu, Eugen Barbu, Ov	Poets
8	Eseu, Traducere, Nr, Prezentare, Emisiune, Manual, Scrisoare	Writing types
9	Mircea Eliade, Eliade, Eseu, Mit, Călinescu, Național, Blaga	Essays
10	Piesă, Teatru, Caragiale, Dramaturgie, Dramatic, Scenă, Spectacol	Theatre
11	Film, Modern, Stil, Fenomen, Clasic, Real, Existență	Movie
12	Domnul, Domn, Instituție, Membru, Nicolae Manolescu, Alegere, Opoziție	Politics
13	Noica, Cioran, Paul Goma, Eseu, Nae Ionescu, Memorie, Filosofie	Philosophy
14	Liric, Personaj, Expresie, Viziune, Sentiment, Erou, Uman	Expressing feelings
15	Național, European, Patapievici, Francez, Europa, Editură, Franța	Europe
16	Ediție, Călinescu, Cronica, Inedit, Cuprinde, Cercetare, Traducere	Chronicle
17	Comunism, Regim, Rău, Călinescu, Comunistă, Ideologie, Libratate	Communism
18	Premiu, Premiul, Leu, Juriu, Acorda, Premiile, Eminescian	Prizes
19	Sat, Dezvoltare, Socialistă, Copil, Nuvelă, Aspect, Erou	Villages
20	Reportaj, Liric, Cronică, Cântec, Traducere, Mihai Beniuc, Călinescu	Reportage

After LDA was trained on the entire set of events, an importance to each topic was assigned for every year, and then sorted by importance. This assignment is performed as the sum of topic probabilities for each event in that year. Thus, the evolution of the importance of these topics is shown in Fig. 3. The missing years are substituted with a linear function based on the known neighboring years. Only 7 emblematic topics were selected for this visualization; the remaining topics showed a similar trend to one of those selected.

Interesting trends are captured by the topic evolution analysis. In the beginning of the 1950s, the most prominent topic has ID 2, which is mainly about socialism (frequent words are "muncitor", "socialist", "clasă", "erou", etc.). This is due to the influence of the Russian Soviet Union which aimed to create "the new human", aligned with their socialist vision and started with cultural press propaganda, driven mainly by young writers or writers with a left-party vision. However, its importance drops significantly at the beginning of the 1960s, which indicates a moment of change in the relationships with the Russian Soviet Union (known as the moment of "cooling of brotherly relations", started by Gheorghe Gheorghiu-Dej and continued by president Nicolae Ceaușescu). Although it is still the communist era, the literature field distances itself from communism at the beginning of 1960s. In this period, events shift towards topics 16, 20 and 11 which are focused on literature; this announces a new generation, with European and Global literary values, and also the moment when part of the Romanian great writers returned from the Exile. In the 1990s, the main topics are 6, 12 and 1. Topic 1 and 6 contain a lot of words related to dissidence in the communist period. For instance, topic 1 refers to the author Paul Goma, an author well-known for his critique of the communist, and which generated many debates on recovering our literary past values. Therefore, communism dissidence is highly present in the post communism events.

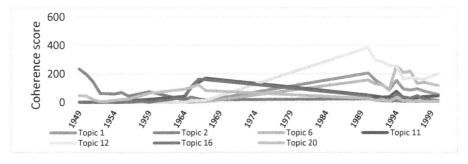

Fig. 3. The evolution of topics occurring in CVLR.

4.2 Providing Event Recommendations

User data is required for providing personalized recommendations. Information is stored in the user profile, based on the following flow: user searches, based on keywords, for some specific events; after browsing through them, the user is able to mark one or more events and a list of events of interest is stored in the user profile. The system recommends other events within the same topics, based on the previously entries. A sample of this flow is described below. For example, the user searches for the following keywords (1):

$$['premiu', 'pentru', 'socialism', 'juriu', 'pământ', 'și', 'sat',] \qquad (1)$$

The search query is initially filtered using spacy model trained for Romanian Language from the ReaderBench Python library, and the filtered query is the following (2):

$$['premiu', 'socialism', 'juriu', 'pământ', 'sat'] \qquad (2)$$

The final list of keywords (only content words) is afterwards passed on to each topic, and a corresponding weight is computed. Afterwards, the weights are ordered in descending order, and only the relevant topics are kept. In the list of top topics, the weight percentage of each topic is calculated, and a maximum number of events is returned. For the provided example, the corresponding values for top topics are displayed in Table 2.

Table 2. Top Topics Corresponding Values based on a list of keywords

Topic Id	Weight	Weight percentage	Events no. to display	Top words in topic
18	.0476	64.99%	6	premiu, leu, juriu, acorda, premiat
4	.0126	17.2%	2	pământ, patrie, inimă, munci, sat
19	.0067	9.19%	1	sat, dezvoltare, socialist, copil, nuvelă
2	.0063	8.61%	1	muncitor, socialist, clasă, realism, socialism

As it can be observed, the most prominent topic within the provided list of keywords is topic 18, which has as top words some of the words provided directly in the search query: "premiu" (eng. "prize") and "juriu" (eng., "jury"). Also, results are similar for the other returned topics, which have top words similar to the provided keywords. The final results are displayed as ordered events (based on their weight, in descendent order) within each topic. One of the most relevant returned events is the following (3):

Ecouri despre premianții Academiei Române apar și în „ Luptătorul bănățean”: „ Înalta prețuire a oamenilor de știință și cultură” pentru clasa muncitoare, ajunsă la putere, revoluționând și cultura, odată cu modul de producție” s-ar fi reflectat în decernarea premiilor Academiei pentru cele mai valoroase creații științifice, literare și artistice.

$$(3)$$

Users are also able to store events as favorites in their profile. After building it, users can query for recommendations based on the events they are interested in. In this case, the system checks for potentially relevant events and a weight for each topic is calculated. Afterwards, a strategy similar to the one employed by the search engine is used to provide personalized recommendations: topics are ordered descendent by weight, a weight percentage is calculated for each topic, and a number of events, in this case excluding the ones already stored by the user, is retrieved.

5 Conclusions and Future Work

Shifting the Romanian literature to the digital era is an ambitious effort which includes multiple approaches and methods. This paper introduces NLP and IR techniques in order to determine the emerging topics from the Chronology of Romanian Literary across time. Moreover, we propose a solution to improve the search for events in CVLR, together with semantic recommendations. The current work shares similar goals with previously performed analyses on the General Romanian Dictionary of Literature [12].

Future work will be conducted to include the missing years from CVLR. In addition, the recommender system will be enhanced by taking into account further details about users, their search history, and a more comprehensive profile in order to provide more tailored recommendations. Moreover, designing an intuitive user interface and publishing the search engine online is one of our main priorities.

Acknowledgements. This work was supported by a grant of the Romanian National Authority for Scientific Research and Innovation, CNCS – UEFISCDI, project number PN-III 54PCCDI / 2018, INTELLIT – "Prezervarea și valorificarea patrimoniului literar românesc folosind soluții digitale inteligente pentru extragerea și sistematizarea de cunoștințe".

References

1. Manning, C.D., Raghavan, P., Schütze, H.: Introduction to Information Retrieval, vol. 1. Cambridge University Press, Cambridge (2008)
2. Persen, W.C.A.R.: A Recommender System for Collaborative Knowledge. books.google.com 1 (2009)
3. Dagadita, M., Bancu, C., Dascalu, M., Dobre, C., Trausan-Matu, S., Florea, A.M.: ARSYS - article recommender system. In: 14th International Symposium on Symbolic and Numeric Algorithms for Scientific Computing (SYNASC 2012). IEEE, Timisoara (2012)
4. Blei, D.M., Ng, A.Y., Jordan, M.I.: Latent dirichlet allocation. J. Mach. Learn. Res. **3**(4–5), 993–1022 (2003)
5. Ricci, F., Rokach, L., Shapira, B., Kantor, P.B.: Recommender Systems Handbook, p. 845. Springer, Boston (2011). https://doi.org/10.1007/978-0-387-85820-3
6. Tang, T.Y., McCalla, G.: Smart Recommendation for an Evolving E-Learning System: Architecture and Experiment. Int. J. E-learn. **4**, 105–129 (2005)
7. Zaiane, O.R.: Building a recommender agent for e-learning systems. In: International Conference on Computers in Education, Proceedings, p. 5 (2002)
8. Klasnja-Milicevica, A., Boban Vesina, M.I., Budimac, Z.: E-Learning personalization based on hybrid recommendation strategy and learning style identification. Comput. Educ. **56**, 885–899 (2011)

9. Hoffman, M., Bach, F.R., Blei, D.M.: Online learning for Latent Dirichlet Allocation. In: Advances in Neural Information Processing Systems, p. 10 (2010)

10. Röder, M., Both, A., Hinneburg, A.: Exploring the space of topic coherence measures. In: Proceedings of the Eighth ACM International Conference on Web Search and Data Mining, pp. 399–408. ACM (2015)

11. Manouselis, N., Drachsler, H., Vuorikari, R., Hummel, H., Koper, R.: Recommender Systems in Technology Enhanced Learning. Springer, New York (2014). https://doi.org/10.1007/978-1-4939-0530-0

12. Neagu, L.-M., Cotet, T.-M., Dascalu, M., Trausan-Matu, S., Badescu, L., Simion, E.: Semantic author recommendations based on their biography from the General Romanian Dictionary of Literature. In: 7th International Workshop on Semantic and Collaborative Technologies for the Web, in Conjunction with the 15th International Conference on eLearning and Software for Education (eLSE 2019), pp. 165–172. "CAROL I" National Defence University Publishing House, Bucharest (2019)

A Web-Based Platform for Building PBL Competences Among Students

Hans Hüttel[1,2,3,4](✉), Dorina Gnaur[1,2,3,4], Thomas Ryberg[1,2,3,4],
and Jette Egelund Holgaard[1,2,3,4]

[1] Department of Learning and Philosophy, Aalborg University, Aalborg, Denmark
`hans@cs.aau.dk, dg@learning.aau.dk, ryberg@hum.aau.dk, jeh@plan.aau.dk`
[2] Department of Computer Science, Aalborg University, Aalborg, Denmark
[3] Department of Communication and Psychology,
Aalborg University, Aalborg, Denmark
[4] Department of Planning, Aalborg University, Aalborg, Denmark

Abstract. Problem-based learning (PBL) is at the heart of all degree programmes at Aalborg University and is most often project-organized. Experience shows that it is a challenge to develop the competences necessary for students to carry out PBL and requires systematic reflection of the part of students. The PBL Exchange/stud platform is a web-based platform intended for sharing student reflections and experience concering problem-based learning. In this paper we describe PBL Exchange/stud and our experience with introducing it in guided interventions in degree programmes at Aalborg University. The main challenge faced with PBL Exchange/stud turned out to be that of building a stable community of student users.

Keywords: Problem-based learning · Crowdsourcing · Community building

1 Introduction

At Aalborg University, the degree programmes are based around problem-based learning, and in most cases this takes the form of a project-based approach. Students use a variety of Internet-based infrastructures for sharing their experiences with PBL projects, and research results indicate that students generally informal infrastructures originally intended for other purposes, such as Facebook and Pinterest, for many of their PBL activities [8]. This informal digitalization of PBL may be beneficial for the project process but it also leads to risks. In particular, informal traditions and ways of seeing the learning process may emerge that lead to a form of ritualization that is detrimental to actual learning [1].

Another challenge is that the sharing of experience only happens within well-defined communities, usually among students within the same degree programme or even within the same year. This is despite the fact that many experiences are similar across degree programmes and years.

© Springer Nature Switzerland AG 2020
E. Popescu et al. (Eds.): SETE 2019, LNCS 11984, pp. 175–182, 2020.
https://doi.org/10.1007/978-3-030-38778-5_20

There are many different ways of viewing the same kinds of challenges in the project process, but most students never become aware of the fact that many students from different degree programmes face the very same problems that they face and may be able to contribute to their understanding of the situation through a different perspective.

In this paper we describe the PBL Exchange/stud platform and our experience with it. The goal of this web-based platform has been to support student processes of reflections on and sharing of experiences with PBL. PBL Exchange/stud is a structured space in which communication can be carried out by students and in which experience can be shared across years and degree programmes and achieve a form of permanence. Moreover, the goal has been to involve lecturers and project supervisors through guided activities. PBL Exchange/stud is inspired by previous work on a platform for PBL supervisors [2]. A major difference is that activity within PBL Exchange/stud is to be initiated through interventions from teaching staff.

In the rest of this paper we describe the central features of the PBL Exchange/stud platform, our use of it through guided interventions and our reflections on the outcome of these.

2   Soft Skills and Crowdsourcing

The kinds of skills needed in collaborative efforts such as problem-based projects are examples of what is now known as "soft skills", and for the past 20 years there have been different initiatives to define and promote such skills. Often one speaks of "21st century skills" in education [3,5,12]. These are not thought of as specific to a particular degree programme or subject area but are skills that concern information and communication; civic literacy, global awareness, cross-cultural skills, and critical and inventive thinking.

PBL Exchange/stud is based on *crowdsourcing* and therefore also supports the important soft skills of knowledge-sharing and co-creating knowledge. This is a collaborative technique for exploring, exposing and evaluating a problem setting and the process and product dimensions involved. The best-known example is probably Wikipedia.

Moreover, PBL Exchange/stud explicitly focuses on a question- and answer-based format for building and exchanging knowledge and thereby emphasises the importance of and principles of dialogue – an important soft skill.

In group-based PBL projects at Aalborg University, all of these skills are of particular importance both as competences to be used within the projects themselves and as learning goals.

3   The PBL Exchange/stud Platform

PBL Exchange/stud is a system inspired by StackExchange [11] and its question- and answer-based format. It allows all users to

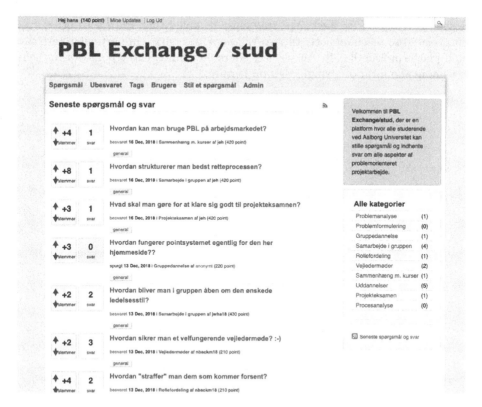

Fig. 1. Screenshot of the PBL Exchange/stud user interface. The interface lists the most recent questions asked and shows the scores (in pale green boxes). (Color figure online)

- ask questions
- answer questions
- comment answers and questions that are already in the system
- upvote and downvote questions, answers in the system

In this way, PBL Exchange/stud makes use of a gamification principle that allows uses to collect points and thereby get additional rights as users. Moreover, and importantly, the notion of votes should create a decentralized model of quality control. A screenshot of PBL Exchange/stud can be seen in Fig. 1.

The PBL Exchange/stud platform was originally based on the Question2Answer codebase [6] that was also used for the PBL Exchange meant for PBL supervisors [2]. This codebase used for the first version of the system is written in PHP and uses a mySQL database. The reason for choosing this codebase initially was that Question2Answer already supported quite a few of the features: Categorization of questions and answers and user-defined tagging as well as a reputation-based voting system.

On the other hand, Question2Answer turned out to have a codebase of poor modularity, which made extensions and modifications difficult to incorporate.

Most importantly, PBL Exchange/stud must be able to interface with other systems related to teaching activities at Aalborg University – in particular with the main platform Moodle [4]. All services share a common entry point for authentication in the form of a single sign-on feature.

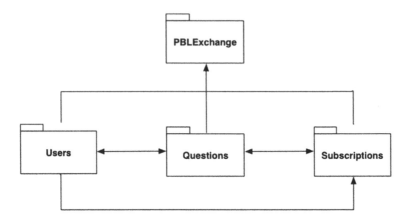

Fig. 2. The four main modules of PBL Exchange/stud

As part of the joint effort with PBL Exchange meant for PBL supervisors, we decided to re-implement a version of PBL Exchange/stud using the Python-based Django framework. This framework was chosen because it can help ensure plugability and ease of reusability of Python code. This allows us to incorporate a collection of new features, including multilingual support and mail notifications.

Using the Django framework allowed us to build the structure around modules, where we for modules such as the authentication module, could use existing modules that had already been tested. The system architecture of PBL Exchange/stud showing the four main modules is shown in Fig. 2. The four modules are written to be independent. Some functionality of each module may require another module to be active, but this is not required. An example of this is the questions module, which only activates the scoring system if the users module is present. The PBLExchange module forms as the base of the site, defining the front page and the base layout that the other modules extend.

4   The Interventions

The challenge of developing, maintaining and extending competences within PBL exist both at the undergraduate and postgraduate level; postgraduate students in Denmark may come from other institutions that have no tradition for using problem-based learning. For this reason we decided to study how the PBL Exchange/stud platform could be useful in the setting of teaching activities whose stated goal has been to get students to develop PBL competences.

In the project, we introduced students to PBL Exchange/stud in the following degree programmes.

- The undergraduate degree programme in computer science, 4th semester.
- The first year of the degree programmes at the Faculty of Design and Technology, which has a course whose learning goals are to develop students' PBL competences and getting them to reflect on their own project process.
- The masters degree programme in learning and change. The student body here is highly diverse; a large proportion of the students have no previous experience with PBL, as they hold undergraduate degrees from other institutions.

In the undergraduate degree programme in computer science, the second author is the semester coordinator for the projects at this semester and has in the past observed that knowledge sharing with a project group is often an issue, as there are two major learning objectives that students often fail to connect well.

In the first-year undergraduate degree programme the lecturer responsible for the PBL course introduced PBL Exchange/stud to students. This was done at an early stage by means of a short presentation of the system and were then encouraged to generate as many questions as they could within 15 min. The results of the reflections were later used by each group in the process analysis that documented the project process that they carried out. The attitude was generally positive but interest in using the system eventually waned.

In the masters programme in learning and change, students were encouraged to use the material that they would produce using PBL Exchange/stud to their learning portfolios.

5   A Critical Look at the Interventions

Unfortunately, the interventions all turned out to be more complicated than expected. We had assumed that a major challenge would be one of allaying any fears that students might express. This was not the case. Rather, it turned out to be difficult to get students to use the system on a regular basis. An unexpected situation arose, when students from different degree programmes began interacting. Unfortunately, the students appeared not be respond well to questions from other degree programmes.

5.1   The Challenge from Existing Internet-Based Fora

Students already share or communicating within their semester cohorts using informal Internet-based fora such as Facebook [10]. It is therefore a challenge to persuade students to use another system together with students they might not know. We tried to meet this by incorporating PBL Exchange/stud into ongoing study activities as already described.

However, previous studies at Aalborg University indicate [8] that there is a tension in introducing systems and study-related learning activities that sit somewhere between the formal and informal. A study of a platform for student portfolios and subject related discussions [9], showed that students initially responded that the activities needed to align with the formally accredited course activities, rather than being voluntary. However, when activities were implemented as formal requirements in the course, many students regarded the system as yet another (and ultimately more cumbersome) way of handing in assignments, not as an opportunity to engage in subject-related reflections and discussions.

Similarly, Ryberg and Davidsen [7] reported how they established a well-functioning platform for community, interaction and knowledge sharing across a cohort of first-semester students but that the interactions and use of the platform dwindled as the teachers left the environment and no activities were promoted or formally required any longer.

5.2 Scaffolding as a Means of Community Building

Teacher-led scaffolding and incorporation of PBL Exchange/stud into courses and learning activities can be a valid strategy for generating participation. However, the intention for PBL Exchange/stud is not that it should hinge on becoming part of formal courses, but instead become a student-led community.

One way to go bridge teacher-led scaffolding with a more student-driven led platform could be to question whether the scaffolding should change focus from a more instrumental approach (scaffolding the use of the system) to a more value-based approach (scaffolding the sense-making of the system). In such an approach, a deeper understanding of students' motivation drives the scaffolding process.

We need to understand the intrinsic as well as the extrinsic motivations that drive students and identify occasions that appear meaningful to students [13].

As an example, the invention at the first year of study clearly showed that it was not only a question of raising students' awareness about the system or providing students with competences to use the system – one also had to create an occasion where students experience that the use of the system creates added value. Thereby scaffolding has to address what a meaningful occasion would be for the students. In the case of the first semester students, an extrinsic source of motivation was that students should use PBL Exchange/stud as a PBL experiment to be reported and credited in their PBL portfolio. Students however, did not respond easily to this.

Informal dialogue with students indicated the inquiry-based platform was not totally in alignment with how they were trained to work with PBL experiments. Students work with PBL experiments based on self-experienced problems and found it hard to go from this to a general question that would lead to useful answers in their specific context. This points to the importance of first claryfing the context and then formulating an appropriate question.

Moreover, at least in the case of first-year students, it was not obvious to them why they should give priority to answers from their fellow students when they had experienced members of teaching staff to draw on. Therefore, scaffolding should seek out situations where students would naturally want to learn from the experience of other students. Still, students could be asked to systematically document and reflect on their experiences with PBL Exchange/stud, and if one made sure that students got credit for such an activity, this could be an extrinsic motivation.

6   Conclusions and Further Work

We have presented PBL Exchange/stud, a dialogue-based system for sharing reflections among students that carry out group-based PBL projects. The system has been used experimentally in four settings involving students at Aalborg University.

An obstacle that became highly visible was that of adopting the system and forming a stable base of users; interest in using PBL Exchange/stud dwindled after the initial presentation of the system. Much of the exchange of ideas and sharing of experience appeared to happen informally, and students often found it easier to simply ask their students sitting next door. It is highly important to understand the intrinsic and extrinsic motivations that drive students to use and adopt fora and design suitable means of scaffolding based on this.

At the system level, there is also room for improvement. International students with no previous experience of PBL are a particularly interesting and important future target group for the platform. An important part of the ongoing implementation work will therefore be to extend the new Django codebase for PBL Exchange/stud with machine translation between Danish and English.

Moreover, the miscommunication that was sometimes caused by students from different degree programmes should be dealt with. Just as importantly, we intend to add the ability to set up separate fora dedicated to specific degree programmes, years or semesters.

References

1. Hüttel, H., Gnaur, D.: If PBL is the answer, then what is the problem? J. Probl. Based Learn. High. Educ. **5**(2), (2017). https://doi.org/10.5278/ojs.jpblhe.v5i2.1491
2. Hüttel, H., Gnaur, D., Hairing Klostergaard, A., Blegmand, G.: A new platform for question-based sharing of supervision competencies in problem-based learning. In: Rodrigues, A., Fonseca, B., Preguiça, N. (eds.) CRIWG 2018. LNCS, vol. 11001, pp. 177–184. Springer, Cham (2018). https://doi.org/10.1007/978-3-319-99504-5_14. http://dblp.uni-trier.de/db/conf/criwg/criwg2018.html#HuttelGKB18
3. McComas, W.F.: "21st-Century Skills", p. 1. SensePublishers, Rotterdam (2014). https://doi.org/10.1007/978-94-6209-497-0_1
4. Moodle. http://www.moodle.org

5. NEA: Preparing 21st century students for a global society: an educator's guide to the "four cs" (2012). http://www.nea.org/tools/52217.htm

6. Question2Answer. https://www.question2answer.org

7. Ryberg, T., Davidsen, J.: Establishing a sense of community, interaction, and knowledge exchange among students. In: Kergel, D., Heidkamp, B., Telléus, P., Nowakowski, S., Rachwal, T. (eds.) The Digital Turn in Higher Education. Springer, Wiesbaden (2018). https://doi.org/10.1007/978-3-658-19925-8_11

8. Ryberg, T., Sørensen, M.: Sociale medier i undervisning og uddannelse: potentialer og problematikker. Læring og Medier 12(21), 1–11 (2019). https://doi.org/10.7146/lom.v12i21.112894. (in Danish)

9. Ryberg, T., Wentzer, H.: Erfaringer med e-porteføljer og personlige læringsmiljøer. Dansk Universitetspaedagogisk Tidsskrift 11, 14–19 (2011)

10. Sørensen, M.T.: The students' choice of technology a pragmatic and outcome-focused approach. In: Kergel, D., Heidkamp, B., Telléus, P., Rachwal, T., Nowakowski, S. (eds.) The Digital Turn in Higher Education. Springer, Wiesbaden (2018). https://doi.org/10.1007/978-3-658-19925-8_12

11. Stackexchange. http://www.stackexchange.com

12. Uskoković, V.: Flipping the flipped: the co-creational classroom. Res. Pract. Technol. Enhanc. Learn. 13(1), 11 (2018). https://doi.org/10.1186/s41039-018-0077-9

13. Wenger, E.: Communities of Practice: Learning, Meaning, and Identity (Learning in Doing: Social, Cognitive and Computational Perspectives), pbk. edn. Cambridge University Press (1999). http://www.amazon.de/Communities-Practice-Cognitive-Computational-Perspectives/dp/0521663636/ref=wl_it_dp_v?ie=UTF8&coliid=IDPFVX4U6T022&colid=1SYIKSJ6TTEE3

Reconstructing Scanned Documents for Full-Text Indexing to Empower Digital Library Services

Melania Nitu[1], Mihai Dascalu[1(✉)], Maria-Iuliana Dascalu[2], Teodor-Mihai Cotet[1], and Silvia Tomescu[3]

[1] Computer Science Department, University Politehnica of Bucharest,
313 Splaiul Independentei, 060042 Bucharest, Romania
melania.nitu@yahoo.com, mihai.dascalu@cs.pub.ro,
teodor_mihai.cotet@stud.acs.upb.ro
[2] Department of Engineering in Foreign Languages, University Politehnica of Bucharest,
313 Splaiul Independentei, 060042 Bucharest, Romania
maria.dascalu@upb.ro
[3] Central University Library of Bucharest, 1 Boteanu Street, 010027 Bucharest, Romania
slvtomescu@gmail.com

Abstract. The digital era raises new challenges for traditional library services in which information has to be delivered and supported by technology-enhanced systems. The increasing need for rapid access to information requires librarians to re-evaluate the way they develop, manage and deliver resources, as well as services. However, most information extraction systems are not designed to work with PDF files generated after Optical Character Recognition, and several problems are encountered while trying to properly restructure the recognized text, for example: disruption of paragraphs, improper page breaks, or loss of content structure. This paper introduces a pre-processing pipeline designed to support university libraries to adequately index old document collections. The extracted text is indexed into Elasticsearch which facilitates the search for relevant documents, based on keywords. The information extraction system is designed to assist librarians in the digitization process by enabling a systematic review of documents, which leads to more accurate representations of the indexed files.

Keywords: Preprocessing pipeline · Text extraction · Text indexing · Unstructured documents

1 Introduction

The digital services provided by libraries have emerged from the need to easily retrieve relevant information from the wide range of existing physical and electronic documents. Our project is aimed to facilitate the digitization process of the Central University Library of Bucharest, which currently hosts over 2 million physical volumes [1], for information retrieval purposes and integration in an e-learning environment. In the current global context driven by advanced technologies [2], it is recognized that data preprocessing is

E. Popescu et al. (Eds.): SETE 2019, LNCS 11984, pp. 183–190, 2020.
https://doi.org/10.1007/978-3-030-38778-5_21

a critical part of any text mining, Natural Language Processing (NLP) and Information Retrieval (IR) system.

This paper proposes an implementation of extraction mechanisms from unstructured file formats, data indexing, and search for relevant documents based on keywords, stages for which text processing techniques play a significant role. A processing pipeline consists of several stages, each centered on a specific type of operation. Most information extraction systems were not designed to work on Portable Document Format (PDF) files in which the content is often mixed with publication metadata or semi-structured text, thus introducing additional NLP challenges. Moreover, the absence of effective means to extract text from these PDF files represents a struggle for researchers relying on published literature as a primary source of information. We focus on the fundamental text preprocessing stage, represented by an information extraction system that has the potential to assist humans in the text extraction task, enabling a systematic review before the indexing stage.

The following state-of-the-art section highlights existing approaches in terms of modern text processing techniques. The preprocessing stages and our pipeline are presented in the Method section, starting with the used corpora, text parsing and preprocessing algorithms, followed by document indexing. The obtained results are reported in the following section, while conclusions and the roadmap of future work are outlined next.

2   Related Work

The growing need to efficiently find and extract information from documents led to the development of various text mining tools. However, many of these tools were mainly designed to extract information from text-based documents, like JSON and other formats [3], while today a considerable part of the literature is published and distributed in PDF format. The well-known Acrobat DC is one of the most widely used software for pdf text extraction and processing. Despite its capabilities, the features are not free and there is few freely available information on the employed algorithms.

In the following, we briefly present a selection of the most popular PDF extraction tools for comparison purposes, along with their features. Depending on the presented tool, the output format of the processed file can be TXT (pdftotext, LA-PDFText, PdfMiner, PdfBox), XML (pdftohtml, pdftoxml, pdf2xml, PdfMiner, PDFExtract, pdfXkt, pdf-extract, pdfx), HTML (pdftohtml, pdf2xml, PdfMiner, pdfXkt) or JSON (Icecite [4]). Table 1 presents an overview of the above tools' features. If a feature is fully provided by the tool, it is represented with "X"; otherwise it is noted by "-".

Most of the existing text processing tools were designed to extract text from formatted PDF layouts. Neji framework [5] was built for biomedical concept recognition in journal publications, while Maciocci [6] conducted a study on data extraction from scientific manuscripts in formatted PDF files using computer vision techniques and developed the ScienceBeam tool. Yet the challenge remains; the processing of non-formatted PDF files, which is currently a popular research subject in the field.

Related approaches for text extracting features in unstructured PDF files were presented by Hassan & Baumgartner [7] who proposed three methods based on layout segmentation for data extraction: conversion to a structured format, ontology-based wrapping, and spatial reasoning. Other researchers approached the non-formatted files issue

Table 1. Features of the most popular PDF text extraction tools.

Tool/feature	Description	Output format	Paragraph boundaries	Semantic roles	Diacritics	Hyphenated words	Read order
pdftotext	Converts PDFs to plain text, without recognizing the boundaries of the paragraph or the delimitation of the text body - http://www.xpdfreader.com/	txt	-	-	X	X	X
pdftohtml	Transforms the PDF to xml or html format, being able to split the text into lines, extracts characters with diacritics as two characters, without identifying the paragraphs or hyphenated words https://sourceforge.net/projects/pdftohtml	HTML, XML	-	-	-	-	X
pdftoxml	Converts PDFs to XML, splitting content into blocks (which do not correlate to paragraphs), text lines and words, while ligatures, diacritics and hyphenated words are not handled - https://sourceforge.net/projects/pdf2xml	XML	-	-	-	-	X
pdf2xml	Uses Apache Tika and pdfotext to extract text and combines the result of both tools to improve the identification of word boundaries - https://bitbucket.org/tiedemann/pdf2xml	HTML, XML	X	-	-	X	X
LA-PDFText	Processes full-text scientific articles and extracts logical text blocks based on user-defined rules (defined for each article layout) [9]	txt	-	X	-	-	X
PdfMiner	Converts the PDF file into plain text, xml or html format, while analyzing the file structure; diacritics and hyphenated words are not processed properly - https://github.com/euske/pdfminer	txt, XML, HTML	X	-	-	-	X
PDFExtract	One of the most effective tools, is capable to identify the semantic roles in scientific articles: title, abstract, headings and paragraphs, well-handling hyphenated words and diacritics - https://github.com/oyvindberg/PDFExtract/	XML	X	X	-	-	X
PdfBox	A well-known Apache java library used for converting PDF files to plain text; it cannot identify the paragraph boundaries and cannot merge hyphenated words, but it can handle characters with diacritics - https://pdfbox.apache.org/	txt	-	-	X	-	X
pdfXkt	Built on top of Pdfbox, converts PDF files to XML or HTML, and can split the content into blocks, lines, words and characters; diacritics and hyphenated words are not being handled accurately - https://github.com/tamirhassan/pdfxtk	HTML, XML	-	-	-	-	X

(*continued*)

Table 1. (*continued*)

Tool/feature	Description	Output format	Paragraph boundaries	Semantic roles	Diacritics	Hyphenated words	Read order
pdf-extract	Converts files to XML and split the PDF content into text lines, can recognize reference sections and split them into individual references - https://github.com/CrossRef/pdfextract/	XML	-	-	-	-	X
pdfx	Rule-based tool that studies layouts and fonts to build a geometrical model of the PDF file, being capable to identify titles, sections and tables - http://pdfx.cs.man.ac.uk/	XML	-	X	X	X	X

into stages: started with a layout analysis and continued with segmentation, character and structure recognitions [8].

3   Method

3.1   Corpus

The current corpus consisted of 55 books in PDF format, written in Romanian language, provided by Central University Library of Bucharest. The input data is represented by a set of scanned books on which Optical Character Recognition (OCR) was performed. The resulting PDFs do not follow a specific format, so we are working with a set of non-formatted PDFs. There are many challenges when working with non-formatted PDFs. As a result of the OCR phase, we have encountered different font sizes and font types on the same page, in one text line or in one paragraph, and different styles for headers and footers in the same book, which created difficulties in adjusting the preprocessing pipeline algorithm.

3.2   Processing Pipeline

A high-level overview of the modular architecture corresponding to our PDF Processing Pipeline is presented in Fig. 1. The input data consists of unformatted PDFs obtained via OCR, that are further processed into a JSON object by identifying metadata and the table of contents, establishing the paragraph boundaries, rebuilding hyphenated words, extracting images, and identifying tables. The workflow continues with the validation phase, where the JSON object is converted into HTML and displayed in an editable format to enable users to correct the outcome. Once corrected, the HTML is transformed back into a JSON object and the processed item is indexed using Elasticsearch (https://www.elastic.co/products/elasticsearch) which facilitates the search for relevant documents based on keywords. Apache PdfBox library is used as a main technology for text extraction task because it allows the facile extraction of Unicode text from PDF files, as well as position and font features.

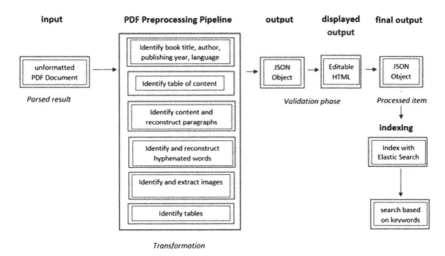

Fig. 1. PDF processing pipeline.

Given an unformatted PDF book, the first step of the preprocessing pipeline algorithm is the parsing phase, where the logical text blocks are being identified. The text extraction can be a challenging task in unformatted files, as the text is rendered in different formats. Determining the correct reading order of words is an essential step for the text extraction. Words order within a line is easily correlated with the position of the words on the page, while the order between lines can be difficult to identify on two-column layouts. This challenge is addressed by using PdfBox which successfully handles reading order, the translation of ligatures, and the characters with diacritics. The document is parsed on lines, identifying relevant sections and metadata within the book: chapter titles, headings, paragraphs of the body text content, images, tables, and the table of contents. Paragraph boundaries are rebuilt, whereas hyphenated words are merged. The book title, the author, and the publishing year are extracted from the first page (if present) and are passed to the JSON object before the processing phase. In the processing workflow, the refined text is sent to the user interface by converting the JSON object into editable HTML and displaying it using TinyMCE customized text area, allowing the user to edit the text before saving the file. The saved form of the processed text is converted to JSON and sent to Elasticsearch for indexing.

We experimented several approaches to properly extract metadata. The first model uses the table of content to identify the chapter titles and their associated pages, splitting the content into titles and paragraphs. In contrast, the second model identifies the dominant font type and size on a page which is associated to the body content. Each time a different font is encountered, the corresponding text is considered chapter title or heading. A more detailed overview on the algorithms is presented in the next paragraphs.

The algorithm for table of content (TOC) parsing consists of three main steps: (a) the identification of TOC's first page, (b) pattern validation, and (c) reconstruction of TOC boundaries. In order to identify the first page of the table of content, we start from the premise that its title should match one of the keywords from our dictionary. However, due to the condition of the original documents and as a result of Optical Character

Recognition phase, the words may contain white spaces or symbols or may be split on multiple lines; this imposed additional challenges and an additional validation phase using regular expression was introduced. As a general observation, most TOC lines in our dataset are ending with digits representing the start page of the chapter. Therefore, a condition for the pattern validation was created. Moreover, the TOC is found in the first or last 10 pages of a book, which helped us create a heuristic for the identification of TOC boundaries. Furthermore, TOC entries are parsed using a regular expression to correctly extract the chapter title and the associated page range.

The second approach is used to identify chapters and paragraphs based on most common font. The method relies on PDFTextStriper from pdfBox to strip the text, ignoring its formatting. The text is analyzed line by line, based on font information (font name and font size), as well as text position on the page. The data for each line is stored in a list and the text is associated with body content or title content by comparing the predominant font on the page, with each line. As a convention, the text having a font smaller or equal in size than the most common font is considered part of a paragraph. Because the dataset contains very old documents having unformatted layouts, we encountered different fonts and different sizes within the same paragraph, within the same line or even within the same word. Since our goal is to group the text content into titles and paragraphs, the small font differences within a line are ignored, and only the predominant font is considered.

After iterative experiments, the two models were combined into one robust tool which improved individual performances by easily adapting to the structure of most PDF books. Moreover, a mechanism for image extraction was implemented; the images are saved into a local folder, and a tag is inserted in the place where the image was extracted.

4   Results

Starting from the corpus of 55 unformatted PDFs, we disregarded 18 books with severe problems while assessing accuracy (i.e., percentage of correctly extracted document metadata, including table of contents); thus, we were left with a collection of 37 items.

The evaluation of the proposed pipeline on the processed books is detailed in Table 2: 18 books had a processing accuracy of 100%, 22 over 90%, 25 over 80%, and only 9 under 50%. The separation of document headings in the unformatted PDFs on a corpus of 37 processed books had an overall precision of 78%, a recall of 75%, while the overall F-score was 73%. The overall high accuracy of the PDF processing pipeline argues for its applicability within the digitization process.

An in-depth overview on the causes of the problematic documents is presented in the following section. Within the 18 disregarded books we identified the following issues:

1. poor format, as a result of OCR process;
2. un-numbered pages inserted between the numbered pages of the book;
3. same font and same font size for titles and headings the whole book;
4. no separation between titles and content;
5. no table of contents.

Table 2. Count of documents having a statistical measure (Accuracy, Precision, Recall, F-score) higher than the imposed threshold.

Threshold	Accuracy	Precision	Recall	F-score
100%	18	23	20	19
Over 90%	22	27￩	22	24
Over 80%	25	28	26	26
Over 50%	28	28	27	26
Under 50%	9	9	9	11

A more detailed distribution of the problematic books with an accuracy below 4% across the previously identified issues is presented in Table 3.

Table 3. Distribution of identified issues within the disregarded books.

	Count of books exhibiting a specific issue				
	Issue #1	Issue #2	Issue #3	Issue #4	Issue #5
Number of affected books	7	5	4	9	15

Table 4 introduces an evaluation of the proposed preprocessing pipeline while relating to three other state of the art tools. For evaluation purposes, we randomly choose 2 books from the well-performing set and 2 books from the bad-performing set, and we assessed the accuracy for headings and content separation. The proposed preprocessing pipeline performed better than the other tested tools on the well-performing book set, while on the bad-performing set PDFExtract had a higher accuracy for one of the tested books.

Table 4. Performance evaluation in comparison with other existing tools.

Tools	Features	WB1	WB2	BB1	BB2
Pdftotext	_R_DH	66.1%	71.4%	0%	5.2%
PDFExtract	PRSDH	72.09%	98%	3%	23.4%
pdfx	_RSDH	63.8%	44.8%	1.08%	6.39%
Our tool	PRSDH	77.47%	100%	4.04%	9.94%

P-paragraph boundaries, R-reading order, S-semantic roles, D-diacritics, H-hyphenated words, WB-well performing book, BB-bad performing book

5   Conclusions and Future Work

This paper presents a pipeline designed to process unformatted PDFs as a principal tool to assist humans in the digitalization process for a library, later to be used as a search and recommendation engine for learners. Two processing algorithms were implemented and tested on a dataset of scanned and OCRed books and, as a result of the preliminary testing phase, the two algorithms were combined into one processing pipeline which exhibited an accuracy of over 70%. However, a number of 18 books out of the 57 books from our corpus were difficult to process due to the impossibility to separate the headings and the content based on the font type, font size, page numbering, table of content, or position of the text on the page.

In terms of future improvements, a spellchecking module will be added, which has the purpose to correct potential errors in the text body, an issue frequently encountered after performing Optical Character Recognition. Additional heuristics will be introduced to tackle footnotes, page headers and footers.

Acknowledgement. This work was supported by a grant of the Romanian Ministry of Research and Innovation, CCCDI - UEFISCDI, project number PN-III-P1-1.2-PCCDI-2017-0689/"Lib2Life - Revitalizarea bibliotecilor si a patrimoniului cultural prin tehnologii avansate"/"Revitalizing Libraries and Cultural Heritage through Advanced Technologies", within PNCDI III.

References

1. Biblioteca Centrala Universitara Carol I. http://www.bcub.ro/home/biblioteca-in-cifre/biblioteca-in-cifre-la-31-decembrie-2018. Accessed 16 Aug 2019
2. Cervone, H.F.: Emerging technology, innovation, and the digital library. OCLC Syst. Serv. Int. Digit. Libr. Perspect. **26**(4), 239–242 (2010)
3. Schouten, K., Frasincar, F., Dekker, R., Riezebos, M.: Heracles: a framework for developing and evaluating text mining algorithms. Expert Syst. Appl. **127**, 68–84 (2019)
4. Korzen, C.: Icecite (2017). https://github.com/ckorzen/icecite. Accessed 16 Aug 2019
5. Santos, A., Matos, S., Campos, D., Oliveira, J.L.: A curation pipeline and web-services for PDF documents. In: CEUR Workshop Proceedings, vol. 1650. http://ceur-ws.org/Vol-1650/smbm16San-tos.pdf. ISSN 1613-0073
6. Maciocci, G.: ScienceBeam - using computer vision to extract PDF data. https://elifesciences.org/labs/5b56aff6/sciencebeam-using-computer-vision-to-extract-pdf-data. Accessed 16 Aug 2019
7. Hassan, T.: Baumgartner, R.: Intelligent text extraction from PDF documents, pp. 2–6 (2005). https://doi.org/10.1109/cimca.2005.1631436
8. Sasirekha, D., Chandra, E.: Text extraction from PDF document. In: IJCA Proceedings on Amrita International Conference of Women in Computing, AICWIC, no. 3, pp. 17–19 (2013)
9. Ramakrishnan, C., Patnia, A., Hovy, E., Burns, G.: Layout-aware text extraction from full-text PDF of scientific articles. Source Code Biol. Med. **7**(1), 7 (2012)

Curating Educational Resources for Homework Management: A Support Prototype

Andreea-Isabela Bala, Stefania-Carmen Dobre, and Elvira Popescu$^{(\boxtimes)}$

Computers and Information Technology Department, University of Craiova, Craiova, Romania
{cdobre,epopescu}@software.ucv.ro

Abstract. Learning content curation plays an important role given the increasing amount of educational resources available on the Web. The process implies searching, collecting, annotating, filtering, organizing and sharing relevant resources for a specific learning context. Our aim is to provide a support platform which allows both teachers and students to become content curators, leveraging various levels of expertise. More specifically, we propose a system dedicated to homework management, called EdReHo, which allows the collection and sharing of educational resources needed to understand and solve assignments. When teachers create an assignment in EdReHo, they can recommend also a set of resources relevant for that topic, which are aimed to supplement the mandatory course material. The students can also add useful resources and share them with peers, becoming more actively involved in the process and benefitting from the "learning by searching" approach. The paper describes the EdReHo system prototype in terms of concept, features and implementation and illustrates its main functionalities.

Keywords: Learning content curation · Educational resources · Assignment management · Learning by searching · Student engagement

1 Introduction

Learning content curation refers to the identification, organization and contextualization of the most relevant information for a target group of students. The process implies the search and collection of educational resources from multiple sources, filtering the most suitable information for learners' needs and structuring it to facilitate comprehension. The value of the content can be further enhanced by adding a suggestive title, an explanatory description or relevant tags. Subsequently, the content can be shared with students and stored for future reference [3, 8].

Given the abundance of educational resources available on the Web, the role of content curator becomes essential for the teacher. At the same time, students can also be involved in the process. On one hand, they should be able to provide feedback on the content, by rating or commenting on it; thus they get more actively engaged with their learning and offer insights to the instructor [3]. On the other hand, students can become content curators themselves, searching for relevant resources and sharing them with peers. The process of searching and filtering information can foster learning [4]; in

© Springer Nature Switzerland AG 2020
E. Popescu et al. (Eds.): SETE 2019, LNCS 11984, pp. 191–197, 2020.
https://doi.org/10.1007/978-3-030-38778-5_22

addition, by annotating resources with meaningful terms, students create a personalized classification, facilitating subsequent retrieval [9].

In this context, we aim to provide a support platform for the learning content curation process. In particular, homework assignments are learning activities which generally require additional educational resources for the students. Hence, we propose a platform specifically tailored to homework management: on one hand it aims to help teachers curate learning resources and link them to homework assignments; thus, relevant resources are provided to the students just when they are searching for the information [3]. On the other hand, the system provides a learning space for the students, where they can act as content curators and share resources with peers. In addition, the platform is designed to support communication and feedback between students and teachers with respect to the homework activities. A prototype of the system, called EdReHo (**Ed**ucational **Re**sources for **Ho**mework), has already been developed, as detailed further on.

The rest of the paper is structured as follows: Sect. 2 presents an overview of related work, Sect. 3 describes the EdReHo prototype in terms of concept, functionalities and implementation, and Sect. 4 includes some conclusions and future research directions.

2   Related Work

In what follows, we discuss some relevant systems proposed in the literature, focusing especially on retrieving, collecting, searching, organizing, tagging, rating and sharing learning resources.

Paper [2] presents a platform for language learning in which educational resources consist in links retrieved from social bookmarking sites; the search is done automatically by the system, based on keywords attached by the teacher to each learning activity. When accessing such a learning activity, the student is presented with a list of 10–15 links, which they have the option to like or dislike; links are subsequently filtered based on the number of votes received from the learners.

Another system that provides the option of searching resources through various Web 2.0 services (such as YouTube, SlideShare, Blogger, Delicious etc.) is described in [7]. LearnWeb2.0, as it is called, allows the students to retrieve and store resources of interest, organize them in folders, bookmark, tag, rate, comment and share them with peers. Students can form groups around various topics of interest, in which they collect resources on a particular subject.

Automatic searching is also proposed in [1], by means of a federated search engine which helps students retrieve resources from various services (MIT OCW or OpenER courseware, Blogger, Technorati, YouTube, Slideshare etc.). Learners can organize resources into collections, tag, rate and share them with peers. A filtering option is provided, based on the popularity of the resources (in terms of the number of comments, links, saves, likes, ratings, votes, views, shares, trackbacks etc.).

A similar approach is presented in [9]; Edu3R system allows students to search through various learning object repositories (Ariadne, comPADRE, Connexions, LOR-NET, Merlot, OCW, OER etc.) and save resources of interest. These can be subsequently tagged, rated and shared with peers. A collaborative filtering mechanism is also included, which recommends learning resources based on student similarity.

A somewhat different approach, based on social tagging, is proposed in [5]. ASK-LOST 2.0 platform offers students the possibility to submit and tag learning objects and organize them in personal collections; they can also search, rate and comment on educational resources and access them via tag clouds. Moreover, students can also follow their peers and receive updates regarding the educational resources and tags created by them.

In addition to the dedicated systems presented above, some general-purpose existing services have been used for learning content curation, such as MediaWiki [10] or social bookmarking systems (Diigo, Delicious, Bibsonomy) [6].

In most of the above platforms, the selection of learning resources is done either by the students [1, 5, 7, 9] or by the teacher [2]. What we propose in our EdReHo system is to allow both teachers and students to become learning content curators, thus combining various levels of expertise. Furthermore, our platform is centered on homework management, so resources are aggregated and organized based on a very specific topic of interest; students are more engaged in searching for resources, as this helps them to solve their course assignments. Moreover, by allowing manual addition of the links, the system emphasizes the active role of the students, based on the "learning by searching" approach [11]; this also means that the source is not confined to a predefined set of learning object repositories and/or Web 2.0 services. More details regarding the EdReHo platform are included in the next section.

3 EdReHo Prototype

3.1 Concept, Features and Implementation

EdReHo is a web application designed to provide learning content curation support for both teachers and students. The aim is to allow the collection and sharing of educational resources needed to understand and solve homework assignments. When a teacher proposes an assignment, he/she should be able to recommend also a set of resources relevant for that topic. These resources are aimed to supplement the mandatory course material and could take various forms, both formal and informal, such as: additional lecture slides, developer guides, tutorials, video demonstrations, blog posts, source code examples on GitHub, StackOverflow answers etc. In addition, students could also search for useful resources on the web and share them with peers in case of group assignments. Peers' recommendations have the potential to be very relevant, as they reflect the preference of fellow students in a relatively homogenous learning community (e.g., a class centered around the same course, in which students have similar learning backgrounds) [9].

In addition, the teacher can always access the resources added by the students to an assignment and provide feedback if needed; in case of a useful and relevant resource, the instructor can choose to save it to his/her own collection of resources and link it to that particular assignment in the future. Conversely, in case of an incorrect or irrelevant resource, the teacher can use the built-in comment feature to signal this issue to the students. The possibility to add comments to assignments also encourages student communication and interaction with peers and with the instructor.

Furthermore, EdReHo allows both students and teachers to tag and rate resources. Tagging facilitates labeling and categorization of resources; subsequent retrieval is also made easier by adding meaningful keywords. Tags also provide a personalized classification, which is relevant to the learning community [5]. In addition, the quality of the resources can be assessed both by students and instructors, by means of a simple 1 to 5 rating scale.

Some more details and illustrations of EdReHo functionalities are included in the following subsection. As far as the implementation is concerned, EdReHo was developed using mainly JavaScript as programming language. The following technologies were used on the client side: *Vue.js* (an open source JavaScript framework for building the user interface), *Pug.js* (a template engine used to inject data to produce HTML content) and *Stylus* (a dynamic stylesheet preprocessor language providing an efficient and expressive way to generate CSS). The server side is based on *Node.js* (an asynchronous event driven JavaScript runtime environment designed to build scalable web applications) and *Express.js* (the de facto standard server framework for *Node.js*), together with *MongoDB* (a document-oriented database for storing all persistent data).

3.2   Illustrating EdReHo Functionalities

When accessing EdReHo system, the instructor can choose between two main tasks: managing resources or managing homework, as illustrated in Fig. 1.

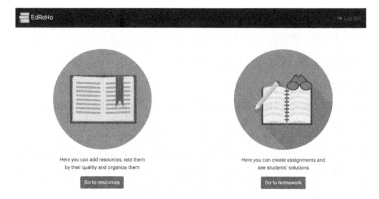

Fig. 1. EdReHo - Teacher welcome page

The resource management module offers support for learning content curation and enriching the learning resources database. Thus, the instructor can save a resource of interest by providing the link (URL) together with a title, a description, a set of tags and a rating. Subsequently, the teacher can visualize the list of resources and search /filter them (as displayed in Fig. 2).

The homework management module allows the instructor to create homework assignments and link recommended resources to them, as shown in Fig. 3. The teacher can also visualize the list of assignments, including the resources and comments added by the students and communicate with the learners if needed. Finally, the instructor can also access students' solutions to the homework and evaluate them by providing a grade and a feedback.

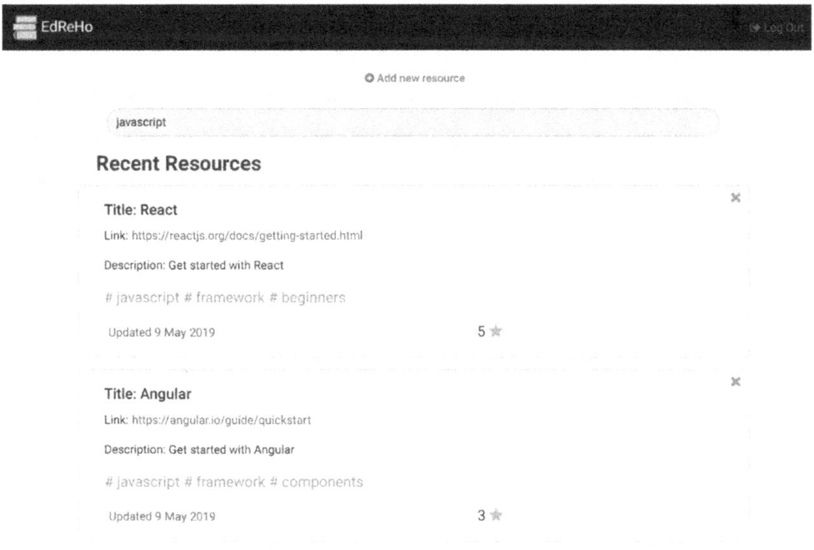

Fig. 2. EdReHo Teacher functionalities - Search for resources

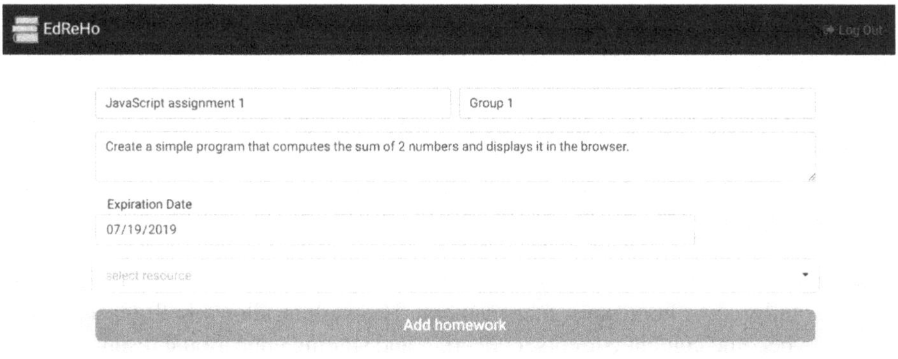

Fig. 3. EdReHo Teacher functionalities - Create homework and add resources

The student can also act as learning content curator in EdReHo. The system provides the same functionalities with respect to resource management (adding, visualizing and searching educational resources). As far as homework is concerned, the student can visualize the list of assignments and select the one she/he prefers to solve. Subsequently, the learner can add some relevant resources for the assignment (in addition to the ones recommended by the teacher) and share them with peers; comments can also be posted to an assignment, ensuring communication with the teacher and fellow students (as illustrated in Fig. 4).

Finally, the student can also submit a solution for an assignment (and upload a corresponding file); once the solution is assessed by the teacher, the learner can visualize

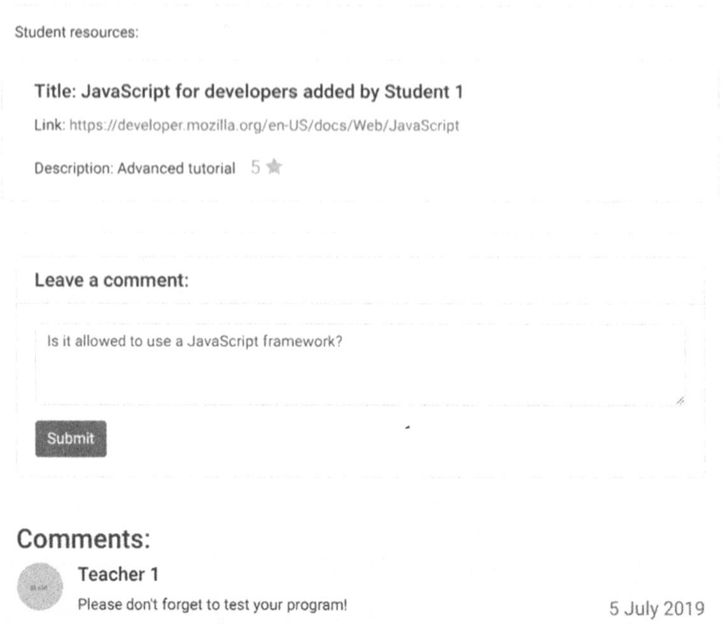

Student resources:

Title: **JavaScript for developers added by Student 1**

Link: https://developer.mozilla.org/en-US/docs/Web/JavaScript

Description: Advanced tutorial   5 ☆

Leave a comment:

Is it allowed to use a JavaScript framework?

Submit

Comments:

Teacher 1

Please don't forget to test your program!   5 July 2019

Fig. 4. EdReHo Student functionalities - Add resources and comments

the feedback and grade. In addition, the system also sends email notifications to the learners when their solutions are evaluated by the instructor.

4 Conclusion

We designed and implemented EdReHo, a support prototype for curating educational resources, tailored to homework management. The system allows both teachers and students to become content curators, collecting and sharing educational resources relevant for a homework assignment. The process of searching, filtering, rating and tagging resources has the potential to increase students' engagement and critical thinking.

The next step is to experimentally evaluate the platform in various course settings. In addition, we plan to extend EdReHo with a recommender module, which can suggest resources of interest based on student's profile. A guided tagging approach could also be included, by automatically proposing keywords based on the resource content.

References

1. Chatti, M.A., Anggraeni, Jarke, M., Specht, M., Maillet, K.: PLEM: a Web 2.0 driven long tail aggregator and filter for e-learning. Int. J. Web Inf. Syst. **6**(1), 5–23 (2010)
2. Dettori, G., Torsani, S.: An approach to exploit social bookmarking to improve formal language learning. In: Popescu, E., Li, Q., Klamma, R., Leung, H., Specht, M. (eds.) ICWL 2012. LNCS, vol. 7558, pp. 1–10. Springer, Heidelberg (2012). https://doi.org/10.1007/978-3-642-33642-3_1

3. Gutierrez, K.: Why You Should Use Content Curation in Your L&D Strategy? (And How to Do It) (2018). https://www.shiftelearning.com/blog/content-curation-learning-and-development
4. Jansen, B.J., Booth, D., Smith, B.: Using the taxonomy of cognitive learning to model online searching. Inf. Process. Manage. **45**, 643–663 (2009)
5. Kalamatianos, A., Zervas, P., Sampson, D.: ASK–LOST 2.0: a web-based tool for social tagging of digital educational resources. In: Proceedings of 9th IEEE International Conference on Advanced Learning Technologies (ICALT 2009), pp. 157–159 (2009)
6. Kiu, C., Lim, E.: Social bookmarking systems to enhance students' learning process. In: Proceedings of 3rd International Conference on Science in Information Technology (ICSITech 2017), pp. 413–417 (2017)
7. Marenzi, I., Zerr, S.: Multiliteracies and active learning in CLIL - the development of LearnWeb2.0. IEEE Trans. Learn. Technol. **5**(4), 336–348 (2012)
8. Pink, A.: Content Curation for Learning. https://anderspink.com/documents/content-curation-book.pdf (2017)
9. Popescu, E., Buse, F.E.: Supporting students to find relevant learning resources through social bookmarking and recommendations. In: Proceedings of 18th International Conference on System Theory, Control and Computing (ICSTCC 2014), pp. 458–463 (2014)
10. Verhaart, M.: Curating digital content in teaching and learning using wiki technology. In: Proceedings of 12th IEEE International Conference on Advanced Learning Technologies (ICALT 2012), pp. 191–193 (2012)
11. Zhang, X.: Searching interactions and perceived learning. In: Zaphiris, P., Ioannou, A. (eds.) LCT 2016. LNCS, vol. 9753, pp. 245–255. Springer, Cham (2016). https://doi.org/10.1007/978-3-319-39483-1_23

UMLL (User Modeling and Language Learning)

The Analysis of Worldwide Research on Artificial Intelligence Assisted User Modeling

Xieling Chen[1], Dongfa Gao[2], Yonghui Lun[3], Dingli Zhou[4], Tianyong Hao[4(✉)], and Haoran Xie[5(✉)]

[1] Department of Mathematics and Information Technology,
The Education University of Hong Kong, Hong Kong SAR, China
s1131872@s.eduhk.hk
[2] School of Information Science and Technology, Guangdong University of Foreign Studies,
Guangzhou, China
gaodf@gdufs.edu.cn
[3] Guangzhou Huagong Information Software Co., LTD., Guangzhou, China
wingfai_lun@163.com
[4] School of Computer Science, South China Normal University, Guangzhou, China
zhoudingli1999@126.com, haoty@m.scnu.edu.cn
[5] Department of Computing and Decision Sciences, Lingnan University,
Hong Kong SAR, China
hrxie2@gmail.com

Abstract. Information and communication technologies is being heralded as a catalyst for educational innovations. Artificial intelligence (AI) assisted user modeling has attracted great increasing interests from the academia with a growing research articles available. In this article, a bibliometric analysis of scientific literature concerning AI assisted user modeling was carried out. 333 articles from Web of Science were retrieved and analyzed to comprehensively understand trends and developments of the research field. Specifically, we analyzed the articles in terms of article count and citation count, influential journals, subjects, authors, and keyword occurrence. Finally, special attention was paid to the study of leading countries/regions and institutions. Findings of this work are useful in helping scholars as well as practitioners better understand the development trend of research of AI assisted user modeling, as well as being more aware of the research hotspots.

Keywords: Artificial intelligence · User modeling · Bibliometric analysis · Research hotspots · Topic evolution

1 Introduction

In the era of media-suffused environment, information and communication technologies are being heralded as catalyst for educational innovations in various spheres of life [1]. Diversified emerging technologies such as Artificial Intelligence (AI) provide underlying infrastructure to create enormous potential educational innovations. Such innovations are significantly stimulating the development of tools

© Springer Nature Switzerland AG 2020
E. Popescu et al. (Eds.): SETE 2019, LNCS 11984, pp. 201–213, 2020.
https://doi.org/10.1007/978-3-030-38778-5_23

and systems for interaction purposes, for example, intelligent tutoring systems, computer aided assessment, and computer mediated communication [2]. With the ability of providing rich features about users, user modeling is of great significance for the development of interactive systems as to offer various adaption effects [3, 4]. Different types of user activities can be recorded and used to identify regularities in user paths with the use of data mining and machine learning, which can be further integrated to implicitly and dynamically generate user models [3]. For example, classification techniques can map user information into different groups for the representation of various user profiles [5].

Emerging interdisciplinary research towards AI assisted user modeling has attracted increasing interests from the academia with a growing research articles available. It is of need to handle the information to uncover important issues. Although there are reviews concerning the adoption of data mining to user modeling within web-based personalized educational systems [6–8], none of them is conducted by the use of quantitative approach. And further, important issues, e.g., how do the research studies distribute by year, who are the most active researchers and institutions, and what are the foci and hotspots related to the field, have not been uncovered.

As a commonly adopted technique in the field of library and information sciences, bibliometric analysis has long been regarded as an effective method for mapping scientific articles in relation to a specific area [9]. It explores the distribution of articles based on given categories such as topic, research subject, author, or country using quantitative and statistical approaches. Bibliometric analysis have been widely used to investigate research trend of a specific field recently [10–19].

This study aims to bibliometrically evaluate, academic articles about AI assisted user modeling research published in Web of Science between 2001 and 2018. These articles are analyzed and evaluated based on a number of perspectives (publication year, research subjects, journals, authors, institutions, and countries/regions, as well as keywords) and are employed to uncover major research issues and trends in the area.

2   Materials and Methods

ISI Web of Science (WOS) database was utilized to collect research articles concerning AI assisted user modeling, since it is the most authoritative academic publication and citation repository. A retrieval field Topic (TS) in WOS, referring to title, abstract and/or keywords, was used. The article retrieval was conducted in March 25, 2019. To acquire relevant academic articles, an essential step was to prepare keywords lists for both AI and user modeling research in education area. The identified keywords were then used to retrieve articles from the database. Referring to the work of Hassan et al. [20], we followed the following steps to obtain relevant keywords for both AI and user modeling research. Step 1: A list of seed keywords closely related to user modeling research in education area was provided by domain experts. Step 2: A query containing the seed keywords was constructed with a restriction of Web of Science Category concerning 'education' or 'educational' to retrieve articles with keywords matched against title, abstracts, and author defined keywords. A part of the query to retrieve articles related to user modeling research in education area was ('user model*' OR 'user interface model*' OR 'learner model*' OR 'student model*' OR 'adaptable system*' OR 'learning model*'…). Step 3: Co-occurred author defined keywords from the retrieved articles were presented to domain experts to help identify and add relevant ones to the initial seed keywords. Likewise, we followed the same steps to acquire of keyword query for AI research.

The search query was used and further restricted based on the following conditions: (1) articles published during the period 2001–2018; (2) articles of "ARTICLE" type; (3) articles written in English; (4) articles of Science Citation Index Expanded and Social Sciences Citation Index. According to the above restrictions, 424 articles with full bibliographic information and annual citations were retrieved. In order to include articles that are highly related to our research target, domain experts carried out a filtering procedure based on their expertise and knowledge of the research field. After filtering, 333 articles were obtained and categorized based on different elements including number of scientific articles per year, allocation by journal and subject category, as well as allocation by country/region and institution.

With referring to the work of Zawacki-Richter and Latchem [21], we used terms extracted from title and abstract for keywords analysis. Additional, given the fact that article keywords are commonly considered to represent key focus of a piece of study, and are able to uncover research topics and trends by integrating frequency [22, 23], we also included keywords of articles to perform a word cloud analysis using WordArt[1]. In the figure created, font sizes represented frequencies of keywords. To perform the word cloud adequately and effectively, keyword preprocessing was conducted. Firstly, abbreviations were replaced by their full names according to article content (e.g., CALL was replaced by 'computer assisted language learning', EFL was replaced by 'English as a foreign language', and AI was replaced by 'artificial intelligence'). Secondly, all keywords were unified as lowercase, and were separated if compound words existed. Thirdly, keywords such as 'model', 'modeling', 'article', and 'using' were removed due to little contribution to the study. In addition, duplicated keywords in semantics (e.g., 'behaviour' and 'behavior') were merged. We then applied Term Frequency-Inverse Document Frequencies (TF-IDF) to filter out unimportant keywords. Only keywords with a TF-IDF value greater than a threshold (0.01 in this study) were kept for analysis. To explore topic evolution, articles were associated with three consecutive time periods: 2001–2006 (39 articles), 2007–2012 (113 articles), and 2013–2018 (181 articles). The number of keywords displayed in the figures was in proportion to the article counts for each period. Thus, for the three periods, number of keywords displayed were 25, 75, and 150, respectively.

The citation count of a scientific article reflects the impact of the research in a scientific community [23]. Thus, the citation count was applied in this paper as an analytical metric to estimate the academic level of a journal, country/region, institution, or author via H-index in the research field. H-index is defined as H, meaning that H of one's articles has at least H citations each [24]. A higher H-index value generally indicates a higher scientific achievement. We also used Mann-Kendall test [25] to examine if there are significant trends in the usage of keywords. Such trend analysis was performed using an R software package *trend*.

---

[1] https://wordart.com/.

3   Results and Discussions

3.1   Article and Citation Trends

Articles of the utilization of AI techniques in user modeling research is not available until 2001 in WoS, thus the exploration period of the research field is from 2001 to 2018. Figure 1 shows the trends of article and citation counts. We can find that on the whole, the article count experiences an increasing trend in fluctuation, from 2 in 2001 to 44 in 2018. There is a dramatic drop of article count in 2014. As for citation count, it increases continuingly till 2017, however, the number drops slightly in 2018. This may be partially due to the fact that it takes time for new articles to be cited. Two polynomial regression curves with *year* as an independent variable x are fitted for article and citation trends, respectively. Comparing with the regression model of citation count ($R^2 = 96.47\%$), the fitting effect of the regression model for the article count is less effective with a goodness of fit as only 68.96%. In total, the research field is gaining more and more attention, and is still under development.

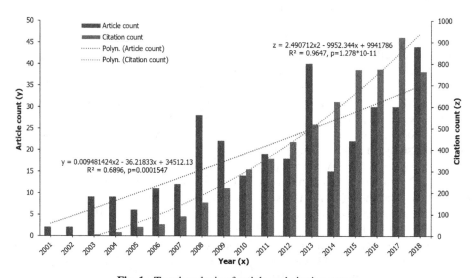

Fig. 1. Trend analysis of article and citation counts

3.2   Research Subject and Journal Distributions

The WoS subject category taxonomy is utilized for the analysis of research subject distribution. The 333 articles are distributed in 22 subjects in total . Figure 2 shows the top 10 subjects of articles, *Education & Educational Research* is the dominate subject since articles retrieved are restricted to education relevant domain. It is worth noting that *Computer Science, Interdisciplinary Applications* is ranked at 2nd. The two subjects contribute 69.60% in total to the research field.

The 333 articles are identified to be published in 75 journals. Table 1 displays the top 15 journals by H-index. They together account for 31.23% of the total articles. *Computers & Education* is the dominate journal with an H-index value up to 30 and an article count of 71. Other top journals include *Educational Technology & Society* and *IEEE Transactions on Learning Technologies*. Further referring to Fig. 3 on both article count and H-index, the dominate role of *Computers & Education* is significant.

Table 1. Top journals ranked by H-index

Journal	H	AC (R)	TC (R)	ACP (R)	IF (Q)	5-year IF
Computers & Education	30	71 (1)	2,801 (1)	39.45 (4)	4.538 (Q1)	5.568
Educational Technology & Society	16	45 (2)	923 (2)	20.51 (14)	1.767 (Q2)	2.326
IEEE Transactions on Learning Technologies	9	32 (3)	333 (3)	10.41 (28)	1.869 (Q2)	2.5
British Journal of Educational Technology	7	8 (9)	121 (8)	15.13 (21)	2.729 (Q1)	3.142
Interactive Learning Environments	7	15 (5)	151 (6)	10.07 (29)	1.604 (Q2)	1.722
IEEE Transactions on Education	5	6 (11)	92 (10)	15.33 (20)	1.6 (Q2)	1.88
ETR&D-Educational Technology Research and Development	5	9 (7)	220 (4)	24.44 (10)	1.728 (Q2)	2.396
Journal of Computer Assisted Learning	4	6 (11)	82 (11)	13.67 (22)	1.859 (Q2)	3.055
International Journal of Engineering Education	4	14 (6)	51 (14)	3.64 (47)	0.575 (Q4)	0.663
Computer Applications in Engineering Education	4	16 (4)	118 (9)	7.38 (36)	1.153 (Q3)	0.973
Journal of Educational Psychology	4	5 (13)	129 (7)	25.80 (9)	4.433 (Q1)	6.197
Educational and Psychological Measurement	3	3 (16)	41 (18)	13.67 (22)	1.663 (Q2)	2.301
Computer Assisted Language Learning	3	5 (13)	24 (27)	4.80 (45)	1.928 (Q1)	2.366
Eurasia Journal of Mathematics Science and Technology Education	3	9 (7)	30 (23)	3.33 (48)	0.903 (Q3)	N/A

Abbreviations: R: ranking position; H: H-index; AC: article count; TC: citation count; ACP: citation count per article; IF (Q): impact factor and JCR quartile in category for year 2017.

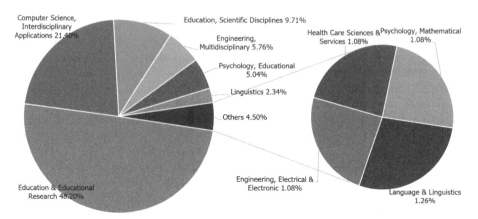

Fig. 2. The distribution of top 10 subjects of the retrieved articles.

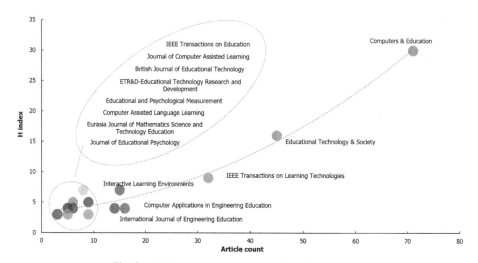

Fig. 3. H-index and article count of the listed journals

3.3   Analysis of Country/Region, Institution, and Author

58 countries/regions have participated in the 333 research articles. Table 2 displays the top 16 countries/regions ranked by H-index. Taiwan is the dominate region with an H-index value up to 29 (81 articles), followed by the USA (18 H-index, 72 articles). The two countries/regions together contribute 37.97% of the research field.

According to the comparison of ACP values between internationally collaborated articles and non-internationally collaborated articles, for countries/regions such as the USA, Canada, and UK, their ACP values of internationally collaborated articles are higher than that of non-internationally collaborated articles. This indicates that international collaboration can potentially improve their research quality. However, for countries/regions such as Taiwan and Australia, the ACP values of internationally collaborated articles are lower than that of non-internationally collaborated articles.

Table 2. Top countries/regions ranked by H-index

Name	H	AC (R)	TC	ACP (R)	IC (%)	ACP	
						IC	NIC
Taiwan	29	81 (1)	2,498	30.84 (8)	7.41	18.83	31.80
USA	18	72 (2)	1,027	14.26 (19)	26.39	17.58	13.08
Australia	8	14 (7)	223	15.93 (16)	42.86	11.83	19.00
Canada	7	17 (5)	193	11.35 (26)	64.71	12.91	8.50
Greece	7	11 (9)	200	18.18 (13)	18.18	4.00	21.33
UK	6	15 (6)	155	10.33 (28)	46.67	12.86	8.13
Germany	6	7 (11)	172	24.57 (10)	57.14	24.50	24.67
Singapore	6	7 (11)	108	15.43 (18)	42.86	20.67	11.50
Turkey	6	24 (3)	341	14.21 (20)	12.50	0.33	16.19
Argentina	5	5 (19)	333	66.60 (1)	0	NA	66.60
Belgium	5	7 (11)	122	17.43 (14)	28.57	26.00	14.00
Spain	5	18 (4)	170	9.44 (31)	38.89	3.00	13.55
Netherlands	4	7 (11)	141	20.14 (11)	57.14	19.50	21.00
China	4	12 (8)	186	15.50 (17)	50.00	20.33	10.67
Portugal	4	7 (11)	90	12.86 (22)	28.57	12.50	13.00
Serbia	4	9 (10)	103	11.44 (25)	44.44	17.75	6.40

Abbreviations: R: ranking position; H: H-index; AC: article count; TC: citation count; ACP: citation count per article; IC: articles with international collaboration; NIC: articles without international collaboration.

398 institutions have participated in the research work, yet 76% of them have only one research article. Table 3 displays the top 16 institutions ranked by H-index, among which 9 are from Taiwan, again demonstrating a dominate position and contribution of Taiwan. *National Cheng Kung University* and *National Taiwan University of Science and Technology* are top two institutions.

National Council for Science and Technology and *Chung Hua University* have high ACP values (78.00 and 78.25) although with relatively less articles (4 articles each), indicating the high quality of their research articles. For most institutions, the international collaboration rates are higher than 50%, especially *National Council for Science and Technology*, *Athabasca University*, and *Chung Hua University* with an international collaboration rate of 100%. The ACP values of internationally collaborated articles for most institutions are higher than that of articles without international collaboration.

936 authors have participated in the research articles, yet 91% of them have only one research article in the dataset. Table 4 displays the top 18 authors ranked by H-index, among which 9 are from Taiwan. *Gwo-Jen Hwang* and *Chih-Ming Chen* are top two

Table 3. Top institutions ranked by H-index

Institutions	Country/region	H	AC (R)	TC	ACP	IC(%)	ACP	
							IC	NIC
National Cheng Kung University	Taiwan	9	12 (1)	331	27.58	58.33	33.57	19.20
National Taiwan University of Science and Technology	Taiwan	8	11 (2)	707	64.27	90.91	70.30	4.00
National Central University	Taiwan	6	7 (5)	251	35.86	71.43	29.00	53.00
National University of Tainan	Taiwan	6	10 (3)	338	33.80	90.00	33.56	36.00
National Taiwan Normal University	Taiwan	6	7 (5)	211	30.14	57.14	20.75	42.67
National Chengchi University	Taiwan	6	7 (5)	478	68.29	71.43	36.80	147.00
National Chiao Tung University	Taiwan	6	8 (4)	172	21.50	87.50	22.86	12.00
University of Piraeus	Greece	5	6 (8)	135	22.50	50.00	36.00	9.00
Nanyang Technological University	Singapore	5	5 (10)	83	16.60	40.00	24.00	11.67
National Council for Science and Technology	Argentina	4	4 (12)	312	78.00	100.00	78.00	NA
University of Sydney	Australia	4	4 (12)	98	24.50	NA	NA	24.50
Athabasca University	Canada	4	5 (10)	123	24.60	100.00	24.60	NA
Chung Hua University	Taiwan	4	4 (12)	313	78.25	100.00	78.25	NA
Ming Chuan University	Taiwan	4	4 (12)	70	17.50	75.00	14.67	26.00
Middle East Technical University	Turkey	4	4 (12)	298	74.50	50.00	13.00	136.00
The University of Memphis	USA	4	6 (8)	94	15.67	83.33	13.80	25.00

Abbreviations: R: ranking position; H: H-index; AC: article count; TC: citation count; ACP: citation count per article; IC: article with international collaboration; NIC: article without international collaboration.

Table 4. Top authors ranked by H-index

Authors	C	H	AC (R)	TC	ACP	Authors	C	H	AC (R)	TC	ACP
Gwo-Jen Hwang	Taiwan	9	10 (1)	661	66.10	*Detmar Meurers*	Germany	3	3 (10)	47	15.67
Chih-Ming Chen	Taiwan	6	7 (2)	647	92.43	*Maria Virvou*	Greece	3	4 (6)	28	7.00
Analia Amandi	Argentina	5	5 (3)	333	66.60	*Kuo-En Chang*	Taiwan	3	3 (10)	124	41.33
Shian-Shyong Tseng	Taiwan	5	5 (3)	118	23.60	*Nian-Shing Chen*	Taiwan	3	4 (6)	120	30.00
Jun-Ming Su	Taiwan	4	4 (6)	88	22.00	*Chih-Yueh Chou*	Taiwan	3	4 (6)	104	26.00
Chin-Chung Tsai	Taiwan	4	5 (3)	341	68.20	*Chenn-Jung Huang*	Taiwan	3	3 (10)	43	14.33
Patricio Garcia	Argentina	3	3 (10)	291	97.00	*Yueh-Min Huang*	Taiwan	3	3 (10)	158	52.67
Silvia Schiaffino	Argentina	3	3 (10)	291	97.00	*Yao-Ting Sung*	Taiwan	3	3 (10)	124	41.33
Roger Nkambou	Canada	3	3 (10)	36	12.00	*Luiz Amaral*	USA	3	3 (10)	47	15.67

Abbreviations: R: ranking position; H: H-index; C: Country/region; A: article count; TC: citation count; ACP: citation count per article; IC: articles with international collaboration; NIC: articles without international collaboration.

authors. It is worth noting that *Patricio Garcia* and *Silvia Schiaffino* have high ACP values (97.00 each) although with relatively less articles (3 articles each), indicating the high quality of their research articles.

3.4 Research Topic and Evolution Analysis

Top frequently used terms in different time periods are identified, as shown in Table 5. For the period 2001–2018, the top terms ranked by frequency include 'environment' (44.74%), 'adaptive' (41.14%), and 'intelligent' (40.84%). From the trend test results in the table, terms such as 'adaptive' 'performance', and 'technology' have experienced a significant growth over the study periods, while terms 'web' and 'information' have experienced a significant decreasing trend.

Figure 4 depicts the major terms covered in the articles in each time period. For period 2001–2006, less terms are involved due to limited articles available. Top important terms include 'intelligence', 'tutoring', 'web', and 'learner'. For period 2007–2012, top important terms include 'learner', 'intelligence', 'tutoring', and 'environment'. For period 2013–2018, top important terms include 'environment', 'adaptive', 'education', 'data', 'performance', and 'self'. By comparing the three periods, some interesting findings are as follows. Firstly, terms such as 'education' and 'educational' are gaining constant attention, indicating that they are always main foci in the research. Secondly, terms such as 'adaptive', 'environment', 'data', 'self', and 'performance', are becoming more and more important. This indicates that there are growing interests among scholars in user adaptive learning research. Further, terms such as 'intelligence' and 'tutoring' are getting less and less attention with time going on. In addition, some terms have experienced sudden change of attention. For example, term 'web' enjoys great attention in the first period, however, it disappears suddenly in the latter two periods. Comparing with the first and last periods, term 'learner' gets the most importance in the second period.

Table 5. Top frequently used terms for different periods of time

2001–2018					2001–2006		2007–2012		2013–2018	
Terms	%	Mann-Kendall test			Terms	%	Terms	%	Terms	%
		Z	p	trend						
environment	44.74	0.2666	0.7898	↑	intelligent	53.85	learner	47.79	environment	48.62
adaptive	41.14	2.3518	0.0187	↑↑	tutoring	48.72	intelligent	46.90	adaptive	45.30
intelligent	40.84	−1.8966	0.0579	↓	web	48.72	tutoring	41.59	education	40.88
learner	39.94	−0.5705	0.5683	↓	learner	46.15	environment	38.94	performance	40.88
education	38.74	0.3433	0.7314	↑	environment	43.59	performance	36.28	data	36.46
tutoring	37.84	−1.7057	0.0881	↓	knowledge	41.03	adaptive	35.40	analysis	35.91
performance	35.74	3.461	0.0005	↑↑↑↑	adaptive	38.46	education	35.40	educational	35.91
knowledge	34.23	−1.0641	0.2873	↓	education	38.46	e-learning	35.40	intelligent	34.25
analysis	33.63	1.2138	0.2248	↑	information	38.46	reserved	34.51	knowledge	33.70
educational	32.73	0.1137	0.9095	↑	content	35.90	knowledge	32.74	learner	33.70
technology	30.33	2.6192	0.0088	↑↑↑	design	33.33	web	31.86	tutoring	33.15
computer	29.43	−0.6081	0.5431	↓	educational	33.33	analysis	30.97	technology	32.04
data	29.43	1.5202	0.1285	↑	analysis	30.77	computer	30.09	design	30.39
design	28.53	−0.5694	0.5691	↓	technology	30.77	course	30.09	computer	29.28
process	28.23	0	1	–	computer	28.21	process	29.20	different	28.18
course	27.63	0.8002	0.4236	↑	development	28.21	content	28.32	process	28.18
web	27.33	−2.0513	0.0402	↓↓	domain	28.21	information	28.32	achievement	26.52
e-learning	25.83	0.1895	0.8497	↑	tool	28.21	educational	27.43	course	26.52
different	25.53	1.2527	0.2103	↑	course	25.64	technology	27.43	teaching	25.97
content	24.02	0.2280	0.8197	↑	issue	25.64	support	25.66	group	25.41
information	24.02	−2.1242	0.0337	↓↓	process	25.64	design	23.89	developed	24.86
support	23.42	−1.7082	0.0876	↓	support	25.64	time	23.89	strategy	24.31
teaching	23.12	0.4942	0.6212	↑	application	23.08	user	23.89	self	23.20
reserved	21.92	−1.7841	0.0744	↓	focus	23.08	different	23.01	individual	22.10
individual	21.62	1.4811	0.1386	↑	framework	23.08	evaluation	23.01	school	22.10

Abbreviations: %: percentage of articles; p: significance level; –: no significant change of trend. ↑(↓): increasing (decreasing) trend but not significant with an p value > 0.05, ↑↑(↓↓), ↑↑↑(↓↓↓), ↑↑↑↑(↓↓↓↓): significantly increasing (decreasing) trend with p value < 0.05, < 0.01, and < 0.001 respectively.

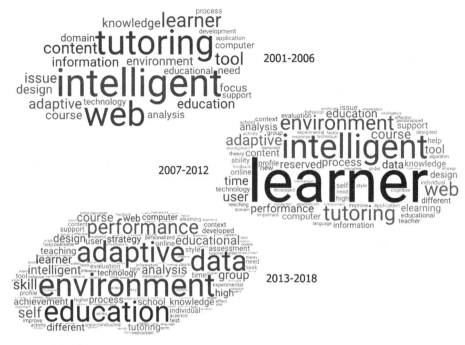

Fig. 4. Term evolution during year 2001–2006, 2007–2012, and 2013–2018.

4 Conclusion

This study presents the analysis of articles in the research field of AI assisted user modeling during years 2001–2018 from a bibliometric point of view. Based on the 333 retrieved articles, this paper recognizes influential authors, institutions, countries/regions, as well as journals and subjects, and reveals distribution and evolution of topics. Trend analysis of article count indicates a continuing development of the research field. The analyzing results can potentially benefit scholars in the field by raising their aware of the research status and research topic evolution. Admittedly, in this study, only WoS was adopted to retrieve research articles. Thus, further investigations would be needed to include more relevant articles indexed by other databases like Scopus.

Acknowledgements. This work was supported by National Natural Science Foundation of China (No.61772146).

References

1. Mwanza, D., Engeström, Y.: Pedagogical Adeptness in the Design of E-Learning Environments: Experiences from the Lab@ Future project. In: E-Learn: World Conference on E-Learning in Corporate, Government, Healthcare, and Higher Education, pp. 1344–1347. AACE (2003)

2. Leow, F.T., Neo, M.: Interactive multimedia learning: innovating classroom education in a Malaysian University. Turkish Online J. Educ. Technol.-TOJET **13**(2), 99–110 (2014)

3. Papatheocharous, E., Belk, M., Germanakos, P., Samaras, G.: Towards implicit user modeling based on artificial intelligence, cognitive styles and web interaction data. Int. J. Artif. Intell. Tools **23**(02), 1440009 (2014)

4. Brusilovsky, P., Millán, E.: User models for adaptive hypermedia and adaptive educational systems. In: Brusilovsky, P., Kobsa, A., Nejdl, W. (eds.) The Adaptive Web. LNCS, vol. 4321, pp. 3–53. Springer, Heidelberg (2007). https://doi.org/10.1007/978-3-540-72079-9_1

5. Wu, X., Kumar, V., Quinlan, J.R., Ghosh, J., Yang, Q., Motoda, H., et al.: Top 10 algorithms in data mining. Knowl. Inf. Syst. **14**(1), 1–37 (2008)

6. Mobasher, B.: Data mining for web personalization. In: Brusilovsky, P., Kobsa, A., Nejdl, W. (eds.) The Adaptive Web. LNCS, vol. 4321, pp. 90–135. Springer, Heidelberg (2007). https://doi.org/10.1007/978-3-540-72079-9_3

7. Pierrakos, D., Paliouras, G., Papatheodorou, C., Spyropoulos, C.D.: Web usage mining as a tool for personalization: a survey. User Model. User-Adap. Inter. **13**(4), 311–372 (2003)

8. Eirinaki, M., Vazirgiannis, M.: Web mining for web personalization. ACM Trans. Internet Technol. (TOIT) **3**(1), 1–27 (2003)

9. Pérez-Acebo, H., Linares-Unamunzaga, A., Abejón, R., Rojí, E.: Research trends in pavement management during the first years of the 21st century: a bibliometric analysis during the 2000–2013 period. Appl. Sci. **8**(7), 1041 (2018)

10. Song, Y., Chen, X., Hao, T., Liu, Z., Lan, Z.: Exploring two decades of research on classroom dialogue by using bibliometric analysis. Comput. Educ. **137**, 12–31 (2019)

11. Chen, X., Wang, S., Tang, Y., Hao, T.: A bibliometric analysis of event detection in social media. Online Inf. Rev. **43**(1), 29–52 (2019)

12. Hao, T., Chen, X., Li, G., Yan, J.: A bibliometric analysis of text mining in medical research. Soft. Comput. **22**(23), 7875–7892 (2018)

13. Chen, X., Liu, Z., Wei, L., Yan, J., Hao, T., Ding, R.: A comparative quantitative study of utilizing artificial intelligence on electronic health records in the USA and China during 2008–2017. BMC Med. Inform. Decis. Mak. **18**(5), 117 (2018)

14. Chen, X., Lun, Y., Yan, J., Hao, T., Weng, H.: Discovering thematic change and evolution of utilizing social media for healthcare research. BMC Med. Inform. Decis. Mak. **19**(2), 50 (2019)

15. Chen, X., Ding, R., Xu, K., Wang, S., Hao, T., Zhou, Y.: A bibliometric review of natural language processing empowered mobile computing. Wireless Communications and Mobile Computing, **2018** (2018)

16. Chen, X., Xie, H., Wang, F.L., Liu, Z., Xu, J., Hao, T.: A bibliometric analysis of natural language processing in medical research. BMC Med. Inform. Decis. Mak. **18**(1), 14 (2018)

17. Chen, X., Hao, J., Chen, J., Hua, S., Hao, T.: A bibliometric analysis of the research status of the technology enhanced language learning. In: Hao, T., Chen, W., Xie, H., Nadee, W., Lau, R. (eds.) SETE 2018. LNCS, vol. 11284, pp. 169–179. Springer, Cham (2018). https://doi.org/10.1007/978-3-030-03580-8_18

18. Chen, X., Weng, H., Hao, T.: A data-driven approach for discovering the recent research status of diabetes in China. In: Siuly, S., et al. (eds.) HIS 2017. LNCS, vol. 10594, pp. 89–101. Springer, Cham (2017). https://doi.org/10.1007/978-3-319-69182-4_10

19. Chen, X., Chen, B., Zhang, C., Hao, T.: discovering the recent research in natural language processing field based on a statistical approach. In: Huang, T.-C., Lau, R., Huang, Y.-M., Spaniol, M., Yuen, C.-H. (eds.) SETE 2017. LNCS, vol. 10676, pp. 507–517. Springer, Cham (2017). https://doi.org/10.1007/978-3-319-71084-6_60

20. Hassan, S.U., Haddawy, P., Zhu, J.: A bibliometric study of the world's research activity in sustainable development and its sub-areas using scientific literature. Scientometrics **99**(2), 549–579 (2014)

21. Zawacki-Richter, O., Latchem, C.: Exploring four decades of research in computers & education. Comput. Educ. **122**, 136–152 (2018)
22. Zhong, S., Geng, Y., Liu, W., Gao, C., Chen, W.: A bibliometric review on natural resource accounting during 1995–2014. J. Cleaner Prod. **139**, 122–132 (2016)
23. Gimenez, E., Salinas, M., Manzano-Agugliaro, F.: Worldwide research on plant defense against biotic stresses as improvement for sustainable agriculture. Sustainability **10**(2), 391 (2018)
24. Hirsch, J.E., Buela-Casal, G.: The meaning of the H-Index. Int. J. Clin. Health Psychol. **14**(2), 161–164 (2014)
25. Mann, H.B.: Nonparametric tests against trend. Econometrica J. Econometric Soc. **13**(3), 245–259 (1945)

Analyzing the Influence of Academic Papers Based on Improved PageRank

Chang Ji, Yong Tang, and Guohua Chen$^{(\boxtimes)}$

School of Computer Science, South China Normal University, Guangzhou, China
jimmy_flower@foxmail.com, ytang@m.scnu.edu.cn, chenguohua1984@qq.com

Abstract. The number of papers, published in different fields, is continually increasing, but the quality of papers varies widely. Scholars evaluate the quality and influence of a paper by the number of times the paper was cited, but the result of this citation quantity method is not accurate enough especially for new papers. Our society needs an accurate, objective and fair evaluation of papers. To address these problems, this article presents a method for evaluating the impact of papers. We analyze the influence of each academic paper in the citation network based on the improved PageRank algorithm and combined with the personal influence of the authors and the published date. Thus, this method tends to select high-quality authors and high-quality citations as high-impact papers. The comparison results showed that our method outperformed the traditional method of citation number and PageRank algorithm.

Keywords: Analyzing influence · Influence of academic papers · PageRank · Influence of authors

1 Introduction

The academic influence has always been a high concern of research scholars, and it plays a decisive role in fund application, talent plan declaration and so on. The influence of papers is an important part of academic influence. High-impact papers often give authors a better reputation and inspire others, even lead to a new field. The importance of high-impact papers is obvious, so the key question is how to judge whether these are high-impact papers, therefore, the evaluation method is particularly important. In general, two methods are commonly used to evaluate the value of the impact of the paper. One is based on the Impact Factor (IF) of journals [1], the other one is based on the citation number [2,3].

A high-IF journal not always publishes high-impact papers, thus, the journal IF is not suitable for the assessment of the impact of papers [4]. The key point of journal IF is based on citation number. The more citation journals obtain, the higher IF journals have. So without the number of citations, the IF of journals makes no sense. The number of times the papers were cited can reflect the papers' influence under some certain conditions, but there are still some issues.

© Springer Nature Switzerland AG 2020
E. Popescu et al. (Eds.): SETE 2019, LNCS 11984, pp. 214–225, 2020.
https://doi.org/10.1007/978-3-030-38778-5_24

The first issue is new papers are less cited than the old, old papers have longer exposure time, so the citation numbers are bigger than new papers generally. This will lead to a special situation, an old paper is considered to be more influential than a new paper by the method of citation number, but this is not true in reality. Second issue is the different periods of citation have different meanings, it has been claimed in [5] that short-term citations can be considered as currency at the research front, whereas long-term citations can contribute to the codification of knowledge claims into concept symbols. In order to solve these problems, this article studies some related content.

We mentioned two issues above. For the first issue, this article proposes a method that combines the authors' impact. Influence of authors is an important indicator of the paper's influence. For those authors who have published many high-impact papers, their next new paper may also be high-impact too. So we can roughly infer the impact value of the author's new papers when we get the impact value of the author. For the second issue, this article suggests a method that considers the year interval of two papers (paper and its reference). For the evaluation of papers, short-term citations are not significant as long-term citations, so we can combine the year interval to weight the impact value that reflects the different citations.

The contribution of this paper is that we adopt the GapYear-Rank approach to improve the existing evaluation methods we have discussed, combining the authors' influence and the structure in the citation network.

2   Related Work

The indicators of papers influence and calculation methods are attracting argues for a long time, we discuss these related three issues. They are the relationship between citation and papers' influence, the difference between short-term and long-term citations, and the method of calculating influence. We will discuss these issues in the rest.

According to research by Filippo Radicchi et al. [6], when scientists have enough information and can indeed make objective and fair choices, their judgment on the impact of papers is consistent with the number of papers been cited. That is to say, papers with more citation have greater influence. A paper, although released in a high IF publication for a few years, and it is rarely quoted, indicating that whether it is released or not, except for the author himself, it's the same for peers. In other words, this paper has little influence on the development of the subject area [7]. So a high-impact paper usually has more citation, evaluating papers according to the number of citation is a proper way to work.

There is a difference between short-term citation and long-term citation, the summary of [5] shows that a majority of the indicators used for the evaluation for the papers and journals are biased towards short-term impact, it can be expected to lead to a selection bias that is skewing the results of evaluations in favor of short-term impact. It may lead scholars to prefer to publish papers on popular topics for higher impact factor to improve the reputation and influence of himself while ignoring some other important topics and underestimating some scholar who made real contributions in some unpopular field. There is a special case, called sleeping beauties [8]. Sleeping beauty in science refers to a paper whose importance is not recognized for decades after publication. Its citation history exhibits a long hibernation period followed by a sudden spike of popularity. Considering these conditions and this issue, this article separates these conditions and carries out different processing to make the evaluation of papers more objective and fair.

PageRank algorithm is one of the methods that Google used to evaluate the webpages' impact to improve the quality of web search engines [9]. It helps Google a lot in the search engine field and dictates the rules for everyone else [10]. This algorithm has been widely applied not only to rank web search results but also to rank the academic papers [11]. PageRank is a mathematical algorithm that evaluates the quality and quantity of links to a webpage. This evaluation helps it to determine a relative score of the page's importance and authority [12]. This algorithm draws on the general method of evaluating the importance of papers in academia, by using the data about citation to evaluate the web-page, so using PageRank algorithm to evaluate the influence or quality of papers is a backtracking practice and suitable method.

The basic idea of PageRank is based on two assumptions. One is the quantity assumption, if page x is linked by more pages, it means that the more important x is. Another is the quality assumption, if the page y is linked by a higher quality page, it means that the quality of y is higher. Intuitively, *qq.com* created by *Tencent* is a famous, popular, high-impact page in China, reflected by the fact that many pages link it. Likewise, pages prominently pointed to from *qq.com* are themselves probably important [13]. Let *PR(x)* represent the importance of page x, so we can use the out-links of page x to calculate the *PR(x)*. Generally speaking, we pre-give an initial PR for each web page as *1*, and N is the total number of web's out-link. For example, *Nx* is the out-degree of page x. since the physical meaning of the PR is the access probability of a web page. Let *By* represent the set of pages pointing to y. In each iteration, propagate the ranks as follows:

$$PR(y) = \sum_{x \in By} \frac{PR(x)}{Nx} \qquad (1)$$

But there are two special situations should be concerned. One is that some selfish web-pages which do not have any out-link except itself, its value of PR will only increase while iterating. Another is web-pages do not have out-link including itself, all the PR will become zero while iterating. Both of them are unreasonable. To solve these special situations, we can image real people who surf on the internet, while facing these web-pages, they won't be trapped here. We assume that they have a certain probability of inputting URL to jump to a random web-page directly, and the probability of jumping to each web-page is the same, and we use α to represent the probability. The improved formula is as follows:

$$PR(y) = \frac{1-\alpha}{M} + \alpha \sum_{x \in By} \frac{PR(x)}{Nx} \qquad (2)$$

M is the number of all web-pages. This modification improves the quality of PageRank by considering the influence of all web-pages to page y, the value is $(1-\alpha)/M$, so the beginning PR should be multiplied by α. Now we turn this formula into matrix form and PR represent the one-dimensional array about all web-pages' PR:

$$PR = \begin{bmatrix} (1-\alpha)/M \\ (1-\alpha)/M \\ \vdots \\ (1-\alpha)/M \end{bmatrix} + \alpha \begin{bmatrix} l(p_1,p_1) & \cdots & l(p_1,p_M) \\ \vdots & \ddots & \vdots \\ l(p_M,p_1) & \cdots & l(p_M,p_M) \end{bmatrix} PR \qquad (3)$$

If the page i doesn't link the page j, the $l(p_i,p_j) = 0$ for each j. the matrix should satisfy one condition:

$$\sum_{i=1}^{M} l(p_i,p_j) = 1 \qquad (4)$$

Larry sets α to 0.85.

The practice has proved that PageRank performed well in ranking web-pages' impact, there are some differences while applying this method in ranking papers' impact. It will be discussed in the next section.

3   The Method

3.1   Overview of Proposed Evaluation Methods

Our proposed evaluation method combines the influence of the authors, this method considers the relationship among the papers in the citation network and evaluates the influence of authors by their papers. The process for the proposed method comprises five steps: (1) cleaning dataset and structuring it into database, (2) calculating the initial papers' PR in citation network by using PageRank, (3) calculating the authors' impact value by initial papers' PR, (4) calculating the initial papers' PR from authors' impact value and (5) calculating the papers' final PR by using improved PageRank named GapYear-Rank. An overview of the procedure for the proposed method is shown in Fig. 1.

3.2   Calculating Author Impact

We get initial papers' PR by using traditional PageRank algorithm, it could not be accurate and the evaluation of the new paper is not friendly, but it is enough to calculate the author's impact factor. We have considered the order of authors, every one paper has many authors and authors have a different contribution, our

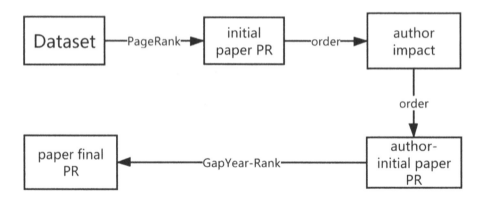

Fig. 1. The procedure of the evaluation method.

main point is the more you contribute, the more points you add. The first author can get all the impact value of the paper, the second author can get half of that, we especially take the corresponding author into consideration, and treat them as the second author. These formulas are as follows:

$$\text{paperAuthor}(x) = PR(x) \times 2^{\text{order}-1} \tag{5}$$

$$\text{correspondingAuthor}(x) = PR(x) \times \frac{1}{2} \tag{6}$$

$$author(z) = \frac{\sum_{x \in z} \text{paperAuthor}(x) + \text{corresponding Author}(x)}{N_z} \tag{7}$$

$PR(x)$ is the initial PR of paper x, $paperAuthor(x)$ is the authors of paper x, the *order* is the authors' order when published on publication, *correspondingAuthor(x)* is the corresponding author of paper x, and always the last author of the paper. *Author(z)* is the authors' impact factor, Nz is the total number of author z's score records, and z is each author. While calculating all the *paperAuthor(x)* and *correspondingAuthor(x)*. Finally, adding all scores of each author to average and get all the authors' impact factor.

3.3   Calculating Initial PR of Paper

After we get all the authors' impact, we can assign initial PR values to all papers by the authors, whether it is a new paper or an old paper, we only care about the composition of the authors and their corresponding impact scores. Just as we calculate the authors' impact, we consider the authors' order as well. The first author contributes the biggest part of a paper, the second contributes less than the first, and so on. We use the same formula as calculating authors in calculating Initial PR:

$$\text{Init}_{PR(x)} = \sum_{z \in x} author(z) \times 2^{order-1} \tag{8}$$

We use *InitPR(x)* to represent the initial value of the paper based on the authors' impact, and add all the processed *author(z)* from paper x to get all the *InitPR(x)*. This operation solves the problem of cold start in PageRank and makes the result of evaluation more accurate and reasonable. But it is not enough to use the variable of author impact to evaluate the paper, we still need a citation network in the next work.

3.4 GapYear-Rank

We solved the issue of new published papers' evaluation. To be more accurate for distinguishing the differences of short-term citation and long-term citation, we considered the year interval between the paper and the reference, and weighted calculation to achieve an effect, that is, short-term citation based on the author's impact, long-term citation based on the citation network. We named the improved algorithm based on PageRank as GapYear-Rank. The formula of weight in GapYear-Rank is as follows:

$$\text{weight}_{x,y} = \frac{\log_2\left(\frac{y\,\text{ear}(x) - y\,\text{ear}(y)}{30} + 1\right) + 3}{4} \tag{9}$$

Weight$_{x,y}$ is the weight of paper x and reference y, *year(x)* is the published year of paper x. Because the biggest value of *year(x)* – *year(y)* is 70 in the dataset, by using this formula, we control the weights value range from 0.75 to 1.18, and with the interval increases, the weight is also increasing. And put the weights in PageRank algorithm in the matrix such as (10).

$$\begin{bmatrix} \text{weight}_{p_1,p_1} \times l\,(p_1,p_1) & \cdots & \text{weight}_{p_1,p_M} \times l\,(p_1,p_M) \\ \vdots & \ddots & \vdots \\ \text{weight}_{p_M,p_1} \times l\,(p_M,p_1) & \cdots & \text{weight}_{p_M,p_M} \times l\,(p_M,p_M) \end{bmatrix} \tag{10}$$

And we initiated the first iteration matrix of papers' PR based on the authors' impact, high impact author has a larger base in the GapYear-Rank algorithm's iterations, this can solve the issue of new paper has a smaller cited number. The weight in GapYear-Rank algorithm can solve the issue of citation in a different term.

4 Experimental and Results

4.1 Experimental Data

AMiner is designed to search and perform data mining operations against academic publications on the Internet, using social network analysis to identify connections between researchers, conferences, and publications [14], it also provides some open datasets. Our dataset comes from the Citation Network Dataset of AMiner [15]. We choose the smaller dataset that contains 629,814 blocks. Each block contains the following information: (1) Index: every paper has unique index value, (2) Title: paper's title, (3) Year: the published year of paper, (4) Author: authors who participated in the publishing of this paper, (5) Reference: the index of references of this paper (there are multiple lines, with each indicating a reference). Table 1 is a basic outline of the data obtained.

Table 1. Summary of the dataset.

Data name	Block number
Paper	629814
Citation	629614
Author	1337943

Paper is every individual paper, Citation contains the paper's index and reference's index, Author is the authors of each paper are stored separately. Based on this dataset, we write three tables into a MySql database and generate two tables in the process of calculating PR.

4.2   Experimental Results

In this section, we demonstrate the most influential papers from experiments that used ten papers based on Citation numbers, PageRank and GapYear-Rank, shown in Tables 2, 3 and 4. We compare the performances of PageRank and GapYear-Rank in Fig. 2. The x-axis indicates the release year distribution for nearly eight decades, the y-axis shows the PR value of each paper.

Table 2. Top 10 ordered by papers' impact based on Citation number.

Rank	Title	Year	First author	#citations
1	Introduction to algorithms	1990	Thomas T. Cormen	814
2	Compilers: principles, techniques, and tools	1986	Alfred V. Aho	788
3	C4.5: programs for machine learning	1993	Adele Goldberg	645
4	Smalltalk-80: the language and its implementation	1983	Adele Goldberg	587
5	A relational model of data for large shared data banks	1970	E. F. Codd	566
6	Time, clocks, and the ordering of events in a distributed system	1978	Leslie Lamport	560
7	The nature of statistical learning theory	1995	Vladimir N. Vapnik	553
8	Pattern Classification (2nd Edition)	2000	Richard O. Duda	523
9	The art of computer programming, volume 1 (3rd ed.): fundamental algorithms	1997	Donald E. Knuth	521
10	The art of computer programming, volume 2 (3rd ed.): seminumerical algorithms	1997	Donald E. Knuth	504

Table 3. Top 10 ordered by papers' impact based on PageRank.

Rank	Title	Initial PR	Year	First author	#citations
1	Recovery semantics for a DB/DC system	1.14138e-04	1973	Charles T. Davies	17
2	Recovery scenario for a DB/DC system	1.12686e-04	1973	Lawrence A. Bjork	9
3	The art of computer programming, volume 2 (3rd ed.): seminumerical algorithms	1.09098e-04	1997	Donald E. Knuth	504
4	A method for obtaining digital signatures and public-key cryptosystems	1.08851e-04	1978	R. L. Rivest	366
5	The art of computer programming, volume 1 (3rd ed.): fundamental algorithms	1.06766e-04	1997	Donald E. Knuth	521
6	A relational model of data for large shared data banks	1.04805e-04	1970	E. F. Codd	566
7	Programming semantics for multiprogrammed computations	6.48747e-05	1966	Jack B. Dennis	122
8	Principles of interactive computer graphics (2nd ed.)	6.25748e-05	1979	Robert F. Sproull	224
9	Report on the algorithmic language ALGOL 60	5.75248e-05	1960	J. W. Backus	79
10	Ethernet: distributed packet switching for local computer networks	5.57950e-05	1976	Robert M. Metcalfe	176

Table 4. Top 10 ordered by papers' impact based on authors' impact and GapYear-Rank.

Rank	Title	Final PR	Year	First author	#citations
1	A relational model of data for large shared data banks	6.13085e-05	1970	E. F. Codd	566
2	A method for obtaining digital signatures and public-key cryptosystems	5.84014e-05	1978	R. L. Rivest	366
3	The art of computer programming, volume 2 (3rd ed.): seminumerical algorithms	4.03362e-05	1997	Donald E. Knuth	504
4	Introduction to algorithms	3.82750e-05	1990	Thomas T. Cormen	814
5	The art of computer programming, volume 1 (3rd ed.): fundamental algorithms	3.81922e-05	1997	Donald E. Knuth	521
6	Compilers: principles, techniques, and tools	3.28422e-05	1986	Alfred V. Aho	788
7	Principles of interactive computer graphics (2nd ed.)	3.19992e-05	1979	Robert F. Sproull	224
8	C4.5: programs for machine learning	3.19656e-05	1993	Adele Goldberg	645
9	The nature of statistical learning theory	3.14446e-05	1995	Vladimir N. Vapnik	553
10	Time, clocks, and the ordering of events in a distributed system	3.11257e-05	1978	Leslie Lamport	560

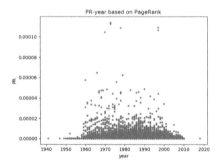
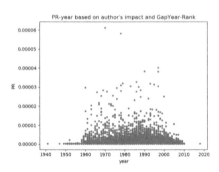

Fig. 2. The PR score of all papers based on PageRank algorithm and the author's impact with GapYear-Rank algorithm.

We find that the citation number of the third paper is 50 times more than the second paper from the Table 3. That is because the nine papers which cited the second paper are all high quality, their average value of initial PR has reached 1.90513e-05, at the same time, the average value of third paper is 7.69379e-07, so the second paper entered the top 10 by high quality, and the third paper entered the top 10 by huge quantity.

From Table 4, we will find that there are eight papers in both leaderboards while comparing with Table 2, and five papers while comparing with Table 3. It shows that the results of the three methods in this paper are generally close.

Table 5 shows the top 10 influential authors through our calculation based on the initial PR score of papers, author Charles T. Davies and author Lawrence A. Bjork are published only one paper but entered the top 10, the reason is that the method which we choose the top 10 authors is based on the average score of authors' published papers' initial PR, author Charles T. Davies, and Lawrence A. Bjork are both published a high impact value paper, so they could get high author's impact by their paper.

Table 5. Top 10 ordered by authors' impact based on initial papers' impact.

Order	Author Name	Number of papers published	Score
1	Donald E. Knuth	60	2.91248e-04
2	C. A. R. Hoare	74	2.05424e-04
3	E. F. Codd	17	1.46780e-04
4	Leslie Lamport	68	1.36488e-04
5	Peter J. Denning	144	1.36314e-04
6	Edsger W. Dijkstra	42	1.26873e-04
7	Niklaus Wirth	37	1.16712e-04
8	R. L. Rivest	9	1.14377e-04
9	Charles T. Davies	1	1.14138e-04
10	Lawrence A. Bjork	1	1.12686e-04

4.3   Experimental Results Analysis

The results of Tables 2, 3, and 4 are generally similar. But among them, the differences in Table 3 are more obvious, the citation number in the first and second rows of the table is less than other rows. In order to more intuitively refer to all data, we have made a distribution of the different number of the top papers based on these methods in Fig. 3. It is not difficult to find that the citation number line differs greatly from the other two lines, and the citation number line is roughly at the center of the two lines. From the variance analysis of the citation number of different years in Table 6, we find that the result of the citation number is larger than other methods in each column. It means the result of citation number has a large fluctuation in different years, which is unreasonable because high-impact papers always appear in a period of time. To some extent, the smaller variance results are fairer. Therefore, according to Fig. 3 and Table 6, PageRank and GapYear-Rank performed better than the citation number. That is because PageRank and GapYear-Rank also consider the relationship between citation networks, that is to say, these two methods not only take the quantity but also the quality into consideration.

But even the variance results of PageRank is smaller than GapYear-Rank, we can't conclude that the PageRank is better than GapYear-Rank, cause they both consider the citation numbers and citation relationships. So we are supposed to analyze deeper data.

We will find different PR score distributions from the two subgraphs in Fig. 2, we take some examples to illustrate the differences. The 9th top paper in GapYear-Rank, which is ranked 29th in PageRank has 553 cited papers, the cited number in ten years only accounted for 164, about 29.66% of the total, but in 2008 and 2009, the cited number has reached for 235, about 43.50% of the total. So this paper is probably the sleeping beauty we mentioned above, similar situations have appeared in other papers, such as the 8th and 10th top paper in GapYear-Rank, both of them are sleeping beauties and the 8th paper which titled *C4.5: programs for machine learning* has a great influence on the field of machine learning. From these results, we find that GapYear-Rank is better to find the influential papers and rank them in higher rankings.

Table 6. Variance data for different methods under different numbers.

Method	Top100	Top1000	Top10000	Top40000	Top100000
Citation Number	2.445535762	20.30101754	202.5769801	777.8393557	2043.0992805
PageRank	1.658073083	13.79588818	162.0823311	696.7836399	1851.0328457
GapYear-Rank	1.664412891	14.22866585	166.9732560	717.2119285	1860.0888123

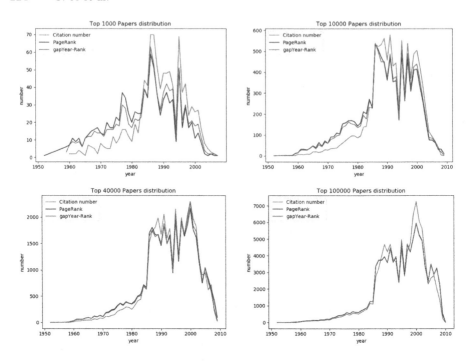

Fig. 3. The distribution of the different number of top papers based on these methods.

5   Conclusion

The vast amount of information currently available makes it important for researchers to rank the influence of papers. We improved the PageRank algorithm by considering the year interval into the matrix for iteration and changing the initial matrix of papers' PR on authors' impact. Our result, which based on GapYear-Rank algorithm combined authors, displays a more accuracy and objective result than the PageRank algorithm or rank by cited number. That means the author's impact and year interval of its citation are both effective approaches to analyze the papers' influence. Compared with the method by cited number rank, our method is more focus on the quality of the relationship in the citation network. Compared with the method by PageRank, our method is more care about the paper itself. So we combine the advantage of both method and could get a better rank of papers in our experiment. In the next work, we plan to combine the venue information or international IF score of the journal and construct the multi-level citation network to take the direct-quote and indirect-quote into consideration.

References

1. Du, M., Bai, F., Liu, Y.: PaperRank: a ranking model for scientific publications. In: 2009 WRI World Congress on Computer Science & Information Engineering, vol, 4, pp. 277-281 (2009). https://doi.org/10.1109/CSIE.2009.479
2. Beel, J., Gipp, B.: Google scholar's ranking algorithm: the impact of articles' age (an empirical study). In: 2009 Sixth International Conference on Information Technology: New Generations, pp. 160–164 (2009). https://doi.org/10.1109/ITNG.2009.317
3. Beel, J., Gipp, B.: Google scholar's ranking algorithm: the impact of citation counts (an empirical study). In: 2009 Third International Conference on Research Challenges in Information Science, pp. 439–446 (2009). https://doi.org/10.1109/RCIS.2009.5089308
4. Mariethoz, G., Karssenberg, D., Grana, D.: Who cares about impact factor?. J. Comput. Geosci. **115**, iii–iv (2018)
5. Leydesdorff, L., Bornmann, L., Comins, J.A., Milojevic, S.: Citations: indicators of quality? The impact fallacy. J. Front. Res. Metrics Analytics **1**, 1 (2016)
6. Radicchi, F., Weissman, A., Bollen, J.: Quantifying perceived impact of scientific publications. J. Informetrics. **11**(3), 704–712 (2017)
7. Wen, S.: Papers with more citations may not be influential. News. China Science Daily. 2 (2017)
8. Ke, Q., Ferrara, E., Radicchi, F., et al.: Defining and identifying Sleeping Beauties in science. Proc. Nat. Acad. Sci. U.S.A. **112**(24), 7426 (2015)
9. Liang, Y., Li, Q., Qian, T.: Finding relevant papers based on citation relations. In: Web-age Information Management, pp. 403–414 (2011). https://doi.org/10.1007/978-3-642-23535135
10. SEO PowerSuite: Beginner's Guide to Google PageRank: How It Works & Why It Still Matters in 2018. https://www.link-assistant.com/news/page-rank-2018.html. Accessed 20 Jul 2019
11. Gipp, B., Beel, J., Hentschel, C.: Scienstein: a research paper recommender system. In: Proceedings of the International Conference on Emerging Trends in Computing (ICETIC 2009), pp. 309–315 (2009)
12. Son, J.: Seoung Bum Kim: academic paper recommender system using multilevel simultaneous citation networks. J. Decis. Support Syst. **105**, 24–33 (2018)
13. Haveliwala, T.H: Topic-sensitive PageRank. In: International Conference on World Wide Web, pp. 517–526 (2002). https://doi.org/10.1145/511446.511513
14. Tang, J., Zhang, J., Yao, L., et al.: ArnetMiner: extraction and mining of academic social networks. In: Proceedings of the ACM SIGKDD International Conference on Knowledge Discovery and Data Mining, ACM, pp. 990–998 (2008). https://doi.org/10.1145/1401890.1402008
15. AMiner: Citation Network Dataset. https://www.aminer.cn/citation. Accessed 20 Jul 2019

A Systematic Review of Frameworks for Coding Towards Classroom Dialogue

Yu Song[1], Tianyong Hao[2(✉)], Zhinan Liu[1], and Zixin Lan[1]

[1] School of Education, South China Normal University, Guangzhou, China
sungyuepku@foxmail.com, newzhinan@foxmail.com,
cherrylam0114@foxmail.com
[2] School of Computer Science, South China Normal University, Guangzhou, China
haoty@m.scnu.edu.cn

Abstract. Classroom dialogue, characterized by its interactive features and verbal encounters between teachers and students or among students, has been commonly used in teaching and learning. This paper conducted a systematic review of the coding frameworks used in the examination of classroom dialogue. We discussed over three main issues relating to the development of coding frameworks: linguistic ethnography versus sociocultural approach, coding units and levels, and objects of coding. The review indicates that there are six themes that a dialogic framework should encapsulate in its categories, which are prior knowledge, personal information, analysis, generalization, speculation and uptakes. With this knowledge, scholars and practitioners would become more competent in designing or selecting frameworks.

Keywords: Classroom dialogue · Coding frameworks · Systematic review · Themes

1 Introduction

Classroom dialogue, characterized by its interactive features and verbal encounters between teachers and students or among students, has been commonly used in teaching and learning (Howe 2017). In literature, the term has been elaborated using various conceptualizations and terminologies, for example, accountable talk, dialogic teaching, assessment conversation, instructional dialogue and talk (Howe and Abedin 2013). Nevertheless, many of these terminologies are intended to indicate similar situations and share identical theoretical foundations, which can be shown in the following ways. Firstly, most work has been founded on the socio-cultural theory proposed by Vygotsky (1978), which bridges the relationships between thought, action, communication and culture (Alexander 2015; Howe and Abedin 2013). Secondly, language has been highlighted as a key medium for transmitting information from one mind to another, and for jointly constructed knowledge (Mercer 2010). Thirdly, a three-step pattern, initiation-response-feedback (IRF), as illustrated by Sinclair and Coulthard (1975), typically captures the patterns within these dialogic activities (Alexander 2017). Fourthly, people generally

© Springer Nature Switzerland AG 2020
E. Popescu et al. (Eds.): SETE 2019, LNCS 11984, pp. 226–236, 2020.
https://doi.org/10.1007/978-3-030-38778-5_25

believe that classroom dialogue is beneficial in terms of fostering thinking and learning, and particularly facilitates deep processing of knowledge (Howe et al. 2019). Making effective use of dialogue to increase students' learning achievement has been the main aim of research. A definition proposed by Howe and Abedin (2013) referring to classroom dialogue as the kind of communication in which one individual addresses another individual or individuals and at least one addressed individual replies, is broad enough to encapsulate many of these commonalities.

The number of publications on classroom dialogue has increased dramatically during the past 20 years, and interests in research on, and practical applications of, classroom dialogue has grown around the world (Song et al. 2019). When considering dialogue, scholars usually use the codes that emerge from specific scripts or they design a framework that is specific to their special research interests. Various coding frameworks, instruments and specific codes have been developed, which has made cross-study comparisons difficult, and has prevented the field from exerting the greater influence on policy and practice (Hennessy et al. 2016). Therefore a systematic review of the coding frameworks used in the examination of classroom dialogue is greatly needed in order to allow the emergence of typical themes, forms and functions across the frameworks. Scholars and practitioners would become more competent in designing or selecting frameworks.

2   Data Selection

This sample selection was based on a previous work of the authors (Song et al. 2019). 'Classroom' and its two associated terms 'whole-class' and 'small-group' were taken as one set of keywords and 'dialogue' and associated terms, 'dialogic', 'discourse', 'conversation', 'discussion', 'language', 'interaction', 'talk', 'communication' and 'speaking' acted as the other set of keywords in literature search. Publications were retrieved from the most important bibliometric database, Web of Science (WoS), and 3,914 publications were filtered after computer retrieval and artificial preprocessing. We checked these publications and retained the ones showing complete or parts of coding frameworks, which resulted in 51 articles remaining for reviewing. The follows information was systematically reviewed: name of instruments, contexts of the use of instruments (i.e. educational contexts and cultural contexts), coding domains, specific codes, and evaluation of frameworks (i.e. reliability and validity). A summary of the main coding domains is listed in Fig. 1.

3   The Analysis of Coding Framework Themes

As indicated in Howe et al. (2019), characteristics of classroom dialogue should display in order to optimize student outcomes. The review of publications indicates that there are six themes that a dialogic framework should encapsulate in its categories (see Table 1). Firstly, there should be categories that take account of *prior-known information*, which includes standard-referenced knowledge, rule-governed answers and a repetition of previous knowledge (see e.g. Alexander 2017; Chinn et al. 2000; Ruiz-Primo 2011). Standard-referenced knowledge is that which can be judged right or wrong with reference to textbooks or knowledge that teachers have taught before; rule-governed

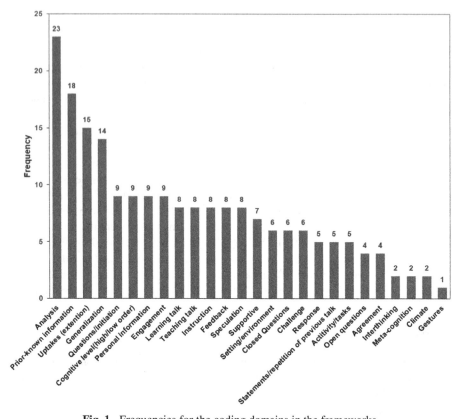

Fig. 1. Frequencies for the coding domains in the frameworks

dialogue is concerned culturally recognized explanations and solutions to a problem of an algorithmic kind which student(s) are expected to know or should be able to compute; repetition of previous knowledge refers to the dialogue narrating or describing previous contributions made by other students or teachers. It usually only requires recitation to contribute this kind of dialogue and does not involve a complicated process of thinking, which is recognized at a low-cognitive level (Chin 2006). Dialogue in this theme aims to help students obtain information, concepts, basic knowledge, facts, and to learn basic methods and ground rules.

The second theme deals with *personal information*, which is further divided into the categories of personal experience, imagination, subjective opinions and feelings/emotions (see e.g. Boyd and Markarian 2011; Fisher 2007; Galton et al. 1999; Hennessy et al. 2016). Dialogue coded as personal experience is an invitation or providing events in the speaker's life that are not assumed to be known to other participants; imagination is personal response of an imaginative kind to a situation or work of art; subjective opinions are what the speaker personally believes about a topic or situation of personal concern; feelings/emotions invites or describe affective and sensitive states. This kind of dialogue aims to help students express individual thoughts, emotions, opinions and feelings.

The third theme shown in coding frameworks is concerned with *analysis*, which can further be found in evaluation, explanation/justification and exemplification (see e.g. Boyd and Markarian 2011; Dolin et al. 2018; Hennessy et al. 2016; Nystrand et al. 2003). Evaluation is used to request or provide an opinion about how useful or appropriate another person's contribution (in words or action) has been; explanation/justification refers to an argument to support a preceding contribution or to show that it was reasonable or appropriate; exemplification requests more information, including examples, to supplement existing, relatively simple information or to illustrate a point that has just been made. Dialogue of this kind is characterized by the use of deductive reasoning and making knowledge explicit and easy to understand. The setting of codes in this theme aims to support students in digging deeper into their ideas and reasoning, and in abstractly separating a whole into its constituent parts in order to study the parts and their relationships.

The fourth theme is that coding should show the *coordination* of information, and summarization, comparison and connection are its main specific embodiments (see Alexander 2008; Kumpulainen and Lipponen 2014; Mercer and Littleton 2007; Reznitskaya and Gregory 2013). Summarization is a condensed statement of what has been said by one or more participants or the provision of only the main information; comparison refers to dialogue that examines the similarities or differences in knowledge and information; connection assesses whether dialogue builds and explores the relationships between things and information. This kind of dialogue helps students focus, connect, coordinate and reflect, and promotes deep learning. It is a process of formulating general concepts by reasoning from detailed facts and involves inductive reasoning and the development of ideas.

The fifth theme concerns *speculation*, which refers to dialogue that considers possibilities, going beyond the current state of knowledge but with a theoretical or factual basis (see e.g. Chin 2006; Mortimer and Scott 2003; Nystrand 1997; Ruiz-Primo 2011). This kind of dialogue supports students' generation of new ideas and develops creative abilities.

The sixth theme is that categories should be able to assess how teachers and students use *uptakes* (see e.g. Mortimer and Scott 2003; Ruiz-Primo 2011; Wells and Arauz 2006). The issue here concerns the way in which the previous response by somebody is taken up by others. Uptake can be realized in a comment that explicitly recognizes the previous response and builds on it in some way; or it can be manifested in a question that asks the previous responder to elaborate on what s/he has said. Extension of talk provides a constructive supplement based on previous talk, rather than simply a repetition of a previous articulation (see e.g., Alexander 2008; Nystrand 1997; O'Connor et al. 2015; Rojas-Drummond et al. 2010). The inclusion of this theme aims to encourage students to listen carefully to their peers' ideas; to build on, think and reason with others.

Table 1. Themes emerged from a review of dialogic frameworks

Themes	Codes in the dialogic frameworks
Prior-known information	Narrate, rote, recitation, exposition (Alexander 2017); Closed questions, direct speaker nominations, didactic statements, revoicing of student language, direct prompting (Boyd and Markarian 2011); repetitions (Chinn et al. 2000); provides background information (Dwyer et al. 2016); precise question, leading question, something missing (Ellegaard et al. 2017); sharing previous knowledge or experience (Fisher 2007); recasts, repetition, introduce authoritative perspective (Hennessy et al. 2016); reference back, reference to wider context (Howe et al. 2019); recall facts, providing information, offer ideas and solutions (closed) (Jay et al. 2017); factual questions, personal connection (Jie et al. 2016); knowledge (Lee and Irving 2018); direct, Closed questions (Lefstein et al. 2015); factual (Muhonen et al. 2017); fact, rule-governed answer, report of public event (Nassaji and Wells 2000); teaching social rule, teaching academic skill (National Institute of Child Health and Human Development Early Child Care Research Network 2002); learning basic skills (Nichd and Bonnie 2005); describing processes or reactions, definitions, stating laws, principles, terms, models, symbols, knowledge from everyday life (Podschuweit et al. 2016); recitation, revoice, rephrase/repeat (Robin 2018); tapping into diverse types of knowledge, type of information asked in the question (Ruiz-Priomo 2011); linking Concepts (Smith et al. 2013); reviewing, rote recall, previous conversation, memory/prior knowledge, fact, rule-governed answer (Wells and Arauz 2006)
Personal information	Everyday talk, imagine (Alexander 2017); open questions, inauthentic questions (Boyd and Markarian 2011); open question (Ellegaard et al. 2017); sharing experience, imagining and seeing things in the mind's eye (Fisher 2007); offer ideas and solutions (open) (Galton et al. 1999); invite opinions/beliefs/ideas (Hennessy et al. 2016); imagine (Jay et al. 2017); turn-taking management (Jie et al. 2016); open questions, presentation (Lefstein et al. 2015); experiential, imaginative, affectional, view (Muhonen et al. 2017); experience, imagination, opinion (Nassaji and Wells 2000); negative with peers, positive/neutral with peers, positive/neutral with teacher, negative with teacher (Nichd and Bonnie 2005); emotional engagement, emotional support (Pöysä et al. 2018); imagination, personal opinion, opinion (Wells and Arauz 2006)
Analysis	Explain, analyze, evaluate, justify, discuss, reasoning (Alexander 2017); explications (Boyd and Markarian 2011); precise valuing, precise correction (Dolin et al. 2018); facilitates reasoning, encourages students to provide evidence from text (Dwyer et al. 2016); wondering question (Ellegaard et al. 2017); giving examples (Fisher 2007); generative mechanisms, reasoning activities, acknowledgement, frames, forestall/secure, forestall/remove (Harney et al. 2017); ask for explanation or justification of another's contribution, invite building on/elaboration/(dis)agreement/evaluation of another's contribution or view, ask for explanation or justification, ask for elaboration or clarification, explain or justify another's contribution, explain or justify own contribution (Hennessy et al. 2016); elaboration, reasoning, elaboration of previous contributions, reasoned discussion of competing viewpoints (Howe et al. 2019); asking for clarifications (Hulsman and Vloodt 2015); why question, explain, evaluate, justify (Jay et al. 2017); comments (Jie et al. 2016); explanation/examples (Lee and Irving 2018); explain, elaborated feedback, explain, elaborated feedback (Lefstein et al. 2015); argumentational, expositional (Muhonen et al. 2017); Conventional explanation, explanation, amplification, justification (Nassaji and Wells 2000); learning analysis/inference (Nichd and Bonnie 2005); level of evaluation (Nystrand et al. 2003); analysis and inquiry; describing and justifying arrays of causes, giving reasons for linear chains of causes and effects or reaction schemes, justifying results or steps within a process, justifying factors of influence, deductive reasoning, calculations with multiple steps (Podschuweit et al. 2016); explain, analyse, evaluate, evidence of reasoning (Robin 2018); analysis of the interaction, analysis of the discourse, analysis of problem-solving (Rojas-Drummod et al. 2003); offering explanations, elaborating, offering explanations (Ruiz-Primo 2011); elaborated explanations, reasoning words (Soter et al. 2008); analysis/explanation, commenting (Wells and Arauz 2006); teacher explanation (Xie and Cao 2010)

(continued)

Table 1. (continued)

Themes	Codes in the dialogic frameworks
Coordination	Summarising (Dolin et al. 2018); Prompts students to make text-to-self connections, Draws out students' knowledge and experience, Synthesizes/ summarizes (Dwyer et al. 2016); Making connections and seeking relationships (Fisher 2007); Synthesise ideas, Compare/evaluate alternative views, Link learning to wider contexts (Hennessy et al. 2016); Simple coordination, Reasoned coordination, Linkage and coordination across contributions (Howe et al. 2019); Summarizing (Hulsman and Vloodt 2015); Summing up and refocusing (Jie et al. 2016); Asking children to sum up, Summing up (Jadallah et al. 2011); Connection, Summarize (Nassaji and Wells 2000); Describing or completing commonalities and differences, (Podschuweit et al. 2016); Summarizing (Ruiz-Priomo 2011); Relating a student's response to another student's response, Promoting students' questions and comments about a student's contribution, Comparing and contrasting students' ideas/contributions (Ruiz-Priomo 2011); Connection (Wells and Arauz 2006)
Speculation	Speculate (Alexander 2017); Speculate (Jay et al. 2017); Invite possibility thinking based on another's contribution, Invite possibility thinking or prediction, Speculate or predict on the basis of another's contribution, Speculate or predict, Propose resolution (Hennessy et al. 2016); Extrapolation (Mortimer and Scott 2003; Aguiar et al. 2010); Hypothetical (Muhonen et al. 2017); Conjecture, Prediction (Nassaji and Wells 2000); Speculate (Robin 2018); Speculation, Prediction, Conjecture (Liu et al. 2010)
Uptakes	Expand, clarify thinking (Alexander 2017); explore, dialogue (Alexander 2017); inter-thinking, redirecting, tie-ins (Boyd and Markarian 2011); extension by responsive questioning, focusing and Zooming (Chin 2006); uptake (Dolin et al. 2018); clarifies students' ideas (Dwyer et al. 2016); explicit correction, clarification requests, repair, needs-repair (Heift 2004); Build on/clarify others' contributions, clarify/elaborate own contribution (Hennessy et al. 2016); Asking for clarification (Jadallah et al. 2011); expand question (Jay et al. 2017); asking for clarification, fostering independence (Jie et al. 2016); uptake questions, repeat or repair question (Lefstein et al. 2015); uptake, repair, recast, translation, clarification request, metalinguistic feedback, elicitation, explicit correction, repetition (Lyster and Ranta 1997); accepts or clarifies student comments (Macgregor and Atkinson 2002); continuation (Mortimer and Scott 2003; Aguiar et al. 2010); uptake (Nystrand and Gamoran 1991); uptake (Nystrand et al. 2003); rephrasing, clarifying, elaborating, summarizing, and repeating help to verify students' responses, debugging (Ruiz-Priomo 2011); clarifying, relating a student's response to another student's response, comparing and contrasting students' ideas/contributions, connecting the discussion (conversation) to the learning goal (Ruiz-Priomo 2011); teacher invites students to expand on an utterance (Rojas-Drummond et al. 2013); uptake (Soter et al. 2008); clarification request, accept plus uptake (Wells and Arauz 2006)

4 The Analysis of Coding Framework Issues

People hold controversial views with regard to several main issues, which has led to the variety of coding forms and functions. The issues are illustrated first, together with a justification of our positionality.

(1) **Linguistic ethnography versus sociocultural approach**
Mercer (2010) shows that the research on classroom dialogue is mainly based on two approaches: linguistic ethnography and sociocultural approach. Coding frameworks developed according to the first approach usually closely examine a short

purposefully selected excerpt and use codes that emerge from a transcript (Rampton 2009). This usually employs a linguistic ethnography and allows adequate contextual detail and linguistic characteristics of dialogic teaching and learning to be examined (Lefstein 2008). In contrast, coding frameworks based on the sociocultural approach are more fundamental than those addressing language use and look beyond the surface forms of dialogue to demonstrate the relationship between language and thoughts (see e.g. Chin 2006; Fisher 2007; Muhonen et al. 2017). As a learning method, the ultimate goal of involvement in classroom dialogue is that it should prompt thinking and learning (Alexander 2017; Howe 2017). According to the socio-cultural approach, knowledge is a socially mediated product and can be built collaboratively between teacher and students or among students themselves (Mercer and Dawes 2014). Coding frameworks should be able to account for how dialogue acts as a social and cognitive mediation, and to elaborate the process of narrating, expressing, analysing, generalizing, speculating and constructing knowledge. From the review, more than 80% of publications have used the sociocultural approach when assessing classroom dialogue. We agree with the view of the majority that dialogue should go beyond its role as a linguistic tool in order to make important contributions to improving the quality of the teaching–learning process. This requires consideration of the cognitive function of language when developing or selecting coding frameworks.

(2) **Coding units and levels**

The unit of coding and analysis varies across studies. Dialogue can be coded at a single word, a sentence, or sentences in which at least one characterization or function is clearly identifiable (Chin 2006; Wells and Arauz 2006). Some coding frameworks focus on specific dialogic strategies or specific knowledge-building techniques (e.g. Alexander 2017; Hennessy et al. 2016). Others are broader when it comes to assessing dialogic activities or interactive behaviours during classroom teaching and learning (e.g. Galton et al. 1999; Jay et al. 2017; Mortimer and Scott 2003). Levels of coding are also different, and coding can be applied at a macro level or a micro level to elicit multi-dimensional information. Researchers, such as Saville-Troike (2003) and Hennessey et al. (2016), have used an ethnography of communication, which has established a system of hierarchical levels of analysis consisting of 'communicative acts' (CA) at a micro level; these are embedded within 'communicative events' (CE) at a meso level; which are in turn part of broader 'communicative situations' (CS) at a macro level. Some others, for example, Wells and Arauz (2006) and Nystrand et al. (2003) have proposed a five-level coding in which from the macro to micro levels there are episodes, sequences, exchanges, moves and acts. Howe et al. (2019) distinguish two levels of measurement of dialogue, turn-level coding and lesson-level ratings.

The selection of unit and levels of coding depends on research interests and at the same time, is influenced by methodology choice (Mercer 2010; O'Connor et al. 2015). A broad, macro-level coding is adaptable to large sample studies and quantitative analysis (Howe et al. 2019). It is time-consuming and costly to conduct data collection and analysis when using a detailed and micro-level coding framework (Gillies and Nichols 2015). Scholars tend to use qualitative research methods and work with a small number of students and teachers, thus the results are less likely to be generalizable to, or comparable with, other contexts (Gillies and Baffour 2017). Nevertheless, it allows us to move from merely describing frequencies or modelling in order to better explain what happens in the classroom (Bakeman and Gottman 1997), and to keep track of how knowledge is constructed collaboratively across time (Mercer and Dawes 2014). There seems to be a tension between the varied levels of coding. With the development of methodological technology (e.g. AI), it is likely that multiple levels and units of coding will be conducted with the large samples involved. The field of dialogue research has much to gain by using interdisciplinary research methods.

(3) **Objects of coding**

There are a number of frameworks focusing exclusively on the teacher's talk (e.g. Fisher 2007) or on that of student (e.g. Norman 1992; Mercer 2000; Mercer et al. 2004). In comparison, a few others have encompassed all utterances expressed either by the teacher or the students, and this seems to be a more recent trend (e.g. Howe et al. 2019; Hennessey et al. 2016). We are inclined to the second way of coding for the reason that teachers' and students' talk are more often connected to, or influenced by, each other. Although student talk must be our ultimate preoccupation because of its role in the shaping of thinking, learning and understanding, it is largely through the teacher's talk that the student's talk is facilitated, mediated, probed and extended - or, all too often, inhibited (Hennessy et al. 2016; Kumpulainen and Wray 2003). At the same time, teachers' initiations and feedback will be more effective only when appropriate to students' learning requirements and based on students' dialogue (Gillies and Baffour 2017).

5 Conclusion

Classroom dialogue, acting as a frequently used method for teaching and learning, has attracted much interest around the world and publications in this field keep increasing. The choice of coding frameworks matters in the assessment of dialogic teaching and learning. Various coding frameworks, instruments and specific codes have been developed, which has made cross-study comparisons difficult. This paper conducted a systematic review of the coding frameworks used in the examination of classroom dialogue. The review indicates that three issues are closely related to the development or choice of frameworks: linguistic ethnography versus sociocultural approach, coding units and levels, and objects of coding. At the same time, six main themes emerged from many of these codes and these should be encapsulated in a coding framework, which are prior knowledge, personal information, analysis, generalization, speculation and uptakes. With this knowledge, scholars and practitioners would be more competent in designing or selecting frameworks. Findings would be more feasible for comparisons across different educational and cultural contexts, which will make it possible for the field to exert greater influence on policy and practice.

Acknowledgements. This work was supported by National Natural Science Foundation of China (No. 61907017) and the Guangdong Philosophy and Social Science Foundation (No. GD18XJY23).

References

Aguiar, O.G., Mortimer, E.F., Scott, P.: Learning from and responding to students' questions: the authoritative and dialogic tension. J. Res. Sci. Teach. **47**(2), 174–193 (2010)

Alexander, R.J.: Essays on Pedagogy. Routledge, London (2008)

Alexander, R.J.: Teaching and learning for all? The quality imperative revisited. Int. J. Educ. Dev. **40**, 250–258 (2015)

Alexander, R.J.: Developing dialogue: process, trial, outcomes. Paper of 17th Biennial EARLI Conference, 31 August 2017, Tampere, Finland (2017)

Bakeman, R., Gottman, J.M.: Observing Interaction: An Introduction to Sequential Analysis. Cambridge University Press, Cambridge (1997)

Boyd, M.P., Markarian, W.C.: Dialogic teaching: talk in service of a dialogic stance. Lang. Educ. **25**(6), 516–534 (2011)

Chinn, C.A., O'Donnell, A.M., Jinks, T.S.: The structure of discourse in collaborative learning. J. Exp. Educ. **69**(1), 77–97 (2000)

Chin, C.: Classroom interaction in science: teacher questioning and feedback to students' responses. Int. J. Sci. Educ. **28**(11), 1315–1346 (2006)

Dolin, J., Bruun, J., Nielsen, S.S., Jensen, S.B., Nieminen, P.: The structured assessment dialogue. In: Dolin, J., Evans, R. (eds.) Transforming Assessment. CSER, vol. 4, pp. 109–140. Springer, Cham (2018). https://doi.org/10.1007/978-3-319-63248-3_5

Dwyer, J., Kelcey, B., Berebitsky, D., Carlisle, J.F.: A study of teachers' discourse moves that support text-based discussions. Elem. School J. **117**(2), 285–309 (2016)

Ellegaard, M., Damsgaard, L., Bruun, J., Johannsen, B.F.: Patterns in the form of formative feedback and student response. Assess. Eval. High. Educ. **43**(5), 727–744 (2017)

Fisher, R.: Dialogic teaching: developing thinking and metacognition through philosophical discussion. Early Child Dev. Care **177**(6–7), 615–631 (2007)

Galton, M., Hargreaves, L., Comber, C., Wall, D., Pell, T.: Changes in patterns of teacher interaction in primary classrooms: 1976-96. Br. Edu. Res. J. **25**(1), 23–37 (1999)

Gillies, R.M., Nichols, K.: How to support primary teachers' implementation of inquiry: teachers' reflections on teaching cooperative inquiry-based science. Res. Sci. Educ. **45**(2), 171–191 (2015)

Gillies, R.M., Baffour, B.: The effects of teacher-introduced multimodal representations and discourse on students' task engagement and scientific language during cooperative, inquiry-based science. Instr. Sci. **45**(4), 493–513 (2017)

Harney, O., Hogan, M., Quinn, S., et al.: Investigating the effects of peer to peer prompts on collaborative argumentation, consensus and perceived efficacy in collaborative learning. Comput. Support. Collab. Learn. **12**(3), 307–336 (2017)

Heift, T.: Corrective feedback and learner uptake in call. Recall **16**(1), 37–66 (2004)

Hennessy, S., et al.: Developing a coding scheme for analysing classroom dialogue across educational contexts. Learn. Culture Soc. Interact. **9**, 16–44 (2016)

Howe, C., Abedin, M.: Classroom dialogue: a systematic review across four decades of research. Camb. J. Educ. **43**(3), 325–356 (2013)

Howe, C.: Advances in research on classroom dialogue: commentary on the articles. Learn. Instr. **48**, 61–65 (2017)

Howe, C., Hennessy, S., Mercer, N., Vrikki, M., Wheatley, L.: Teacher-student dialogue during classroom teaching: does it really impact upon student outcomes? J. Learn. Sci. **28**(4–5), 462–512 (2019)

Hulsman, R.L., Vloodt, J.V.D.: Self-evaluation and peer-feedback of medical students' communication skills using a web-based video annotation system. Exploring content and specificity. Patient Educ. Couns. **98**(3), 356–363 (2015)

Jadallah, M., et al.: Influence of a teacher's scaffolding moves during child-led small-group discussions. Am. Educ. Res. J. **48**(1), 194–230 (2011)

Jay, T., et al.: Dialogic Teaching: Evaluation Report and Executive Summary. Education Endowment, London (2017)

Jie, Z., Shahbaz, M., Chunling, L., Richard, C.A.: What makes a more proficient discussion group in English language learners' classrooms? Influence of teacher talk and student backgrounds. Res. Teach. Engl. **51**(2), 183–207 (2016)

Kumpulainen, K., Wray, D.: Classroom Interactions and Social Learning: From Theory to Practice. Routledge, Abingdon (2003)

Kumpulainen, K., Lipponen, L.: Building on the positive in children's lives: a co-participatory study on the social construction of children's sense of agency. Early Child Dev. Care **184**(2), 211–229 (2014)

Lee, S.C., Irving, K.E.: Development of two-dimensional classroom discourse analysis tool (CDAT): scientific reasoning and dialog patterns in the secondary science classes. Int. J. STEM Educ. **5**(1), 5 (2018)

Lefstein, A.: Changing classroom practice through the English National Literacy Strategy: a micro-interactional perspective. Am. Educ. Res. J. **45**(3), 701–737 (2008)

Lefstein, A., Snell, J., Israeli, M.: From moves to sequences: expanding the unit of analysis in the study of classroom discourse. Br. Edu. Res. J. **41**(5), 866–885 (2015)

Liu, Y.F., Zhao, Y.: A study of teacher talk in interactions in English classes. Chin. J. Appl. Linguist. **33**(2), 76–86 (2010)

Macgregor, S.K., Atkinson, T.R.: Facilitating learner interactions in the two-way video classroom. J. Educ. Technol. Syst. **31**(1), 45–62 (2002)

Mercer, N.: Words and Minds: How We Use Language to Think Together. Routledge, London (2000)

Mercer, N., Dawes, L., Wegerif, R., Sams, C.: Reasoning as a scientist: ways of helping children to use language to learn science. Br. Edu. Res. J. **30**(3), 359–377 (2004)

Mercer, N., Littleton, K.: Dialogue and the Development of Children's Thinking: A Sociocultural Approach. Routledge, Abingdon (2007)

Mercer, N.: The analysis of classroom talk: methods and methodologies. Br. J. Educ. Psychol. **80**(1), 1–14 (2010)

Mercer, N., Dawes, L.: The study of talk between teachers and students, from the 1970s until the 2010s. Oxf. Rev. Educ. **40**(4), 430–445 (2014)

Mortimer, E., Scott, P.: Meaning Making in Secondary Science Classroomsaa. McGraw-Hill Education, London (2003)

Muhonen, H., Rasku-Puttonen, H., Pakarinen, E., Poikkeus, A.M., Lerkkanen, M.K.: Knowledge-building patterns in educational dialogue. Int. J. Educ. Res. **81**, 25–37 (2017)

Nassaji, H., Wells, G.: What's the use of "triadic dialogue"? An investigation of teacher-student interaction. Appl. Linguist. **21**(3), 376–406 (2000)

National Institute of Child Health and Human Development Early Child Care Research Network: The relation of global first-grade classroom environment to structural classroom features and teacher and student behaviors. Elem. School J. **102**(5), 367–387 (2002)

Nichd, E., Bonnie, K.: A day in third grade: a large-scale study of classroom quality and teacher and student behavior. Elem. School J. **105**(3), 305–323 (2005)

Norman, K.: Thinking Voices: The Work of the National Oracy Project. Hodder and Stoughton, London (1992)

Nystrand, M., Gamoran, A.: Instructional discourse, student engagement, and literature achievement. Res. Teach. Engl. **25**(3), 261–290 (1991)

Nystrand, M.: Dialogic instruction: when recitation becomes conversation. In: Opening Dialogue: Understanding the Dynamics of Language and Learning in the English Classroom, pp. 1–29 (1997)

Nystrand, M., Wu, L.L., Gamoran, A., Zeiser, S., Long, D.A.: Questions in time: investigating the structure and dynamics of unfolding classroom discourse. Discourse Process. **35**(2), 135–198 (2003)

O'Connor, C., Michaels, S., Chapin, S.: "Scaling down" to explore the role of talk in learning: from district intervention to controlled classroom study. In: Socializing Intelligence Through Academic Talk and Dialogue, pp. 111–126 (2015)

Podschuweit, S., Bernholt, S., Brückmann, M.: Classroom learning and achievement: how the complexity of classroom interaction impacts students' learning. Res. Sci. Technol. Educ. **34**(2), 142–163 (2016)

Pöysä, S., Vasalampi, K., Muotka, J., Lerkkanen, M.K., Poikkeus, A.M., Nurmi, J.E.: Teacher–student interaction and lower secondary school students' situational engagement. Br. J. Educ. Psychol. **89**(2), 374–392 (2018)

Rampton, B.: Interaction ritual and not just artful performance in crossing and stylization. Lang. Soc. **38**(2), 149–176 (2009)

Reznitskaya, A., Gregory, M.: Student thought and classroom language: examining the mechanisms of change in dialogic teaching. Educ. Psychol. **48**(2), 114–133 (2013)

Robin, A.: Developing dialogic teaching: genesis, process, trial. Res. Pap. Educ. **33**(5), 561–598 (2018)

Rojas-Drummod, S., Pérez, V., Vélez, M., Gómez, L., Mendoza, A.: Talking for reasoning among Mexican primary school children. Learn. Instr. **13**(6), 653–670 (2003)

Rojas-Drummond, S., Littleton, K., Hernández, F., Zúñiga, M.: Dialogical interactions among peers in collaborative writing contexts. In: Educational Dialogues: Understanding and Promoting Productive Interaction, pp. 128–148 (2010)

Rojas-Drummond, S., Torreblanca, O., Pedraza, H., Vélez, M., Guzmán, K.: 'Dialogic scaffolding': enhancing learning and understanding in collaborative contexts. Learn. Culture Soc. Interact. **2**(1), 11–21 (2013)

Ruiz-Primo, M.A.: Informal formative assessment: the role of instructional dialogues in assessing students' learning. Stud. Educ. Eval. **37**(1), 15–24 (2011)

Saville-Troike, M.: Extending "communicative" concepts in the second language curriculum: a sociolinguistic perspective. In: Culture as Core: Interdisciplinary Perspectives on Culture in the Second Language Classroom, pp. 3–17 (2003)

Sinclair, J.M., Coulthard, M.: Towards an Analysis of Discourse: The English Used by Teachers and Pupils. Oxford University Press, Oxford (1975)

Smith, M.K., Jones, F.H., Gilbert, S.L., Wieman, C.E.: The classroom observation protocol for undergraduate STEM (COPUS): a new instrument to characterize university STEM classroom practices. CBE Life Sci. Educ. **12**(4), 618–627 (2013)

Song, Y., Chen, X., Hao, T., Liu, Z., Lan, Z.: Exploring two decades of research on classroom dialogue by using bibliometric analysis. Comput. Educ. **137**, 12–31 (2019)

Soter, A.O., Wilkinson, I.A., Murphy, P.K., Rudge, L., Reninger, K., Edwards, M.: What the discourse tells us: talk and indicators of high-level comprehension. Int. J. Educ. Res. **47**(6), 372–391 (2008)

Vygotsky, L.: Interaction between learning and development. In: Readings on the Development of Children, vol. 23, no. 3, pp. 34–41 (1978)

Wells, G., Arauz, R.M.: Dialogue in the classroom. J. Learn. Sci. **15**(3), 379–428 (2006)

Xie, Z.Y., Cao, X.: Construction three-dimensional observation system of teacher-student interaction behavior in classroom and practice. In: International Conference on Education Technology & Computer. IEEE (2010)

Application of Parallel Corpus to Teaching Style and Translation

Lu Tian[1,2(✉)]

[1] School of Interpreting and Translation Studies, Guangdong University of Foreign Studies,
Guangzhou, China
ivytianlu@gdufs.edu.cn
[2] Center for Translation Studies, Guangdong University of Foreign Studies, Guangzhou, China

Abstract. This paper is a detailed account of the application of parallel corpus to the teaching of style and translation. Facilitated by corpus tools, a quantitative and qualitative comparative analysis of the translation of narrative markers, a key style of Chinese full-length vernacular fictions, is thoroughly demonstrated. Through the class learning, students are expected to be aware of the pseudo oral storytelling feature of Chinese vernacular fictions and understand that narrative markers, as crucial narrative devices ensuring the cohesion and coherence of the text and more importantly, reflecting the style of the genre, require proper rendition in translation. It concludes that the introduction of parallel corpus to Style and Translation class obtains positive effects. On the one hand, parallel corpus provides abundant authentic bilingual data for observation; on the other hand, convenient searching tools help sort out the desired data in an accurate and swift manner, thus facilitate class demonstration and discussion.

Keywords: Parallel Corpus · Style and Translation · Narrative marker · Chinese full-length vernacular fiction · *Hong Lou Meng*

1 Introduction

Style is considered the fingerprint of a piece of writing, showing its essential linguistic characteristics and reflecting the preference and choice of the writer in language use. Such characteristics can be observed on all aspects—vocabulary, syntax, rhetoric, structure, etc. In translation, it is important for translators to be aware of the style of the source text (ST) and then properly retain it or justifiably deal with it otherwise in the target text (TT). In this process, the translator, as the creator of the target text, may inevitably bring his or her own style into the translated work.

As style can be observed through repetitive linguistic features, corpus together with its various retrieval and concordance tools provides an effective method for discovering and analyzing such features, thus facilitating the discussion and study of the style of the text. This paper is an account of the application of *the Chinese-English Parallel Corpus of Hong Lou Meng* to the teaching of translating narrative markers, a key style of Chinese vernacular fictions, in the module of Style and Translation for postgraduates of Translation Studies in a Chinese university.

© Springer Nature Switzerland AG 2020
E. Popescu et al. (Eds.): SETE 2019, LNCS 11984, pp. 237–245, 2020.
https://doi.org/10.1007/978-3-030-38778-5_26

2   Teaching Objectives and Methodology

This class aims to cultivate students' awareness of and sensitivity to narrative markers and guide them to probe into the proper retention and presentation of such a key style of Chinese vernacular fictions in translation. *Hong Lou Meng (HLM)* or *A Dream of the Red Mansions* was adopted for case study as the novel is widely acknowledged as one of the most significant vernacular fictions in Chinese literature. *The Chinese-English Parallel Corpus of Hong Lou Meng* and relevant retrieval tools including Editplus and ParaConc are adopted for efficient and convenient extraction and calculation of desired parallel data.

The Chinese-English Parallel Corpus of Hong Lou Meng consists of the 120-chapter Chinese text and three representative English translated texts [1]. The three English texts are respectively translated by Yang Xianyi and Gladys Yang, David Hawkes and John Minford, and H. Bencraft Joly. They will be referred to as Y's, H's and J's hereafter. While J's is not a complete translation of the novel as the translator only translated the first fifty-six chapters, both of the other two versions are full translation containing 120 chapters.

Aided by ParaConc, a parallel corpus retrieval tool, narrative markers and their translations can be easily sorted out from the original text and the three English translated texts and the frequency of each expression automatically calculated. Then, detailed comparison and analysis are carried out under the framework of Halliday's Systemic-Functional Grammar in order to evaluate the presentation of the narrative features of *HLM* in its three translation versions. In addition, students are also guided to note the style of each translator in rendering this narrative mechanism and learn possible methods in translating Chinese vernacular fictions as such in the future.

3   Narrative Markers in Full-Length Vernacular Fiction

As its name suggests, full-length vernacular fiction, or *zhanghui xiaoshuo* in Chinese, is characterized by division of the fiction into chapters and episodes. Influenced by the oral narrative feature of story-telling performance, Chinese vernacular fictions retain a series of narratological and stylistic characteristics of oral narrative performance. One of such characteristics is the adherence to a particular set of formulas at the beginning and the end of a chapter or an event [2]. These expressions are the "style markers" of the fiction and "call for more careful investigation" [3]. In this study, these expressions are specified as "narrative markers" [4]. Examples of such markers include "huashuo" (word say), "qieshuo" (but say), "zhijian" (only see), "buti" (no mention), etc. These seemingly formulaic clichés, on the one hand, indicate the involvement of a pseudo-storyteller, in effect indicating the author's conception of the whole story especially on how to deal with the relationship between the author and the reader [5]; on the other hand, they function as connections between plots, making clear of the background, characters, scenes, or even the storyteller's comments [6]. Therefore, narrative markers are not simply dispensable ornaments but crucial narrative devices in the division of sessions and integration of the whole fiction [7].

According to the locations they appear in the text, narrative markers can be generally divided into three categories—beginning markers, ending markers and turning markers.

3.1 Beginning Markers

In Chinese vernacular fictions like *HLM*, when an event is recounted, a repetition is always made reminding the reader of the on-going event. Superfluous and omissible as they may seem, such expressions represent an important narrative feature indicative of the style of the genre. The most conspicuous repetition in Chinese vernacular fictions appears at the beginning of a chapter recounting what has been mentioned in the previous chapter.

"Huashuo" is one of the most frequently used beginning markers. However, despite the 88 occurrences of "huashuo" in the ST of *HLM*, Y's only keeps three of them and renders them as "as we saw". According to Halliday's Systemic-Functional Grammar, "huashuo" is a verbal process which shows the impact of storytelling tradition on Chinese full-length vernacular fictions, while "as we saw" is a behavioral process which suggests that the narration is more like a performance. Such an adjustment perhaps caters the need of literature writing but fails to reflect the storytelling feature of *HLM*. Figure 1 below shows the parallel texts of "huashuo" and its translations in the three English versions.

	ST	H's	Y's	J's
1				
2	话说凤姐和宝玉回家，	When Bao - yu and Xi - feng were	After Xifeng and Baoyu reached	Pao - yu and lady Feng，we will now ex
3	话说秦业父子专候贾家	In the last chapter we left Qin Ban	Qin Ye and his son did not have	But to return to our story．Mr．Ch^in，th
4	话说金荣因人多势众，	Outnumbered，and hard pressed	With heavy pressure on him anc	We will now resume our story．As the p
5	话说凤姐正与平儿说话	Jia Rui ^s arrival was announced w	While Xifeng was talking to Ping	Lady Feng，it must be noticed in contin
6	话说宁国府中都总管来	When Lai Sheng，the Chief Stews	When the news that Xifeng was	When Lai Sheng，be it noticed in contin
7	话说贾妃回宫，次日见回奏	On the day following the Imperial (	The day after her return to the P	The Chia consort，we must now go on t
8	话说贾琏谢凤姐儿说有	Hearing that Xi - feng wanted to cc	Hearing that Xifeng wanted to cc	Chia Lien，for we must now prosecute c
9	话说宝玉养过了三十三	By the time the thirty - three days	After thirty - three days ^ convale	After thirty days ^ careful nursing，Pao
10	话说林黛玉正自悲泣	TO CONTINUE OUR STORY，As	As Daiyu was weeping，the gat	Lin Tai - yu，we must explain in taking (
11	话说袭人见不了自己吐的	WE told in the last chapter how，	Baoyu was so absorbed by his f	Pao - yu，so our story runs，was gazin
12	话说林黛玉与宝玉角口	Dai - yu，as we have shown，regr	Daiyu for her part was also remc	Lin Tai - yu herself，for we will now resu
13	话说袭人见了自己吐的	A cold feat came over Aroma whe	When Xiren saw the blood on th	But to proceed．When she saw on the
14	话说袭人见贾母、王夫	WHEN she saw that Grandmother	As soon as the others had left，	When Hsi Jen saw dowager lady Chia，
15	话说贾母自王夫人处回	WHEN Grandmother Jia got back	The Lady Dowager went back fr	Ever since dowager lady Chia's return
16	话说众人见平儿来了，	PATIENCE，you will recall，had j	On Pinger ^s return she was asl	Upon seeing，the story explains，P^ing
17	话说宝玉听了，忙进来	HEARING that he was wanted，B	Baoyu hurried over at this summ	As soon as Pao - yu，we will now expla
18	话说众人看演《荆钗记》	BAO - YU having now taken his p	Baoyu was sitting with the girls	But to resume our narrative．
19	话说凤姐儿正在忙他平儿	As we were saying at the end of tf	They were offered seats and Pin	Lady Feng，we will now go on to explai
20	话说林黛玉直到四更将	IT was not，we observed in the las	Daiyu did not fall asleep till near	Lin Tai - yu，to resume our story，droρ
21	话说王夫人听见邢夫人	HEARING that Lady Xing had arriv	She had no choice but to go in ;	As soon as Madame Wang，so runs ou
22	话说香菱见众人正白笑	WHEN Caltrop saw the cousins t	When Xiangling discovered the c	Hsiang Ling，we will now proceed，perc
23	话说薛宝钗道：	I THINK We ought to have a fixed	We must have some sort of orc	But to continue．
24	话说平儿陪着凤姐儿吃	Having kept Xi - feng company whi	After eating with Xifeng and wait	But let us pick up the clue of our story．
25	话说王夫人唤他	Obedient to the summons，Bao -	Baoyu hurried to his mother as	as summoned，to find that she war
26	话说她三人因见探春等	Our last chapter concluded with T	The subject of conversation was changed at the arrival of Tanchun and Xi
27	话说宝玉听说贾母等因	Hearing that his grandmother and	Baoyu put on a coat and went over with his cane to pay his respects to

Fig. 1. Parallel texts of "huashuo" and its translations

"Huashuo" is dealt with in more variety in H's where it is presented two dozen times in the TT, roughly accounting for a quarter of the total occurrences in the ST. No specific rule is found in terms of the translator's selection of which ones to translate and which ones not to. In other words, it seems that Hawkes & Minford were quite casual in picking narrative markers for translation. Despite this defect, their endeavor to show the variety of language can be readily discovered. Generally, H's expresses the meaning of "huashuo" from three points of view—"we", "you", and "story". Table 1 shows the detail.

Table 1. Hawkes & Minford's translation of "huashuo"

Subject (signifier)	Signified	Predicator	Process
"we"	narrator (author) & narratee (reader)	left	material
		(have) shown	material
		told	verbal
		(were) saying	verbal
		observed	mental
		saw/(have) seen	mental
"you"	narratee (reader)	(will) recall	mental
"our last chapter"	story	conclude	material
		told	verbal
"it"		(was) told	verbal
		(may be) remembered	mental
"our story"		(had) reached	material

Table 1 shows that in rendering the narrative marker "huashuo", H's adopts expressions in three categories as the subjects of clauses. The starting point of information shifts from "we", which refers to the author and the reader or the narrator and the narratee, to "you", simply the reader or narratee. Another alternative is to start with reference to the "story" by employing subjects including "our last chapter", "our story" and the pronoun "it". As far as predicators and the associated processes are concerned, H's again adopts a variety of devices, including material, verbal, and mental processes, in flashbacking the content of the previous chapter despite the fact that "huashuo" is unanimously verbal in the ST.

It is worth noting that in some chapters H's capitalized each letter of the very first word, for instance "WHEN Caltrop saw the cousins…". However, the translator did not follow this practice throughout the whole translation, and hardly could any criteria be figured out as which ones to capitalize and which ones not to. Moreover, in two chapters the text begins with "TO CONTINUE OUR STORY", an all-letter-capitalized phrase to function as the beginning markers.

In comparison, J's is the most significant in that it, in one way or another, retains the meaning of "huashuo" in all the chapters where it appears in the ST. Its renditions are summarized in Table 2.

As is shown in Table 2, J's mainly takes two categories of subjects in rendering "huashuo"—"we" referring to the narrator (author) and narratee (reader), and "story" in diverse forms. As to the predicators, most predicators present the material process. With a detailed look at the goals of these processes, it is found that they mainly fall into two kinds—"our story" and "our narrative". Both explicitly reflect the story-telling origin of Chinese vernacular fictions and ensure the continuity of narrative. In addition, similar to H's, J's also employs "to-infinitive" to start a chapter. Examples of such expressions include "But to proceed/continue", "But to resume/return to our narrative/story" and

Table 2. Joly's translation of "huashuo"

Subject (signifier)	Signified	Predicator	Process
"we"	narrator (author) & narratee (reader)	explain	material
		resume	material
		go on	material
		prosecute	material
		pick up	material
		take up	material
		proceed	material
		saw	mental
		notice	mental
"it"	story	runs	material
		added	material
"our/the story"		runs	material
		explains	material
		goes	material
"our narrative"		says	verbal
		noticed	mental

"But to return to our narrative". In all, expressions like these are employed up to ten times in J's in conveying the meaning of "huashuo", which is much more than that in H's despite the fact that J's only covers the first 56 chapters of the 120-chaptered novel.

In summary, among all the three translations of the beginning marker "huashuo", J's stands out in conveying its narrative function and having all of them translated. Both H's and J's adopt a variety of language devices in expressing "huashuo" in English and sometimes employ additional explanatory words for narrative, which makes the TTs not as concise as the ST.

3.2 Ending Markers

As the counterpart of beginning markers, ending markers are used to mark the ending of a chapter or an event. At the end of each chapter in Chinese vernacular fictions, there is usually an intentional suspense imitating the end of an oral performance, which aims to arouse the curiosity and interest of the audience so that they will come back and pay for the performance.

"Xiahui fenjie" (next chapter explain) is a typical ending marker, appearing 106 times in *HLM*. Along with this ending marker, the narrator sometimes intentionally drops some hints on what will happen next. The way to translate "xiahui fenjie" in the three translated texts is various, reflecting the translators' understanding of the textual and narrative functions of narrative ending markers. In H's, literal translation is adopted, and the sentence structures vary as the contextual situation changes. While there is almost no ellipsis in translating this set phrase, H's seldom presents any narratological nature of this ending marker.

In Y's, a variety of linguistic devices including conditional clause, passive voice and modal verbs indicating strong degree of imperative are adopted. For instance, the ending marker is translated as "If you want to know what followed, read the next chapter" and "To know whether she lived or died, you must read the next chapter." The main clauses in both sentences are imperative. The use of modal verb "must" in the second sentence indicates a strong suggestion. The subordinate clause in the first sentence and the adverbial phrase in the second are respectively conditional and purposeful, which on the one hand function as connections between chapters in content, on the other hand play the role of arousing the audience's curiosity. In this sense, Y's does well in preserving the narratological characteristics of Chinese vernacular fictions through the translation of narrative ending markers.

In J's rendition of "xiahui fenjie", appellation and interrogative are adopted, which highlights the interpersonal function of the narrative expression. For instance, the translation of "qieting xiahui fenjie" in J's is "But, reader, listen to the explanation contained in the next chapter." The use of "reader" and "listen to" indicates both the interpersonal relationship between the writer and the reader as well as that between the story-teller and the listener in a pseudo-story-telling scene, reflecting the legacy of storying-telling tradition in Chinese full-length vernacular fictions. Moreover, interrogative is widely used in J's, which expresses a strong degree of appeal to the audience. For instance, "But reader, do you want to know the sequel?" In this sense, J's successfully reproduces the pseudo-storytelling scene which traditional Chinese vernacular fictions originate from. Just as their functions in the ST, the ending markers in J's play the role of summarizing the previous story and arousing the curiosity of the audience.

3.3 Turning Markers

Apart from beginning and ending markers discussed above, some narrative markers are employed within the narrative of an event indicating turns in plot. We name these markers "turning markers". If beginning and ending markers indicate the normal start and finish of an event, turning markers suggest the beginning and ending of acts, when an intrusion by an unexpected person or event is often involved. Facilitated by turning markers, the narrator changes the focus of narrative and advances the plot. For this reason, turning markers are not dispensable narrator's clichés as beginning and ending markers look like but crucial devices weaving the rise and fall of the plot.

Some turning markers show interruptions to speeches and indicate the time of events. Examples of such markers are "yiyu weiliao", "shuohuashi", "shuohuajian", "zhengshuozhe", etc. Their respective frequencies in the ST are shown in Table 3.

In this class "yiyu weiliao" (one speech not finish) was taken as an example to illustrate the translation of narrative turning markers. With corpus tools, it can be found from the data that "yiyu weiliao" is always followed by phrases like "zhiting" (only hear), "zhijian" (only see), "hujian" (suddenly see), etc. to show transitions of events. Because of its substantial function in narration, almost all "yiyu weiliao" are rendered in all the three English versions. Of its forty-one occurrences in the ST, Y's only leaves one

Table 3. Frequency of some turning markers in *HLM*

Turning marker	yiyu weiliao	shuohuashi	shuohuajian	zhengshuozhe
Frequency	41	15	4	119

untranslated and H's two. J's re-presents all the twenty-two markers in the first fifty-six chapters.

Figure 2 shows the concordance of "yiyu weiliao" and its translations sorted by ParaConc, which greatly enhances the accuracy and efficiency of data retrieval. For easier observation and comparative analysis, the sorted data was exported and opened in Excel with clearer display of the parallel data. Figure 3 is a snapshot of the parallel texts of "yiyu weiliao" and its translations shown in Excel.

Fig. 2. The concordance of "yiyu weiliao" and its translations in ParaConc

In both Y's and H's, the adverbial phrase "just then" is adopted ten and four times respectively in rendering "yiyu weiliao" to indicate the time of event, making the TTs look brief. In addition, H's uses the prepositional phrase "(just) at that (very) moment" fourteen times, much more than the only one adoption in Y's. Both expressions have similar functions and pragmatic effects. It is interesting to find that "at once" is coincidentally

Fig. 3. Parallel texts of "yiyu weiliao" and its translations shown in Excel

adopted in both translations in handling a same text, which shows the influence of context on translators' choice. Other mostly adopted expressions include adverbial clauses of time with words such as "as", "while", and "before" as the conjunctions. Generally speaking, H's and Y's show great similarity in the rendering of "yiyu weiliao".

J's way of handling "yiyu weiliao" is unitary. They are all put into adverbial clauses. Among its twenty-two occurrences, sixteen are put in inverted order. Adverbs such as "scarcely", "hardly" and "barely" are alternatively adopted with frequencies of nine, nine and four respectively. Although renditions as such make the texts appear a bit redundant, J's best presents the narrative function of turning markers in bringing sudden intrusions into the scene in focus.

3.4 Summary

In translating *Hong Lou Meng,* though the omission of narrative markers may not necessarily make much difference to the flow of the story, it will run the risk of losing a key style of this Chinese classical vernacular fiction in terms of narration. After detailed comparative analysis of the three English versions, it is discovered that all the three English versions have their gains and losses in the translation of the narrative markers under discussion. With the aim to help foreign readers learn the language, J's excels in the proportion of narrative markers retained in the translated text whereas the other two versions only keep less than a half. As far as the specific translation methods are concerned, Joly is found to prefer the use of clauses, so the TT tends to be long and redundant. This is in accord with the fact that J's overall length is longer than the other two. In comparison, the language of Y's is the most concise. As it focuses more on the function of expressions, Y's is not confined to the literal meaning of narrative markers.

H's pays attention to the diversity of language use, so there is usually more than one way to translate a same narrative marker.

4 Conclusion

The narrative feature is an important style of a fiction. Translation of literature works should pay attention to the retention of the narrative flavor of the original text. Unlike fictions of many other countries, Chinese full-length vernacular fictions feature in the narratological characteristics of oral narrative performance. The most distinctive evidence is the use of narrative markers. Although these formulaic expressions are sometimes regarded as "storyteller's clichés", they are stylistically crucial narrative devices functioning as connections between episodes and indicating the involvement of the narrator. Therefore, they need to be properly introduced to the western readers via translation.

This class of Style and Translation focuses on the translation of narrative markers in *Hong Lou Meng*, a representative masterpiece of Chinese classical full-length vernacular fictions. To facilitate teaching, *the Chinese-English Parallel Corpus of Hong Lou Meng* was used. The authentic data provide abundant and trustworthy material for discussion. Meanwhile, the retrieval tools make information extraction convenient and efficient. They help swiftly sort out the narrative markers under discussion and accurately show the frequency of each expression as well as the co-text of each hit thus making the comparative study of narrative markers among different versions easier and effective.

Acknowledgements. The work was substantially supported by The National Social Science Fund of China (Project No. 19BYY125).

References

1. Liu, Z.Q., Tian, L., Liu, C.P.: The compilation of Hong Lou Meng Chinese-English parallel corpus (《红楼梦》中英文平行语料库的创建). Contemp. Linguist. **10**(4), 329–339 (2008)
2. Zhao, H.H.: The Uneasy Narrator: Chinese Fiction from the Traditional to the Modern. Oxford University Press, Oxford (1995)
3. Leech, G., Short, M.: Style in Fiction: A Linguistic Introduction to English Fictional Prose, 2nd edn. Pearson Education Limited, Harlow (2007)
4. Liu, Z.Q., Tian, L.: Narrative markers in Hong Lou Meng and their translations—a corpus-based study (《红楼梦》叙事标记语及其英译——基于语料库的对比分析). Foreign Lang. Res. **1**, 106–110 (2009)
5. Chen, P.Y.: The Conversion of Narrative Patterns of Chinese Novels (中国小说叙事模式的转变). Shanghai People's Publisher, Shanghai (1988)
6. Yu, X.H.: Research on the Classical Vernacular Fictions (古代白话小说研究). Anhui People Press, Hefei (2005)
7. Plaks, A.H.: Chinese Narrative. Peking University Press, Beijing (1995)

The Design and Application of an Web-Based Online Examination System

Jilu Jiang[1], Baoxian Wu[2], Liang Chang[1], Kui Liu[3]($\boxtimes$), and Tianyong Hao[2]

[1] Audit Governance and Risk Control Research Center, School of Accounting,
Guangdong University of Foreign Studies, Guangzhou, China
jiangjl@gdufs.edu.cn, changlianggdufs@163.com
[2] Guangzhou Key Laboratory of Big Data and Intelligent Education, School of Computer
Science, South China Normal University, Guangzhou, China
876354386@qq.com, haoty@m.scnu.edu.cn
[3] Network and Modern Educational Technology Center,
Guangzhou University, Guangzhou, China
liukui@gzhu.edu.cn

Abstract. Online examination has been used more and more widely in the education and other fields due to its advantages of efficiency, convenience, and fairness. This paper proposes a new web-based online examination system, which utilizes PHP, Ajax and other technologies to implement online examination functions, including testing question collection, user management, online testing, real-time score calculation, answer checking, and result analysis. Particularly, an automated test paper generation module was designed and integrated. The system has been applied to a course involving more than 1000 students per semester at Guangzhou University of Foreign Studies. It has been proved to save efforts of teachers and students, demonstrating its effectiveness in assisting teaching and learning.

Keywords: Online examination system · PHP · Automated test paper generation · Web-based · User management

1 Introduction

Education is at the strategic position of priority development in many countries. The Ministry of Education of China advocates that education should be geared to modernization, the world, and the future. The educational tools in terms of information and technology deserves more attention [1]. Consequently, there is a need that education should actively adapt to the development of science and technology worldwide, and make fully use of computer and network technology [2]. Currently more and more education researchers apply information technologies, particularly text mining methods, to education. For example, Chen et al. and Song et al. used bibliometric technique and topic modelling to study academic research output in education field [3–5]. Wang et al. designed interactive exercises by using a software for corpus-based English learning [6]. Dun et al. utilized a topic mining method to discover user intention from query text [7].

© Springer Nature Switzerland AG 2020
E. Popescu et al. (Eds.): SETE 2019, LNCS 11984, pp. 246–256, 2020.
https://doi.org/10.1007/978-3-030-38778-5_27

As an essential part of education, examination is an vital means of testing the performance of students in mastery of teaching content as well as verifying the performance of teachers during teaching process [8]. In addition, examination can help students to consolidate what they have learned and to supplement missing or incomplete knowledge points. Besides, it provides teachers with feedbacks for assisting to adjust their teaching materials and improve corresponding teaching strategies.

Traditionally, a printed paper-based examination generally goes through a long process containing several stages. Firstly, a teacher needs to design a style of test paper, arrange examination contents and print test papers. After that, the teacher reports examination schedule to the university, which arranges the examination time and location. Students then take examinations as scheduled. After that, the teacher collects all the test papers and marks each of them manually to calculate examination scores. Finally, students are notified with their final scores [9]. However, there are some disadvantages of the examination in printed paper-based way, such as long time, high cost of physical papers, low examination efficiency, etc.

Moreover, in a printed paper-based examination, students have difficulties in knowing correct and incorrect answers of test questions to enhance their learning performance. Stergiopoulos et al. [10] compared the performance of electronic examination systems with traditional printed-paper examinations. The results showed that students participated in electronic examination systems performed better, and electronic examinations could improve teaching efficiency as well. Compared with traditional printed paper-based examinations, modern online examination systems can solve some ingrained problems through utilizing internet technology. Benefied from the widespread distribution of the internet and the computer technology with gradual maturity, online examinations break through the limitation of time and geography [11]. Students can take examinations at different times and places. Besides, an online examination system can not only select questions randomly to prevent plagiarism and generate an examination automatically and promptly but also update a question bank continuously to benefit future examinations. For example, Ayo et al. [12] proposed a Nigerian e-examination model, potentially preventing examination cheating, which remains one of drawbacks of traditional examinations.

Due to the significant benefits of online examination systems, many scholars have conducted various researches on design and implementation of online examination systems. Yuan et al. [13] designed an online examination system based on the Browser/Server framework for the evaluation of computer basic operational skills, which promoted the development of basic computer education. Zhang et al. [14] designed a computer skill assessment system with a management capability concerning with practical computer skills. With the development of computer technology, online examination systems have continuously been developed and improved. Abubakar and Adebayo [15] implemented a set of electronic examinations in Nigeria to prevent students from bad behaviors to some extent. In order to avoid cheating and reflect the fairness of examinations, Ko et al. [16] designed an examination system to monitor the status of students during examinations. Yu [17] developed an electronic test system, which analyzed testing results, rolled out textbook randomly and separated teaching from testing. All of existing researches reflect the advantages and the tendency of utilizing online examination systems in the internet and technology era.

Through the investigation of existing online examination systems in Chinese mainland, some situations have been discovered as follows: The online examination systems are mainly utilizing general computer-based techniques. Most of test papers are created by utilizing a random sampling strategy. At the end of examination, scores are recorded without any further deep analysis. Therefore, based on the investigations, this research tries to design an online examination system based on a new strategy for automated test paper generation. This system is characterized by a list of features including: (1) The examination system is applied to the evaluation of accounting course learning. (2) The system serves not only for examinations but also for periodically exercises. (3) Question banks are created based on a knowledge graph. (4) A new automated test paper generation strategy is proposed and implemented.

2 System Architecture

System requirements are firstly analyzed to ensure reliability and safety. The system mainly uses a Model-View-Controller (MVC) framework to separate data processing, data representation, program input and output controls. In the framework, controller is responsible for forwarding requests and processing requests, and view is for graphical interface design, while model implements functions and algorithms, data management and database design. The framework not only makes system program structure clear and flexible but also reduce the degree of coupling among functions. Moreover, the framework enhances dynamic programming and simplifies subsequent modifications and expansions of the system.

Based on the analysis, the system is designed with a list of modules. Each of the modules corresponds to a list of functions. The overall architecture of the online examination system design is shown as Fig. 1. In addition, this system is developed and tested in WAMP general application environment, which is a set of open source softwares that are commonly used to build websites or services. WAMP contains an integration of Apache, Mysql, MariaDB, Perl, PHP, and Python.

2.1 System Modules

In the system architecture, there are three user centers associating with a list of modules. A student user center includes personal information maintenance, examination participant, and score view. A teacher user center includes personal information maintenance, student management, class management, and so on. An administrator user center contains all the modules of teacher user center with additional modules such as teacher management and class management. In general, the major modules of the system consists of student management, class management, question bank management, examination management, automated test paper generation, score management, teacher management, etc. Some of the essential modules are described as follows, and the automated test paper generation module is specifically introduced in Subsect. 2.2.

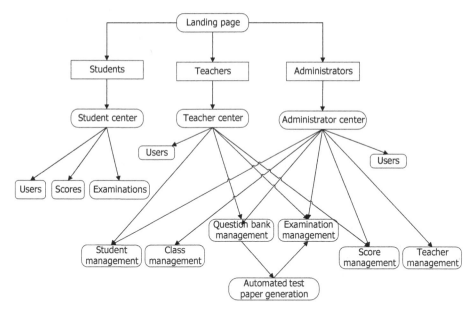

Fig. 1. The overall architecture of the proposed online examination system.

(1) Student management module. Administrators or teachers can insert, edit, delete and search students in the system using the module. Each student has basic information including student number, user name, associated class, courses, etc. Since it is time-consuming and error-prone to add students to the system one by one, the system provides a convenient way by reading all students' information from a batch of file. After logging in the system with a user name and password, a student can view personal user center to maintain his/her information including password reset, personal icon modification, etc.

(2) Question bank management module. The question bank contains four types of objective questions including blank filling, single-choice, multiple-choice, and true-false. Permitted users can search, add, modify and delete questions. Each question contains a question title, multiple candidate answer options, correct answer, as well as a difficulty level and its coverage in corresponding textbook. Considering teachers may not have enough database knowledge, the system also provides a friendly user interface to operate the module intuitively and conveniently.

(3) Examination management module. Teachers or administrators can initiate, modify, suspend, and terminate an examination in the module. A teacher can indicate the name of the examination, duration, coverage of textbook, students, score sheet, etc. to create a new examination. He/she can then design a detailed test paper manually or using the automated test paper generation function. After that, the teacher can suspend and modify the examination information. When students log into the examination system, they can find a list of currently available examinations and choose one to start an online test.

(4) Score management module. When a student completes an online examination, the system calculates a final score automatically by comparing student's answers with correct answers and displays the score to the student. At the same time, the user can choose to view the correct answers or view the wrong questions for learning improvement. The test score, associated with students' information, and examination information are recorded into the database. Teachers and administrators can view overall scores, sort student by scores, search the score of a particular student, modify scores, and output scores in a certain format. By measuring the scores, a teacher can adjust his/her teaching plan and teaching scheme accordingly to improve teaching performance.

2.2 Automated Test Paper Generation

Test paper generation is an essential procedure for the success of an examination [18]. Traditionally, test papers are designed by teachers manually and empirically. After that, the teachers need to manually read and score test papers collected from students. During this process, teachers usually face a heavy working load particularly when there are many students involved in the course. Moreover, fairness remains a concern when there are multiple teachers with different classes for the same course since teachers may design various test papers. In that case, score distributions of students in different classes may be much diverse even though they took the same course. Consequently, an algorithm is demanded to avoid the issue and generate test papers automatically by online examination systems to improve efficiency.

There are some algorithms used in conventional online systems. Generally, questions are randomly selected from a question bank according to the requirements of question forms and scopes. Although the fairness of the test is guaranteed to some extent and students can take examination without geographical restrictions, the algorithms fail to diversify difficulty degrees. Therefore, examinations based on the algorithms may not achieve stratifying evaluation results without appropriate design of difficulty distributions.

In our system, a new algorithm for automated test paper generation is proposed considering both difficulty distribution and knowledge point distribution of questions. Based on a pre-designed question bank, the algorithm is built by a group of teachers in the same course collaboratively. On the basis of the practice and analysis of relevant course knowledge points, teachers have designed a scheme of question bank, including a list of question dimensions, such as question forms, question difficulty levels, question scope, associated knowledge points, and a detailed representation of a question. Based on the question bank, a knowledge graph is created, which is a series of different linked sub-graphs presenting knowledge points and their relations. By this means, the relations of knowledge points are structured and the questions associated with the knowledge points are connected. The whole process of automated test paper generation in our online examination system is shown in Fig. 2.

During the test paper generation, our system enables the creation of traditional manual test papers and also provides a module of automated test paper generation based on the algorithm and a knowledge graph. According to test scope, examination location, question difficulty level, knowledge point distribution, and other requirements, the module randomly selects questions from the question bank according to a list of rules comforting the requirements to generate a test paper automatically. For example, teachers may limit question forms and the number of questions, the scope of textbook, the knowledge points, the difficulty distribution of questions. The test questions are automatically extracted from the question bank according to the examination requirements.

After that, the module organizes the selected questions by following some rules to generate a test paper automatically. For instance, the total of single-choice questions are 20 thus 10 questions are needed.

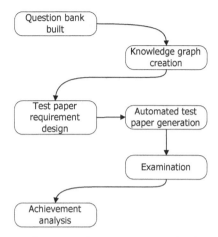

Fig. 2. The process of automated test paper generation in our online system.

In the implementation of the module, three software or frameworks LAMP, J2EE, and .Net are compared. Considering the development cost and efficiency, we used the open source LAMP.

3 System Implementation

The usage of system functions needs user permission and authorization. When a user tries to login the system, account name, password, user role, and verification code are required. When he/she enters the information in the login page, the system sends an Ajax request to the server to verify the account, password, verification code and other information. If the error happened, an error message is displayed on the login page. If user information is correct, the login is successful and the corresponding user interface is loaded and displayed.

In order to prevent malicious attacks, the system uses the verification code technology in the user login interface. Nowadays, there are many kinds of verification codes on the Internet, such as characters, voices, and question and answer. Users can visually recognize verification code information and input the form to submit the website for verification. In our system, a more straightforward method is used to generate a 4-digit verification code. Although the system login test and other problems become troublesome after the introduction of the verification code, this feature is necessary for system security. Besides, users can tick "remember me" function when logging in so that user password information is stored in the cookie for 24 h and no repeated password input is needed for the convenience of user login.

Teachers and system administrators can enter the system backend to manage data after user authorization on the login interface. Due to different permissions of teachers and administrators, all data management modules are separated. In the backend, teachers can perform student management, class management, question bank management, examination management, score management, and maintain personal information. In addition to the modules, system administrators can add, delete, and modify teacher modules.

(1) Student management module. System administrators and teachers have the right to use the student management module. Figure 3 shows a screenshot of the user interface of the student management module.

Fig. 3. The screenshot of the student management module.

System administrators or teachers can add or delete student information through clicking the add button on the student management page. When they input a student's name, student number, and password, select a class, and click the Add button, the information of a student can be added through Javascript code verification. For student deletion, in the operation of the last column of student records on the student management page, there is a delete icon corresponding to an Ajax request sending to remove the corresponding record. At the same time, the system supports the function of batch deletion, that is, deleting multiple pieces of data at the same time by clicking "checkbox" before the relative records.

(2) Class management module. System administrators or teachers have permission to enter the module for the management of class information. They can add classes, delete classes, modify class information, or search for classes with the input of a class name. The detailed operations of the management actions are similar to that of the student management module.

(3) Question bank management module. Question bank management model consists of single-choice questions, multiple-choice questions, true-false questions, and blank filling questions. Taking single-choice question management as an example, a screenshot of the user interface is shown as Fig. 4. Teachers or system administrators could add or modify single-choice questions, delete or bulk delete single-choice questions and search for single-choice questions based on single-choice questions or chapters. Multiple-choice questions management and true-false questions management are similar to that of single-choice management.

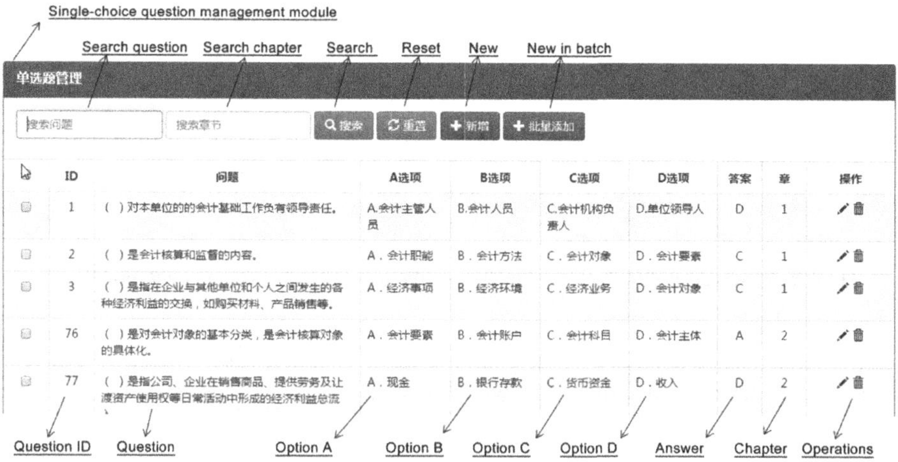

Fig. 4. A screenshot of the single-choice question management in the question bank management module

(4) Examination management module. System administrators and teachers have full access to the examination management module. As conventional operations, they can add examination information, delete an examination, modify examinations, or search for examinations based on their names. A screenshot of the examination management module is shown as Fig. 5.

(5) Score management module. System administrators and teachers have full access to the score management module. Similarly, they can search or modify students' scores on the score management user interface. Meanwhile, they can view some statistical analysis of students' scores including the average scores for every question, and the changes of student's performance on every knowledge point compared with that in the past examination, etc.

(6) Teacher management module. System administrators have permissions to enter the teacher management module and they can add, delete, modify teacher information, or search for teachers based on the basic information of teachers.

(7) Examination module. After user information authorization, students can enter the user-side of the module to take examinations, maintain personal information, and check individual examination scores. Figure 6 shows the user interface of an ongoing online examination. The page displays the information of examination name, time requirement, test questions in single-choice, multiple-choice, blank filling and true-false types, etc. When a student completes the test paper, he/she can click the submit button and the system automatically calculates the score of the test paper automatically in real time.

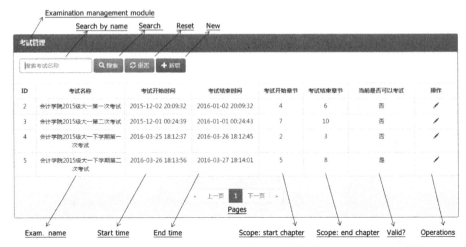

Fig. 5. A screenshot of the user interface of the examination management module.

The page also has an automated time counting-down function with JavaScript. The test paper will be automatically submitted when the examination time is used up.

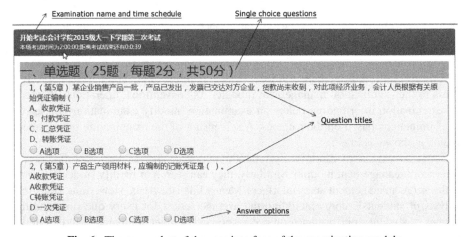

Fig. 6. The screenshot of the user interface of the examination module.

4 Conclusion

As the wary of learning change, more and more people acquire the knowledge they need through internet. Examination systems have gradually transformed from means based on traditional printed-paper to the online one. This paper introduces a new online examination system containing an automated test paper generation method that has been applied to a university with more than 1000 students per semester for two years. The system has implemented most of the major functions and modules for the completion of an online examination systems. However, it still has some limitations such as the lack of automatic scoring for objective questions, for this is a highly challengeable and open problem. More efforts will be made to improve its capability to adapt to different needs of online examinations in the future.

Acknowledgements. This work was supported by Natural Science Foundation of Guangdong Province (2018A030310051), Science and Technology Plan of Guangzhou (201804010296), and Ministry of Education Humanities and Social Sciences Research Youth Project (18YJCT90146).

References

1. Zhu, J.W.: Implementation of an online examination management system based on .NET framework. Master's thesis, Chengdu University of Electronic Science and Technology, 7–11 (2009)
2. Hao, T., Chen, W., Xie, H., Nadee, W., Lau, R. (eds.): SETE 2018. LNCS, vol. 11284. Springer, Cham (2018). https://doi.org/10.1007/978-3-030-03580-8. ISSN 0302-9743, ISBN 978-3-030-03579-2
3. Chen, X., Hao, J., Chen, J., Hua, S., Hao, T.: A bibliometric analysis of the research status of the technology enhanced language learning. In: Hao, T., Chen, W., Xie, H., Nadee, W., Lau, R. (eds.) SETE 2018. LNCS, vol. 11284, pp. 169–179. Springer, Cham (2018). https://doi.org/10.1007/978-3-030-03580-8_18
4. Chen, X., Wang, S., Tang, Y., Hao, T.: A bibliometric analysis of event detection in social media. Online Inf. Rev. **43**(1), 29–52 (2019)
5. Song, Y., Chen, X.L., Hao, T.Y., Liu, Z.N., Lan, Z.X.: Exploring two decades of research on classroom dialogue using bibliometric analysis. Comput. Educ. **137**(2019), 12–31 (2019)
6. Wang, X., Hao, T.: Designing interactive exercises for corpus-based English learning with Hot Potatoes software. In: Huang, T.-C., Lau, R., Huang, Y.-M., Spaniol, M., Yuen, C.-H. (eds.) SETE 2017. LNCS, vol. 10676, pp. 485–494. Springer, Cham (2017). https://doi.org/10.1007/978-3-319-71084-6_57
7. Dun, Y.J., Wang, N., Wang, M., Hao, T.Y.: Revealing learner interests through topic mining from question-answering data. Int. J. Distance Educ. Technol. (IJDET) **15**(2), 18–32 (2017)
8. Ren, D.Y.: Design and implementation of course examination system based on .Net. Shandong University (2018)
9. Jiang, L.Z.: Development of Java programming online examination system. Comput. Knowl. Technol. **2019**(07), 142–144 (2019)
10. Stergiopoulos, C., Tsiakas, P., Triantis, D., et al.: Evaluating electronic examination methods applied to students of electronics. Effectiveness and comparison to the paper-and-pencil method. In: IEEE International Conference on Sensor Networks, Ubiquitous, and Trustworthy Computing (SUTC 2006), vol. 2 (2006)
11. Pang, G.M., Yuan, J.M.: WEB-based online examination system. Friends Sci. **10**(29), 121–122 (2009)
12. Ayo, C.K., Akinyemi, I.O., Adebiyi, A.A., Ekong, U.O.: The prospects of e-examination implementation in Nigeria. Turk. Online J. Distance Educ. - TOJDE **8**(4), 125–135 (2007). ISSN 1302-6488, Article No. 10
13. Yuan, Z.M., Zhang, L., Zhan, G.H.: A novel web-based online examination system for computer science education. In: 33rd ASEE/IEEE Frontiers in Education Conference, S3F-7–S3F-10 (2003)

14. Zhang, L., Zhuang, Y.T., Yuan, Z.M., Zhan, G.H.: A web-based examination and evaluation system for computer education. In: Sixth IEEE International Conference on Advanced Learning Technologies (ICALT 2006), pp. 120–124. IEEE (2006)
15. Abubakar, A., Adebayo, F.: Using computer based test method for the conduct of examination in Nigeria: prospects, challenges and strategies. Mediterr. J. Soc. Sci. 5(2), 47 (2014)
16. Ko, C.C., Cheng, C.D.: Secure Internet examination system based on video monitoring. Internet Res. 14(1), 48–61 (2004)
17. Singh, S.K., Tiwari, A.K.: Design and implementation of secure computer based examination system based on B/S structure. Int. J. Appl. Eng. Res. 11(1), 312–318 (2016)
18. Cen, G., et al.: A implementation of an automatic examination paper generation system. Math. Comput. Model. 51(11–12), 1339–1342 (2010)

A Text Mining Application in Operation Management Course Teaching

Yingying Qu[1], Zihang Liang[1], Wenxiu Xie[2], and Xinyu Cao[3(✉)]

[1] School of Business, Guangdong University of Foreign Studies, Guangzhou, China
jessie.qu@gdufs.edu.cn, leungzihong@gmail.com
[2] Department of Linguistics and Translation, City University of Hong Kong,
Kowloon, Hong Kong SAR, China
vasiliky@outlook.com
[3] China National Institute of Standardization, Beijing, China
caoxy@cnis.ac.cn

Abstract. Sharing bicycle, as one of the hottest and newest industries in recent years, has drawn much dramatic attention from society. In the operation management course in this paper, students are expected to analyze the interview texts and investigate the problems occurred in sharing bicycle with corresponding suggestions. A list of interview texts from sharing bicycle users in Guangzhou Higher Education Mega Center are collected and analyzed. TF-IDF, as a widely used text mining method, is applied to extract frequently used key words for a qualitative analysis. Finally, ten key problems are identified and summarized, which provide government suggestions about supervision, such as user-centered management, user experience improvement, user interest protection, and deposit management.

Keywords: Text mining · TF-IDF · Content analysis · Operation management course

1 Introduction

The sharing bicycle is an emerging transport that provides users with another environmentally friendly and convenient travel option to make up for the slow and crowded traditional public transport [1]. According to the incomplete statistics from the Ministry of Transport, there are more than 16 million sharing bicycles on the market from 2010 to 2018 [2]. The number of users of sharing bicycles in China was 28 million in 2016, but increased to 235 million in 2017, with a growth rate of 632.1% [3]. The explosive growth not only drives China's sharing economy, but also expands the global sharing bicycle market. According to Cheetah Data, the weekly active penetration rate of the global sharing bicycle industry increased by 1258% in 2017. From 2016 to 2018, Alibaba, Ant Financial and DiDi have conducted nearly 10 rounds of financing (nearly $1.5 billion) to OFO, which is the largest sharing bicycle company in China [4].

However, the massive capital inflows and market competition created fake booms and bubbles. As more and more cities strengthened the regulation of sharing bicycle

E. Popescu et al. (Eds.): SETE 2019, LNCS 11984, pp. 257–266, 2020.
https://doi.org/10.1007/978-3-030-38778-5_28

management, its market demand drops abruptly. In 2018, the Beijing Municipal Commission of Transport issued an order banning the sharing bicycles from being on market. This act was later followed by the cities of Shanghai, Guangzhou and Shenzhen. As the market shrank in 2018, the problem of excess capacity among bike suppliers is gradually exposed. In the first half of 2018, a large number of sharing bicycle enterprises went bankrupt. The operating income of OFO Company decreased by 82.3% [5].

In the context of a shrinking market, the remaining sharing bicycle companies are exploring the appropriate direction for future development. Therefore, the OFO, as a representative company, is frequently taken as an example in the course teaching of operation management to help students understand the existed problems in the operation management of sharing bicycle industry, which plays a crucial role in enterprise transformation learning.

Instead of focusing on the identification of key factors in sharing bicycle operation, this paper uses real-life interviews as teaching and learning activities to contextualize the research topic. Exiting research mainly explored the quantitative relationships among critical factors in OFO operation decision making [6]. For example, Chen and Li (2018) discussed factors influencing customers' willingness to use sharing bicycles from the perspective of rational behaviour theory and a technical acceptance framework model [7]. Fan and Cao (2018) analyzed the interactive relationship among sharing bicycle users [8]. However, qualitative research on sharing bicycle remains extremely rare. Therefore, the operation management course teaching is used in this research and students are required to use qualitative methods to analyze interview texts from OFO users in the local communities. Through the utilization of a text mining method, students identified a list of existing problems, which are further summarized and explained in current sharing bicycle industry.

2 Background

Qualitative analysis clarifies the text structure and the subject relationships inside the texts through reading, comprehension, interpretation and summary. It relies much on the researchers' subjective understanding and processing [9]. Content analysis method, however, is an analytical method that describes content texts by objective and quantitative data [10]. It improves the reliability of research by quantitative statistics of text elements (symbols, punctuation marks, characters and sentences) and the occurrence frequencies of these elements. Although it brings in the objective indicators, the criteria of evaluation and classification of contents still involve a great deal of subjective judgments, which can produce deviations to research results. Content analysis, which is limited to the statistics of elements, is difficult to explore the deep-seated and hidden relationship among texts and the text sampling, while computer-aided content analysis bridges the gap.

Computer-aided content analysis relies on the processing and conversion of texts with the assistance of programming to transform unstructured text data into structured ones for research and management [11]. It eliminates deviation in the subjective text comprehension through machine learning and data mining in text similarity, by which the criteria on text classification and evaluation can be universal. With the development of the algorithms, the classification accuracy of texts can be improved. In this sense, computer-aided content analysis method plays a vital role in qualitative research.

TF-IDF is an important natural language processing method in computer-aided content analysis, which is the product of the Inverse Document Frequency (IDF) and the Term Frequency (TF). Term frequency refers to the frequency of specific words. The higher the term frequency of a word, the more it appears in the text, which indicates that the word is more relevant to the theme of the text. However, while computing the frequency of a term, all words are considered equally important which may not effective to filter out stop words, such as "some", "is" and "of". Theses stop words may be irrelevant to the research objective in spite of high term frequency. As a result, the inverse document frequency is introduced, by which the term frequency can be weighted based on the coverage or universality of the words. Therefore, the TF-IDF can not only mine relevant key words, but also filter out common stop words as much as possible.

Given a set of documents D, a specific word w_i, and a document d_j that $d_j \in D$, the calculation of TF-IDF value is shown as Eq. (1).

$$TF_{i,j} = \frac{n_{i,j}}{\sum_k n_{k,j}} \tag{1}$$

$n_{i,j}$ is the occurrence frequency of the word w_i in the document d_j, $\sum n_{k,j}$ is the total number of all words in the document.

There are many options for the base number of the logarithm part in IDF. In this paper, 10, as the most commonly used base number, is adopted. The Equation of IDF is shown as follows:

$$IDF_i = lg \frac{|D|}{1 + \{j : w_i \in d_i\}} \tag{2}$$

In Eq. (2), the numerator $|D|$ is the total number of documents, and the denominator $\{j : w_i \in d_i\}$ represents the number of documents containing the word w_i. In case the word w_i does not exist in the document, $1 + \{j : w_i \in d_i\}$ is used as the denominator to prevent the denominator from being 0. In conclusion, the Equation of TF-IDF is shown as follows:

$$TF - IDF_{i,d} = TF_{i,j} \times IDF_i \tag{3}$$

3 Data

The course reading materials of the OFO operation management are released to students, which contain eight randomly selected interviews from sharing bicycle users in Guangzhou Higher Education Mega Center. The interviews are conducted in Chinese and the total materials are over thirty pages, with 21984 Chinese characters. The interview texts are expected to analyze and answer the following questions:

(1)   Does the interviewee know about OFO sharing bicycle?
(2)   What are the life changes to the interviewees brought by OFO?
(3)   What are the respondents' satisfaction and dissatisfaction about the sharing bicycle industry?

(4)   What do respondents think of the current price of OFO?
(5)   What do respondents think of the current pricing of sharing bicycle?
(6)   What do the interviewees think of the deposit management?
(7)   Did the interviewees violate the regulations on OFO bicycles usage?
(8)   How should the government regulate the sharing bicycle industry?
(9)   What are the respondents' view on the relationship between the government and the sharing bicycle industry?
(10)   Do respondents think that the government should be involved in the pricing of sharing bicycles? How should it participate?
(11)   What other areas should the government intervene in the sharing bicycle industry?

TF-IDF requires a necessary data pre-processing procedure. For English texts, the following principles are applied: (1) uniform case; (2) remove punctuations; (3) remove digital symbols; (4) remove short words shorter than the specified length; (5) remove stop words; (6) stemming, which means the adjective form and the past tense of the word are transformed to the root of the word. After above steps, the text document is constituted with a number of unique terms.

Due to the large differences between Chinese and English grammatical structures, this paper adopts principles of partial data pre-processing before the calculation of TF-IDF: (1) remove punctuations; (2) remove digital symbols; (3) remove expletives; (4) remove single words and retain terms that contain more than two words and less than four words; (5) remove stop words and repeated words in interview materials.

4   Results and Comparison

4.1   Results of Manual Encoding in Nvivo

The eight interview documents were analyzed by a software NVivo through manual encoding. After decomposing and encoding, the following ten coding categories are determined, as shown in Table 1, including bicycle delivery, bicycle quality, the way of charge, misuse, privacy protection, changes in life, usage frequency, urban governance, storage place and deposit management. In the table, reference number refers to the times of number that this code is occurred among the eight interview texts. The weighted coverage rate means the coverage rate of a node in NVivo in a single text multiplied by the coverage rate of the documents containing this node in the total number of documents. The weighted coverage rate reflects the overall coverage of a node in ten documents and is calculated by applying Eq. (4).

$$R_{wc} = \frac{|\{a : C_i \in d_c\}| \sum R_i}{|D|} \tag{4}$$

$R_{w,c}$ is the weighted coverage rate of a particular node, and $|\{a : C_i \in d_c\}|$ is the number of documents that contain the node. $\sum R_i$ the sum of coverage rate of the node in all documents. The denominator $|D|$. is the number of documents in D.

The identified words and their frequencies analyzed by Nvivo are shown in Table 2. The shortest term length in Chinese is two. "Change" is as the most frequently occurred

Table 1. The selected text encoding of interview texts

Coding categories	Reference No.	Weighted coverage rate	Text encoding
Bicycle delivery	13	1.75%	Control quantity, everywhere, available anytime, not enough to increase supply
Bicycle quality	16	1.43%	Just so-so, not bad or good, unsatisfied, bad, damaged seats
Way of charge	74	16.74%	Use for free, not clear, uniform price, price rise, charge by time, charge by distance,
Misuse	20	3.97%	Unlock, no strong limit, park anywhere, privatization, damaged, park within the yellow line
Payment security	28	4.94%	Flow of money, Identity Card, GPS system, location information, divulge
Changes in life	26	5.06%	To subway, to bus stop, to school, to library or for internship, go shopping, short traveling, self-decided, convenient
Usage frequency	13	2.40%	Ever used, used very often, during working days and holidays, used three or four times
Urban governance	25	5.20%	Public facilities, protection, discard, urban environment, park anywhere, crowded, run the red light, safety hazard
Storage place	35	6.03%	Storage place, pick-up place, not fixed, unavailable, park permission, poor service quality
Deposit management	71	13.7%	Return at any time, return deposit, convenient, Alipay binding, illegal fund-raising, concerned with bankruptcy, usage frequency

word that appears 350 times, followed by the word "Government. All of the respondents expressed a strong desire for government intervention. Combined with the third and fifth ranked words "Deposit" and "Pricing", it reflects that the users want the government to supervise pricing mechanism and deposit management.

However, the results generated by Nvivo are not concentrated enough. There is dramatic diversity among the 14 ranked words with higher frequencies generated by Nvivo. In addition, Nvivo cannot filter out stop words from the texts, thus it contain deviations caused by the preference of each interviewer. Moreover, some long compound words in Chinese are usually incorrectly identified as multiple short words by Nvivo, and therefore the results are affected because of the false recognition.

Table 2. The identified words and their frequencies in the interview texts

Words	Counts	Weighted percentage	Similar words
Change	350	1.58%	Become, partial, produce, get, improve, restore, strengthen, alleviate, reduce, solve, carry on, destroy, obtain, confirm, set up, raise, promote, unify, limit, shape, influence
Government	183	2.14%	Public administration
Deposit	151	1.77%	Cash pledge
Enterprise	138	1.62%	Company
Pricing	136	1.59%	Price rate
Place	135	0.77%	Location, scope, function, area, advantage, status
Management	94	0.69%	Management, supervise, trade, operation, competition, control, permission
Privacy	80	0.94%	Right of privacy
User	77	0.90%	Consumer
Information	75	0.88%	Report, news
Regulation	72	0.84%	Stipulation
Comparison	67	0.79%	Contrast
Intervention	56	0.66%	Interpose
System	56	0.66%	Regime, institution

4.2 Results of TF-IDF Method

The TF-IDF value indicates the importance of a word in a single document. Therefore, the larger the value is, the more important the word is. However, a lesser value of TF-IDF does not necessarily mean the word is not important. Most of TF-IDF applications are conducted positively, by which the targeted text analysis is conducted on the result of maximum value. However, through the reverse application of TF-IDF, we can not only find out the key theme of eight interview texts, but also test the reliability of the key points.

Four interview texts were randomly taken for TF-IDF computation. Ten words with the highest frequencies in each interview document were selected. In Table 3, those terms with negative TF-IDF value were marked in bold type. For the Equation of TF-IFD calculation, the result can be negative when IDF value is negative. The number of documents $|D|$ is a constant, which equals to 8. If TF-IDF is negative, it means the tagged terms are mentioned in all eight interview texts.

From the result, it is found that government intervention and deposit management are the most vital words to which the students need to pay more attention, in addition to the theme of the interview - "sharing" and "bicycle".

Table 3. TF-IDF results by interview 1–4 text

Document	Term	Counts	#Documents	TF	IDF	TF-IDF
Interview 1 (325 words)	Facilities	8	1	0.02	0.6	0.015
	Public	8	4	0.02	0.2	0.005
	Convenient	10	6	0.03	0.06	0.002
	Regulation	8	6	0.02	0.06	0.001
	Place	6	6	0.02	0.06	0.001
	Price	12	7	0.04	0	0
	Government	**8**	**8**	**0.02**	**−0.05**	**−0.001**
	Deposit	**10**	**8**	**0.03**	**−0.05**	**−0.002**
	Sharing	**16**	**8**	**0.05**	**−0.05**	**−0.003**
	Bicycle	**26**	**8**	**0.08**	**−0.05**	**−0.004**
Interview 2 (91 words)	Quality	4	2	0.04	0.43	0.019
	Place	2	1	0.02	0.6	0.013
	Problem	3	6	0.03	0.06	0.002
	Price	5	7	0.05	0	0
	Deposit	**4**	**8**	**0.04**	**−0.05**	**−0.002**
	Enterprise	**5**	**8**	**0.05**	**−0.05**	**−0.003**
	Bicycle	**7**	**8**	**0.08**	**−0.05**	**−0.004**
	Government	**7**	**8**	**0.08**	**−0.05**	**−0.004**
	Sharing	**8**	**8**	**0.09**	**−0.05**	**−0.004**
Interview 3 (333 words)	Users	10	4	0.03	0.2	0.006
	Regulation	10	6	0.03	0.06	0.002
	Location	7	6	0.02	0.06	0.001

(*continued*)

Table 3. (*continued*)

Document	Term	Counts	#Documents	TF	IDF	TF-IDF
	Company	9	7	0.03	0	0
	Price	7	7	0.02	0	0
	Deposit	**12**	**8**	**0.04**	**−0.05**	**−0.002**
	Bicycle	**13**	**8**	**0.04**	**−0.05**	**−0.002**
	Government	**15**	**8**	**0.05**	**−0.05**	**−0.002**
	Sharing	**27**	**8**	**0.08**	**−0.05**	**−0.004**
Interview 4	Gradient	7	1	0.03	0.6	0.016
(263 words)	Minute	5	1	0.02	0.6	0.011
	Privacy	8	4	0.03	0.2	0.006
	University	5	3	0.02	0.3	0.006
	Charge	5	3	0.02	0.3	0.006
	Intervention	6	5	0.02	0.12	0.003
	Government	**8**	**8**	**0.03**	**−0.05**	**−0.002**
	Deposit	**13**	**8**	**0.05**	**−0.05**	**−0.003**
	Bicycle	**22**	**8**	**0.08**	**−0.05**	**−0.004**
	Sharing	**23**	**8**	**0.09**	**−0.05**	**−0.004**

5   Discussion

5.1   Government Regulation

From the results, it is found that users want government to solve the destruction of market rules and the disorder of market pricing mechanism caused by vicious competition among sharing bicycle companies. There are two main factors that lead to vicious price competition in sharing bicycle industry: (1) some companies dominate the market in transaction; (2) these advantageous companies lower regulatory standards in market competition [12]. Sharing bicycle services failed to differentiate among companies. The market segmentation and market positioning are also quite similar with each other, thus the strategy of corporate mainly focuses on how many bicycles can occupy the market quickly. This strategy uses capital erosion of other competitors' market share to achieve higher returns and more funding in the future, especially when it survives as a monopoly in the market [13]. However, as the funds are mainly used for marketing, the daily maintenance are largely cut. As a result, obvious regression occurs in the management of the sharing bicycle industry. This is the reason why the problems mentioned in the interview occurred, in which the maintenance of damaged bicycles cannot be kept up, and the bicycles are parked anywhere without being recycled.

As the society steps into the era of big data, users pay more attention to their personal privacy information, which can bring unprecedented value to enterprises. There are four ways to disclose users' personal privacy information in company's daily operation: data collection, secondary use of data, misuse of data, and unauthorized use of data [14]. Due to the demand of rent price calculation, sharing bicycle enterprises have an advantage in collecting and tracking customers' data. If customers want to use the sharing bicycle service, they have to exchange their private information in transaction. Consequently, the results reflect that users hope the government to strengthen the supervision on enterprises' collection and usage of personal privacy information.

5.2 Deposit Management

The results point out the necessity of government's supervision on deposit. The lack of regulation and guidance on deposit in sharing bicycles industry are caused by insufficient supervision of relevant regulatory authorities [15, 16]. The sharing bicycle industry has been developed rapidly in China since 2017. The expansionary speed with capital support is far beyond the prediction of government departments and financial regulators. Due to the immature financial technology, when it comes to the deposit transactions with fast turnover and large amount of information, the relevant departments do not have effective means to supervise the transaction data.

Although it is reasonable for enterprises to charge users' deposit as a pledge, many users are still concerned about the safety of the deposit. That the users pay the deposit as a pledge does not mean the users agree with how-to-use the deposit by enterprises. Users are concerned that the usage of deposit will change the ownership, since the enterprises make profits by investing the deposits. However, the risk of loss will be transferred to the users if the investment fails. If the deposit does not have the function of currency circulation, it should have not been flowed into the market [17, 18]. As an asset, the flow of deposit can create more value. In this regard, as long as the use of deposit is reasonable and legal, and an agreement has reached between enterprises and users on the ownership and the right to use, the deposit flowing into the market will have a positive effect [19].

6 Conclusion

As one of the hottest and newest industries in recent years, sharing bicycle is often used in the course teaching of operation management. In this paper, a text mining analysis on interview text data from users of OFO sharing bicycle in Guangzhou Higher Education Mega Center was conducted. The highly frequently used words were identified by using a TF-IDF method to investigate the existing problems occurred in sharing bicycle industry. A number of key problems including government supervision and deposit management are summarized and analyzed to provide policy suggestions to the government.

Acknowledgements. This paper is supported by the science and technology plan of Guangzhou (No. 201804010296) and Natural Science Foundation of Guangdong Province, China. (No. 2018A030310051).

References

1. Singla, A., Santoni, M., Bartók, G.: Incentivizing users for balancing bike sharing systems. In: AAAI 2015 Proceedings of the Twenty-Ninth AAAI Conference on Artificial Intelligence, pp. 723–729 (2015)
2. Su, J.: Sharing economy: drivers, problems and prospects. J. Xinjiang Normal Univ. **39**(02), 126–131 (2018). (Philosophy and social sciences edition)
3. China sharing economy development report (2019). http://www.sic.gov.cn/News/557/9904.htm
4. Ai Media: Special research on 2018 China's Sharing bicycle development status report (2018). http://www.iimedia.cn/63243.html
5. Li, K.: Study on the development countermeasures of urban shared bicycle from the perspective of sharing economy. City **3**, 66–69 (2017)
6. Li, M.: Marketing research on Shared Bicycle. Financial Industry (academic edition) **5**, 121–123 (2017)
7. Chen, C., Li, X.: A study on the influencing factors of citizens' willingness to use Shared bicycles. J. Manag. **15**(11), 1601 (2018)
8. Fan, Y., Cao, Y.: Sharing of legal responsibilities among users under sharing mode-a case study of sharing bicycles. Tianjin Law **3**, 1–6 (2018)
9. Qiu, J., Zou, F.: Research on content analysis. Chin. Libr. J. **2**, 12–17 (2004)
10. Noble, H., Smith, J.: Qualitative data analysis: a practical example. Evid. Nurs. **17**(1), 2 (2014)
11. Marshall, H.: Horses for courses: facilitating postgraduate research students' choice of Computer Assisted Qualitative Data Analysis System (CAQDAS). Contemp. Nurse **13**(1), 29–37 (2002)
12. Tan, Y.: Exploration and prevention of "bottom line competition" in shared bicycle. Price Theory Pract. **3**, 36–40 (2017)
13. Zhang, Y., Liu, X., Zhang, H.: Urban public bicycle system in China: current situation, problems and countermeasures. China Dev. **13**(5), 74–79 (2017)
14. He, M., Liang, X.: Can the system and mechanism of sharing platform promote consumers' continuous willingness to share? – influence mechanism of institutional trust on shared platforms. Financ. Econ. Rev. **236**(8), 75–84 (2008)
15. Deng, D., Li, Z.: Study on the nature and supervision of shared bicycle deposit management. J. Southwest Jiaotong Univ. **18**(04), 94–100 (2017). (social science edition)
16. Guo, P.: Bike-sharing: collaborative governance in Internet technology and public services. J. Pub. Adm. **14**(3), 1–10 (2017)
17. Liu, Y.: Analysis on the development of Shared Bicycle. Financ. Times **8**, 251 (2017)
18. Wu, M., Cheng, N., Li, L.: Public welfare and business of shared bicycle from the perspective of rent and deposit management. Price Theory Pract. **5**, 136–138 (2017)
19. Song, J.: An analysis on regulatory issues of deposit management for shared bicycles. Gansu Finance **4**, 27–30 (2017)

Leveraging Neural Network for Online Learning Performance Prediction and Learning Suggestion

Yingshan Shen[1], Weiwei Liu[1], Qiumei Wu[1], Ruiyang Chen[1], and Kui Liu[2](✉)

[1] School of Computer Science, South China Normal University, Guangzhou, China
shenys@m.scnu.edu.cn, 674960668@qq.com, 1014894992@qq.com,
243189663@qq.com
[2] Network and Modern Educational Technology Center, Guangzhou University, Guangzhou,
China
liukui@gzhu.edu.cn

Abstract. Learning performance analysis is such a research field that draws much attention from researchers though it has just been emerged in recent years. On the one hand, analyzing learning behaviors can help learners to choose their learning methods and allocate their study time in a more appropriate way. On the other hand, learning analysis can provide valuable feedbacks for teachers and administrators to improve teaching efficiency and quality. This paper studies and analyzes more than 640,000 learning data from the MOOC platform edX. A tree-based model along with an information gain measure is applied to identify the usefulness of data features. A back-propagation neural network model is further adopted to train data and achieve a prediction model of learning performance. In addition, a genetic algorithm calculates learning score conditions and return feedbacks as suggestions to learners. Experiment results demonstrate the effectiveness of the utilization of the methods in the predication of online learning performance.

Keywords: Neural network · Genetic algorithm · Learning prediction · Suggestion

1 Introduction

With the fast development of information technology in education area, dramatically increasing of educational data has been accumulated. The data has attracted more and more attentions from both academic researchers and industry engineers as the data is an essential source to measure the quality of education and analyze learning behaviors. For example, Song et al. utilized a bibliometric analysis to explore the research on classroom dialogue in the past two decades [1]. By analyzing a large number of data collected during the teaching and learning processes, various learning styles of learners and different situations of learning environments can be discovered [2]. These findings can further reveal the significance of improving learning efficiency through feedbacks and predictions of learners' learning trends [3]. There are a variety of online education

© Springer Nature Switzerland AG 2020
E. Popescu et al. (Eds.): SETE 2019, LNCS 11984, pp. 267–279, 2020.
https://doi.org/10.1007/978-3-030-38778-5_29

platforms, e.g., Moodle, Blackboard, MOOC, etc., containing a large amount of learning record data including the information of learning behaviors, emotional states, facial features, cognitive activities, attention levels and so on. The data sources for learning analysis are widespread and the data types are extraordinary diverse [4].

Learning analysis technology can be used to evaluate the quality of online courses and performances. For teachers and administrators, it provides more specified methods and targeted teaching interventions of students on the basis of data analysis [5, 6]. For researcher, it can be used as an effective tool to find out the learning situations of individual students and the utility status of online learning [7]. For technical developers, it helps to optimize the user interface design of learning management systems, discover the relationship between frequency and usage paths of each module in a learning management system, and develop better functions of systems according to the needs of software engineers to carry out appropriate learning analysis technology [8].

Among the learning technology, machine learning algorithms are frequently applied to learning analysis and data prediction [9]. Recently, new machine learning algorithms particularly deep learning methods are receiving more and more attentions in domain applications. For example, Back-Propagation (BP) neural network, as one of artificial neural networks, is used in many prediction scenarios, such as lottery opening prediction [10], vehicle speed prediction [11] and its optimization, building insulation material performance prediction [12], short-term traffic flow prediction [13] to improve chaotic genetic algorithm, etc. All these applications are oriented to daily life and the BP neural network has demonstrated suitable performances.

Therefore, this paper tries to apply a BP neural network model for online learning analysis. In addition, there is a large-scale open online course learning platform edX, which is created by MIT University and Harvard University in 2012. There are more than 640,000 learning behavior records, which are initially analyzed by using a logistic regression algorithm, where the learners' ability to complete learning tasks is predicted [14]. Moreover, many literatures report the usage of genetic algorithms for application optimization. For example, a robust global optimization search algorithm has been widely used in combinatorial optimization, signal processing, machine learning and other aspects of predictive controls. Therefore, this paper applies a BP neural network model for the prediction of learning performance as well as applies a genetic algorithm for the prediction analysis of learning data for learning behavior suggestion.

2 The Methodology

The approach that analyze education data and make suggestions for online learning is described in this section. We firstly apply a decision tree algorithm to automatically discovery learning data attributes/features that have different impacts on learning results. A BP feed forward neural network model is then applied to train a model containing learning behaviors of learners to find out the correlation between learners' learning behaviors and final performance in terms of scores. Based on these correlations and a genetic algorithm, the estimation of learning cost required for the prediction of expected learning score is implemented. The corresponding goal-oriented learning behavior suggestion is thus made based on these predicted results. The processes and related methods for the learning predication and suggestion is described below in detail.

2.1   A Decision Tree Model for Feature Selection

In order to achieve a more accurate prediction of online learning performance, a widely used measure, information gain, along with a tree-based data mining model are used to distinguish data attributes/features having much or less influence on the learning results.

Information gain is mainly used to measure the impacts of a feature on a classification target. In the measure, the essential criterion is to define how much information a feature can bring to a classification target. The more information it brings, the more important the feature is. For a feature, the amount of information changed between the beginning and the ending is the total information that this feature brings to the system. The information quantity is so-called entropy. The stronger the information gain of a certain influence feature for a classification target (such as learning performance score in this study), the greater impact of the influence on that classification target generally.

The volume of information gain for a decision tree model is often used to judge the impacts of various data on performance values in the decision tree. There are precedents in learning analysis and prediction by using decision tree model for data analysis. For example, the decision tree ID3 algorithm is used to predict whether the students can pass the exam [15]. Predict the results of the general English examination of public courses for undergraduate [16]. Chanchary et al. used association rule mining and decision tree classification to discover the relationship between learners' using behavior in learning management system and their final scores [17]. In most of these documents, decision tree model is used to roughly predict whether a course achieve the standard or not, which reflects the value of decision tree model in learning analysis to a certain extent. However, it also proves that the idea of information gain, which is the support of classification rules of decision tree algorithm, has good reliability in dealing with classification problems.

It also proves that the idea of information gain, which is support of classification rules of decision tree algorithm, has better reliability in dealing with classification problems.

The information attributes of data are task-related. For classification tasks, the information contained value y is calculation as Eq. (1),

$$Info(y) = \ln p(y) \tag{1}$$

where $p(y)$ is the probability of y occurrence. The smaller $p(y)$ is, the larger of amount of information contained in y.

Entropy is a measure widely used in information theory that describes the purity of any sample data set. It is defined as the expected value of information. A data set S can be divided into m classes, where information entropy is the expected value of the information contained in a randomly obtained label as Eq. (2).

$$E(S) = -\sum_{i=1}^{m} p(y_i) ln p(y_i) \tag{2}$$

Assuming that $E(S_{aim})$ is the entropy of the m class for the target data and S_i ($i = \{0, 1, 2...\}$) is another entropy of target classification using other classification strategies. The $Gain[i]$ is the information gain about S_{aim} obtained by classifying data according to data item S_i. When the information gain value is larger, the greater correlation between data item S_i and data item S_{aim} is. Popularly, the information gain $Gain$ is a quantification of the degree of association between S_i data and S_{aim} data. The higher the value of $Gain[i]$, the closer relationship between S_i and S_{aim} is. Assume that n classes can be obtained by classified data according to S_i, the $Gain$ value is calculated using the Eq. (3) as follows:

$$Gain[i] = E(S_{aim}) - \sum_{n=1}^{k} E(S_{in}) \tag{3}$$

2.2 A BP Neural Network Model for Prediction

We use a BP neural network model to train our online learning data set and get the trained neural network for the prediction of learning performance. The BP neural network is the way of recurrent error calculation algorithm which is an error back propagation algorithm added on the basis of ordinary artificial neural network [3]. The idea is to use output error to estimate the error of first layer of output layers, and then use this error to estimate the error value of previous layer, so as to obtain the estimated error of all layers. The error estimation here can be understood as partial derivatives, through which the connection weights of each layer are adjusted, and then the output errors are recalculated with the adjusted connection weights until the output errors meet the requirements or the number of iterations overflow a set value. Its essence is the dynamic adjustment of connection weights through adjusting the weights of each layer of error partial derivative, and finally make the error output meeting established requirements. Figure 1 is the flow chart of the BP neural network model. Due to the space limitation, the details of the model is not be described in this paper.

2.3 A Genetic Algorithm for Suggestion

Conventional learning suggestions only put forward some comments for improving learning performance. It is difficult for learners to visually and quickly understand how much help can be obtained from those learning suggestions. Specific suggestions for learning objectives are generally missing in existing suggestion systems. Moreover, accurate prediction of academic performance and its related suggestions based on learning behaviors through learning analysis can further promote the allocation of learners' energy in learning, enable learners to achieve their expected learning goals more efficiently to maximize personal value and to improve the efficiency of social operation to a certain extent.

The essence of learning suggestion is the specific and accurate comment details on particular learning aspects. The learning suggestions are carried out by utilizing a genetic algorithm. The genetic algorithm, on the one hand, eliminates the trouble of reverse decomposition of complex neural networks to find a target value. On the other hand, if only reverse decomposition of a trained neural network substitution operation can only achieve a target and the value is fixed. However, using genetic algorithm not only can obtain multiple predications on necessary learning features, but also can acquire dynamic solutions according to the principle of the genetic algorithm. Through these dynamic solutions, we can identify new learning experiences which are different from previous ones.

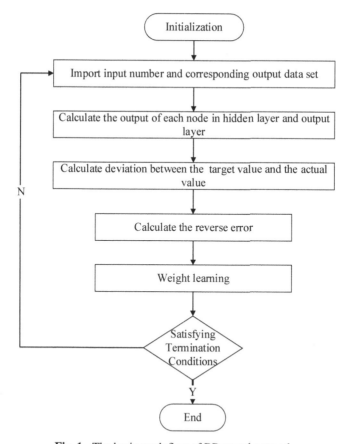

Fig. 1. The basic work flow of BP neural network.

From the training results of the neural network, final prediction score is calculated based on seven aspects, such as the number of learning chapters, the number of days of course visits, the number of course interactions, etc. The trained formula of the neural network is derived by function named *BPnet* (*N*), in which *N* is the data items of the seven aspects, and the function returns the result value learning *grade*. Equation (4) is used to implement the predication of certain expected feature values.

$$GA(A, grade) = X(grade) = BPnet(N), N = \{A, X\} \qquad (4)$$

In the equation, *A* refers to the known data items, *grade* refers to the value of target score, *X* refers to an expected feature, *N* is a set of factors that affect the final score value in the trained neural network. *N* is composed of *A* and *X*. From the trained neural network *BPnet*, the genetic algorithm *GA* is computed. The approximated feature value achieved with the goal *grade* is obtained by the recursively genetic algorithm.

When the expected feature X contains multiple items, there are several combinations of solutions with large deviations in the solution set of X. Furthermore, some of the combinations deviate from actual needs, which requires a system to repeat siftings the combination of these solutions in order to get the best suggestion. In this paper, each data in the training data set is sorted, 1/4 of the first and last data are excluded, and the average of half data in the middle is obtained as the value of each data (mid). When X has multiple items, the weight W of each group of solutions is obtained by using the Eq. (5). n denotes the number of combinations of different solutions, m is the number of combinations of solutions that are artificially restricted for optimal selection, and k defines the serial number of data items.

$$W_n = \sum_{i}^{i \in k} (x_n[i]/mid[i]), n = \{0, 1, 2..m\} \tag{5}$$

3   Experiments and Results

3.1   Data Pre-processing

The data are from edX[1], which is a MOOC online course learning platform, containing learning reports from Harvard University and MIT during 2010 to 2013. All the data contains learning information of participants, including course registered time, the last login time, the number of course interactions, course visit days, video chips playing frequency, the end time of each learning chapter, forum posting number, etc. The relevant personal information of learners, such as course identify, grade, user identify, country, educational background, date of birth, gender and so on, is also included. A total number of 640,000 records are used in this research. After filtering out invalid data, such as incomplete data, 74,000 records are finally used as a data set.

Learning effort refers to the measurable value of behavior that learners put in to achieve the learning goal of mastering a knowledge point, such as learning time, learning comprehension ability and other objective factors. It is worth to discuss that how to minimize the input learning cost and maximize the learning effect. In addition to the traditional factors affecting the learning cost, some new elements, such as the length of online learning, the number of questions answered, the timeliness of submitting homework, the frequency of online browsing, the frequency of downloading learning resources and watching teaching videos, the number of posts, etc., are included in the following experiments.

For the purpose of data mining, the data set is being pre-processed. The preprocessing consists of the following aspects:

(1)   There are 16 disciplines of courses recorded in the edX data set. For the convenience of data processing, all course identify (ID) belongs to the 16 course disciplines are renumbered to be 1–16.

---

[1] https://www.edx.org/about-us.

(2) For the existing missing value cases particularly on the academic qualifications attribute, different levels of academic qualifications are mapped to a list of sequential numerics. For example, missing values and incorrect values are mapped to 0, while the secondary school qualification is set to be 1, secondary school is set to be 2, and undergraduate is set to be 3, etc.
(3) The null value or missing value of gender attribute is labelled to 0 while male is 1 and female is 2.
(4) Age information is not directly available but it can be calculated from year of birth. According to the release time of the data, all the year of birth information is transferred to the actual age of learners. However, there are some false cases, such as 2011–2013. We therefore set them as a special mark. After that, since 20 years old is an essential age in this research, all the age lower than 20 is set as 1 and every increase of 5 years obtains an additional 1 based on the base value.
(5) Others information such as nationality are removed considering that the information has no practical reference value in this study.

Afterwards, all the data items with 0 or null values are filtered out. A sample raw data from the edX MOOC platform and the corresponding pre-processed data are shown in Fig. 2.

B	C	D	E	F	G	H	I	J	K	L	M	N	O	P	Q	R	S	T
userid_[	registeri	viewed	explore(	certified	final_cc	LoE_DI	YoB	gender	grade	start_tin	last_eve	nevents	ndays_a	nplay_vi	nchapte	nforum	roles	incompl
MHxPC13(	1	0	0	0	United Stat	NA	NA	NA	0	#######	#######		9			0		1
MHxPC13(	1	1	0	0	United Stat	NA	NA	NA	0	#######			9		1	0		1
MHxPC13(	1	0	0	0	United Stat	NA	NA	NA	0	2013/2/8	#######		16			0		1
MHxPC13(	1	0	0	0	United Stat	NA	NA	NA	0	#######			16			0		1
MHxPC13(	1	0	0	0	United Stat	NA	NA	NA	0	#######			16			0		1
MHxPC13(	1	1	1	0	United Stat	NA	NA	NA	0	#######	#######	502	16	50	12	0		
MHxPC13(	1	0	0	0	United Stat	NA	NA	NA	0	2013/2/8			16			0		1
MHxPC13(	1	1	0	0	France	NA	NA	NA	0	2013/1/1	#######	42	6		3	0		
MHxPC13(	1	1	0	0	United Stat	NA	NA	NA	0	#######	#######	70	3		3	0		
MHxPC13(	1	1	0	0	United Stat	NA	NA	NA	0	#######			12		3	0		1
MHxPC13(	1	1	0	0	United Stat	NA	NA	NA	0	#######	#######	17	2		2	0		
MHxPC13(	1	1	0	0	United Stat	NA	NA	NA	0	#######	#######	32	1		3	0		
MHxPC13(	1	1	0	0	United Stat	NA	NA	NA	0	#######			2		2	0		1
MHxPC13(	1	1	0	0	United Stat	NA	NA	NA	0	#######	#######	78	5		4	0		
MHxPC13(	1	1	0	0	United Stat	NA	NA	NA	0	#######	#######	75	14	5	2	0		
MHxPC13(	1	1	0	0	United Stat	NA	NA	NA	0	#######	#######	11	2	2	1	0		

A	B	C	D	E	F	G	H	I	J	K	L	M	N	O
1	2HxPC130	0	Nigeria	4	4	2	0.06	2012/12/21	2013/3/13	455	7	11	5	0
1	2HxPC130	0	United Sta	4	0	1	0.02	2013/2/11	2013/3/3	494	6	46	2	1
1	2HxPC130	1	Spain	4	3	1	0.51	2013/1/26	2013/4/5	2194	11	146	5	0
1	2HxPC130	0	Other Eurc	4	4	1	0.02	2012/12/22	2013/3/7	286	4	19	1	0
1	2HxPC130	1	United Sta	3	2	1	0.86	2013/2/11	2013/5/6	5508	25	651	11	0
1	2HxPC130	0	Other Eurc	4	3	1	0.39	2013/1/15	2013/3/26	3514	17	348	7	0
1	2HxPC130	1	United Sta	3	2	1	0.88	2013/1/15	2013/5/12	5636	41	323	10	0
1	2HxPC130	1	India	2	1	1	0.59	2012/12/21	2013/5/8	1313	9	2	7	0
1	2HxPC130	0	Other Afri	3	3	1	0.44	2013/2/2	2013/4/7	3735	17	17	7	0
1	2HxPC130	0	United Sta	0	0	0	0.18	2013/2/13	2013/6/5	1564	10	122	7	0

Fig. 2. Examples of raw data (top panel) containing learning information from the edX MOOC platform and the corresponding pre-processed data (bottom panel).

3.2 The Results

By applying the decision tree method with the information gain measure, as described in Subsect. 3.1, the edX data can be computed to filter out invaluable attributes. From the processing result on the edX data set, the attributes of the number of learning chapters, course visits, course interactions, video playback times, course id, forum posts, education, age and gender have a less impacts on learners' final performance. Among them, age and gender have the lowest influences. Therefore, it can be preliminarily concluded that age and gender have little influence on the final learning scores, thus they are removed from the dataset in the following experiments. The settings and the result of using the decision tree model is shown as Table 1.

Table 1. The settings of the decision tree model and the result using the model.

Model settings	Growth Method	CRT
	Independent variable	Learning score
	Dependent variable	The number of course interactions, course visit days, video chips playing frequency, the time of learning chapter, forum posting number, grade, educational background, age, gender, course ID
	Verification	None
	Maximum tree depth	10
	Minimum case in parent node	100
	Minimum case in sub-node	50
Running result	Independent variables include	The number of learning chapters, the days of course landing, the number of course interactions, course visit days, video chips playing frequency, course ID, forum posting number, educational background, age, gender
	Number of nodes	71
	Number of terminal nodes	36
	Depth	8

In accordance with the BP neural network model, the total of 74,000 data of edX records is split into three datasets, training data (70%), validation data (15%) and testing data (15%). According to the result of attribute/feature selection, the number of learning chapters, course visiting days, course interaction times, video playback times, course id, forum posting numbers and academic qualifications are taken as input conditions. By applying the BP neural network, the learning scores of learners are predicted. Table 2 demonstrates the predicted learning scores corresponding to each online course for example learners.

Since the output derivation of the trained BP neural network can be regarded as a linear problem, the genetic algorithm can obtain satisfactory results when the number of iterations is larger enough to solve the linear problem. We therefore conduct an experiment on 1,000 randomly selected samples. The calculated result of error rate after 10,000 iterations closes to 0.

Table 2. Examples of final learning score predication corresponding to courses for different learners.

Course id	Educational background	Number of course interactions	Days of course visiting	Times of video playback	Learning chapters	Numbers of forum posting	Predicted learning score
1	4	455	7	11	5	0	0.06
1	4	494	6	46	2	1	0.02
1	4	2194	11	146	5	0	0.51
1	4	286	4	19	1	0	0.02
1	3	5508	25	651	11	0	0.86
1	4	3514	17	348	7	0	0.39
1	3	5636	41	323	10	0	0.88
1	2	1313	9	2	7	0	0.59
1	3	3735	17	17	7	0	0.44
1	0	1564	10	122	7	0	0.18
1	4	4414	33	322	11	0	0.93
1	0	1681	15	87	4	0	0.2
1	2	1723	21	2	9	0	0.6
1	2	6683	33	1512	12	0	0.78
1	3	1377	5	4	5	0	0.45
1	4	118	3	13	1	0	0.03
1	2	225	5	106	2	0	0.01
1	3	971	5	46	5	0	0.15
1	3	2719	17	58	9	0	0.6

The error histogram is shown as Fig. 3, where *Targets* represents the actual value, *Outputs* denotes the output values calculated using the trained neural network based on the training data and validation data. *Errors* is calculated by *Targets* minus *Outputs*, as the horizontal axis in the figure. The vertical line in the middle of the histogram represents zero error. Accordingly, the distribution of errors on the training, validation, and test data can be visualized and analyzed.

In addition, to better analyze the errors, error ranges are calculated, as shown in Table 1. It shows that the result of whole error prediction accounts for the vast majority within 0.1 (nearly 70%). However, the error is within 0.05 accounting for more than 50% in proportion (Table 3).

From the above experiments, it can be seen that the prediction accuracy using the BP algorithm is relatively reliable to some extent by viewing the low error values. Thus, it is feasible to select the features that have great influence using information gain as well as to predict learning performance in terms of score.

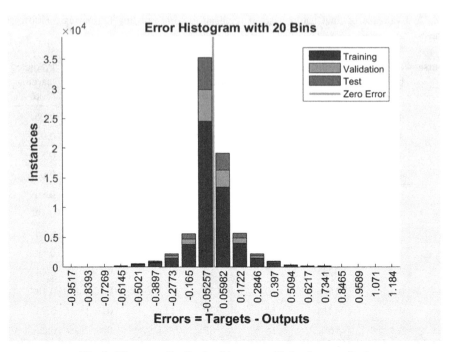

Fig. 3. The error distribution histogram (Color figure online)

Table 3. The error ranges and their corresponding proportion.

Error range	Proportion
<1.00	7.6%
<0.30	3.34%
<0.25	4.82%
<0.20	6.3%
<0.15	9.15%
<0.10	15.23%
<0.05	52.96%

A system containing the described prediction and suggestion functions is designed and implemented in our project. A screenshot of the system user interface is shown as Fig. 4. The system can automatically select features with the lowest weight W value as the optimal solution, which is translated into suggested learning behavior as feedbacks to learners. The large rectangle in red color shows the detailed suggestions of learning behaviors for current learner if he/she expects to obtain a distinction score (0.087424) under current learning progress.

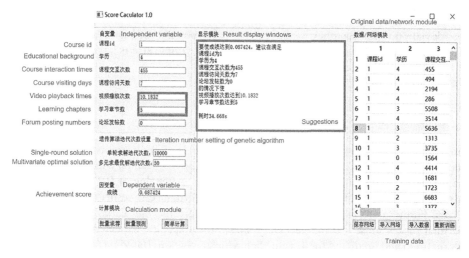

Fig. 4. Demonstration of operation results

3.3 Complexity Discussion

In this processing of research, it is found that so complexity by using decision tree, neural network and genetic algorithm to build the model which is relatively high. There are several problems in the prediction and suggestion of learning performance as follows:

(1) There are many factors affecting a student's test scores, which can't depend on a small amount of data recorded to a large extent. On the one hand, in addition to the recorded learning behavior factors, some sudden situations for individual students will also affect learners' performance, then affecting the predicted results.

(2) On the other hand, because of too many factors, many common learning behaviors or related data that affect learning outcomes cannot be recorded, thus affecting the comprehensiveness and accuracy of prediction. At present, there are widely accepted recording standards technology of online learning behavior such as xAPI, but in fact it is very difficult to use these standards of technology to achieve real academic performance prediction.

(3) It Lacks of publicly available research and learning datasets. From the point of this papers, most of the data come from the private data of online learning system or distance education platform in universities. It is difficult for external researchers to obtain valuable research data. Although the widespread use of MOOC platform has created a large number of online learning records, due to privacy protection and other factors, users' using data is not fully public. There are only 16 courses on Edx platform and education data in UCI database are published by Harvard University and Massachusetts Institute of Technology. However, there are some problems in these data, such as low data quality and few reference factors.

(4) When the amount of data used in the experiment is small, there may be a large deviation in the accuracy of the results. This study is based on learning large data technology for learning and analysis. When the sample size is large enough, it can significantly improve the prediction accuracy.

4 Conclusions

This paper targets at online learning prediction and learning behavior suggestion for improving learning performance of learners. A decision tree method with an information gain measure are applied for data feature selection. After that, a BP neural network model is adopted for the prediction of learning performance in terms of final learning scores. Furthermore, with the help of a genetic algorithm, the features that influence the final scores most and the necessary values for a specific expected learning score are analyzed and predicted for learning behavior suggestion. Based on 640,000 learning records of online courses from edX, the experiments are conducted and the results show that almost 70% of the prediction with errors remain within 0.1, indicating the high prediction accuracy. Therefore, this work provides a potential way for effective online learning performance prediction and learning behavior suggestion.

With the rapid development of big data technology, and the opening and collection of data, it also received wide attention of the mining and analysis of educational data. With the further development of data collection and openness, the accurate learning prediction will be more accurate. Therefore, the paper can build learner's standard learning model through learning analysis technology, use standardized source data to predict and suggest, improve the accuracy of prediction results, make more accurate recommendation, and help learners to conduct personalized learning more effectively, improve the efficiency of online learning.

References

1. Song, Y., Chen, X.L., Hao, T.Y., Liu, Z.N., Lan, Z.X.: Exploring two decades of research on classroom dialogue using bibliometric analysis. Comput. Educ. **137**(2019), 12–31 (2019)
2. Qu, Y., Yu, Z., Cong, H., Hao, T.: Pedagogical principle based e-learning exploration: a case of construction mediation training. In: Huang, T.-C., Lau, R., Huang, Y.-M., Spaniol, M., Yuen, C.-H. (eds.) SETE 2017. LNCS, vol. 10676, pp. 539–547. Springer, Cham (2017). https://doi.org/10.1007/978-3-319-71084-6_63
3. Kashiwao, T., Nakayama, K., Ando, S., et al.: A neural network-based local rainfall prediction system using meteorological data on the Internet: a case study using data from the Japan Meteorological Agency. Appl. Soft Comput. **56**, 317–330 (2017)
4. Lou, W.: The research of high-dimensional data mining technology for big data. Shanghai University (2013)
5. Chen, E., Heritage, M., Lee, J.: Identifying and monitoring students' learning needs with technology. J. Educ. Students Placed Risk **2010**(3), 309–332 (2010)
6. Wang, X., Hao, T.: Designing interactive exercises for corpus-based English Learning with Hot Potatoes software. In: Huang, T.-C., Lau, R., Huang, Y.-M., Spaniol, M., Yuen, C.-H. (eds.) SETE 2017. LNCS, vol. 10676, pp. 485–494. Springer, Cham (2017). https://doi.org/10.1007/978-3-319-71084-6_57

7. Gu, X.Q., Zhang, J.L., Cai, H.Y.: Learning analysis: emerging data technology. J. Distance Educ. **30**(01), 18–25 (2012)

8. Wei, S.P.: Learning analysis technology: mining the value of educational data in the age of big data. Mod. Educ. Technol. **02**, 5–11 (2013)

9. Hao, T., Chen, W., Xie, H., Nadee, W., Lau, R. (eds.): SETE 2018. LNCS, vol. 11284. Springer, Cham (2018). https://doi.org/10.1007/978-3-030-03580-8. ISSN 0302-9743, ISBN 978-3-030-03579-2

10. Tu, Y.: Application of BP neural network in welfare lottery prediction. Intelligent Computing Branch of China Operational Research Society. Third China Intelligent Computing Congress. Intelligent Computing Branch of China Operational Research Society, vol. 2009, no. 4, pp. 16–19 (2009)

11. Xie, H.: Prediction of driving condition for plug-in hybrid electric vehicles. Chongqing University, Chongqing, China (2014)

12. Shu, Y., Gu, B.W., Zhang, Y.Q.: Performance prediction of building thermal insulation materials based on bp neural network algorithm. Build. Energy Conserv. **04**, 52–55 (2017)

13. Lun, Z.M.: Short-term traffic flow prediction based on BP neural network optimized by modified chaotic genetic algorithms. Comput. Program. Skills Maintenance **05**, 18–20 (2017)

14. He, C.K., Wu, M.: Analysis and prediction of learning behavior of educational big data based on edX Platform. Distance Educ. China **06**, 54–59 (2016)

15. Li, D.Z., Du, L.Y.: Application of data mining-based student performance prediction. Heilongjiang Sci. Technol. Inf. **7**, 156–157 (2017)

16. Sun, L., Cheng, Y.X.: Research and realization of learning achievement prediction of network education in the big data era - taking the english examination for undergraduate public courses as an example. Open Educ. Res. **21**(03), 74–80 (2015)

17. He, W.: Examining students' online interaction in a live video streaming environment using data mining and text mining. Comput. Hum. Behav. **29**(1), 90–102 (2013)

An Empirical Study of Corpus-Based Translation Teaching in Higher Vocational Colleges in China

Wen Zhao[1] and Yuanyuan Mu[2,3(✉)]

[1] Basic Teaching Department, Fuyang Vocational and Technical College, Fuyang, China
389060617@qq.com
[2] School of Foreign Studies, Hefei University of Technology, Hefei, China
390842884@qq.com
[3] Center for Translation Studies and Specialized Corpora, Hefei University of Technology, Hefei, China

Abstract. This paper analyzes the current situation of corpus-based translation teaching, and highlights the necessity and advantages of using corpora to facilitate translation teaching in vocational colleges in China. The development of corpus not only provides an unprecedented wide range of text materials for language research, but also promotes further development of various research fields of linguistics. The teaching research based on corpus is conducive to expanding and deepening translation research, promoting translation practice and improving the quality of translation and translation teaching. This research also applies a corpus-based online translation teaching and learning platform in translation courses of a vocational college and summarizes a "data-driven" mode of translation teaching and learning assisted by corpora.

Keywords: Corpus · Translation teaching · Vocational colleges

1 Introduction

Translation studies had not been integrated with corpus linguistics for a long time until the 1990s. Corpus-based language teaching has become a new teaching mode with the development of information technology. In English translation teaching, in addition to the mass storage of teaching corpus, the data emission generated by corpus can also be archived, counted, analyzed and described quantitatively with the help of a certain technical support, so as to find out the translation problems that tend to occur during students' learning, or to find and verify the rules of translation performance characteristics of students at a certain stage, or even get the rules of the development of translation ability of a specific group of students. In addition to the statistics and analysis of the characteristics of students' translations, teachers can also combine keyboard recording software such as Trans log, Input log or Camtasia and other screen capture software to dynamically track and record students' translation process, and explore students' translation behaviors or the reasons behind their behaviors.

© Springer Nature Switzerland AG 2020
E. Popescu et al. (Eds.): SETE 2019, LNCS 11984, pp. 280–284, 2020.
https://doi.org/10.1007/978-3-030-38778-5_30

In our case study, we focus on the application of corpus in translation teaching in higher vocational colleges in China. At the present stage, higher vocational colleges pay more attention to students' oral and writing ability in language teaching and learning. However, more has been required about students' translation ability due to objective factors. Therefore, the quality of translation teaching in higher vocational colleges is in urgent need of improvement. With an empirical study, this paper discusses the applicability of corpus in higher vocational English translation teaching. Assisted by an online translation teaching/(self-)learning platform, teachers can take a guiding role to select and mark the corpus to suit their teaching purposes and students' translation levels. Based on the explorations in real translation teaching environment, this paper summarizes the "data-driven" mode to inspire the translation teaching in higher vocational colleges.

2 An Overview of Corpus-Based English Translation Teaching

In the 1990s, there are several trends of translation studies that have shifted from a prescriptive approach to a descriptive one. These trends inevitably lead to the gradual development of descriptive translation studies. In this context, corpus-based translation research has emerged. Mona Baker is a core representative of a group of cutting-edge scholars who advocated corpus translation research. Baker [1] applied relevant research results of corpus to translation studies and has made considerable achievements in the field of translation studies and translation teaching. The application of corpus can not only drive students' learning enthusiasm and make classroom teaching subjects diversified, but also reduce the obstacles in translation teaching, encouraging students to learn translation knowledge better and hence improving their translation ability, and thereby promote the quality of translation teaching and facilitate the standardization in translation teaching. It can be seen that the application of corpus in English translation teaching is not only the need of English curriculum reform, but also the need of students to improve their translation competence. In short, the construction of the corpus of translation teaching can be extended to the scientific research module to study and promote teaching.

In recent years, the construction of translation teaching corpus has attracted much attention in this field. One of the corpus-based online translation teaching and learning platform has been developed by Professor Zhu Chunshen and Dr. Mu Yuanyuan's research team. This platform comprises: (1) corpus-construction (including text-annotation, exercises with explanation of answers, and knowledge-based topical boards); (2) the knowledge management system; and (3) electronic program design to interconnect all the aforementioned components for inter-module navigation online [2]. The Platform has been used in actual teaching of translation and has generated a series of studies [3–5].

The platform relies on the development of bilingual corpus and adopts SAAS multi-tenant service architecture to ensure the isolation of user data and fill the gap of domestic and foreign computer-aided translation teaching software. Its corpus is real and vivid, with complete classification and rich sources. In its platform, the annotated words are keywords extracted from various text phenomena and translation methods. It is an original and strictly defined system used to identify and describe the texts and cultural phenomena that can be used for corpus annotation. There is a total of 200 labeled keywords, covering 9 categories currently. Each keyword is strictly defined, and its theoretical support comes from functional linguistics, textual linguistics, stylistics, translation studies, etc. The purpose of corpus annotation guided by annotated keywords is to avoid impressionistic comments, and to enhance the teachability of translation methods and skills by displaying the explanatory power of texts.

3   The Empirical Research of Corpus-Based Translation Teaching in Vocational Colleges

Corpora provide resource support for English translation classes in higher vocational colleges. Corpora contain real language materials used by people in various language communication situations, provide objective examples of the actual use of language, intuitively reflect the use of language, and have strong realistic and social characteristics. In corpus-based English translation teaching in vocational colleges, teachers can avoid the phenomenon of lacking objective scientific basis by relying on intuition or teaching experience in traditional translation teaching, which not only fully demonstrates the characteristics of high-vocational translation teaching, but also provides a lot of real language materials as support for it.

Compared with the traditional teaching mode of indoctrination, the corpus-based English teaching in vocational colleges can transform the role of teachers from traditional knowledge indoctrinator to the guide and organizer of students' learning of translation. The "data-driven learning" method proposed by Johns [6] is an advanced computer-aided teaching method based on corpora. It advocates that the students learn the actual usage of a word, a sentence pattern or a grammatical phenomenon by observing real linguistic phenomena and observing, analyzing and summarizing a large number of contexts.

In line with the data-driven learning mode, the online translation teaching and learning platform, ClinkNotes Online Platform, is adopted by the authors as the empirical research in the teaching of vocational college courses. With the help of this platform, the learning process is exploratory, discoverable and independent, which is in line with the current trend of education. The enthusiasm and initiative of higher vocational students can be brought into play, and the research thinking and practical ability can be cultivated, so as to learn translation more effectively.

In this empirical research design, the authors use corpus materials which are closely related to vocational settings in the teaching for students of different majors. As shown in Fig. 1, the corpus-based online translation teaching platform includes a corpus with the classification of various topic themes, which can be mapped with various vocational fields for students in different majors. For instance, corpus materials related to scenic spots and tourism industry can be used as vivid teaching samples for students majoring in tourism management.

The corpus can be marked and saved to suit different teaching purposes. Before the class, the teachers can release the searched corpus to the teaching platform for students' preview, or assign the corpus to students in the form of practice text. They can also mark the corpus of translation skills that need to be explained according to the translation level of students. During the teaching and learning process, students can click all the markers on the screen to find the explanations of knowledge points in a certain sentence of the text (Fig. 2).

Fig. 1. Topic themes of the ClinkNotes platform

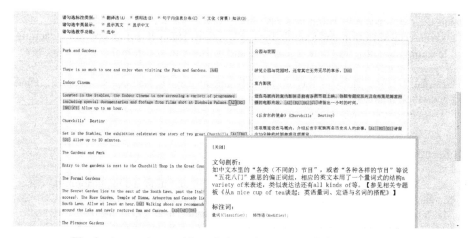

Fig. 2. Annotations and knowledge points of the ClinkNotes platform

Inspired by Tim Johns' data-driven learning process, vocational students' learning process facilitated by the corpus-based online translation teaching platform is shown in Fig. 3. According to different vocational settings, teachers search in the corpus for relevant corpus topics. Then under a certain topic category, teachers can select text data for students to learn. In the next step, students are guided by teachers to learn knowledge points (keywords) and detailed annotations of translation methods and language phenomena. Finally, the knowledge points and annotations can be related to translation in a certain vocational setting, so that students can give feedbacks and have reflections on what they can learn for translation in a specific vocational setting.

As an empirical tool, this online translation teaching and learning platform has become a powerful method in translation teaching for vocational students.

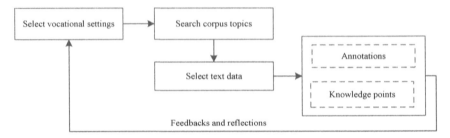

Fig. 3. Students' learning process

4   Conclusion

As an emerging technology, corpus has a wide application prospect and has made great achievements in language teaching. The application of corpus in translation teaching is undoubtedly a great breakthrough in this field. The authors have conducted an empirical study in the teaching of translation for students of a vocational college, and have generated the data-driven learning process which focuses on the vocational characteristics of text material selection and knowledge explanation. This will set an operable teaching and learning mode for translation teaching and learning in vocational colleges in China.

Acknowledgements. The work was substantially supported by The National Social Science Fund of China (Project No.19BYY125).

References

1. Baker, M: Corpus linguistics and translation studies: implication and application. In: Baker, M., et al. (eds.) Text and Technology: In Honor of John Sinclair, no. (1), pp. 233–250 (1993)
2. Mu, Y., Tian, L., Yang, W.: Towards a knowledge management model for online translation learning. In: Hao, T., Chen, W., Xie, H., Nadee, W., Lau, R. (eds.) SETE 2018. LNCS, vol. 11284, pp. 198–207. Springer, Cham (2018). https://doi.org/10.1007/978-3-030-03580-8_21
3. Zhu, C., Mu, Y.: Towards a textual accountability-driven mode of teaching and (self-) learning for translation and bilingual writing: with special reference to a CityU online teaching platform. Chin. Translators J. **2**, 56–62 (2013)
4. Tian, L., Mu, Y., Yang, W.: Designing a platform-facilitated and corpus-assisted translation class. In: Hao, T., Chen, W., Xie, H., Nadee, W., Lau, R. (eds.) SETE 2018. LNCS, vol. 11284, pp. 208–217. Springer, Cham (2018). https://doi.org/10.1007/978-3-030-03580-8_22
5. Zhu, C., Wang, H.: A corpus-based, machine-aided mode of translator training: ClinkNotes and beyond. Interpreter Translator Trainer **5**(2), 269–291 (2011)
6. Johns, T.: Data-driven learning: the perpetual challenge. In: Teaching and Learning by Doing Corpus Analysis, pp. 105–117. Brill Rodopi (2002)

Species Assignment for Gene Normalization Through Exploring the Structure of Full Length Article

Ruoyao Ding, Huaxing Chen, Junxin Liu, and Jian Kuang[✉]

School of Information Science and Technology, Guangdong University of Foreign Studies,
Guangzhou, China
ruoyaoding@outlook.com, 937057048@qq.com, 438152470@qq.com,
jiankuang2648@126.com

Abstract. Gene normalization is a process of automatically detecting gene names in the literature and linking them to database records. It is critical for improving the coverage of annotation in gene databases. Automatic association of a gene with a species, also known as species assignment, is an essential step of gene normalization. In this article, we propose a new species assignment method which explores the structure of full length article. Experimental results show our method outperforms state-of-art systems on full length article level species assignment. Thus, we believe our work can be used in the process of full length article gene normalization.

Keywords: Species assignment · Gene normalization · Full length article

1 Introduction

Biological experimental results are usually described in published literature. In order to conduct and interpret their own experiments, researchers need to find the information of their interest from the research literature. However, with the rapid growth of biomedical publications, molecular biology has become an information-saturated field. Manually extracting information from the literature is a time-consuming and labor-intensive process. As a result, a major focus of bioinformatics research is to automatically extract information from published literature, using text mining techniques.

In order to comprehensively annotate gene records and to support queries from biologists from a variety of backgrounds who may use different names to refer to a gene of interest, curators of knowledge bases, such as UniProt Knowledgebase (UniProtKB) [1], need to capture the full range of names and symbols by which a gene is known. Automatic detection of gene names in the literature and their linkage to gene database records, also known as gene normalization, is being developed as an alternative to the time-consuming practice of manual extraction of names. Since gene database records are species-specific, deciding which species the gene belongs to is an essential and critical step for gene normalization. Wei et al. [2] conclude that accuracy of species assignment is critical for the overall performance on the gene normalization task. When the species

© Springer Nature Switzerland AG 2020
E. Popescu et al. (Eds.): SETE 2019, LNCS 11984, pp. 285–290, 2020.
https://doi.org/10.1007/978-3-030-38778-5_31

is incorrectly assigned, clearly a wrong database accession number will be assigned to the gene. This not only results in false positives but false negatives as well.

Identifying species names in biomedical text is not particularly challenging by itself. For example, both Linnaeus [3] and Organism Tagger [4] have reported more than 95% F-measure in the task of species name identification. However, associating recognized species mentions to other biological entities, e.g., gene mentions, remains challenging. SR4GN [5] is a well-known and state-of-art system that assigns species to gene mentions. It has been adopted by many gene normalization tools such as GenNorm [2] and GNormPlus [6]. However, despite the structures of full length article and abstract are quite different, SR4GN uses the same rules which are developed based on abstract for species assignment in the full length article. In this paper, we propose a new method which explores the structure of full length article for the species assignment process. Experimental results show our method outperforms SR4GN on full length article level species assignment.

2   Methodology

In order to investigate how to assign species to genes in full length articles, we studied the annotations in the full length articles from BioCreative III gene normalization training set [7], drew observations and developed our algorithm for species assignment accordingly.

2.1   Observations

We drew the following observations, which are helpful for developing the species assignment algorithms.

(1) Different sections of the article have different roles. For example, the setups of the experimental study are usually described in the methods section, while the results of the experimental studies are usually described in results section. Thus, the relevant species information can be found in the methods section and mentions of the species do not need to be found in the results section at all. On the other hand, the species mentioned in the background section may or may not be relevant for normalization of genes mentioned in the results section.

(2) Many articles describe one or more experimental studies that are focused on genes from a single species, even when genes from multiple species are mentioned in the article. Out of the 32 articles we have studied, only 4 articles (PMC 2048754, 2443158, 2579434, and 2631505) conducted their research on genes from more than a single species. We observed that the genes used in the experiments and their species are identifiable from the methods section and that such species (if there is a single one) can be used for species assignment in the results section. However, if a particular gene's mentions correspond to different species, we noticed that authors usually provide that information in immediate context. For example, in PMC 2396500, the experimental study is focused on genes from Arabidopsis thaliana. When genes from other species are used for comparison purpose, mentions such as "human DDB2" and "DDB1 in mammalian" were used.

(3) For the detection of species from the methods section, we observed that such species are often mentioned in the titles of the methods subsections, or in the beginning of the methods section or subsections, where authors introduce how they conduct their research. Thus, the position (e.g., title of method subsections) and the identification of textual patterns involving species in the first 1–2 sentences of the method subsections can be used to identify the species.

2.2 Algorithm

Based on the three observations, we developed the following species assignment rules for full length article. The overview of our algorithm is shown in Fig. 1.

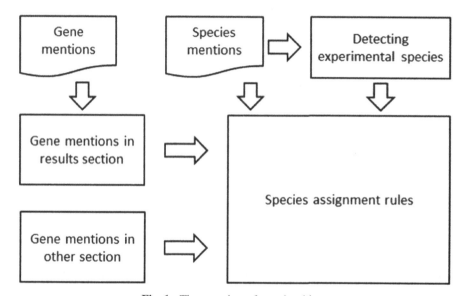

Fig. 1. The overview of our algorithm.

For genes that are mentioned in the results section, we first detect the species of the genes used in the experiments. The detection of species is handled by dictionary matching, using a species dictionary built from NCBI Taxonomy. These species are detected from the Methods sections and will be called the experimental species. We identify the experimental species if they appear in: (1) the titles of the methods subsections, and (2) the first two sentences of the methods subsections and adjacent to phrases such as "sample", "derived from", "carried out", "harvesting" while extracting the species names. For example, in PMC 2423616, sentence which describes experimental species is "MEFs were prepared by harvesting embryonic stage 14.5 mice".

We described how species being assigned to gene mentions in the results sections as follow. The most straightforward case is when only one experimental species is detected. Like the case of major species in our species assignment process for abstracts, this experimental species will be used as the default choice for genes in the result section. It can be overridden by immediate species context, i.e., in cases where the gene mention includes (1) species prefix, (2) species in the same noun phrase or (3) has an attached prepositional phrase with the species name (we will discuss these three rules in detail below).

If multiple experimental species or no experimental species is detected, then we hypothesize that the species for a gene mention would be explicitly stated in the results section. Thus, this situation becomes similar to an abstract which is read before the methods. Therefore, in this case, each subsection in the result section will be treated like an abstract and the rules will be applied the same way they were designed for the other sections. The rules are developed based on our previous work [8], as shown below.

(1) Prefix. If a gene mention has a species prefix, we assign the species based on the prefix. e.g., 'AtAurora1' would be assigned the species 'Arabidopsis thaliana'.
(2) Same noun phrase. If a gene mention and species are in the same noun phrase, we assign that species to the gene mention. e.g., 'Arabidopsis TOC1/PRR1 gene' would be assigned the species 'Arabidopsis thaliana.
(3) Attached prepositional phrase. If a species appears in a prepositional phrase that is attached to the noun phrase containing a gene, we assign that species to the gene mention.
(4) Species in the same sentence. A gene mention is assigned to a species that occurs in the same sentence.
(5) Species in the title and in the MeSH terms. If there is only one species in the title and the MeSH terms, we will assign it to the rest of the gene mentions in the article.

3   Results and Discussion

Currently, there is no corpus available for full length article level species assignment. To evaluate the performance of our method, we use the BioCreative III gene normalization corpus. The corpus consists of a gold standards test set that includes 50 articles which are annotated manually. The annotations are in the form of Gene ID and PMCID pairs. Thus, if there are more than one Gene IDs corresponding to one unique gene name, there is no information that indicates the species for each of the gene mentions. For this reason, we cannot evaluate the recall precisely.

Therefore, we run our system and SR4GN on these articles from the BioCreative III gene normalization gold standards test set and manually analyze the system outputs for species assignment errors (errors caused by other process, e.g., gene mention recognition, are not included). Table 1 shows the number of TPs, FPs and FNs of our method and SR4GN.

We analyzed the errors of our species assignment algorithm, and found that these errors mainly correspond to cases where no experiment species is detected and no species information from immediate context can be used. In these cases, some low confidence rules will be applied, e.g., species in the same sentence. This causes both FPs and FNs. Other errors involved mentions of homologs, where multiple genes were mentioned

Table 1. Performance of the species assignment process.

	# of TPs	# of FPs	# of FNs
Ours	296	43	31
SR4GN	213	61	58

together but from different species. Overall, the results indicate that our algorithm yields good performance in the species assignment process. One possible improvement can be detecting species name from presence of cell line names. If multiple species are detected in this manner from all Methods subsections, we can see if specific genes are associated with them. Techniques used in conjunction with specific genes can also be associated with species but currently we have not implemented this aspect.

4 Conclusion

We have described a new method of species assignment for full length article. We proposed a concept, called experimental species, as a default species in the article, especially in the results section. We also explored the structure of full length article by treating different sections of full length article differently. Evaluation shows that our method yields good performance and outperforms SR4GN, a well-known and state-of-art system that assigns species to gene mentions. We believe our method can be extended for other text mining tasks that are applied on full length articles. In the future, we plan to conduct additional evaluation to further illustrate the significance of exploring the structure of full length article.

Acknowledgements. The work was supported by Guangdong University of Foreign Studies (299-X5219112, 299-X5218168).

References

1. The UniProt Consortium: UniProt: the universal protein knowledgebase. Nucleic Acids Research, 45(D1), D158–D169 (2017)
2. Wei, C.-H., Kao, H.-Y.: Cross-species gene normalization by species inference. BMC Bioinform. **12**(Suppl 8), S5 (2011)
3. Gerner, M., Nenadic, G., Bergman, C.M.: LINNAEUS: a species name identification system for biomedical literature. BMC Bioinform. **11**, 85 (2010). https://doi.org/10.1186/1471-2105-11-85
4. Krallinger, M., Leitner, F., Rodriguez-Penagos, C., Valencia, A.: Overview of the protein-protein interaction annotation extraction task of BioCreative II. Genome Biol. **9**(Suppl 2), S4 (2008). https://doi.org/10.1186/gb-2008-9-s2-s4
5. Wei, C.-H., Kao, H.-Y., Lu, Z.: SR4GN: a species recognition software tool for gene normalization. PLoS ONE **7**(6), e38460 (2012)
6. Wei, C.-H., Kao, H.-Y., Lu, Z.: GNormPlus: an integrative approach for tagging genes, gene families, and protein domains. Biomed. Res. Int. **2015**, 918710 (2015)

7. Lu, Z., Kao, H.-Y., Wei, C.-H., Huang, M., Liu, J., Kuo, C.-J., Wilbur, W.J.: The gene normalization task in BioCreative III. BMC Bioinform. **12**(Suppl 8), S2 (2011)
8. Ding, R., Arighi, C.N., Lee, J.-Y., Wu, C.H., Vijay-Shanker, K.: pGenN, a gene normalization tool for plant genes and proteins in scientific literature. PLoS ONE **10**(8), e0135305 (2015)

ETLTL (Educational Technology for Language and Translation Learning)

Blended Learning Approach in English Language Teaching – Its Benefits, Challenges, and Perspectives

Blanka Klímová[✉] and Marcel Pikhart

Department of Applied Linguistics, Faculty of Informatics and Management,
University of Hradec Kralove, Hradec Kralove, Czech Republic
{blanka.klimova,marcel.pikhart}@uhk.cz

Abstract. At present, blended learning (BL) is commonly used in majority of the institutions of higher learning since it appears to have a positive impact on student learning outcomes and brings a number of benefits for the whole educational process. This is also true for English language teaching (ELT). In ELT, the BL approach offers more opportunities for exposure, discovery, and use of target language. In addition, the BL approach is especially suitable for distant students, who due to their work commitment cannot be involved in full-time English language study. However, recently there has been a shift from the online courses used as counterparts to traditional instruction in the BL approach towards the use of mobile applications. The findings show that such a BL approach (i.e., a combination of mobile learning via mobile applications and traditional instruction) is particularly effective in vocabulary learning. However, such an approach demands even more rigorous teaching methods and strategies, as well as a more elaborate and meaningful context within which learning can take place. Therefore, future research should focus on the exploration of effectiveness of this new BL approach.

Keywords: Blended learning · Traditional instruction · Mobile learning · English · Students · Benefits

1 Introduction

Blended learning (BL) is nowadays a well-established methodology. The term itself was firstly officially defined by Bonk and Graham [1] in 2006. They defined BL as *learning systems that combine face-to-face instruction with computer mediated instruction.*

Generally, the BL approach aims to optimize student learning [2]. On the one hand, there is more support and interactions online. On the other hand, it is expected that the BL approach will enhance the quality of contact classes provided that students can benefit from online learning activities and resources [2].

According to research studies [3–8], the BL methodology seems to be effective since it brings several benefits for educational process, which are as follows:

© Springer Nature Switzerland AG 2020
E. Popescu et al. (Eds.): SETE 2019, LNCS 11984, pp. 293–298, 2020.
https://doi.org/10.1007/978-3-030-38778-5_32

- flexible learning and teaching (i.e., learners can access their learning materials from anywhere and at any time and according to their own pace, and teachers can flexibly modify students' material, which they access online);
- improved pedagogy (it is assumed that well-thought use of new technologies contributes to better use of relevant teaching methods);
- more frequent and timely feedback since feedback can be provided online;
- more learning resources, which are provided online;
- learners are expected to be more responsible for their learning, which might increase their intrinsic motivation;
- collaboration among students and between students and teacher can be promoted more often;
- use of new teaching methods and strategies enhanced by new technologies may enhance learner performance;
- BL approach seems to be more cost-effective than the traditional, face-to-face teaching.

Overall, the BL approach appears to be more effective than the use of only traditional instruction. This was also confirmed by the findings of recent meta-analytic study by Vo et al. [9]. Apart from the effectiveness of BL on learner performance in the institutions of higher learning, they demonstrated that the effect of the BL approach is considerably higher for the so-called STEM disciplines (i.e., hard disciplines such as chemistry or public health) than for the so-called non-STEM disciplines (i.e., soft disciplines such as English or psychology). Furthermore, Dziuban et al. [10] compared face-to-face instruction, blended learning, and online learning and discovered that the BL approach contributed to better learning outcomes than the fully online approach. In addition, in some subjects the BL approach was more beneficial than the traditional one.

2   Blended Learning in English Language Teaching (ELT)

In ELT, the BL approach offers more opportunities for exposure, discovery, and use of target language (cf. [11]). In addition, the BL approach is especially suitable for distant students, who due to their work commitment cannot be involved in full-time English language study. Moreover, Siew-Eng and Muuk [12] indicate that the BL approach in English classes is especially used to improve students' writing, reading and speaking skills. Nevertheless, Klimova [7] in her study on the effectiveness of the BL approach in the Course of Business English, revealed that the BL approach had not improved students' learning outcomes although students were satisfied with the proposed blended learning strategy. The same was true, for example, for study by Tosun [13]. This is probably in line with Vo et al. study [9] on the effectiveness of BL in non-STEM disciplines as described above.

There is no unanimous consensus on how much learning should be done in class and how much learning students should perform online. For instance, according to Dudeney and Hockly [14], a blended language learning course consists of 75% delivered online and 25% delivered through face-to-face instruction. However, BL can also serve only as support to face-to-face classes [7].

For a long time, BL in ELT was perceived as a combination of eLearning courses and face-to-face instruction [15–17]. However, nowadays, with the emergence of mobile devices, especially smartphones, BL is becoming more a combination of mobile learning and face-to-face instruction. In comparison with eLearning, mobile learning enables students to learn ubiquitously from anywhere and at any time, on their own pace. In addition, the main advantage is its easy portability. However, in comparison with the eLearning modality, on the one hand, mobile learning phases are shorter, but on the other hand, they are more frequent [18]. Currently, pure mobile applications are the most widely used applications in the English mobile learning context [19]. Although this kind of BL approach aims to enhance all four language skills, i.e., listening, reading, speaking, and writing, research studies show that it is particularly effective in vocabulary learning [20–28] because vocabulary can be split into smaller segments, which is suitable for designing the content of smartphones. Smartphone applications are becoming widely used in learning thanks to their proved benefits such as improved knowledge retention and increased student engagement [26, 27].

Thus, as research above indicates, there is a shift from the eLearning component of BL to a more informal and interactive mobile learning component of BL (Fig. 1).

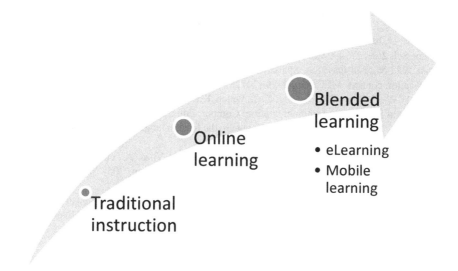

Fig. 1. Development of learning modalities

However, such an approach demands even more rigorous teaching methods and strategies, as well as a more elaborate and meaningful context within which learning can take place. In addition, the content itself must be tailored to learner needs in order to motivate them to use a mobile application on a daily basis [29, 30].

3   Conclusion

The findings of this overview article indicate that the emergence of new technologies constantly influences the development of new learning modalities, which attempt to respond to it. For further research into other aspects of the emergence of new technologies and blended learning, business communication and eLearning see the research of Pikhart [31–41]. At the moment, blended learning experiences a new phase of its development by including mobile learning as valuable counterpart to traditional, face-to-face teaching. This new BL approach, however, will need new challenging pedagogical methods in order to enhance the effectiveness of the learning outcomes. Therefore, future research should focus on the exploration of effectiveness of this new BL approach.

Acknowledgments. This study is supported by the IGS project 2019, run at the Faculty of Informatics and Management, University of Hradec Kralove, Czech Republic.

References

1. Bonk, C.J., Graham, C.R.: The Handbook of Blended Learning Environments: Global Perspectives, Local Designs. Joosey-Bass/Pheiffer, San Francisco (2006)
2. Kose, V.: A blended learning model supported with web 2.0 technologies. Procedia Soc. Behav. Sci. **2**(2), 2794–2802 (2010)
3. Khan, A.I., Noor-ul-Qayyum, Shaik, M.S., Ali, A.M., Bebi, C.V.: Blended learning process in education context. MECS **9**, 23–29 (2012)
4. Porter, W.W., Graham, C.R., Spring, K.A., Welch, K.R.: Blended learning in higher education: institutional adoption and implementation. Comput. Educ. **75**(6), 185–193 (2013)
5. Hubackova, S.: Blended learning – new stage in the foreign language teaching. Procedia Soc. Behav. Sci. **197**, 1957–1961 (2015)
6. Frydrychova Klimova, B.: Blended learning. In: Mendez Vilas, A., et al. (eds.) Research, Reflections and Innovations in Integrating ICT in Education, pp. 705–708. FORMATEX, Spain (2009)
7. Klimova, B.: Evaluation of the blended learning approach in the course of business English – a case study. In: Huang, T.-C., Lau, R., Huang, Y.-M., Spaniol, M., Yuen, C.-H. (eds.) SETE 2017. LNCS, vol. 10676, pp. 326–335. Springer, Cham (2017). https://doi.org/10.1007/978-3-319-71084-6_37
8. Klimova, B., Simonova, I., Poulova, P.: Blended learning in the university English courses: case study. In: Cheung, Simon K.S., Kwok, L.-f., Ma, Will W.K., Lee, L.-K., Yang, H. (eds.) ICBL 2017. LNCS, vol. 10309, pp. 53–64. Springer, Cham (2017). https://doi.org/10.1007/978-3-319-59360-9_5
9. Vo, H.M., Zhu, C., Diep, N.A.: The effect of blended learning on student performance at course-level in higher education: a meta-analysis. Stud. Educ. Eval. **53**, 17–28 (2017)
10. Dziuban, C., Hartman, J., Moskal, P., Sorg, S., Truman, B.: Three ALN modalities: an institutional perspective. In: Bourne,, J., Moore, J.C. (eds.) Elements of Quality Online Education: Into the Mainstream, pp. 127–148 (2004)
11. Tomlinson, B.: Comments on Part 4. In: Tomlinson, B., Whittaker, C. (eds.) Blended Learning in English Language Teaching: Course Design and Implementation (2013). https://www.teachingenglish.org.uk/sites/teacheng/files/pub_D057_Blended%20learning_FINAL_WEB%20ONLY_v2.pdf

12. Siew-Eng, L., Muuk, M.A.: Blended learning in teaching secondary schools' English: a preparation for tertiary science education in Malaysia. Procedia Soc. Behav. Sci. **167**, 293–300 (2015)

13. Tosun, S.: The effects of blended learning on EFL students' vocabulary enhancement. Procedia Soc. Behav. Sci. **199**, 641–647 (2015)

14. Dudeney, G., Hoskly, N.: How to Teach English with Technology. Pearson Education Limited, Harlow (2007)

15. Hubackova, S., Semradova, I.: Comparison of on-line teaching and face-to-face teaching. Procedia Soc. Behav. Sci. **89**, 445–449 (2013)

16. Simonova, I., Kostolanyova, K.: The blended learning concept: comparative study of two universities. In: Cheung, Simon K.S., Kwok, L.-f., Shang, J., Wang, A., Kwan, R. (eds.) ICBL 2016. LNCS, vol. 9757, pp. 302–311. Springer, Cham (2016). https://doi.org/10.1007/978-3-319-41165-1_27

17. Frydrychova Klimova, B., Poulova, P.: Forms of instruction and students' preferences - a comparative study. In: Cheung, Simon K.S., Fong, J., Zhang, J., Kwan, R., Kwok, L.F. (eds.) ICHL 2014. LNCS, vol. 8595, pp. 220–231. Springer, Cham (2014). https://doi.org/10.1007/978-3-319-08961-4_21

18. Mauer, M.: Mobile Blended Learning with eSqirrel (2015). https://eproceedings.epublishing.ekt.gr/index.php/openedu/article/viewFile/62/52

19. Elaish, M.M., Shuib, L., Ghani, N.A., Yadegaridehkordi, E., Alaa, M.: Mobile Learning for English Language Acquisition: Taxonomy, Challenges, and Recommendations, vol. 5, pp. 19033–19047 (2017). IEEE

20. Wu, Q.: Learning ESL vocabulary with smartphones. Procedia Soc. Behav. Sci. **143**, 302–307 (2014)

21. Wu, Q.: Designing a smartphone app to teach English (L2) vocabulary. Comput. Educ. **85**, 170–179 (2015). https://doi.org/10.1016/j.compedu.2015.02.013

22. Basal, A., Yilmaz, S., Tanriverdi, A., Sari, L.: Effectiveness of mobile applications in vocabulary teaching. Contemp. Educ. Technol. **7**(1), 47–59 (2016)

23. Mahdi, H.S.: Effectiveness of mobile devices on vocabulary learning: a meta-analysis. J. Educ. Comput. Res. **56**(1), 134–154 (2017)

24. Rezaei, A., Mai, N., Pesaranghader, A.: The effect of mobile applications on English vocabulary acquisition (2014). https://www.researchgate.net/publication/261246911

25. Song, M., Chen, L.: A review on English vocabulary acquisition and teaching research in recent 30 years in China. Sci. J. Educ. **5**(4), 174–180 (2017)

26. Klimova, B.: Mobile phones and/or smartphones and their apps for teaching English as a foreign language. Educ. Inf. Technol. **23**(3), 1091–1099 (2017)

27. Klímová, B., Berger, A.: Evaluation of the use of mobile application in learning English vocabulary and phrases – a case study. In: Hao, T., Chen, W., Xie, H., Nadee, W., Lau, R. (eds.) SETE 2018. LNCS, vol. 11284, pp. 3–11. Springer, Cham (2018). https://doi.org/10.1007/978-3-030-03580-8_1

28. Klimova, B., Prazak, P.: Evaluation of the effectiveness of the use of a mobile application on students' study achievements – a pilot study. In: Al-Sharhan, Salah A., Simintiras, Antonis C., Dwivedi, Yogesh K., Janssen, M., Mäntymäki, M., Tahat, L., Moughrabi, I., Ali, Taher M., Rana, Nripendra P. (eds.) I3E 2018. LNCS, vol. 11195, pp. 37–44. Springer, Cham (2018). https://doi.org/10.1007/978-3-030-02131-3_5

29. Wang, B.T.: Designing mobile apps for English vocabulary learning. Int. J. Inf. Educ. Technol. **7**(4), 279–283 (2017)

30. Elaish, M.M., Shuib, L., Ghani, N.A., Yadegaridehkordi, E., Alaa, M.: Mobile Learning for English Language Acquisition: Taxonomy, Challenges, and Recommendations, vol. 5, pp. 19033–19047. IEEE (2017)

31. Pikhart, M.: Communication based models of information transfer in modern management - the use of mobile technologies in company communication. In: Proceedings of the 31st International Business Information Management Association Conference, pp. 447–450 (2018)
32. Pikhart, M.: Managerial communication and its changes in the global intercultural business world. In: Special issue on education. SHS Web of Conferences, vol. 37 (2017)
33. Pikhart, M.: Intercultural linguistics as a new academic approach to communication. In: SHS Web of Conferences, vol. 26 (2016)
34. Pikhart, M.: Theoretical foundations of intercultural business communication and their practical consequences. In: SHS Web of Conferences, vol. 26 (2016)
35. Pikhart, M.: Current intercultural management strategies. The role of communication in company efficiency development. In: Proceedings of the 8th European Conference on Management, Leadership and Governance, pp. 327–331 (2012)
36. Pikhart, M.: Communication based models of information transfer in modern management – the use of mobile technologies in company communication. Innov. Manage. Educ. Excell. Through Vis. **2020**, 447–450 (2018)
37. Pikhart, M.: Electronic managerial communication: new trends of intercultural business communication. Innov. Manage. Educ. Excell. Through Vis. **2020**, 714–717 (2018)
38. Pikhart, M.: Managerial communication and its changes in the global intercultural business world. In: Web of Conferences, vol. 26 (2016)
39. Pikhart, M.: Intercultural linguistics as a new academic approach to communication. In: Web of Conferences, vol. 26 (2016)
40. Pikhart, M.: Implementing new global business trends to intercultural business communication. In: Procedia Social and Behavioral Sciences, ERPA 2014, vol. 152, pp. 950–953 (2014)
41. Pikhart, M.: New horizons of intercultural communication: applied linguistics approach. In: Procedia Social and Behavioral Sciences, ERPA 2014, vol. 152, pp. 954–957 (2014)

Investigating Students' Use of a Social Annotation Tool in an English for Science and Technology Course

Jianqiu Tian[✉]

School of Foreign Languages, Peking University, Beijing 100871, China
tianjq@pku.edu.cn

Abstract. This study investigates the linguistic and pedagogical benefits and challenges of using a digital annotation tool (called *Perusall*) to facilitate second language (L2) reading in an advanced English language course at university level. The goals of the study are to analyze the students' reading and annotating behavior, examine the effects of social reading on their understanding of English for science and technology texts and investigate how an L2 teacher might effectively incorporate this activity in his/her classroom. The results indicate that students spent an above average amount of time reading (compared to that reported in the literature) and that most students completed their reading assignments before class with the *Perusall* platform. Moreover, they predominantly used the social reading experience to summarize the sections of the long article, and query fellow students about the meaning of difficult and transitional sentences. *Perusall* allowed students to co-construct meaning and scaffold their learning while engaged in close readings of the science and technology texts outside of the physical classroom. Drawbacks of social reading in this environment are primarily others' comments impeding some students' understanding of the text and students' frustrations with some technical aspects of the *Perusall* tool. Pedagogical suggestions regarding L2 social reading include better integrating students' virtual comments into classroom discussion/activities, and offering more structure for students.

Keywords: Social annotation tool · L2 reading · English for science and technology

1 Introduction

Despite six years or more for English language learning, a majority of EFL students at university level in China, especially students majoring in science and technology, are overwhelmed by the English texts they are expected to read for their major studies. The content and language integrated learning (CLIL) course on science and technology in this research has been given to target the students' reading ability, with reading assignments of articles about 10 pages long each week. The limited class meeting time of two hours a week rendered it necessary to adopt a "flipped" classroom format that requires the students to read the texts before class and saves class time for more interactive activities

© Springer Nature Switzerland AG 2020
E. Popescu et al. (Eds.): SETE 2019, LNCS 11984, pp. 299–309, 2020.
https://doi.org/10.1007/978-3-030-38778-5_33

during which students can be actively engaged with instructors and other students to consolidate their reading skills.

In this context, adequate reading before class is crucial to the success of the course. To address the challenge of the students' poor reading ability, *Perusall*, a digital annotation tool (DAT), was deployed because in the digital environment the learners can not only annotate and mark up a digital text [1–4], but can also share annotations with each other on the same digital documents, and provide feedback on annotations [5, 6] to enhance their reading comprehension.

DATs have been used in science and humanities courses, including language arts courses, to ensure pre-class reading. In language courses the uses of DATs have primarily been carried out with learners in L1 settings (e.g., [7–9]). The handful of studies using DATs in L2 learning and teaching contexts are a language education course for pre-service English-as-a-foreign-language (EFL) teachers [10], an English vocabulary and reading course at university level [11], a course on a Spanish poetry [12] and a beginning level Chinese language course [13]. This study is to be the first to report the use of DATs in an EFL course with a focus on content of science and technology.

2 DAT Research in L2 Contexts

Up to now, a handful of studies have investigated the effects of using DATs in L2 learning and teaching contexts.

In Nor, Azman, and Hamat [10], the nonnative English participants in a pre-service English-as-a-foreign-language (EFL) education course in a university setting in Malaysia were asked to read a supplemental article in English and make annotations on a DAT. The survey after annotation indicates that nearly 85% of the participants reported that sharing notes was essential to their understanding of the article and 77% of the participants noted that highlighting the article facilitated their comprehension.

Tseng, Yeh, and Yang [11] investigated the effects of annotating a text on three different levels of reading: surface-based (understanding basic vocabulary), text-based (understanding specific information within the text), and situation-based (understanding connections between ideas within the text). The researchers found that the participants vary in gains at the three levels: learners who used the annotations to mark vocabulary words made gains at the surface-based level, those who used annotations primarily to comment on the article gained at the text-based level, and those who predominantly used annotations to summarize the text made gains at the situation-based level.

Thoms and Poole [12] analyzed learner–learner interactions within a virtual environment when collaboratively reading Spanish poetry in a Hispanic literature course at the college level from an ecological theoretical perspective [14]. They found three distinct types of affordances in the data: linguistic, literary, and social affordances. The number of literary and social affordances outnumbered the linguistic affordances in students' threaded discussions in collaborative annotation of poems. The primary challenges for learners when engaging in collaborative reading included others' comments impeding some students' understanding of the text, and having to make one's comments distinct from others' comments to avoid being socially viewed as an inactive reader or student. Moreover, the primary pedagogical benefits involve the ability to establish a more open learning community and allowing students to carry out a closer reading of literary texts.

Thoms, Sung and Poole [13] investigates the linguistic and pedagogical benefits and challenges of using a digital annotation tool (called *eComma*) to facilitate second language (L2) reading in a second-semester, university-level Chinese language course. The students primarily query fellow students about the meaning of vocabulary/Chinese characters in the literary texts in the study, and *eComma* allowed students to co-construct meaning and scaffold their close readings of the Chinese literary texts outside of the physical classroom. The challenges encompass the students' frustrations with some technical aspects of the eComma tool and the instructor's concerns about integration of students' social reading experiences outside of the class with in-class discussions/activities. The authors make pedagogical suggestions of adding timing constraints to promote more virtual interaction, better integrating students' virtual comments into classroom discussion/activities, and offering more structure for novice learners.

3 Methodology

This research takes a social constructivist perspective on students' pre-class collaborative reading. Social constructivism suggests that students learn through the process of sharing experiences and building knowledge and understanding through discussion [15]. With this perspective, students in online learning communities [16] collaboratively build knowledge, verbalizing their thinking, building understanding, and solving problems together [17, 18].

The specific research questions are: 1. How do students conduct pre-class reading on *Perusall*, the social learning platform? 2. What is the efficacy of the platform in promoting student learning? And 3. What are the challenges of using *Perusall* for learners?

3.1 Course Context

The study site was an undergraduate English for science and technology course offered at a large comprehensive university in the northern part of China. The course focused on topics in frontiers of science and technology and was offered to students across the university but most students major in science and technology and are freshman or sophomore. Almost all of the students were placed at level C (roughly B2 or C1 with CEFR) in a test (vocabulary, listening and reading) upon university entrance or at equivalent level. The course met once a week for two hours. It was taught in English, and the texts were taken from original English language journals, such as *Scientific American* and *The Economist*; some of the texts had Chinese translations. The course embraced a "flipped" approach, where the students are often engaged in group task and the teacher and the students have face-to-face, whole-class discussions to analyze and interpret the texts.

3.2 Participants

Thirty-eight undergraduate students participated in the study, 28 males and 10 females, ranging in age from 17 to 21 years old. Their native language is Mandarin Chinese. The students brought a portable computer (laptop or tablet) and a smart phone to class to accomplish in-class tasks. The students are in two classes, with twenty in class 1 (15 males and 5 females), and eighteen in class 2 (13 males and 5 females).

3.3   The DAT Tool

The DAT tool in this research is *Perusall*, an online social learning platform designed to promote high pre-class reading compliance, engagement, and conceptual understanding [19]. The instructor creates an online course on *Perusall*, uploading articles or documents, and then creates reading assignments. Students asynchronously annotate the assigned reading by posting (or replying to) comments or questions in a chat-like fashion.

An instructor view of the course home page is shown in Fig. 1. The instructor uploads the reading material to the left-hand side of the page (under Documents) and then creates specific reading assignments from these documents which appear in the right panel.

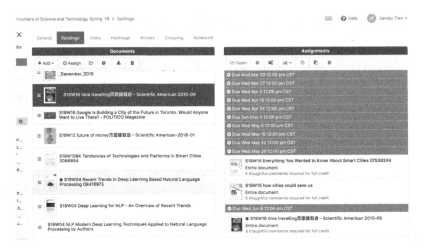

Fig. 1. *Perusall* instructor course view.

Figure 2 shows what a student sees after opening a reading assignment and high-lighting a specific passage on a page in the assignment. A conversation window opens on the right where the student can ask a question or make a comment.

Figure 3 shows a page that has been highlighted and annotated by students. When a student clicks on a specific highlight that highlight turns purple, and the conversation window for that highlight opens on the right.

When a student asks a question about a specific passage, it is automatically flagged with an orange question mark, as shown in Fig. 3. Other students can respond in an asynchronous conversation.

Perusall also has an integrated assessment tool that provides both students and instructors with constant feedback on how students are engaging with the reading assignments.

Moreover, *Perusall* provides many social features (sectioning, avatars, upvoting, email notifications) that are designed to improve the interactions between students. Sectioning allows the division of students into groups, which is suitable for class setting. The avatars of other students and instructors who are viewing the same assignment at the same time appear in the top left hand corner of the screen (Fig. 2), which increases the

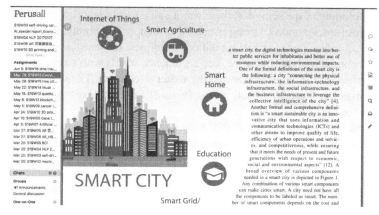

Fig. 2. Page of a reading assignment in *Perusall*.

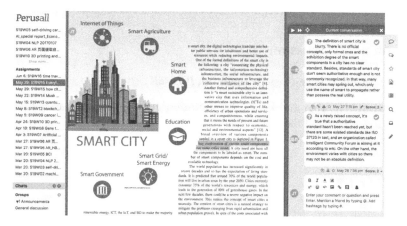

Fig. 3. Reading assignment in *Perusall* showing student highlights and annotations.

social connectivity of the reading experience and encourages students to engage more with the reading (through the software). Upvoting annotations provide feedback on the annotations made by other students in their section. There are two types of upvoting in *Perusall*, the orange question mark to solicit answers by other students and the green checkmark to highlight a particularly helpful explanation. Finally, the email notification feature alerts students not logged into *Perusall* when a classmate has responded to a question or comment they have made.

3.4 Data Collection and Procedures

Data collection took place during the Spring 2019 semester. The students were assigned to read an article or two articles with a total length of about 10 A4 pages on a topic of frontier of science and technology each week via *Perusall* for 14 weeks.

At the beginning of the semester, there was a guide for students on what to annotate, including questions, opinions, strong pieces of evidence, key points, ideas with which you disagree, good or poor supporting data or examples, inconsistencies, key terms or definitions, contrasting points of view, key arguments, words with strong connotations, and figures of speech (images that reveal the writer's feelings). Then the students were required to make at least 5 annotations on *Perusall* for each text before class and be prepared for the reading tasks in class.

In particular, there was a crossover design for the topics *Blockchains* (week 12, shortened as w12 hereafter) and *Quantum Devices* (w13), in which the students made annotations as sections before class and then answered a set of specific or general questions alternately in class. Then the performance in the classroom task was compared between the sections.

Another primary source of data for this study was comprised of students' comments and annotations on *Perusall* when reading articles on 14 topics across the semester. Moreover, statistics were collected from the *Perusall* platform. There is also a survey of the students' behavior and perception of the benefits and challenges of *Perusall*.

4   Result and Discussion

4.1   RQ1: Students' Pre-class Behavior on *Perusall*

Time Spent and Number and Types of Annotations. Using the statistical data collected from *Perusall* it is found that, on average, students spend 6 h viewing the reading for week 13, among which 2.8 h are spent doing active reading on *Perusall* (Fig. 4).

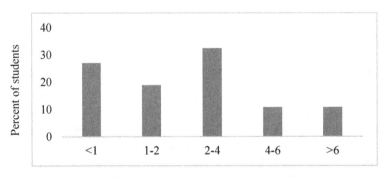

Number of hours spent on active reading

Fig. 4. Histogram of the number of hours students spent on active reading.

The number of annotations students made ranges from 6.4 to 18.0 (Table 1).

As to the types of annotations, those of w12 blockchains include 37 questions, 241 comments and of w13 quantum consist of 25 questions, 243 comments.

The results indicate that students spent an above average amount of time reading (compared to less than 3 h as reported in the literature [19]) and that most students were active in making annotations before class with the *Perusall* platform.

Table 1. Number of annotations student made each week.

Week	W02	W03	W04	W05	W06	W07	W08	W09	W10	W12	W13	W14	W15
Total annotations	441	334	404	503	684	381	297	370	296	278	268	280	243
Average	11.6	8.8	10.6	13.2	18.0	10.0	7.8	9.7	7.8	7.3	7.1	7.4	6.4

What the Students Annotate. Content analysis of the students' annotations for the w13 quantum text on the *Perusall* platform reveals the following types of annotations.

Summary of the text sections. An example reads as follows:

Quantum mechanics *(at the atomic level, certainties-> probabilities, "superposition, entanglement")* ***Applications:*** *(1) Improving atomic clocks' accuracy(entanglement) -> measuring tiny variations in gravity\spot underground pipes\track submarines (2) Permitting messaging without worries about eavesdroppers. (superposition, entanglement) (3) quantum computers (superposition, entanglement)*

English explanation or Chinese translation of word meaning. Here are two examples: *Spookily adv. in an unusual and weird manner //Duplicate* 复制

Comments showing the students' own understanding of words, sentences, etc. A student explains the sentence of "the odds are good; the goods, odd" as follows:

I deem that it has two meanings. First, it represent the odd of atoms of being everywhere. Second it demonstrate the wide application of quantum technology. (sic)

Query and response about the meaning of difficult and transitional sentences. The following example is a part of the original text followed by student query and response.

Born a century ago, this theory is the rule book for what happens at atomic scales, providing explanations for everything from the layout of the periodic table to the zoo of particles spraying out of atom-smashers. (original text)

Query: *What's the meaning of this? (this refers to the "zoo")*

Response: *Maybe it refers to **a place, situation or group marked by crowding, confusion, or unrestrained behaviour**, just like a big zoo with many lively animals. Here in the text, zoo represents a huge number of unpredictable particles.*

Explanation of the content from reference sources. Students also draw on reference tools to gain further understanding of the content, such as:

Quantum mechanics, including quantum field theory, is a fundamental theory in physics which describes nature at the smallest scales of energy levels of atoms and subatomic particles. Classical physics, the physics existing before quantum mechanics, describes nature at ordinary scale. -Wiki

Comments on the ideas in the text. The following paragraph is a student's comment on the current development of the quantum technology.

Actually I was shocked by the numbers of Chinese patents here. In my stereotyped thoughts, US government/companies are devoting huge efforts in this (like Google), but not much are done here (maybe I'm just lacking of information) (maybe our country is trying to overtake in curves?). But the question appear, why China is so lagging in developing quantum computing but have the same and prosperous development in cryptography and sensors? Is it because the poor basis of the Chinese computer chips and that actually delays the computing chip development in quantum?

It can be seen that the types of annotations are consistent with the particular difficulties the part of the text involves or the students' particular interests or understanding. These annotations may help clarify misunderstandings or open space for further discussion, which both potentially facilitate the students' reading comprehension.

How the Student Use *Perusall* to Annotate. The survey indicates that most of the students make annotations when they read for the second time after they figure out the logic of the whole text in the first reading.

They may annotate thesis statements, other key sentences and long sentences that defy understanding, the uncommon word, the understanding of the sentence or the association of social life. When they encounter difficulties, they look at *Perusall* to see if fellow students have asked, or ask questions on *Perusall*. They also answer fellow students' questions.

After reading, students may write a summary, draw mindmaps, paraphrase some sentences, or write a description of the chart.

These steps constitute a loop in which the students read the text in general, followed by detailed reading, which subsequently resulted in enhanced understanding that was consolidated in production tasks.

4.2   RQ2: Efficacy of the Platform in Promoting Student Learning

The question will be answered from two perspectives: the impact of the annotations on the students' understanding, and the students' perceived benefits.

Relationship Between Student Reading Behavior and in-Class Performance. The issues will be approached from the difference in answers to a question about understanding a particular sentence "The odds are good; the goods, odd" in the text of w13 quantum devices.

For this question, no student in Class 1 made any annotation of this point, but for class 2, there was an attempt at explanation, followed by the instructor's comment that encourages other students to pay attention to the sentence, which resulted in an accurate explanation.

The first student: *The following are my understanding of the subtitle: "The odds are good" means the counterintuitive quantum mechanics is very useful while "the goods, odd" means that the products based on quantum mechanics were unexpected at first.*

The instructor: *Good attempt! Yet your explanation for the "odds are good" should be one for "the goods, odd", and an explanation is still pending for "the odds are good".*

The second student: *"the odds" has the meaning of "the degree to which something is likely to happen", and "the odds are good" may mean that quantum technology is very likely to have a promising future.* (NB: This comment is upvoted by the instructor).

The in-class answers to the question indicate that among the 18 students in class 1 who answered the question, only two gave answers that were just close. On the other hand, 5 out of the 17 students in class 2 (with annotations upvoted by the instructor) who submitted an answer made a quite accurate answer. The difference in the in-class task performance seems to suggest that the annotation facilitates the students' attention to and understanding of the part of the text.

Benefits Presented in the Survey. The following quotation is typical of the benefits of *Perusall* students perceived.

Perusall *does contribute to the understanding of reading materials both grammatically and in terms of content, reducing some time for checking words and materials, and strengthening the understanding of certain poorly understood paragraphs. A lot of technical terms and principles would really have been very difficult for people who don't know much about them. The summative comments made by some students are also extremely helpful.*

In a word, the students not only benefited in understanding the literal meaning of the texts, but achieved an enhanced comprehending the content. Moreover, they gained a better overview of the text with the help of other students' summative comments.

4.3 RQ3: Challenges

The student survey reveals challenges both in terms of use and of technology. For challenges with use, some comments on *Perusall* are direct copies of the long wiki or Oxford Dictionary items, which does not represent the actual meaning of the terms/words in the article, or provides little help in understanding the article. Other students suggest that too much information leads to the submersion of useful details. The major technical challenge is that some sentences they want to highlight are difficult to select. And an issue that combines the use and the technology is *Perusall*'s scoring mechanism, which students felt obscure or confusing in making annotations.

From the instructor's perspective, more consideration is necessary for meaningfully bridging students' social reading experiences outside of the class with in-class discussions/activities. Moreover, more structure needs to be provided for the students to achieve better effects.

5 Conclusion and Implications

This study highlights how students in an advanced English CLIL course used a DAT to scaffold each other's understanding of the texts in digital social reading. *Perusall* allowed students to co-construct meaning and scaffold their learning in close readings of the science and technology texts outside of the physical classroom. Drawbacks of social reading included others' comments impeding some students' understanding of the text and students' frustrations with some technical aspects of the *Perusall* tool and the instructor's concerns about meaningfully bridging students' social reading experiences outside of the class with in-class discussions/activities.

Like other exploratory studies that investigate the use of a relatively new tool in L2 contexts, this study has limitations. For one thing, the small sample size does not allow for generalizations to be made about the use of *Perusall* in other EFL courses; clearly, subsequent research efforts need to involve more learners to fully understand the linguistic affordances and pedagogical challenges of using DATs in a CLIL course on science and technology in particular and in L2 contexts in general.

Moreover, the recent proliferation of DATs has resulted in technological features inherent in the tools themselves that need to be improved to provide a more user-friendly experience for students, teachers, and researchers alike. Despite these limitations, this study has revealed the potential benefits and challenges of incorporating social reading in a CLIL English class and hopefully would inspire more research in this area.

Given the dearth of empirical work to date on social reading in L2 contexts other than classroom environments, a number of future research areas is worth exploring. One such area is how L2 digital social reading via DATs affect in-class interactions about L2 texts; in other words, how DATs facilitate linguistic, and science and technology aspects of L2 readings. Moreover, much more empirical work is needed to understand whether or not digital social reading leads to better comprehension of L2 science and technology texts than traditional solitary experiences in most L2 contexts.

References

1. Abraham, L.B.: Computer-mediated glosses in second language reading comprehension and vocabulary learning: a meta-analysis. Comput. Assisted Lang. Learn. **21**(3), 199–226 (2008)
2. Ariew, R., Ercetin, G.: Exploring the potential of hypermedia annotations for second language reading. Comput. Assisted Lang. Learn. **17**(2), 237–259 (2004)
3. Johnson, T.E., Archibald, T.N., Tenenbaum, G.: Individual and team annotation effects on students' reading comprehension, critical thinking, and meta-cognitive skills. Comput. Hum. Behav. **26**(6), 1496–1507 (2010)
4. Kawasaki, Y., Sasaki, H., Yamaguchi, H., Yamaguchi, Y.: Effectiveness of highlighting as a prompt in text reading on a computer monitor. In: Proceedings of the 8th WSEAS International Conference on Multimedia systems and signal processing, pp. 311–315. World Scientific and Engineering Academy and Society (WSEAS), Hangzhou, China (2008)
5. Cadiz, J.J., Gupta, A., Grudin, J.: Using Web annotations for asynchronous collaboration around documents. In: Durand, D.G. (ed.) Proceedings of the 2000 ACM Conference on Computer Supported Cooperative Work, pp. 309–318. ACM, (2000)
6. Jonassen, D.H.: Computers in the Classroom: Mindtools for Critical Thinking. Prentice-Hall, Upper Saddle River (1996)
7. Gao, F.: A case study of using a social annotation tool to support collaboratively learning. Internet High. Educ. **17**, 76–83 (2013)
8. Lu, J., Deng, L.: Examining students' use of online annotation tools in support of argumentative reading. Australas. J. Educ. Technol. **29**(2), 161–171 (2013)
9. Yang, X., Yu, S., Sun, Z.: The effect of collaborative annotation on Chinese reading level in primary schools in China. Br. J. Edu. Technol. **44**(1), 95–111 (2013)
10. Nor, N.F.M., Azman, H., Hamat, A.: Investigating students' use of online annotation tool in an online reading environment. 3L: Lang. Linguist. Lit. **19**(3), 87–101 (2013)
11. Tseng, S.-S., Yeh, H.-C., Yang, S-h: Promoting different reading comprehension levels through online annotations. Comput. Assisted Lang. Learn. **28**(1), 41–57 (2015)
12. Thoms, J.J., Poole, F.: Investigating linguistic, literary, and social affordances of L2 collaborative reading. Lang. Learn. Technol. **21**(2), 139–156 (2017)
13. Thoms, J.J., Sung, K.-Y., Poole, F.: Investigating the linguistic and pedagogical affordances of an L2 open reading environment via eComma: An exploratory study in a Chinese language course. System **69**, 38–53 (2017)
14. Van Lier, L.: The Ecology and Semiotics of Language Learning: A Sociocultural Perspective. Kluwer Academic Publishers, Boston (2004)

15. Vygotsky, L.S.: Mind in Society: The Development of Higher Psychological Processes. Harvard University Press, Cambridge (1980)
16. Downes, S.: Creating an Online Learning Community [PowerPoint Slides]. https://www.slideshare.net/Downes/creating-an-online-learning-community. Accessed 19 Aug 2019
17. Webb, N.M., Nemer, K., Chizhik, A., Sugrue, B.: Using Group Collaboration as a Window into Students' Cognitive Processes. National Center for Research on Evaluation Standards, and Student Testing (CRESST), Los Angeles, CA (1995)
18. Crouch, C.H., Mazur, E.: Peer instruction: ten years of experience and results. Am. J. Phys. **69**(9), 970–977 (2001)
19. Miller, K., Lukoff, B., King, G., Mazur, E.: Use of a Social Annotation Platform for Pre-Class Reading Assignments in a Flipped Introductory Physics Class. Front. Educ. **3**(8), 1–12 (2018)

The Application of Deep Learning in Automated Essay Evaluation

Shili Ge and Xiaoxiao Chen[✉]

Guangdong University of Foreign Studies, Guangzhou 510420, Guangdong, China
geshili@gdufs.edu.cn

Abstract. The shift from Automated Essay Scoring (AES) to Automated Essay Evaluation (AEE) indicates that natural language processing (NLP) researchers respond positively to the request from language teaching field. Writers and teachers need more feedback about writing content and language use from AEE software beside a precise evaluative score. This requirement can be met by the neural network based deep learning technique. Deep learning has been applied in many NLP fields and great success has been made, such as machine translation, emotional analysis, question answering, and automatic summarization. Neural network based deep learning is suitable for AES research and development since AES requires mainly a precise score of writing quality. This can be accomplished with human accurately scored essays as input and scoring model as output with deep learning technology. However, AEE requires more than a score and deep learning can be used to select linguistically meaningful features for writing quality and apply in the AEE model construction. Related experiments already show the feasibility and further research is worth exploring.

Keywords: Automated Essay Evaluation · Automated Essay Scoring · Deep learning · Neural network · Natural Language Processing

1 Automated Essay Evaluation and Deep Learning

Automated Essay Scoring (AES) and Automated Essay Evaluation (AEE) are often used interchangeably but the shift to the latter "indicates that feedback, interaction and an altogether wider range of possibilities for software is being envisioned" in recent years than was seen before [1]. The research and development of AEE pays more attention on the identification and extraction of scoring features, as mentioned in [2] that "a critical goal in e-rater development has been to continue to enrich the system with new features that better reflect the writing construct". Many researchers and developers of AEE systems share the same opinions that feature selection is very important. However, in the end-to-end deep learning algorithm based on neural networks features are directly defined and selected by the algorithm. "Automatically learning features at multiple levels of abstraction allow a system to learn complex functions mapping the input to the output directly from data, without depending completely on human-crafted features" [3]. In AEE research, given the training composition set of scoring model and the score of each composition in the set, the algorithm will automatically extract features from

© Springer Nature Switzerland AG 2020
E. Popescu et al. (Eds.): SETE 2019, LNCS 11984, pp. 310–318, 2020.
https://doi.org/10.1007/978-3-030-38778-5_34

each composition and map them to the score of the composition. Here, the input end is the composition text and the output end is the composition score. The neural network can automatically construct the end-to-end algorithm from the composition text to the composition score. The application of deep learning is not only the result of the development of natural language processing (NLP), but also the historical necessity of the development of NLP

2 Introduction to Deep Learning

Traditional machine learning models, including conditional random fields (CRF), hidden Markov models (HMM), support vector machines (SVM) and so on, are shallow structures. They can basically be considered to have no or only one hidden layer. Because of the lack of structure depth, these models often have poor generalization in fitting complex functions [3]. In addition, traditional machine learning requires constructing features manually, and the step of feature construction has a great impact on the learning effect. Researchers have to spend a lot of time to select the appropriate features and construct rules, and there may be data sparseness problems.

The concept of deep learning can be traced back to the work of G. E. Hinton et al. in 2006 [3]. They point out that deep learning is a process in which a computer learns more complex concepts from simpler concepts through a multi-layer neural network structure [4]. Deep learning model can automatically learn features from large data set without manual intervention, which avoids the cost of manual feature selection, and the accuracy is relatively higher. However, in general, deep learning requires much more computation in its pre-training process than traditional machine learning, and requires much more data and longer model training time.

The earliest artificial neural network is Perceptron model, which was proposed by psychologist Rosenblatt in 1950s and 1960s [5]. Its essence is to model the mathematical model according to the information processing function of human brain. At present, the structure of neural network is evolving continuously, and there are many variants, including Recurrent Neural Network (RNN) and Convolutional Neural Networks (CNN) etc. The structure of neural network used in deep learning includes a large number of neurons. Each neuron is connected with other neurons. Parameters such as the weights between neurons are constantly modified in the process of learning data characteristics. Finally, a learning model that can complete tasks such as classification or prediction is obtained. The basic process of deep learning can be summarized as follows:

(1) Construct a neural network with n layers and initialize network parameters.
(2) Input the untagged training data set into the first layer network, and input the results of the first layer network into the second layer, and so on, until the nth layer network, and output the results.
(3) Compare the network output results with the real results of the training data set, and calculate the error. SGD, ADAM and other optimization methods are adopted to modify the network parameters of all layers to reduce the error.
(4) Repeat steps (2) and (3) until the error meets the requirement.
(5) Accomplish the model for classification or prediction etc.

Among them, steps (2), (3), and (4) are called pre-training stage, which is an important step to build a deep learning model (Fig. 1).

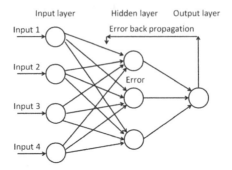

Fig. 1. The basic structure of a neural network.

For the application and research of deep learning in different fields, the following two problems should be solved first:

(1) How to represent the original features of the application domain;
(2) How to choose the appropriate deep learning algorithm [6].

3 Deep Learning in Natural Language Processing

Deep learning has achieved great success in image processing in recent years, and more and more researches have been carried out in the field of natural language with fruitful results. Some representative areas of NLP include machine translation, emotional analysis, question answering, and text summarization etc.

3.1 Machine Translation

Machine translation refers to the process of translating one natural source language into another natural target language by computer. In recent years, the performance of Neural Machine Translation (NMT) has surpassed that of traditional Statistical Machine Translation (SMT), and the research of NMT has become a new paradigm of machine translation.

Kalchbrenner and Blunsom proposed for the first time a new end-to-end Encoder-Decoder structure for machine translation [7]. The machine translation system generates input sentences into vectors with Encoder and then generates the target language with Decoder. At present, most of the NMT systems adopt this kind of Encoder-Decoder structure. When translating, the machine translation system first inputs the original sentences of different lengths into the encoder, which converts them into fixed length vectors, and then inputs the vector into the decoder, which can generate the translation of sentences.

Sutskever et al. proposed the structure of Sequence to Sequence machine translation system [8]. They tried to change the encoder and decoder into Long Short-Term Memory (LSTM) structure. The experimental results show that this structure has more advantages in accuracy than traditional SMT system.

However, since the encoder compresses all the information of the original sentence into a fixed length vector, the longer the original sentence is, the more difficult the system will be to process. In order to solve this problem, Bahdanau et al. first introduced the attention mechanism into NMT system [9]. That is, after the encoder generates a fixed-length vector, the vector is input into the attention layer, a weighted context vector is generated, and then the vector is input into the decoder for decoding. This structure enables the machine translation system to judge which word in the original text is related to the word when it generates the word, which greatly improves the translation performance when translating long sentences. Since then, attention mechanism has been widely applied in NMT systems.

Gehring et al. showed that the performance of the NMT system using CNN as encoder is similar to that of RNN, and the translation speed of the NMT system based on CNN is faster than that of RNN under the same translation accuracy [10]. In the same year, Google's research team proposed a Transformer-based NMT framework, which abandoned the previous CNN or RNN structure and used a Self-Attention-based structure. The framework can perform parallel operations on data during training, avoiding the slow training speed caused by RNN's need to read information sequentially. At the same time, this architecture also enables NMT to achieve greater breakthroughs in translation performance [11]. At present, more and more machine translation systems begin to adopt a framework similar to Transformer.

3.2 Emotional Analysis

Emotional analysis or opinion mining refers to the analysis and reasoning of the text with subjective feelings, and the summary of the emotions that the text wants to reflect. Examples include the analysis of micro-blog information, the emotions contained in the commodity evaluation of shopping websites, and so on. Kim used the multi-channel CNN model, combined with word2vec pre-trained word vector, to classify the emotional sentences of movie reviews, product customer evaluation, etc., and achieved quite good results [12]. Wang et al. proposed the analysis of the emotional polarity of twitter information with the LSTM model [13]. Their experiments show that the accuracy of emotional analysis classifier using LSTM model is better than that using statistical learning classifier even without using the features selected manually.

3.3 Question Answering

Question Answering (QA) is designed to study how to search for answers to specific questions from large-scale text database. Question answering is a complex NLP task, which requires the machine to understand the question first, and then generate the correct answer according to the question. RNN and LSTM networks have relatively limited memory capacity and are unable to deal with longer texts of content or knowledge in question answering. To solve this problem, Weston et al. proposed the framework of a

Memory Network, which consists of a memory m and four components I (input feature map), G (generalization), O (output feature map) and R (response) [14]. The network framework has a great impact on the field of automatic question answering. Kumar et al. proposed a framework of Dynamic Memory Network (DNN) [15]. This framework borrows the structure of memory network and Decoder-Encoder, uses two GRU networks to encode background information and questions respectively, and uses attention mechanism to encode questions and background information, and finally generates answers. The framework achieves good results on the dataset of Facebook's bAbI.

3.4   Automatic Summarization

Automatic summarization refers to the automatic summarization of the main contents of text by computer without changing the original meaning of the text. The applications of automatic summarization include automatic report generation, news title generation, search results preview, etc. There are two main types of automatic summarization. The first one is to extract the content of the original text through keywords, locations and other features. It is called extractive summarization. The second is to generate abstract summarization content by learning a large amount of data through machine learning model. The source of abstract content is not limited to the original content, which is called abstractive summarization. In terms of generative summarization, Rush et al. tried to adopt a similar structure in the field of automatic summarization in view of the success of Encoder-Decoder mechanism and attention mechanism in NMT, and compared it with other types of summarization system, and achieved good results in DUC-2004 task [16]. In the aspect of extractive summarization, Cao et al. proposed Attentive Summarization, which uses the attention mechanism to calculate the correlation between different words in the sentences and the user's query content to remove redundancy [17].

4   Deep Learning in Automated Essay Scoring

4.1   Deep Learning in End-to-End AES

Neural network-based deep learning technology is becoming more and more mature, and its application in automatic essay scoring is also worth exploring.

Alikaniotis et al. constructed a vocabulary representation model by designing an algorithm to learn how certain vocabulary contributes to the essay score; LSTM network was adopted to represent the meaning of the text; and an AES system was designed, which achieved very good results [18]. LSTM network is a variant of RNN, and RNN is usually a multi-layer structure. Multilayer neural networks can automatically learn useful features from data, basic features from low-level structures and higher-level abstract features from high-level structures [19].

On the basis of Collobert and Weston's work [20], i.e., a distributed representation of each word *w* in the local context of the corpus, and adopting the method proposed by Tang [21], Alikaniotis et al. constructed a model that is extended to "capture not only the local linguistic environment of each word, but also how each word contributes to the overall score of the essay" [18]. They call this extended model the "augmented

C&W model". The core function of the model is to capture the "usage" information of vocabulary, that is, to filter out the "under-informative" words, such as *is*, *are*, *to*, *at* and so on. It focuses on the information-rich vocabulary, namely "score-specific word embeddings" (SSWEs). By using SSWEs, continuous vocabulary representation for each essay is obtained, and each essay is treated as a sequence of tokens to explore the use of uni- and bi-directional LSTM networks, and finally these sequences of tokens are embedded into fixed-length vectors. These word vectors representing the essays are input into the linear units of the output layer, and the predicted scores of the essays are obtained.

Alikaniotis et al.'s scoring model was used to evaluate English essays of middle school students from Grade 7 to Grade 10 [18]. The essay dataset consists of 12,976 essays, ranging from 150 words to 550 words, all of which are scored manually to achieve the final score for each essay. The experiment compares several models, and the final results show that SSWE combined with two-layer bidirectional LSTM network achieves the best results.

Another research on AES based on neural network is Taghipour and Ng [22]. In this study, RNN is adopted to complete the training of essay scoring task and scoring model construction.

Taghipour and Ng construct an automated essay scoring model with CNN architecture consisting of five layers: lookup table layer, convolution layer, recurrent layer, mean over time, and linear layer with Sigmoid activation [22]. The first lookup layer projects each word of an essay into a high-dimensional space. The convolution layer is equivalent to a function, which extracts the possible local contextual dependencies from the n-gram vectors transferred from the lookup layer, so as to improve the performance of the scoring system. The recurrent layer first generates the embedding structure, then processes the input data and generates the digital representation of a given essay. "This representation should ideally encode all the information required for grading the essay. However, since the essays are usually long, [...] the learnt vector representation might not be sufficient for accurate scoring". Therefore, this study adopts and compares various deep learning strategies, and finds that LSTM has the best effect. The mean over time layer receives the processing results of the recurrent layer and calculates the average vector of the same length for all the essays. The layer with Sigmoid activation maps the vector into a scalar value, which is the score of the essay.

Taghipour and Ng [22] trained and evaluated the AES model based on deep learning with the same essay dataset as Alikaniotis et al. [18]. The results show that the correlation between the AES results of the model and the scores of the two human scorers is very close, and the correlation coefficient is higher, but still a little lower than that between the two human scorers. Since these two deep-learning-based AES studies are based on the same dataset, a comparative analysis is also made. The Quadratic Weighted Kappa (QWK) of Taghipour and Ng [22] is slightly higher than the best model of the latter study [18].

The greatest advantage of the AES model or system based on the deep learning algorithm of neural network is to avoid the heavy task of constructing evaluation features manually. This method is worth exploring and applying if we consider only the accuracy of essay score in large-scale examinations. However, another important function of writing evaluation is to provide feedback for teachers and writers, that is, the highlights and problems in writing texts. The deep learning method may improve the accuracy of scoring, but from the writing theory, it is difficult to provide convincing arguments.

"The deep architecture of neural network models, however, makes it rather difficult to identify and extract those properties of text that the network has identified as discriminative" [18]. A big problem of the deep learning algorithm based on neural network is that its overall operation is a "black box" structure, and it is usually difficult to find the reason for the results, so it cannot give the feedback of the score.

Although Alikaniotis et al. tried to visualize the process of the neural network, it can be clearly seen from the given example that the words marked as low quality and high quality have little relationship with the quality of the essay [18].

4.2 Deep Learning in Feature Selection

In fact, in order to provide effective feedback for AES, deep learning can also be used to mine the features of essay scoring.

Fu et al. believe that beautiful language is an important feature of students' writing performance, and it should play a certain role in essay scoring [23]. They propose a task of elegant sentence recognition for essay evaluation, which mainly identifies elegant sentences in middle school students' Chinese essays for AES. The research presents a deep neural network combining CNN and Bi-directional LSTM (BiLSTM) networks to recognize grace sentences. The best result of the experiment is that the accuracy rate of elegant sentence recognition is 89.23%. Using elegant sentence features in the AES task can significantly improve the performance of the scoring system. Certainly, elegant sentence has different definitions in different genres. Fu et al. define elegant sentences in Chinese essays of high school students' writing as "vivid language, flexible sentence patterns, rhetorical structures, skillful borrowing and quotation, skillful use of classical Chinese words, etc. [23] " However, other genres, such as Business English, emphasize "simple and clear" [24]. So, it is obvious that there are different definitions for elegant sentences.

Language model has long been used in AES studies and research has proved that RNN can build a very good language model [25, 26]. Kim et al. and Sundermeyer et al. also carry out research of language modeling based on neural networks [27, 28].

Beside language model, syntactical analysis is also important in AES research. Vinyals et al. adopt Sequence to Sequence model, regard the task of parsing as the problem of sequence generation, and use LSTM network to obtain the syntactic tree [29].

On the one hand, the accurate annotation and extraction of these text features can improve the accuracy of essay scoring, and more importantly on the other hand, it can theoretically enhance the validity of AES, and provide efficient and accurate feedback on language use for writers.

5 Summary

In recent years, thanks to the improvement of hardware computing ability, deep learning has been widely used in NLP field. The algorithm model of deep learning has been improved day by day, and has made significant breakthroughs in machine translation and other fields. The development of NLP technology will certainly promote the research and application of AES which belongs to the application of this technology. However, at present, there are still many problems to be solved:

(1) Deep learning learns the probabilistic features of language from corpus instead of semantic features of language. Although deep learning has shown a strong ability in NLP, there is still no perfect theory to explain the principle of deep learning, which means the lack of theoretical support.
(2) Most of the research on NLP based on deep learning currently adopts data-driven approach, and few studies can be closely integrated with linguistic research. In order to enable machines to understand and analyze language in depth, future NLP and linguistics, even cognitive science and other disciplines should promote each other and make up for each other's strengths and weaknesses.

Acknowledgements. This work is financially supported by the Science and Technology Project of Guangdong Province, China (2017A020220002), Graduate Education Innovation Plan of Guangdong Province (2018JGXM39) and the fund of Center for Translation Studies, Guangdong University of Foreign Studies.

References

1. Whithaus, C.: Foreword. In: Shermis, M.D., Burstein, J. (eds.) Handbook of Automated Essay Evaluation: Current Applications and New Directions, pp. vii–ix. Routledge, New York (2013)
2. Burstein, J.: Opportunities for natural language processing research in education. In: Gelbukh, A. (ed.) CICLing 2009. LNCS, vol. 5449, pp. 6–27. Springer, Heidelberg (2009). https://doi.org/10.1007/978-3-642-00382-0_2
3. Bengio, Y.: Learning deep architectures for AI. Found. Trends Mach. Learn. **2**(1), 1–127 (2009)
4. Hinton, G.E., Osindero, S., Teh, Y.W.: A fast learning algorithm for deep belief nets. Neural Comput. **18**(7), 1527–1554 (2006)
5. Rosenblatt, F.: The perceptron: a probabilistic model for information storage and organization in the brain. Psychol. Rev. **65**, 386–408 (1958)
6. Xi, X., Zhou, G.D.: A survey on deep learning for natural language processing. Acta Automat. Sinica **42**(10), 1445–1465 (2016)
7. Kalchbrenner, N., Blunsom, P.: Recurrent continuous translation models. In: Proceedings of the 2013 Conference on Empirical Methods in Natural Language Processing, pp. 1700–1709. Seattle, Washington (2013)
8. Sutskever, I., Vinyals, O., Le, Q. V.: Sequence to sequence learning with neural networks. In: arXiv:1409.3215v3 [cs.CL] (2014)
9. Bahdanau, D., Cho, K., Bengio, Y.: Neural machine translation by jointly learning to align and translate. Proc. ICLR **2015**, 1–15 (2014)
10. Gehring, J., Auli, M., Grangier, D., Dauphin, Y. N.: A convolutional encoder model for neural machine translation. In: Proceedings of ACL, pp. 123–135 (2017)
11. Vaswani, A., et al.: Attention is all you need. In: Advances in Neural Information Processing Systems, pp. 5998–6008 (2017)

12. Kim, Y.: Convolutional neural networks for sentence classification. In: Proceedings of the 2014 Conference on Empirical Methods in Natural Language Processing, pp. 1746–1751 (2014)

13. Wang, X., Liu, Y., Sun, C., et al.: Predicting polarities of tweets by composing word embeddings with long short-term memory. In: Proceedings of the 53rd Annual Meeting of Association for Computational Linguistics and the 7th International Joint Conference on Natural Language Processing, pp. 1343–1353. Stroudsburg, PA (2015)

14. Weston, J., Chopra, S., Bordes, A.: Memory networks. In: Proceedings of ICLR 2015, pp. 1–15 (2015)

15. Kumar, A., Irsoy, O., Ondruska, P., Iyyer, M., Bradbury, J., Gulrajani, I., et al.: Ask me anything: dynamic memory networks for natural language processing. In: Proceedings of the 33th International Conference on Machine Learning, pp. 1378–1387 (2015)

16. Rush, M. A., Chopra, S., Weston, J.: A neural attention model for abstractive sentence summarization. In: Proceedings of EMNLP 2015, pp. 379–389 (2015)

17. Cao, Z., Li, W., Li, S., Wei, F.: Joint learning of focusing and summarization with neural attention. In: Proceedings of 2016 COLING, pp. 547–556 (2016)

18. Alikaniotis, D., Yannakoudakis, H., Rei, M.: Automatic text scoring using neural networks. In: Proceedings of the 54th Annual Meeting of the Association for Computational Linguistics, pp. 715–725. Berlin, Germany (2016)

19. Lee, H., Grosse, R., Ranganath, R., Ng, A.Y.: Convolutional deep belief networks for scalable unsupervised learning of hierarchical representations. In: Proceedings of the 26th Annual International Conference on Machine Learning, pp. 1–8 (2009)

20. Collobert, R., Weston, J.: A unified architecture for natural language processing: deep neural networks with multitask learning. In: Proceedings of the Twenty-Fifth international conference on Machine Learning, pp. 160–167 (2008)

21. Tang, D.: Sentiment-specific representation learning for document-level sentiment analysis. In: Proceedings of the Eighth ACM International Conference on Web Search and Data Mining – WSDM 2015, pp. 447–452. Association for Computing Machinery (ACM) (2015)

22. Taghipour, K., Ng, H. T.: A neural approach to automated essay scoring. In: Proceedings of the 2016 Conference on Empirical Methods in Natural Language Processing, pp. 1882–1891, Austin, Texas (2016)

23. Fu, R., Wang, D., Wang, S., Hu, G., Liu, T.: Elegant sentence recognition for automated essay scoring. J. Chin. Inf. Process. **32**(6), 88–97 (2018)

24. Guffey, M.E., Loewy, D.: Essentials of Business Communication. Cengage Learning, South-Western (2010)

25. Mikolov, T., Kombrink, S., Deoras, A., Burget, L., Cernocky, J.: RNNLM - recurrent neural network language modeling toolkit. In: IEEE Automatic Speech Recognition and Understanding Workshop (2011)

26. Chelba, C., et al.: One Billion Word Benchmark for Measuring Progress in Statistical Language Modeling. Computer Science. arXiv:1312.3005 [cs.CL] (2013)

27. Kim, Y., Jernite, Y., Sontag, D., Rush, A.M.: Character-aware neural language models. In: Proceedings of the Thirtieth AAAI Conference on Artificial Intelligence. arXiv:1508.06615 [cs.CL] (2016)

28. Sundermeyer, M., Ney, H., Schlüter, R.: From feedforward to recurrent LSTM neural networks for language modeling. IEEE/ACM Trans. Audio Speech Lang. Process. **23**(3), 517–529 (2015)

29. Vinyals, O., Kaiser, L., Koo, T., Petrov, S., Sutskever, I., Hinton, G.: Grammar as a foreign language. In: Advances in Neural Information Processing Systems. arXiv:1412.7449 [cs.CL] (2015)

A Teaching Experiment
on a Knowledge-Network-Based Online
Translation Learning Platform

Yuanyuan Mu[1,2] and Wenting Yang[3(✉)]

[1] School of Foreign Studies, Hefei University of Technology, Hefei, China
[2] Center for Translation Studies of Specialized Corpora,
Hefei University of Technology, Hefei, China
[3] School of Foreign Languages, Anqing Normal University, Anqing, China
1339957716@qq.com

Abstract. This paper aims to elaborate on the design and application of an online platform as a knowledge-network-based system for online teaching/(self-)learning of translation in/between English and Chinese. We have two purposes for this research: first, to obtain a good understanding of translation trainees' learning behaviors in the corpus-assisted and knowledge-network-based translation learning setting, in the hope that sufficient data will be collected to draw a model of knowledge-network-based learning. Equally important is our second purpose, which is to initiate a more systematic and in-depth data-based empirical investigation into teaching designs for knowledge-based translation learning. This research conducts an experiment on how teachers can use knowledge nodes to organize online translation learning and how students perceive knowledge-network-based learning. The experiment reveals a rising trend of students' translation quality and they generally hold a positive attitude towards this learning model. Based on theoretical discussions of the platform design rationale and the findings from the teaching experiment, this paper explores how the knowledge-network-based translation learning can assist students in forming more efficient translation learning strategies.

Keywords: Knowledge network · Online translation learning · Corpus-based translation teaching

1 Introduction

With the rapid development of technologies in education practice and research, language teaching has also experienced tremendous progress in terms of technology-enhanced modes. Translation teaching, an advanced form of bilingual teaching, has been faced with challenges and opportunities of computer-assisted and data-based forms. In order to improve the efficiency of translation learning and teaching, an online translation teaching/learning platform, ClinkNotes Online Platform, has been designed and put into

---

The original version of this chapter was revised: the authors' affiliations were corrected. The correction to this chapter is available at https://doi.org/10.1007/978-3-030-38778-5_41

E. Popescu et al. (Eds.): SETE 2019, LNCS 11984, pp. 319–328, 2020.
https://doi.org/10.1007/978-3-030-38778-5_35

use, which includes a knowledge-network-based system with annotations of translation methods for the bilingual corpora and an automatic monitoring system for the tracking of students' learning records and historical performances.

The knowledge base of this project is designed with interdisciplinary approaches with recourse to computer science, knowledge engineering and management, translation studies, functional/text linguistics, language education, etc. to develop a groundbreaking and cost-effective educational paradigm for the teaching/(self-)learning of English-Chinese bilingual text-production in classroom/web-based settings to alleviate the pressure on labor-intensive language/translation courses.

2 Knowledge Network in Translation Learning

2.1 Literature Review on Knowledge Network

The concept "knowledge network" was explicitly put forward by Gągne in 1985. Hereby as a paradigm in conducting research on knowledge management, it has been gradually applied to different disciplines like management, economics and cognitive psychology. With the database of Web of Science and CNKI (China National Knowledge Infrastructure) as literature sources, we firstly searched the papers containing the concept "knowledge network". The retrieving results suggest that the number of the papers published has increased greatly since 2006, mostly in the field of library and information science and science and technology management [1, 2]. There are also some researches that apply the concept "knowledge network" to the educational field in recent years. When we further searched papers containing both "knowledge network" and "teaching", it can be found that most of the papers fall to the field of education technology, more to build macro framework, laying their emphasis on constructing learning cell and learning platform [3, 4], discussing teaching framework [5] and learners' learning trajectories and behavioral patterns [6, 7]; however, there are still not many researches on specific teaching implementations, and even fewer empirical studies on knowledge network's improving learners' abilities in certain aspects. Overall, researches on applying knowledge network to teaching are still at initial stage and recall further development. With translation teaching and learning as example, some scholars have already paid attention to constructing corpus-based network knowledge system and building online platform for translation teaching to improve students' translation ability [8, 9]. But few papers clearly put forward the concept "knowledge network" and verify its feasibility and validity in teaching process.

2.2 Platform Design

The ClinkNotes Online Platform endeavors to build a knowledge management system [10]. The database of this Platform is annotated by using a system of knowledge nodes ("tag-words") [11] derived from the text-analysis, which, in turn, is informed by text-linguistics, systemic-functional linguistics, stylistics, and discourse studies. To facilitate teaching/learning, the electronic system includes: annotations on cultural background knowledge and on textual design, stylistic features/effects, information management, and writing/translating skills; samples for discussion; multiple modes of access to annotated textual phenomena (by: e.g. tagged features, navigation among related features, grouping of the textual manifestations of the same feature); study progress monitoring devices; and tutor-learner communication channels for on-line learning.

As the first attempt of its kind in the field, the cutting edge of this platform lies not in the size of its databases but in its knowledge-based, theoretically-informed delicacy and relevance of annotations and its teacher/learner-friendly data management. This platform endeavors to build a knowledge management system based on the domain-specific ontology for translation/bilingual writing, which features a computable network of inter-related and hierarchically distributed conceptual representations of the knowledge in this field, with "tag-words" as the knowledge nodes to form a roadmap of navigation and also as the keywords to introduce theory-informed annotations (Fig. 1).

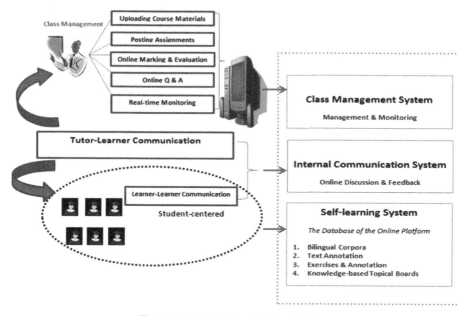

Fig. 1. The ClinkNotes Online Platform

3   The Teaching Experiment

On the corpus-based online translation teaching platform, this project aims at exploring the translation teaching model of knowledge network. To test out its feasibility and validity in improving students' translation ability, we carried out teaching experiment facilitated by ClinkNotes Online Platform.

3.1   Participants

The participants were 23 sophomore students majoring in English. Before joining in the specialized teaching experiment, they had already taken courses on translation between Chinese and English for two semesters. Therefore, they have basic translation knowledge and skills. Also, they had been exposed to online learning before and was basically familiar with online information technology. Each student was well instructed and informed about the operation of the ClinkNotes Online Platform before learning through this platform.

3.2 Procedures

Before the experiment, a Chinese-English translation test was conducted with the help of a Chinese text of about 300 words to pre-test students' translation ability. In the experiment, students were instructed to learn 13 translation knowledge nodes related to the text within a month through the ClinkNotes Online Platform. The knowledge nodes are: (1) Parody; (2) Verb-Present Participle; (3) Idiom; (4) Alliteration; (5) Rhythm; (6) TransferredEpithet; (7) Noun-Pronoun; (8) Echo; (9) Reduplication; (10) Onomatopoeia; (11) Classifier; (12) Metaphor; (13) Intertextuality, covering five categories of translation method, rhetoric, grammar, information distribution within sentences and cultural background knowledge. The knowledge nodes are correlated with other knowledge nodes to form a knowledge network. After learning, students were again assigned to translate the same text as a posttest (Fig. 2).

Fig. 2. The test text

To ensure the reliability and validity of the experiment, students were not informed in advance that the same text would be used for pretest and posttest, and they were also stipulated not to use other electronic resources except the platform during the one-month experiment, here hence to avoid students from referring to the reference translation after the pretest. Students could refer to paper dictionary to complete their translation within a certain limit of time. The test results were scored according to the scoring standards for the translation part of TEM-8 (Test for English Majors, band 8, which is supposed to be for senior students). The weighted scores were made by two teachers and averaged as the final scores of the students being tested. The statistical software SPSS 19.0 was used to compare the mean values of the test results to help understand the changes of students' scores before and after the experiment, so as to test the learning effect of the teaching model.

The study also conducted a questionnaire survey after the test to understand students' self-perception and recognition towards the translation teaching model of knowledge network. The questionnaire was designed according to the Likert Scale, assigning 5 levels of point for different options with 5 the highest recognition and 1 the lowest. Also, one-to-one interviews were made, during which the teacher would ask students questions about the translation task, the platform and their learning experience. Combined all the above explorations, the study then probed into the feasibility of this translation teaching and learning model. The detailed procedures are shown in Fig. 3.

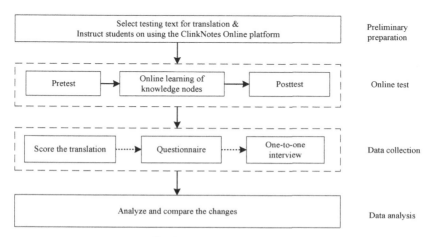

Fig. 3. Research procedures

4 Data Analysis and Discussion

4.1 Score Analysis

According to the scores of the two teachers, the pretest and posttest score of 23 students were calculated and counted. Assisted by SPSS 19.0, Q-Q plot was adopted to test the normal distribution of the scores, the results are shown respectively in Figs. 4 and 5.

As can be seen from Fig. 4, most of the points are allocated around the straight line and the scattered points are basically diagonally straight. Also, the points in the detrended normal Q-Q plot of pretest randomly fall around the zero-scale line, so it can be speculated that the pretest scores of the 23 students are approximately in line with the normal distribution. When observed in the same way, the posttest scores can be taken as normally distributed.

We then applied the paired sample t-test to explore the correlation and significance between the test scores and the knowledge-network-based translation learning model facilitated by SPSS 19.0. Here in this study, the hypothesis and standard should be

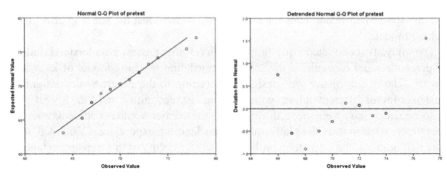

Fig. 4. Q-Q Plot of pretest

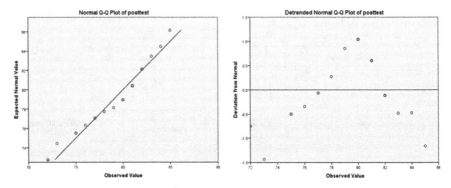

Fig. 5. Q-Q Plot of Posttest

firstly specified. Hypothesis H_0 is that the changes between the two groups of data are not correlated with this translation learning model, while that for H_1 vice versa. Without peculiar requirements, the standard α is set as 0.05 to decide whether to accept H_0 or not. The basic statistical information is shown in Table 1.

Table 1. Statistics of pretest and posttest

	Mean	N	Std. Deviation	Std. Error Mean
Pretest	70.08	23	3.630	.757
Posttest	78.96	23	3.735	.779

As can be observed from Table 1, the mean value of pretest scores is 70.08 and that of posttest scores is 78.96. Combined with the characteristics of normal distribution of students' scores, it indicates that most students' pretest scores are around 70 points while for posttest 79, uprising of about 9 points when compared with pretest.

The paired samples correlations are suggested in Table 2 as above. It can be seen from Table 2 that the correlation value is a positive value 0.507, and $p = 0.014 < 0.05$. With the standard $\alpha = 0.05$, hypothesis H_0 is rejected but H_1 accepted. That is, the changes between the pretest and posttest scores are significantly correlated. A detailed result of the paired samples test is shown in Table 3.

Table 2. Paired samples correlations

	N	Correlation	Sig.
Pair 1 pretest & posttest	23	.507	.014

As can be seen in Table 3, the average difference of pretest and posttest score is 8.870. Meanwhile, the observed $p = .000 < 0.05$, suggesting that statistically H_0 is rejected while H_1 accepted. Combined with the correlations between the two groups of data, it can be stipulated that the knowledge-network-based translation leaning model significantly helps in improving students' posttest scores and the translation quality of students' posttest is improved when compared with that of their pretest.

Table 3. Paired samples test of pretest and posttest

	Paired differences					t	df	Sig. (2-tailed)
	Mean	Std. Deviation	Std. Error Mean	95% Confidence Interval of the Difference				
				Lower	Upper			
Pair 1 pretest-posttest	− 8.870	3.659	.763	− 10.452	− 7.287	− 11.624	22	.000

4.2   Analysis of Questionnaire and One-to-One Interview

A questionnaire survey and one-one-to-one interview were conducted after the test to help further demonstrate the above statistical hypothesis. Totally 23 copies of questionnaire survey were sent out to students and 23 were effectively received with effective rate 100%. According to the evaluation index of the five-level scale, if the option value is between 1 to 2.5 points, it means that the students hold a negative attitude towards the survey item; if 2.5 to 3.5 points, then neutral attitudes and if 3.5 to 5 points, then positive attitudes. The detailed results of the survey items related to knowledge network are listed in Table 4.

The standard deviation of all the survey items, except item 7, is less than 1.00 and their overall number is small, suggesting a relatively low discrete degree in their data distribution with the option of each students closer to the mean score. Also, the mean

Table 4. Questionnaire results

Question item	Statistical counting					Mean	Std. Deviation	Var.
	5	4	3	2	1			
1. How do you think the assigned knowledge nodes are related to the difficult points when re-translate the text?	6	14	2	1	0	4.09	0.72	0.51
2. Do you think the learning of the 13 specific knowledge nodes and their annotation is helpful in completing the assigned translation or not?	3	15	5	0	0	3.91	0.58	0.34
3. From your self-perception, do you think your translation quality is improved or not when you re-translate the same text after learning the 13 knowledge nodes?	3	10	9	1	0	3.65	0.76	0.57
4. There may be one or more knowledge nodes involved in annotating the sample sentences, and there may be other related nodes combined to explicate the translation methods. How do you think of the combination of knowledge nodes?	2	13	6	2	0	3.65	0.76	0.57
5. Does the networked knowledge method by combining knowledge nodes help in translation learning?	3	15	4	1	0	3.87	0.68	0.46
6. Through this online learning, do you agree to the networked knowledge learning method of translation?	6	10	6	1	0	3.91	0.83	0.69
7. The networked knowledge learning method of translation presented in this platform is more accurate and effective than that in traditional classroom learning. Do you agree with this hypothesis?	4	8	6	5	0	3.48	1.02	1.03
8. In your future learning, will you try to consciously cultivate your networked translation learning model based on the knowledge nodes?	7	11	5	0	0	4.09	0.72	0.51

value of all the survey items listed is above 3.5 points, indicating their generally positive attitude towards the listing items. Besides, for all the items, their scores are bigger than 1, showing no students holding a completely negative attitude.

A further probe into the specific survey items is made in combination of the one-to-one interview. From students' self-perception, it is generally believed that the 13 specific knowledge nodes are positively correlated with the difficult points in translation (scoring 4.09). They thought that "when I translate the texts again, I would consciously think about which knowledge nodes could be applied to the text, and I found that some could be directly used in the translation", and thus the knowledge nodes are much helpful in translating (scoring 3.91). Different students held different opinions on what type of knowledge nodes is more helpful, but they generally agreed that many knowledge nodes could help them deal with the difficulties they came across during their pretest, and thereby improving their translation quality when compared with their previous translation (scoring 3.65). This can be well illustrated by their posttest scores, which is consistent with their self-perception. As to the knowledge network interconnected and formed by the 13 nodes, students' acceptance level is relatively high (scoring 3.65). They argued that this combination way of knowledge "let us intuitively understand the connection among different knowledge nodes", "I can master one node while also get to know another", "pretty systematic and overall", "feel like they are in one system", "it much saves my time and energy while learning", etc. Therefore, this way helps in translation learning (scoring 3.87) and students approved of the method for translation learning with the aid of the knowledge network (scoring 3.91).

It is worth noting that in view of the hypothesis put forward in item 7, the mean value of scores is 3.48 points, a little bit lower than 3.5 points. Still, 5 people chose the option scoring 2, and the standard deviation of this item is bigger than the other 7 items, indicating a variation in students' options. A further interview targeting at this item is made to students, especially those holding negative attitude. It is found that their controversial points are mainly in the annotation of knowledge nodes and the explanation of example sentences. Some believed that "it is the first time for me to learn these knowledge nodes. But some nodes are way too professional to understand", and "some nodes are not easy for me to understand, and it becomes even more difficult for me to understand when another node is involved in". Some students held that "there are repeated examples among different nodes. I understand that there may be several nodes in the same example, but I am used to recalling knowledge through examples, and that makes me a little confused." The conflicting part is more concerned about the students, as their learning habits and their knowledge base vary. But overall, students are willing to cultivate this learning model in their future translation learning (scoring 4.09), as "the learning efficiency is relatively high, and I can master several knowledge nodes at the same time".

5   Research Findings and Conclusion

It can be seen from the experiment that according to students' self-perception, the 13 specific knowledge nodes are positively correlated with the difficult points in translation. The students generally accept the knowledge-network-based learning modes.

In fact, based on the learning instructions from the knowledge-network-based experiment, the translation quality of students' posttest is improved when compared with that of their pretest, which, to some extent, testifies the efficiency and effectiveness of knowledge-network-based translation learning platform. However, it should be noted that the familiarity of the test material in the posttest may, to some extent, affect the performance of the students. They may be supposed to achieve a relatively higher score due to familiarity of the text. But it is true that the abovementioned factor cannot determine the overwhelmingly higher score. Since the improvement of the posttest is very significant, we cannot deny the positive function of knowledge-based network in this translation teaching experiment.

With the help of the ontology-based knowledge management system and the monitoring system involved in this platform, we may expect to exploit the ontological representations of the learning environment and provide a mimetic optimization algorithm capable of generating the most effective learning pathway for learners.

Acknowledgements. The work was substantially supported by The National Social Science Fund of China (Project No. 19BYY125).

References

1. Gao, J., Ding, K., Pan, Y., Yuan, J.: Analysis of the research status of knowledge network at home and abroad. Inf. Stud. Theor. Appl. **38**(9), 120–125 (2015)
2. Cai, B., Chen, G., Huang, X.: International research on knowledge network: present situation, hotspot and trend — bibliometrics analyzing based on web of science. J. Xidian Univ. (Social Science Edition). **27**(4), 40–51 (2017)
3. Yang, X., Li, W., Gu, Y.: Research on the construction of knowledge element based teaching resources organization model. Documentation, Inf. Knowl. **1**, 101–107 (2016)
4. Yu, S., Duan, J., Cui, J.: A double spiral deep learning model based on learning cell platform. Modern Distance Education Research. (6), 37–47 + 56 (2017)
5. Yan, Z., Li, M.: Technological pedagogical and content knowledge network — a new knowledge framework for teachers in information age. China Educ. Technol. **4**, 58–63 (2012)
6. Cao, L.: Studies on learning path and learning behavior characteristics in online learning. Distance Educ. China **4**, 25–30 (2014)
7. Yang, X., Li, J., Xing, B.: Behavioral patterns of knowledge construction in online cooperative translation activities. Internet High. Educ. **36**, 13–21 (2018)
8. Zhu, Y., Chen, J.: The theoretical conception and engineering practice of a corpus-based computer-assisted translation. Technol. Enhanced Foreign Lang. Educ. **4**, 52–57 (2015)
9. Zhu, C., Mu, Y.: Towards a textual accountability-driven mode of teaching and (self-) learning for translation and bilingual writing: with special reference to a CityU online teaching platform. Chin. Translators J. **2**, 56–62 (2013)
10. Mu, Y., Tian, L., Yang, W.: Towards a knowledge management model for online translation learning. In: Hao, T., Chen, W., Xie, H., Nadee, W., Lau, R. (eds.) SETE 2018. LNCS, vol. 11284. Springer, Cham (2018). https://doi.org/10.1007/978-3-030-03580-8_21
11. Tian, L., Mu, Y., Yang, W.: Designing a platform-facilitated and corpus-assisted translation class. In: Hao, T., Chen, W., Xie, H., Nadee, W., Lau, R. (eds.) SETE 2018. LNCS, vol. 11284. Springer, Cham (2018). https://doi.org/10.1007/978-3-030-03580-8_22

Design of Discipline Information System for 'Foreign Language and Literature'

Jing He[✉]

Guangdong University of Foreign Studies, Guangzhou 510420, China
mavis23@126.com

Abstract. 'Discipline construction' is the most important and fundamental task of universities, which is based on discipline information management. Since there are no specialized information systems for the discipline of 'Foreign Language and Literature', and the existing systems cannot fully meet today's needs, this paper designs a discipline information system for 'Foreign Language and Literature' on the basis of previous studies, which combines the operation process of the discipline (as an organization) and the features of the discipline (as a research field). The system functions include discipline display, discipline information management, discipline planning, interdisciplinary management, and system management. According to these functions, the system is divided into 2 parts: a website and an information management system, each part consists of 4 basic modules, teaching staff, talent training, scientific research and social services, in which internationalization and interdisciplinary characteristics run through.

Keywords: Information system · Discipline management · Foreign Language and Literature

1 Introduction

The core membership unit in academic systems is discipline-centered [1]. In order to effectively promote the construction of world-class universities and first-class disciplines, the State Council of the PRC issued the "Overall Plan for Coordinating the Promotion of World-Class Universities and First-Class Disciplines" on October 24, 2015. The plan, also known as the "Double-First Class" initiative, aims to ultimately build a number of world class universities and disciplines by the end of 2050, in an effort to make China an international higher education power [2]. On September 21, 2017, Chinese authorities released a selected list of universities, which will participate in the country's construction plan of world-class universities and first-class disciplines. 42 universities colleges will be developed into first-class educational institutions, and 95 universities will focus on building their preponderant disciplines into first-rate ones, including the discipline of 'Foreign Language and Literature' from 6 universities [3]. 'Discipline construction', generally refers to developing a discipline at a university, has entered a period of great change, and its importance has become increasingly prominent in China. It urges universities to set up an information system and management mechanism to promote the development of each discipline on purpose.

E. Popescu et al. (Eds.): SETE 2019, LNCS 11984, pp. 329–334, 2020.
https://doi.org/10.1007/978-3-030-38778-5_36

Of the many who have designed a discipline information system, none has as yet developed an information system especially for 'Foreign Language and Literature', and failed to fully meet the needs of today's users in discipline management. Li has developed a management information system based on VB.NET to look up fast corrective information of disciplines with the help of internet [4]. This system includes six modules: teaching, scientific research, degree management, equipment management, library data, and academic exchange. Wang has designed a web-based information system and applied the date mining technology to the system to make it more intelligent [5]. The system is of a three-tiered structure, which consists by a personal space, a school space and a university space. Its functions include looking for and revising information of academic groups, papers, scientific research projects, academic monographs, and textbooks related to disciplines. Chen has designed a management information system based on ExtJS, consists of five modules: financial support, scientific research, discipline construction, maintenance and system help, the information includes teaching groups, scientific research information, teaching conditions, and talent cultivation information [6]. Li has designed an information management platform based on portal technology, aims to integrate new applications with existing system [7]. The platform mainly carries out the following functions: discipline information display and distribution, academic exchange, tutor management, discipline information management (research interests, team groups, and scientific achievements, teaching conditions, conferences and seminars), project management, and interdisciplinary management. It also provides common functionality such as content aggregation, single sign-on, personal customization, system integration, and full-text search. Gao et al. have designed a discipline information platform for Shanghai University of Finance and Economics [8]. This platform carries out five functions as data base management, discipline programming, discipline information display, discipline evaluation, and system management. These researches mentioned above have laid a foundation for the overall structure and main functional modules of the discipline information system. However, all these information systems are designed at the background of the educational information in China, the main idea of these designs is to save manpower, resources and time. Nowadays, discipline management has become the primary purpose of the system.

2   Discipline Management and Information System

Discipline management is a comprehensive and unified management of the whole process of discipline development and related elements by giving full play to the internal and external effects of discipline system, taking relatively independent or interrelated disciplines as its management object, including three meanings [9]: (i) the management object is an independent discipline or an discipline group consisted by several interrelated disciplines; (ii) the management focuses on the inherent rules, operational mechanism and interdisciplinary linkages of disciplines; (iii) the basic requirement of discipline management is to carry out systematic and comprehensive management, that is, to cover the whole life cycle of the discipline as well as the construction and development evaluation accompanying this process, including the comprehensive and unified management of the elements involved in the discipline, such as teaching, scientific research, social services, resources, and environment. The connotation of discipline management requires that the discipline information system conforms to the discipline rules, covers the whole course of the discipline's life cycle, and serves the integration and development of disciplines.

'An information system (IS) is a set of interrelated components that together collects, processes, stores, analyses, and disseminates data and information in an organization; an information system provides a feedback mechanism to monitor and control its operation to make sure it continues to meet its goal and objectives' [10]. Information system has different types, such as personal IS, group IS, and enterprise IS [10]. A discipline information system can be categorized as a group IS, which improves communications and supports collaboration within a discipline. Based on a general model of an organization [10], this paper attempts to build an organizational model refined to disciplines (see Fig. 1). Information system can support and work in the automated portions of an organizational process of disciplines.

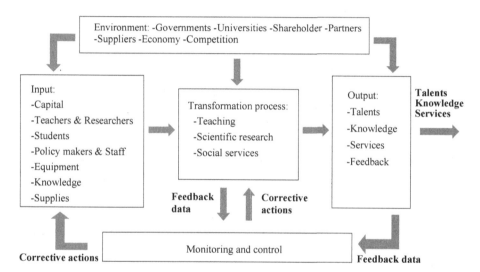

Fig. 1. Organizational model of disciplines.

3   The Discipline of 'Foreign Language and Literature'

The discipline of 'Foreign Language and Literature' covers foreign linguistics and foreign literature research. It takes languages and literature as its main body and extends to translation studies, national and regional studies and cross-cultural studies, within 5 research fields [11]. The second level subjects include English language and literature, Russian language and literature, French language and literature, German language and literature, Japanese language and literature, Indian language and literature, Spanish language and literature, Arabic language and literature, European language and literature, Asian and African language and literature, foreign linguistics and applied linguistics, business English studies, translation studies, comparative literature and cross-cultural studies, foreign language education technology, country and regional studies, etc. [11]. Main features of the discipline are as follows: (i) the research object is divided into two parts: linguistics and literature, which are parallel and relatively independent; (ii) with the obvious characteristics of interdisciplinary and multidisciplinary, the discipline itself is interdisciplinary and developing/integrating with other disciplines; (iii) taking the advantages of languages, it is closely linked with international higher education institutions and has rich international resources.

4 Information System Design of 'Foreign Language and Literature'

4.1 Functional Design

On the basis of Gao et al.'s research [8], in accordance with the disciplinary nature and the actual use demand, this paper gives the design of the information system with functions of personal information management and interdisciplinary management, which are derived from Wang [5] and Li [7]. Based on the above researches, this paper has integrated and refined the functions of the existing discipline information system, the following functional requirements are specifically designed for the discipline information system of 'Foreign Language and Literature'.

Discipline Display. It can be divided into two parts: basic information display and discipline achievements display. The first part shows the basic information of the discipline, includes teachers, research areas and groups, research institutes, academic journals, etc. The second part automatically grasps teaching achievements and research achievements published on the network, include the newest scientific research projects, teaching practices, international academic conferences, etc. Users can leave messages, suggestions and questions, and managers can also reply on the website.

Discipline Information Management (Including Personal Information Management for Teachers). It needs to collect and manage the discipline data comprehensively and accurately, to provide data input and export functions for corresponding needs, and to import data from existing information systems of the whole university by disciplines. At the same time, teachers are encouraged to declare their symbolic achievements made by individuals and research teams in time, and to generate quarterly briefings, annual performance reports of the discipline through the integration of system information, so as to conduct self-evaluation and dynamic monitoring of the discipline, while preparing for the external evaluation.

Discipline Planning. Depending on the two-level management system of school university in China's higher education institutions, it is essential to formulate a medium to long-term strategy for the developments of the discipline, in accordance with the five research areas of linguistics and literature, to clarify the responsibility of the schools and research institutes, by analyzing the data from discipline information system.

Interdisciplinary Management. Interdisciplinary teaching and research should run through the whole discipline information system. Every data in the system should contain discipline participation information to make the system generate the summary report of interdisciplinary achievements automatically.

System Management. Manage users, permissions and default settings for this information system, so that the functional departments and the responsibility departments of the university can real-time view and manage the overall progress of the discipline construction project.

4.2 Module Design

The information system includes two parts: a website for discipline display and a discipline information management system. According to the fourth round discipline evaluation index system in China [12], this system sets up four modules, includes teaching staff, talent training, scientific research and social services, with fourteen secondary indicators, in which internationalization and interdisciplinary characteristics run through (see Fig. 2).

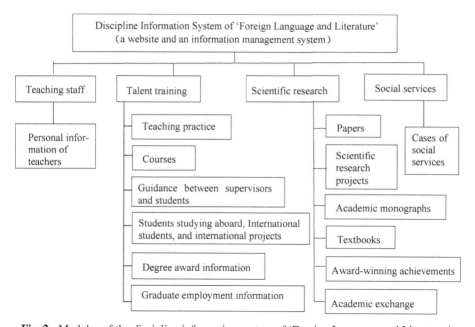

Fig. 2. Modules of the discipline information system of 'Foreign Language and Literature'.

5 Conclusion

Nowadays, 'discipline construction' has become a fundamental task of universities in China, which includes the reorganization of resources, systems, groups and technologies, the information technology requested is more complex and sophisticated, but there is no comprehensive and all-purpose information system for disciplines yet, especially for the discipline of 'Foreign Language and Literature'. Therefore, the author gives the frames of discipline information system of 'Foreign Language and Literature' based on previous studies and the research of disciplines' operation process as a group and the disciplinary nature of 'Foreign Language and Literature'. The system has a website and an information management system, includes functions such as discipline display, discipline information management, discipline planning, interdisciplinary management, and system management, adopts the fourth round discipline evaluation index system, and integrates the characteristics of 'internationalization' and 'interdisciplinary' in each item. It provides a practical and convenient mechanism to promote the development of discipline of 'Foreign Language and Literature' in China.

References

1. Clark, B.R.: The Higher Education System: Academic Organization in Cross-National Perspective, 1st edn. University of California Press, California (1986)
2. The State Council of the People's Republic of China. http://www.gov.cn/zhengce/con-tent/2015-11/05/content_10269.htm. Accessed 24 Oct 2015
3. Ministry of Education of the People's Republic of China. http://www.moe.gov.cn/srcsite/A22/moe_843/201709/t20170921_314942.html. Accessed 21 Sept 2017
4. Li, K.: Design and Construction of Information Management System of discipline construction, 1st edn. Nanchang University, Nanchang (2007)
5. Wang, X.: Analysis and Design of Subject Construction Management System Based on Web, 1st edn. Central South University, Changsha (2008)
6. Chen, R.: Design and Implementation of Discipline Management System based on Ext JS, 1st edn. Huazhong University of Science and Technology, Wuhan (2011)
7. Li, D.: Design and Implementation of Subject Information Management Platform Based on Portal Technology, 1st edn. National University of Defense Technology, Hunan (2011)
8. Gao, L., Hu, Q., Wang, S.: Practice of discipline information platform in promoting discipline construction. Chin. J. ICT Educ. **3**, 73–76 (2014)
9. Zhu, M., Yang, X.: Management of disciplinary programs and development of modern universities. J. Grad. Educ. **6**, 12–18 (2011)
10. Stair, R.M., Reynolds, G.W.: Principles of Information Systems, 13th edn. Cengage Learning, Mexico (2018)
11. The Sixth Discipline Review Group of the Academic Degree Committee of the State Council of PR China. A Brief Introduction to Degree Awarding and Talents Training. 1st edn. Higher Education Press, Beijing (2013)
12. China Academic Degrees Graduate Education information. http://www.cdgdc.edu.cn/xwyyjsjyxx/xkpgjg/283494.shtml#3. Accessed 5 May 2019

AIE-TRST (Artificial Intelligence in Education – Teacher's Role for Student-Centered Teaching)

Simplifying the Validation and Application of Games with Simva

Cristina Alonso-Fernández(✉) ⓘ, Antonio Calvo-Morata ⓘ, Manuel Freire ⓘ,
Iván Martínez-Ortiz ⓘ, and Baltasar Fernández-Manjón ⓘ

Facultad de Informática, Complutense University of Madrid, C/Profesor José García
Santesmases 9, 28040 Madrid, Spain
{calonsofernandez,acmorata}@ucm.es, {manuel.freire,imartinez,
balta}@fdi.ucm.es

Abstract. The suitability of games for learning has been proven for many years. However, effective application of games in education requires two important stages: their initial validation, and their later use in the classroom. Serious games should be validated prior to exploitation to prove their efficacy and usefulness as tools for teachers, via larger experiments that include data collection, either from in-game interactions or from external questionnaires; this, in turn, requires dealing with data privacy regulations and informed consent. Once validated, serious games can then be applied in educational environments, where their effective application is closely linked to the tools and preparation available to the teachers and educators that use them. In this paper, we revise the steps and considerations that need to be dealt with both when conducting experiments with games and, later, when applying them as part of teaching in educational scenarios. For both these stages, we provide guidance and recommendations to simplify stakeholders' tasks, including the use of the tool *Simva*, which simplifies the management of users, questionnaires, privacy, data collection, and storage.

Keywords: Serious games · Games validation · Game-Based learning · Learning analytics · e-Learning

1 Introduction

The application of Game-Based Learning (GBL) has greatly increased in the last years, as many studies have proven the benefits of applying games in educational settings [1]. The interactive nature of games increases the engagement of students in learning activities, motivating them to progress and complete the in-game tasks [2]. This way, students further improve their learning as a consequence of their gameplay. The benefits of games, and in particular of their application in education, have attracted the attention of many stakeholders: from researchers, game developers and designers trying to create games that are effective tools for learning, to teachers, educators and institutions more increasingly willing to apply games as part of their teaching activities. These stakeholders are involved on different parts of the application of games for learning, and consequently face very different issues when carrying out these experiments or applications with games.

© Springer Nature Switzerland AG 2020
E. Popescu et al. (Eds.): SETE 2019, LNCS 11984, pp. 337–346, 2020.
https://doi.org/10.1007/978-3-030-38778-5_37

1.1   Issues for Researchers, Game Designers and Developers

On the one hand, researchers, game designers and developers are trying to promote the application of games in education by conducting experiments to establish their effectiveness and usefulness as a tool for teachers. For this and other purposes, experiments usually include the collection of interactions from students' gameplays. For instance, the authors of [3] provide a practical guide of the use of games in experiments, including the choice of game, event coding, data determination, participants and data collection. These experiments applying games have multiple benefits but also have high costs in terms of time and effort, both during preparation and their later execution. These issues need to be dealt with by whoever oversees the application: commonly game designers, game developers, or researchers. On research applications, these issues are dealt by researchers themselves who do not tend to involve teachers or educators in the process. This way, the researchers conducting these studies take an active role in the use of games, preventing teachers from dealing with these issues. While this simplifies teachers' tasks on these applications, it can also complicate their work in the common case when they are later going to apply the same games on their own.

These experiments generally include the collection of some in-game interaction data from players. The field of Learning Analytics (LA) [4], which has greatly increased since 2011 [5], covers the collection and analysis of data from learning activities to understand and improve learners' processes and contexts. Building up from LA and focusing on serious games, the field of Game Learning Analytics (GLA) extends this to the collection, analysis and display of information on the activities and progress of player-learners. The applications of GLA are wide and varied [6], including, among others, assessment and student profiling. These applications can be used to validate game design, or to gain insights that would otherwise be much harder to obtain [7].

1.2   Issues for Teachers and Institutions

On the other hand, teachers, educators and institutions need effective tools that simplify the application of games in their classrooms. In fact, teachers still find it difficult to integrate this learning approach into their regular practice [8], partly because real, long-term applications of games, necessary need to be managed by teachers on their own with only minimal external support. However, teachers or educators are generally not experts in dealing with software or hardware requirements. Therefore, simplifying teachers' tasks on these real-setting scenarios becomes a crucial step towards the advance of game-based learning.

Authors have identified this issue and try to propose actions to help teachers adopt games. For instance, the work of [9] presents a framework to model the process of teachers' adoption of games. According to this framework, teachers (1) become aware of the innovation to be introduced, (2) focus on adoption and seek more information, (3) engage in activities to measure pros/cons of the innovation and decide whether to include it or not, (4) introduce the innovation and finally, (5) obtain feedback to reinforce their choice. On this work, authors also pointed out several recommendations for teachers to adequately adopt games as part of their teaching practice, including the appropriation of the game by experiencing the activity before taking it to their students. They also found out that rejection of the activity was motivated by fears and issues such as a perceived lack of advantage compared to their previous teaching activity, misuse of the game, or fear of losing control of their students.

The focus of our work is on educational videogames or serious games in general. However, commercial videogames may also be used in education. The study of [10] presents the advantages and disadvantages of using commercial videogames in experiments. Among the advantages they point out, the following are especially significant: ecological validity, lack of implementation times and/or external influence on the implementation, and reproducibility; while disadvantages include that modifications in the games may be difficult or even impossible to conduct, the specificity of the hardware used, and the difficulty of finding a game that is a good fit for a given set of purposes and constraints.

On this paper we revise the considerations that need to be taken into account when (1) conducting experiments with games in real educational scenarios and (2) applying games as part of teaching. We provide guidelines for both researchers or game developers/designers and teachers for both scenarios. These guidelines are presented along with the tool Simva, which simplifies some of the most costly parts of experiments and game applications including questionnaires and data collection, storage, or participants' management. The rest of this paper is structured as follows: Sect. 2 describes considerations when conducting experiments, including the GDPR regulation and the use of informed consents. Section 3 describes considerations for teachers when applying games in their classes. Section 4 presents Simva and its features to simplify experiments for both previous scenarios. Finally, Sect. 5 presents the conclusions of our work.

2 Considerations When Conducting Experiments

Experiments to validate games or apply them in educational settings by external researchers or game developers/designers must deal with several issues at the different phases of the experiments. Even if teachers are present in those experiments, most of these issues will generally fall out of scope of the work of teachers, and should therefore be managed by the experimenters:

1. **Before the experiments**: privacy regulations need to be addressed carefully, including applicable data privacy regulations, such as the General Data Protection Regulation (GDPR) [11]. To ensure their adequate application, anonymization or pseudo-anonymization techniques will commonly need to be applied to the data collected. This requires an anonymization system to be clearly defined and established. Informed consent may also be required in specific contexts, and their characteristics will depend heavily on the type of participants (e.g. minors) and/or the nature of the data to be gathered.
2. **During the experiments**: collection and storage of the data of the experiments need to be dealt with. For this, a clearly established system needs to be defined, including hardware and software requirements. If different data sources are collected for the same user, a way to link all the information collected from the same user must be supplied. If a feedback system is included to display information on the progress

of participants while the activity is being carried out, this system should not hinder privacy.

3. **After the experiments**: once the experiments are completed, some offline aggregated information could provide information of interest for the game developers/designers or researchers. This feedback of the experiences could be provided via aggregated visualizations or with some more complex techniques such as data mining. This data analysis could also be simplified if the system that collects the data does so in a standard format and allows for a user-friendly export of the data. If data is going to be reused or maintained, it should also be defined (e.g. in the informed consent).

In the case of research applications, the previous steps should be guided by an experimental design which defines the purpose of the application and how all issues are going to be dealt with. This experimental design would be defined by researchers, which must also receive informed consent for data collection by the institution where the experiments are going to be conducted (e.g. school). The following subsections detail two of the major issues that need to be dealt with before the experiments, including the GDPR and the informed consents. To this end, Simva can also help to simplify many parts of the issues that arise. These features that Simva includes and can be helpful for researchers, game designers and developers when carrying out these type of experiments are detail in Sect. 4.

2.1 GDPR

Before conducting the experiments, several requirements have to consider including privacy, and legal regulations that may affect how data can and should be collected and stored. These regulations will typically differ depending on the type of users participating in the studies (e.g. minors, participants with intellectual disabilities) and the specific characteristics of the studies, including the type of data to be collected, the collection and storage system.

The new General Data Protection Regulation (GDPR) defines personal data as "any information that relates to an identified or identifiable living individual" [12]. This includes the scenarios where different pieces of information joint together can be related to an individual as well as cases of using pseudo-anonymization. If individuals can not be identified from some data, that data is no longer considered as personal data. It is important to notice that GDPR protects all personal data collected regardless of the system used to store the data (e.g. paper, computer) or to process it (manually or automatically).

2.2 Informed Consent

Informed consent is a procedure to inform and gain permission from participants in a study to collect some personal data prior to the collection [13]. Informed consents are commonly used on the medical domain, but are applied on a broader set of fields. They commonly present the purpose of the collection of the information, as well as its implications and consequences. Usually, informed consents are provided directly to the person data is going to be collected from. However, for specific participants, such as minors or people with certain disabilities, informed consents can be collected from their parents of legal guardians. Although some studies have debated whether children have the capacity to give consent by themselves, the most widely accepted and recommended option is that approval is given by some other responsible adult (e.g. parents or teachers) [14].

The use of informed consents has been required in recent research such as the latest projects of the European Commission. For FP7 projects (years 2007–2013), informed consents were required when participants were minors, patients, immigrants or incapacitated, or when the studies collected any personal data [15]. For the case of minors, those guidelines requested the informed consent of parents or legal representatives, but also the consent of children, with information sheets created according to the age of the participants. For the H2020 program (years 2014–2020), guidelines stated the information informed consents should include (aim of the research, methods, how data will be collected, protected and if it is later going to be reused or destroyed) [16]. For children or people unable to give consent (e.g. mental disabilities), consent is to be obtained from their legally authorized representative.

Figure 1 details some of the issues informed consents should include, as a guideline for researchers creating informed consents. Notice that this is not an exhaustive list, depending on the study, some of this points will not be required (e.g. there may be no benefits or risks) and others may be included. Their order is also optional.

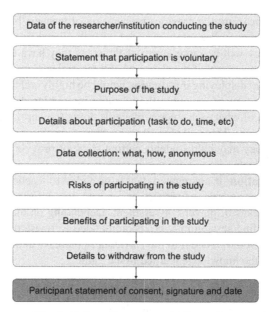

Fig. 1. Informed consent guideline points.

For children, it is recommended that the statement of consent is given by parents or legal representatives. However, as stated before, it could also be interesting to obtain some type of consent by the children themselves if possible, in some terms adapted to their age so they can understand at least the purpose of the study they are going to take part in.

3   Considerations for Teachers Applying Games

The application of games in real scenarios by teachers or educators also includes dealing with several issues at the different stages of the application. Among the steps that teachers need to take into account, we include:

1. **Before the application**: first of all, teachers will have to choose an adequate game that fits the curricula or provides a useful experience for their students. Before taking the chosen game to students, it is recommended that teachers play the game so they have the complete experience and fully understand the tasks that their students are going to be asked to do. If there is any complementary material available (e.g. users' guide), it is also highly recommended that teachers fully read and understand it as it may provide additional context and information about the game and its goals and design. Additionally, teachers may want to assess their students using some external questionnaires. For these cases, the questionnaires should be defined and prepared before the game is played and handed to students at the appropriate times (before and/or after the application). The questionnaires may be handled on paper; on Sect. 4, we present a simpler way to deal with questionnaires using Simva.
2. **During the application**: the previous preparation of teachers by playing the game and/or reading any complementary material will simplify their tasks while students are playing as they will be more aware of the steps they have to do. Additionally, for teachers to keep control of the class and of their students' progress, some way of feedback or system displaying information would be highly welcomed. For instance, if an Analytics System is receiving the in-game interaction data, teachers will be able to keep track of what each student/player is doing (e.g. progress, actions, paths, performance metrics). This will also allow teachers to perform interventions during the gameplays: they may help students getting stuck or provide additional material for advanced students.
3. **After the application**: if aggregated data is provided to teachers (either as global visualizations or as aggregated metrics or reports), this information could be used by teachers as means of players' assessment. Depending on the game content and purpose, a debriefing session may be recommended to revise the content included in the game and even to relate it to the curricula to increase understanding and help students transfer the knowledge learned in the game.

For both previously-described scenarios (carrying out experiments to validate games and effectively applying games in education), the stakeholders involved can benefit of the use of Simva, a tool to simplify scientific validation of games and in general experiments using games. The next section details the features that Simva provides.

4 Simva

Simva is a tool designed to simplify the scientific validation of serious games [17], as well as the assessment of students playing them, both tasks commonly measured via comparison of pre-tests with post-tests. Simva has been already tested on different scenarios to validate games, compare different game versions or carry out recall experiments [18].

Simva includes many features that can help to simplify both researchers, game designers or game developers' tasks when conducting experiments with games on educational settings; and teachers' tasks when applying games in their classes. As part of these applications, Simva can help the different stakeholders to deal with issues including: students' management, students' anonymization, control of access, level of completion, and data storage and management. Details of how Simva helps to deal with those issues are provided below.

Student Management. Simva works with classes of students, to which then provides anonymization features and simplifies assigning questionnaires. Classes of students can be created in Simva providing the number of students per class. The created classes are then kept in Simva where questionnaires can be linked to classes.

Student Anonymization. With class creation, Simva provides the pseudo-anonymous 4-letter random tokens, one per student. These tokens are provided as doc and pdf files to be printed before used. On these files, each token can be cut off to be handled to students before the experiments. For each students, the token is repeated four times, so they can be re-used in several experiments. Additionally, next to each different token, a blank space is available so teachers can write down on their printed papers the name of the student using each token. This way, teachers can relate the information of each token to the student it belongs to, while ensuring privacy as no personal data is input into the system. The bottom-part of Fig. 2 displays an example class list with the anonymous tokens provided for students.

Access Control. Games can be configured to require the anonymous token for players to access the game. If so, the game then checks that there is a class created in Simva where the introduced token is included. When games are configured to include questionnaires in Simva, students will not be allowed to start a questionnaire unless their access token is configured for that questionnaire. Additionally, players will not be able to access the game until the questionnaire prior to the gameplay is completed. This check is also done via Simva.

Level of Completion. While experiments are in play, the class view in Simva provides additional information for stakeholders to keep track of players' progress. On this class view, Simva displays the questionnaires status for each player: started, finished or not configured. This status is displayed for all questionnaires configured (currently a maximum of three questionnaires are available: a pre-test, a post-test and an additional questionnaire). Simva also displays whether interaction data (traces) has been collected. The top part of Fig. 2 displays an examples class in Simva where the three questionnaires are configured for the class. For each student (column "Code" on the left-part),

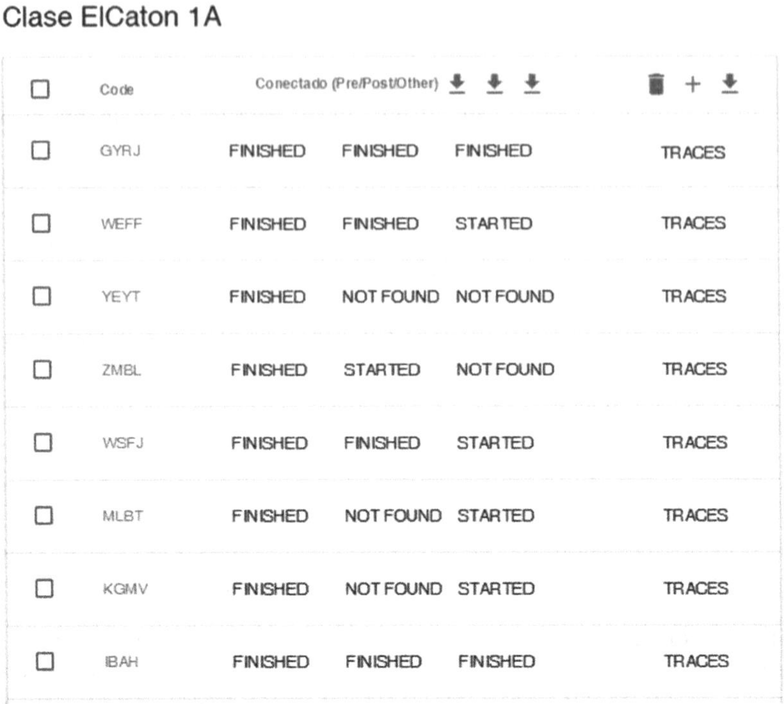

Clase ElCaton 1A

	Code	Conectado (Pre/Post/Other) ⬇ ⬇ ⬇			🗑 + ⬇
☐	GYRJ	FINISHED	FINISHED	FINISHED	TRACES
☐	WEFF	FINISHED	FINISHED	STARTED	TRACES
☐	YEYT	FINISHED	NOT FOUND	NOT FOUND	TRACES
☐	ZMBL	FINISHED	STARTED	NOT FOUND	TRACES
☐	WSFJ	FINISHED	FINISHED	STARTED	TRACES
☐	MLBT	FINISHED	NOT FOUND	STARTED	TRACES
☐	KGMV	FINISHED	NOT FOUND	STARTED	TRACES
☐	IBAH	FINISHED	FINISHED	FINISHED	TRACES

Clase ElCaton 1A:					
No.	Nombre	Código			
1		GYRJ	GYRJ	GYRJ	GYRJ
2		WEFF	WEFF	WEFF	WEFF
3		YEYT	YEYT	YEYT	YEYT
4		ZMBL	ZMBL	ZMBL	ZMBL
5		WSFJ	WSFJ	WSFJ	WSFJ
6		MLBT	MLBT	MLBT	MLBT
7		KGMV	KGMV	KGMV	KGMV
8		IBAH	IBAH	IBAH	IBAH

Fig. 2. Simva screenshots: top part, class view depicting students' anonymous tokens, questionnaires status and traces collected; bottom part, list of students with tokens to be cut and handed to students.

we can see the status of all three questionnaires ("finished", "started" or "not found"). The right-most column provides the traces collected.

Data Storage and Management. Both responses to all configured questionnaires as well as game learning analytics interaction data are sent by the game to and collected in Simva. All this information is identified by the anonymous token introduced by users when accessing the game, so the data is stored in Simva linked to the user token it corresponds to. After the experiments have been completed, stakeholders can download all collected data from Simva, automatically linked from each student together.

5 Conclusions

To promote the application of games in education, both of the major stages must be simplified: first, the experiments carried out to validate and prove the efficacy of these games as learning tools; and then, the teacher's tasks when applying games on their own. For the first stage, researchers or game designers and developers can benefit from automated support that simplifies compliance with data privacy regulations such as the GDPR, and the gathering of informed consent in experiments. In this paper we have provided guidelines for both, and described the use of a tool to greatly simplify the adoption of these guidelines through partial automation: Simva.

Once games are validated as effective, we enter a second stage, where teachers and educators apply them effectively in their classrooms. This, again, requires tools and preparation to manage the game application on their own. For this purpose, we have provided guidelines on the steps that teachers should take before, during and after the application of games. In our experience, these guidelines make teachers more comfortable with the application of games, making them aware of their students' actions and progress while they are playing, and providing them tools to conduct activities after the game that can help students relate the content with the curricula.

Both stages can benefit from the use of Simva. Although the main goal of the tool is to simplify the scientific validation of games, it can also help in everyday classroom uses of serious games by teachers. Simva helps in the questionnaires' management, data collection, users' management and privacy issues.

Future lines of work include testing Simva in more experiments, determining the relative effectiveness of the tool for different stakeholders in each of their tasks, and identifying areas of improvement to further simplify the application of games in educational scenarios.

References

1. Hainey, T., Connolly, T.M., Boyle, E.A., Wilson, A., Razak, A.: A systematic literature review of games-based learning empirical evidence in primary education. Comput. Educ. **102**, 202–223 (2016)
2. Boeker, M., Andel, P., Vach, W., Frankenschmidt, A.: Game-based E-learning is more effective than a conventional instructional method: a randomized controlled trial with third-year medical students. PLoS ONE **8**, e82328 (2013)
3. Järvelä, S., Ekman, I., Kivikangas, J.M., Ravaja, N.: A practical guide to using digital games as an experiment stimulus. Trans. Digit. Games Res. Assoc. **1**, 85–115 (2014)
4. Long, P., Siemens, G.: Penetrating the fog: analytics in learning and education. Educ. Rev. **46**, 31–40 (2011)
5. Long, P., Siemens, G., Gráinne, C., Gašević, D.: Proceedings of the 1st International Conference on Learning Analytics and Knowledge, LAK 2011, 27 February – 1 March 2011, Banff, Alberta, Canada, p. 195 (2011)

6. Alonso-Fernández, C., Calvo-Morata, A., Freire, M., Martinez-Ortiz, I., Fernández-Manjón, B.: Applications of data science to game learning analytics data: a systematic literature review. Comput. Educ. **141**, 103612 (2019)
7. Alonso-Fernández, C., Cano, A.R., Calvo-Morata, A., Freire, M., Martínez-Ortiz, I., Fernández-Manjón, B.: Lessons learned applying learning analytics to assess serious games. Comput. Human Behav. **99**, 301–309 (2019)
8. ProActive: Production of Creative Game-Based Learning Scenarios: A Handbook for Teachers. (2011)
9. Emin-Martinez, V., Ney, M.: Supporting teachers in the process of adoption of game-based learning pedagogy. In: ECGBL 2013-European Conference on Game Based Learning, pp. 156–162 (2013)
10. McMahan, R.P., Ragan, E.D., Leal, A., Beaton, R.J., Bowman, D.A.: Considerations for the use of commercial video games in controlled experiments. Entertain. Comput. **2**, 3–9 (2011)
11. European Commission: 2018 reform of EU data protection rules. https://ec.europa.eu/commission/priorities/justice-and-fundamental-rights/data-protection/2018-reform-eu-data-protection-rules_en
12. European Commission: What is personal data. https://ec.europa.eu/info/law/law-topic/data-protection/reform/what-personal-data_en
13. Musmade, P., et al.: Informed consent: Issues and challenges. J. Adv. Pharm. Technol. Res. **4**, 134 (2013)
14. Gallagher, M., Haywood, S.L., Jones, M.W., Milne, S.: Negotiating informed consent with children in school-based research: a critical review. Child. Soc. **24**, 471–482 (2010)
15. Review, E., Consent, I., Informed, T.: European Commission Ethical Review in FP7. Guidance for Applicants: Informed Consent, pp. 1–7 (2013)
16. ECDGRI: Horizon 2020 programme - guidance how to complete your ethics self-assessment. European Commission of Directorate-General for Research and Innovation (2018)
17. Perez-Colado, I.J., Alonso-Fernández, C., Calvo-Morata, A., Freire, M., Martínez-Ortiz, I., Fernández-Manjón, B.: Simva: simplifying the scientific validation of serious games. In: 9th IEEE International Conference on Advanced Learning Technologies (ICALT) (2019)
18. Alonso-Fernández, C., Perez-Colado, I.J., Calvo-Morata, A., Freire, M., Martinez-Ortiz, I., Fernandez-Manjon, B.: Using Simva to evaluate serious games and collect learning analytics data. In: LASI-SPAIN (2019)

The Robot in the Classroom: A Review of a Robot Role

Violeta Rosanda[1] and Andreja Istenic Starcic[1,2,3](✉)

[1] Faculty of Education, University of Primorska, Koper, Slovenia
violeta.rosanda@gmail.com, andreja.starcic@gmail.com
[2] Faculty of Civil and Geodetic Engineering, University of Ljubljana, Ljubljana, Slovenia
[3] Institute of Education and Psychology, Kazan Federal University, Kazan, Russia

Abstract. The 20th-century was the age of computers and information communication technology; at the beginning of the 21st-century researchers are exploring the use of robots in the classroom. Our review investigates the implementation of copresent social robots with teaching purposes in a classroom setting in areas other than the teaching of subjects that are closely related to the field of Robotics. We are interested in anthropomorphic robots, with an active role in the classroom and capable of human-like activity. With a search of the WOS database and a subsequent manual search in 19 journals we identified 24 relevant articles which have been included in the analysis. Studies mostly include small number of participating learners. In all studies special conditions are established for the robot intervention in a classroom. Most often robots appear in roles as teacher, teacher assistant and Care-Receiving Robot. Robots interventions were conducted by NAO, Saya, RoboThespian, Bioloid, BAXTER, Darwin, NIMA-Robocop, Robosapien, TIRO. Social robots diverge from the computer-mediated communication technologies, as they are not mediating interaction but are partner in interaction. ITSs and ILEs assist teachers in teaching, while the teacher and a robot have a shared presence in the classroom. The copresent social robots perform a social role by interacting with students. Robotic activities are aimed at delivering learning materials and not primarily for individualised teaching, which encompasses the delivery of feedback and the tailoring learning activities for individual learner's needs.

Keywords: Education · Copresent robot · Social robot · Humanoid robot · Android robot · Educational technology · Artificial intelligence · Teacher

1 Introduction

Intelligent tutoring systems (ITSs) and intelligent learning environments (ILEs) support teaching and benefit learning outcomes [1]. By delivering instruction, ITSs and ILEs support learning in diverse social modes for individual or group activities. ITSs and ILEs supported individualised teaching are not limited to an individual student; it is also conducted in small groups, large groups or peer learning. ITSs provide an individualised learning experience in four main ways: monitor appropriateness of student's input in learning process, deliver appropriate complexity of task for students, provide effective

© Springer Nature Switzerland AG 2020
E. Popescu et al. (Eds.): SETE 2019, LNCS 11984, pp. 347–357, 2020.
https://doi.org/10.1007/978-3-030-38778-5_38

feedback based on the pedagogy model, apply interface/s for communication about the domain or the learning contents [2].

This review study of robots in the classroom is focused on copresent robots as physically embodied and physically present in the user's space [3] and social robots as »an autonomous, physically embodied robot that interacts and communicates with humans by following social behaviours and rules attached to its role« [4 p. 628].

Social robots combine artificial intelligence and autonomous behaviours [5]. Social robots diverge from the computer-mediated communication technologies as they are not medium through which humans interact, but a medium with which humans interact [6]. ITSs and ILEs assist teachers in teaching. While the robots' behaviour and their communication are connected with the social role that has been assigned to them [4]. They are hence capable of the appropriate verbal and non-verbal communication. Social robots »can provide supportive behaviour, feedback and recommendations, as well as attention acquisition to assist users in several applications« [7 p. 9].

"Social robots are being designed to deal with human care, health, domestic tasks, entertainment and various other forms of immaterial and material tasks which aim to renew human capacities" [8 p. 12], to take care of children, the elderly, the disabled and the ill [8 p. 14]. They enter the reproduction sphere [8 p. 14]. Social robots are being introduced as aides to the elderly [8–11], as durative assistants [10], in the field of childcare [8, 11], at home [8, 12], in work environments and public spaces [12].

In the health care sphere [11–13] they are used for patients with dementia [11, 13], patients with cognitive/motor disorders [11] and "in critical areas in medical care to automate supervision, coaching, motivation, and companionship aspects of interactions with vulnerable individuals" [11]. In the therapeutic domain [10, 12] they help with autism [10, 11, 13, 14], they are used "as therapeutic tools for children, the elderly, stroke patients, and other special-needs populations requiring personalised care" [15]. Short-term public interaction robots are used as visitors guides and as tour guides in museums [10]. Social robots of the like of robot toys and robot pet companions have the mission of engaging and entertaining the user [10].

Social robots are also used in education; most visibly for vocabulary learning [16] and language learning [16, 17]. As they are capable of communicating and interacting with students [5] and more specifically they are capable of delivering "a learning experience through social interaction with learners" [18], they tend to be applied, tested and studied in a variety of educational areas and purposes.

The introduction of social robots in different areas brings to the foreground the study of human-robot communication [6, 19]. Researchers use them as test subjects, or more precisely as research tools to »examine, validate and refine theories of social and biological development, psychology, neurobiology, emotional and non-verbal communication, and social interaction« [10 p. 20]. Robots could also serve as a tool for understanding humans for example in language processing [17].

At the beginning of the 21st-century researchers are exploring the use of robots in classrooms [14]. It is, more precisely a study of the technical capabilities of the robots with teaching purposes and the Human-Robot Interaction (HRI) rather than research into the pedagogical aspects of the interactions [20, 21].

From the reviews analysed it is clear that the majority of the performed studies focuses on the utilisation of robots in the teaching of foreign languages [14, 17], robotics [14, 22] physics, mathematics [22], language, science and technology [17].

By analysing learning outcomes we see that they are predominantly cognitive [17]: the understanding of concepts in the STEM fields, the development of reasoning, problem-solving, social interaction and teamwork [22]. Studies in high education areas explored the effects of robots on learning outcomes. Said studies focus more on affective outcomes than on cognitive development [18]. However ultimately the effects of robot interventions on learning outcomes are not sufficiently explored [19].

Some studies explore the underpinning learning theory behind robot interventions. In these cases, constructivism is identified as predominant; they, however, lack evidence of its integration in the pedagogical practice [19]. It has been found that, as the learning design is not explored sufficiently, there is a lack of well-defined curriculum and learning material for teachers [17]. The robot activities in the classrooms are also dependent on the level of autonomy achieved by the robot [23] and on the role that has been assigned to the robot. The review of the role of the social robot in the educational sphere highlighted a variety of roles assigned. Among them are: the role of companion, collaborator [10], peer [10, 17, 18], tutor [17, 18], tool [17], presenter, teaching assistant, teacher, novice [18], Care-eliciting Companion [21]; the latter is classified by researchers in our papers as Care-Receiving Robot (CRR).

Our review investigates the implementation of copresent social robots with teaching purposes in a classroom setting in areas other than the teaching of subjects that are closely related to the field of Robotics. We are interested in anthropomorphic robots, with an active role in the classroom and capable of human-like activity. We examine the utilisation of the chosen robot technology evident in the researched studies.

Copresent robots are physically embodied and physically present in the user's space [3]. The physical appearance of a robot is an important factor of HRI [10, 21, 24]. Robots which have their own independent body tend to attract the users' attention [25, 26]. It is hence important that the robot's morphology matches "its intended function" [10 p. 9]. Li (2015) highlights not only the robot's physical embodiment but also the importance of its physical presence in the physical space of the user. Copresent robots combine these two factors. They are persuasive, receive attention and are perceived positively [3].

Social interactions are important in the learning process and cognitive development, this is true also when the robot is present in the learning activity [17, 18]. Elements of human social psychology regulate not only the social interactions between people but also the social interactions between humans and robots [10, 24, 27]. The robot's learning activities can lead to positive educational outcomes only if the students maintain a relationship with the robot [28]. This is in the longer term, a difficult task. It is therefore important that the robot is capable of communicating with the human in a manner appropriate to its role. The presence of the robot in the classroom tends initially, defined as the first two weeks, to cause excitement. The excitement, transforms, in the third and consequent weeks, into a stable interaction and satiation [29].

Long-term interaction capabilities are therefore very important when it comes to the robots used in the classrooms; particularly if the robot is capable of speaking [29]. Considered the time component in the reviewed studies, we believe that it provides the first indicative information about the robotic capability of maintaining the attention of the students and its ability to perform learning activities [20]. The research question of our review study discussed in this paper is: How is robot role and robot type applied in the reviewed studies?

2 Methods

The systematic literature review was conducted from November 2018 to January 2019. Three stages were applied: (a) planning, (b) performing a search in the database and the selection of relevant articles, (c) wrap up with reporting.

In the planning stage, the inclusion and exclusion criteria were defined for the review study. In the planning phase, we decided to start the search in the WOS database and afterwards, we identified the journals which were relevant for a further manual search. The journals were selected based on: references in selected articles and weather the included articles have been indexed in other databases.

The search stage started in November 2018 with the Web of Science (WOS) database. The search terms applied were »robot*« AND »education« OR *learn*« OR »teach* «. The journals with most articles in the WOS were selected.

Based on the results of the automatic search in the WOS database, the relevant journals were selected for further manual. The title and the abstract of the papers identified in the automatic search were then read. The papers were then selected if the inclusion criteria were met. Based on the study of references in the articles, the search also included journals indexed in SCOPUS and IEEE databases. In November and December 2018 we continued with a manual selection within the 19 selected journals.

On the final stage of the search, the selected papers were analysed by reading the whole article. At this stage, we included the papers that matched the following inclusion criteria: the study about copresent social robots with teaching purposes in classroom settings for other curriculum subjects than mechatronics and robotics. We excluded literature matching any of the following exclusion criteria: duplicated publications; only one is kept [30]; studies that deal with the area of mechatronics, robotics learning activities, robot building, robot programming [22]; studies that deal with machine learning (not related to human learning) [19]; the robot is used for healthcare training activities; the robot is used for special education; the robot is used for therapeutic purpose, sickness; researchers made use of zoomorphic robots; researchers made use of telepresence robots, virtual robots or on-screen avatar; material other than scientific articles and articles which do not report on the intervention study. The inclusion criteria were meet by 24 studies, listed in references [11, 25, 26] and references from [31–49]. Papers marked with an * contain two studies each.

The analysis stage took place from January to June 2019. Two papers are reporting the findings. One paper focuses on the research outcomes, the research design, the analysis of journals, educational levels and curriculum areas, participants structure and learner-robot interaction (LRI) time [20]. This paper focuses on the robot role and robot type.

3 Results

The analysis shows a clear increase in the number of research studies of the selected robots being utilised in classrooms during the period 2013–2018 when compared to the 2006–2012 period [20]. The researchers have been addressing 6–12 years old age group most often. This was followed by the 3–5 years old age group. They often designed and performed the research with more than one educational level. None of the reviewed studies dealt with the application of the chosen robot technology in the context of life-long learning [20].

The focus of this analysis was *the robot role*. We analysed the roles that have been assigned to the robot. As the role of the robot was not explicit in all of the analysed studies, we categorised the role of the robot based on the context. In the categorization we used the following roles: teacher [50], teaching assistant [51], tutor [52], CRR [36], peer [53]. In papers that were part of our review study, the robot was used as a teacher (29%), teacher assistant (29%), CRR (17%), tutor (8%), peer (8%), classroom management tool (4%) and tutor/CRR (4%) (Fig. 1).

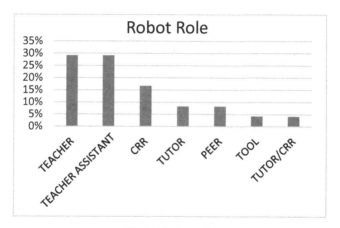

Fig. 1. Robot role

In the reviewed studies, the robot-assisted teaching has been conducted on the delivery of a lesson. Lessons were mainly focused on the teaching of new content (17). Only from five of these cases it is clear that the robot activities were conducted in the context of the learning curricula, in two of them in kindergarten [11]. Only in one of all analysed studies, the pedagogy is in the first plan: "teachers aligned robots with the curriculum-based learning activity rather than the activity with the robot" [35]. Lesson delivery was aimed at classrooms or groups of students. Regarding individualised teaching, in a small number of studies the robot adapted further teaching materials for individual student's needs (6), more often (9) the robot purely provided feedback to students. We can conclude that robot's performance in terms of individualisation identified as the personalisation of lesson progress is rather underestimated. The adaptation of the difficulty level or the content to the student's performance was identified only in 6 studies.

Feedback is instead merely the adaptation of the robot's behaviour based on the answers given by the students.

Analysing *the robot type*, most of the studies (11) in this review worked with the robot NAO, followed by the android Saya (4), RoboThespian (2) and Bioloid (2). All the other robot types and more precisely BAXTER, DARwIn-OP (Darwin), NIMA-Robocop H21 version of NAO, Robosapien, TIRO, have been used only in one research (Fig. 2).

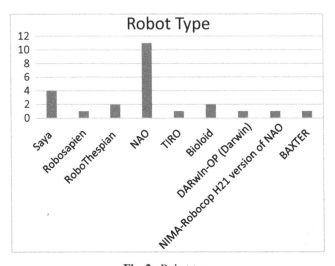

Fig. 2. Robot type

4   Discussion

The robotic teaching activities analysed included a small number of groups in individual research, often specially designed for the experiment and with a small number of students, most often between the ages of 3 and 12 [20]. These activities are, as also indicated by other studies, very rarely a part of the school curriculum [17]. In this context, the robot-learner interaction often takes the form of one-on-one interaction. Therefore, relatively little is known about the learning activities of the selected robotic technology in a realistic context, as a group activity with multiple learners, or with group learning dynamics approaching learning dynamics in a real classroom environment. Ultimately relatively little is known about the learning activities of the selected robotic technology in a real classroom environment [44]. As explained by Verner et al. (2016) "Pedagogical literature provides recommendations for effective instruction, but their application to robot-assisted learning has not yet been developed" [48]. Also, the timing and scale of the robotic activities do not reflect the school's learning realities. The studied robotic activities took the form of a unique session or of a short-lived, fragmented interaction, with students. This does not reflect school realities. The same reasoning and limitations apply to the tasks performed by the robots. The classroom activities performed with the help of robotic technologies were: short, well-defined and well-prepared. Once the activities were implemented in the classrooms human assistance of varied intensity and often diverse in its scope was also required. The scope of an intervention depended on the robot autonomy level. Intense human involvement was required when the robot was operating in a teleoperated or remotely controlled mode, and only minimal intervention was required when it was performing in an autonomous mode [23].

In our review, teleoperated or remotely controlled robots were used in the longest unique interaction sessions (30–60 min) [20]. The length and the continuity of the interaction sessions are ultimately determined by technical limitations [46], the problem of maintaining long-term LRI [29], and the demanding lengthy preliminary preparation. We believe that for all of these reasons, researchers are increasingly aiming to study the dynamics of introducing robots in classrooms rather than focusing their research on examining the effectiveness of robotic activities.

The robot teaching activities were focused on the following domains: science, technology and mathematics, English, geometry, computer science, sign language, subjects of preschool age, stone-age items, mathematics tables, weekly spelling tests, geography and sustainable development [20].

The most commonly used robot types were: NAO, Saya, RoboThespian and Bioloid. The robots predominantly assumed the following roles when performing teaching activities: teacher, teacher assistant and CRR.

During the teaching process, the robot teacher mostly performed only one of the many tasks usually assigned to the human teacher. It was most commonly involved in the teaching of new material (17 studies). The findings indicate that the teaching content was largely out of alignment with respect to the regular curriculum. Only in one survey "teachers aligned the robot with activity rather than the activity with the robot" [35]. The vast majority of the covered studies performed teaching activities outside the scope of the regular curriculum.

While the advantage of using Intelligent tutoring systems is to individualise and tailor the feedback to an individual learner, robotic activities are aimed at delivering learning materials to either a group or an individual. Of the 24 studies, only 6 studies focused on the individualisation in terms of adapting the content for further learning activities (6), while a few (9) purely provided feedback to students.

We believe that defining the robots as performing the teacher role raises, given at the current stage of development of robotic technology, expectations that robots cannot yet meet. Among the open-ended questions, that need to be addressed, before the utilisation of the chosen robot technology in everyday teaching practices, we list not only didactical issues but also LRI [18, 46] and the educational component.

4.1 Conclusions

Social robots diverge from the computer-mediated communication technologies, as they are not mediating interaction but are partner in interaction. ITSs and ILEs assist teacher in teaching, while the teacher and a robot have a shared presence in the classroom. The copresent social robot performs a social role by interacting with students.

Findings of our review study indicate that the research focuses mostly on studying the human-robot interaction [20] in classroom practices. The research targets primarily objectives aimed at advancing robotic technology [21], and it does not necessarily focus on pedagogical outcomes. Robotic activities are aimed at delivering learning materials and not primarily for individualised teaching, which encompasses the delivery of feedback and the tailoring learning activities for individual learner's needs. We conclude that the chosen robot technology has not yet achieved a sufficient technical-developmental phase, to allow for the focus of the research to shift to the educational-pedagogical aspects of the introduction of the robot in the classrooms. The results of the review that we have performed confirm findings of previous studies »the breakthrough of robots in everyday teaching practice is not yet visible« [54 p. 293]. The development of educational robotic technologies is an interdisciplinary practice that urgently needs the input of learning and educational theories. Exploring human learning for the advancement of artificial intelligence and learning analytics will in turn effect in transformation of human learning process [55].

Acknowledgments. The work of Andreja Istenič Starčič was financially supported by Slovenian Research Agency (P2-0210). This research has been conducted for *"The 1st Workshop on Artificial Intelligence in Education - Teacher's Role for Student-centered Teaching - AIE-TRST 2019"* organized by Andreja Istenic Starcic, Manolis Mavrikis, Maria Cutumisu, Cristina Alonso Fernández.

References

1. Ainsworth, S., Grimshaw, S.: Evaluating the REDEEM authoring tool: can teachers create effective learning environments? Int. J. Artif. Intell. Educ. **14**(3) (2004). https://content.iospress.com/articles/international-journal-of-artificial-intelligence-in-education/jai14-3-4-03
2. Du Boulay, B.: Artificial intelligence as an effective classroom assistant. IEEE Intell. Syst. **31**(6), 76–81 (2016). https://cutit.org/yN2nP
3. Li, J.: The benefit of being physically present: a survey of experimental works comparing copresent robots, telepresent robots and virtual agents. Int. J. Hum.-Comput. Stud. **77**, 23–37 (2015). https://cutit.org/QwFV8
4. Edwards, A., Edwards, C., Spence, P.R., Harris, C., Gambino, A.: Robots in the classroom: differences in students' perceptions of credibility and learning between "teacher as robot" and "robot as teacher". Comput. Hum. Behav. **65**, 627–634 (2016). https://cutt.ly/JwdmtVu
5. Jung, S.E., Won, E.: Systematic review of research trends in robotics education for young children. Sustainability **10**(4), 905, 1–24 (2018). https://doi.org/10.3390/su10040905
6. Zhao, S.: Humanoid social robots as a medium of communication. New Media Soc. **8**, 401–419 (2006). https://doi.org/10.1.177/1461444806061951
7. Tsiakas, K., Kyrarini, M., Karkaletsis, V., Makedon, F., Korn, O.: A taxonomy in robot-assisted training: current trends, needs and challenges. Technologies **6**(119), 1–19 (2018). https://doi.org/10.3390/technologies6040119
8. Taipale, S., de Luca, F., Sarrica, M., Fortunati, L.: Robot shift from industrial production to social reproduction. In: Vincent, J., Taipale, S., Sapio, B., Lugano, G., Fortunati, L. (eds.) Social Robots from a Human Perspective. Springer, Cham (2015). https://doi.org/10.1007/978-3-319-15672-9_2. https://cutit.org/8Ziik
9. de Graaf, M.M.A., Allouch, S.B., Klamer, T.: Sharing a life with Harvey: exploring the acceptance of and relationship-building with a social robot. Comput. Hum. Behav. **43**, 1–14 (2015). https://cutit.org/rWPPg

10. Fong, T., Nourbakhsh, I., Dautenhahn, K.: Survey of Socially Interactive Robots. The Robotics Institute Carnegie Mellon University, pp. 1–56 (2002). https://bitlylink.com/cmb3r

11. Fridin, M.: Storytelling by a kindergarten social assistive robot: a tool for constructive learning in preschool education. Comput. Educ. **70**, 53–64 (2014). https://doi.org/10.1016/j.compedu.2013.07.043

12. Ahmad, M.I., Mubin, O., Orlando, J.: A systematic: review of adaptivity in human-robot interaction. Multimodal Technol. Interaction, **3**(14) (2017). https://doi.org/10.3390/mti1030014

13. Kidd, C.D., Breazeal, C.: Effect of a robot on user perceptions. In: IEEE/RSJ International Conference on Intelligent Robots and Systems (IROS) (2004). https://cutt.ly/XwdU0Ew

14. Cheng, Y.W., Sun, P.C., Chen, N.S.: The essential applications of educational robot: requirement analysis from the perspectives of experts, researchers and instructors. Comput. Educ. **126**, 399–416 (2018). https://doi.org/10.1016/j.compedu.2018.07.020

15. Peca, A., Simut, R., Pintea, S., Costescu, C., Vanderborght, B.: How do typically developing children and children with autism perceive different social robots? Comput. Hum. Behav. **41**, 268–277 (2014). https://cutit.org/qrNMO

16. Shiomi, M., Kanda, T., Howley, I., Hayashi, K., Hagita, N.: Can a social robot stimulate science curiosity in classrooms? Int. J. Soc. Robot. **7**, 641–652 (2015). https://doi.org/10.1007/s12369-015-0303-1

17. Mubin, O., Stevens, C.J., Shahid, S., Mahmud, A.A., Dong, J.J.: A review of the applicability of robots in education. Technol. Educ. Learn. **1**, 1–7 (2013). https://doi.org/10.2316/Journal.209.2013.1.209-0015

18. Belpaeme, T., Kennedy, J., Ramachandran, A., Scassellati, B., Tanaka, F.: Social robots for education: a review. Sci. Robot. **3**(21), 1–9 (2018). https://doi.org/10.1126/scirobotics.aat5954

19. Hong, N.W.W., Chew, E., Meng, J.W.S.: The review of educational robotics research and the need for real-world interaction analysis. In: 2016 14th International Conference on Control, Automation, Robotics and Vision (ICARCV), pp. 1–6 (2016). https://doi.org/10.1109/icarcv.2016.7838707

20. Rosanda, V., Istenič Starčič, A.: A review of social robots in classrooms: emerging educational technology and teacher education. Educ. Self Dev. **14**(3), 1–20 (2019). https://doi.org/10.26907/esd14.3.08

21. Sharkey, A.J.C.: Should we welcome robot teachers? Ethics Inf. Technol. **18**, 283–297 (2016). https://doi.org/10.1007/s10676-016-9387-z

22. Benitti, F.B.V.: Exploring the educational potential of robotics in schools: a systematic review. Comput. Educ. **58**, 978–988 (2012). https://doi.org/10.1016/j.compedu.2011.10.006

23. Beer, J.M., Fisk, A.D., Rogers, W.A.: Toward a framework for levels of robot autonomy in human-robot interaction. J. Hum.-Robot Interact. **3**(2), 74–99 (2014). https://doi.org/10.5898/jhri.3.2.beer

24. Phillips, E., Ullman, D., de Graaf, M.M.A, Malle, B.F.: What does a robot look like?: a multi-site examination of user expectations about robot appearance. In: Proceedings of the Human Factors and Ergonomics Society Annual Meeting, vol. 61, pp. 1215–1219. SAGE Publications, Thousand Oaks (2017). https://cutt.ly/1wdmjOs

25. Chin, K.Y., Wu, C.H., Hong, Z.W.: A humanoid robot as a teaching assistant for primary education. In: IEEE Conferences, 2011 Fifth International Conference on Genetic and Evolutionary Computing, pp. 21–24 (2011). https://cutt.ly/CwdmjVn

26. Chin, K.Y., Hong, Z.W., Chen, Y.L.: Impact of using an educational robot-based learning system on students' motivation in elementary education. IEEE Trans. Learn. Technol. **7**(4), 333–345 (2014). https://cutt.ly/mwdmkjq

27. Mathur, M.B., Reichling, D.B.: Navigating a social world with robot partners: a quantitative cartography of the Uncanny Valley. Cognition **146**, 22–32 (2016). https://cutt.ly/hwdmk2b

28. Kanda, T., Hirano, T., Eaton, D.: Interactive robots as social partners and peer tutors for children: a field trial. Hum.-Comput. Interact. **19**, 61–84 (2004). https://cutt.ly/HwdmlGF

29. Kanda, T., Sato, R., Saiwaki, N., Ishiguro, H.: A two-month field trial in an elementary school for long-term human-robot interaction. IEEE Trans. Rob. **23**(5), 962–971 (2007). https://doi.org/10.1109/TRO.2007.904904

30. Spolaôr, N., Benitti, F.B.V.: Robotics applications grounded in learning theories on tertiary education: a systematic review. Comput. Educ. **112**, 97–107 (2017). https://doi.org/10.1016/j.compedu.2017.05.001

31. Akalin, N., Uluer, P., Kose, H.: iSpy-uSign humanoid assisted interactive sign language tutoring games. In: 2013 IEEE RO-MAN: The 22nd IEEE International Symposium on Robot and Human Interactive Communication, pp. 290–291 (2013). https://cutt.ly/Ewdmhc3

32. Alemi, M., Meghdari, A.: The effect of employing humanoid robots for teaching english on students' anxiety and attitude. In: 2014 IEEE, Proceeding of the 2nd RSI/ISM International Conference on Robotics and Mechatronics, pp. 754–759 (2014). https://cutt.ly/fwdmgJa

33. Baxter, P., Ashurst, E., Read, R., Kennedy, J., Belpaeme, T.: Robot education peers in a situated primary school study: personalisation promotes child learning. PLOS ONE **12**(5), 1–23 (2017). https://cutt.ly/YwdmgE9

34. Brown, L.N., Howard, A.M.: The positive effects of verbal encouragement in mathematics education using a social robot. In: 4th IEEE Integrated STEM Education Conference (2014). https://cutt.ly/Jwdmglu

35. Crompton, H., Gregory, K., Burke, D.: Humanoid robots supporting children's learning in an early childhood setting. Br. J. Educ. Technol. **49**(5), 911–927 (2018). https://doi.org/10.1111/bjet.12654

36. Ghosh, M., Tanaka, F.: The impact of different competence levels of care-receiving robot on children. In: 2011 IEEE/RSJ International Conference on Intelligent Robots and Systems, pp. 2409–2415 (2011). https://cutt.ly/SwdmfVm

37. Han, J., Kim, D.: r-Learning services for elementary school students with a teaching assistant robot. In: 2009 4th ACM/IEEE International Conference on Human-Robot Interaction (HRI), pp. 255–256 (2009). https://cutt.ly/Dwdmfmc

38. *Hashimoto, T., Kato, N., Kobayashi, H.: Development of educational system with the android robot SAYA and evaluation. Int. J. Adv. Robot. Syst. **8**(3), 51–61 (2011). Special Issue Assistive Robotics. https://journals.sagepub.com/doi/full/10.5772/10667

39. Hashimoto, T., Kobayashi, H., Kato, N.: Educational system with the android robot SAYA and field trial. In: 2011 IEEE International Conference on Fuzzy Systems, pp. 766–771 (2011). https://doi.org/10.1109/fuzzy.2011.6007430

40. *Hashimoto, T., Kobayashi, H., Polishuk, A., Verner, I.: Elementary science lesson delivered by robot. In: 8th ACM/IEEE International Conference on Human-Robot Interaction (HRI), pp. 133–134 (2013). https://cutt.ly/9wdmfqG

41. Keren, G., Fridin, M.: Kindergarten social assistive robot (KindSAR) for children's geometric thinking and metacognitive development in preschool education: a pilot study. Comput. Hum. Behav. **35**, 400–412 (2014). https://doi.org/10.1016/j.chb.2014.03.009

42. Llamas, C.F., Conde, M.A., Lera, F.J.R., Sedano, F.J.R., García, F.: May I teach you? Students' behavior when lectured by robotic vs. human teachers. Comput. Hum. Behav. **80**, 460–469 (2018). https://cutit.org/QgojI

43. Matsuzoe, S., Tanaka, F.: How smartly should robots behave?: comparative investigation on the learning ability of a care-receiving robot. In: IEEE RO-MAN: The 21st IEEE International Symposium on Robot and Human Interactive Communication, pp. 339–344 (2012). https://cutit.org/PPKyH

44. Matsuzoe, S, Kuzuoka, H., Tanaka, F.: Learning english words with the aid of an autonomous care-receiving robot in a children's group activity. In: The 23rd IEEE International Symposium on Robot and Human Interactive Communication 2014, pp. 802–807 (2014). https://cutit.org/1S2lb

45. Pinto, A.H.M., Tozadore, D.C., Romero, R.A.F.: A question game for children aiming the geometrical figures learning by using a humanoid robot. In: IEEE Conferences, 12th Latin American Robotics Symposium and 2015 Third Brazilian Symposium on Robotics, pp. 228–233 (2015). https://cutit.org/BwXq9

46. Serholt, S.: Breakdowns in children's interactions with a robotic tutor: a longitudinal study. Comput. Hum. Behav. **81**, 250–264 (2018). https://doi.org/10.1016/j.chb.2017.12.030

47. Tanaka, F., Matsuzoe, S.: Children teach a care-receiving robot to promote their learning: field experiments in a classroom for vocabulary learning. J. Hum.-Robot Interact. 78–95 (2012). Inaugural Special Issue: Intersection of Systems Sciences and Human Sciences. https://cutt.ly/IwdmzFT

48. Verner, I.M., Polishuk, A., Krayner, N.: Science class with RoboThespian using a robot teacher to make science fun and engage students. IEEE Robot. Autom. Mag. **23**, 74–80 (2016). https://cutit.org/nyO83

49. You, Z.J., Shen, C.Y., Chang, C.W., Liu, B.J., Chen, G.D.: A robot as a teaching assistant in an english class. In: Sixth IEEE International Conference on Advanced Learning Technologies (ICALT 2006), pp. 87–91 (2006). https://doi.org/10.1109/icalt.2006.1652373

50. Podgoršek, S., Istenič Starčič, A., Kacjan, B.: The foreign teacher's role in ICT supported instruction. Sodobna pedagogika/J. Contemp. Educ. Stud. **70**(136) (2019). https://cutt.ly/Twdmw2S

51. Blatchford, P., Russell, A., Bassett, P., Brown, P., Martin, C.: The Role and Effects of Teaching Assistants in English Primary Schools (Years 4 to 6) 2000–2003. Results from the Class Size and Pupil Adult Ratios. (CSPAR) KS2 Project. School of Psychology and Human Development, Institute of Education, University of London, pp. 1–37 (2004). https://cutt.ly/rwdmcLD

52. Wood, D., Bruner, J.S., Ross, G.: The role of tutoring in problem solving. J. Child Psychol. Psychiatry **17**, 89–100 (1976)

53. Park, H.W., Kima, R.R., Rosenberg, M., Gordon, G., Breazeal, C.: Growing growth mindset with a social robot peer. In: Proceedings of ACM SIGCHI, pp. 137–145 (2017). https://cutt.ly/Xwdmp46

54. Johal, W., Castellano, G., Tanaka, F., Okita, S.: Robots for learning. Int. J. Soc. Robot. **10**, 293–294 (2018). https://doi.org/10.1007/s12369-018-0481-8

55. Istenič, S.A.: Human learning and learning analytics in the age of artificial intelligence. Br. J. Edu. Technol. **50**(6), 1–3 (2019). Special issue editorial

ISTIL ('I Search Therefore I Learn')

Reordering Search Results to Support Learning

Cleber Pinelli Teixeira[1]([⊠]) (iD), Marcelo Tibau[1] (iD), Sean Wolfgand Matsui Siqueira[1] (iD), and Bernardo Pereira Nunes[2] (iD)

[1] Federal University of the State of Rio de Janeiro, Rio de Janeiro, Brazil
{cleber.pinelli,marcelo.tibau,sean}@uniriotec.br
[2] Australian National University, Canberra, Australia
Bernardo.Nunes@anu.edu.au

Abstract. Although many learning activities involve search engines, their ranking criteria are focused on providing factual rather than procedural information. In the context of Searching as Learning, providing factual information may not be the best approach. In this paper, we discuss the relevance criteria according to traditional learning theories to support search engine results reordering based on content suitability to learning purposes. We proceeded on the investigation by selecting some self-proclaimed search literacy experts to answer thoroughly questions about their views on the reordered results. We take into account that literacy expert's judgment may reveal issues regarded to technical side on learning supported by search tools. Experienced users claimed a preference for reliable sources and direct answers to what they are looking for, as they have exploratory skills to overcome information incompleteness.

Keywords: Informal learning · Searching as Learning · Search Engine Result Pages

1 Introduction

Search engines are used to satisfy information needs. When inexperienced users[1] search for new information, they might not be skilled enough to deal with the complexity of capturing, representing, matching and evaluating what they search for, what they need, and what search engines provide them as answers. Then, the user may be affected by a situation known as Anomalous State of Knowledge [4] in which insufficient previous knowledge about the search subject interferes on his/her capability to formulate adequate queries, impairing the results' usefulness. According to Liu et al. [21], 47.19% of search formulation are effective, which means that most initial attempts fail.

It is considered a hard task to properly build a suitable search query [4], and there is also an obstacle to find relevant information within the high volume of retrieved information. Since the number of Search Engine Result Pages (SERPs) increases based on the number of documents that match the terms used, the order in which the content is presented has an essential role. Results based only on matching search terms would rely

---

[1] This study considers as inexperienced users as those with low search literacy or low knowledge domain in the searched subject.

© Springer Nature Switzerland AG 2020
E. Popescu et al. (Eds.): SETE 2019, LNCS 11984, pp. 361–369, 2020.
https://doi.org/10.1007/978-3-030-38778-5_39

on pages based on reference indexes as relevance criteria. These types of criteria may be useful to factual search, in which users look up for information performing navigational or transactional searches tasks.

On the other hand, in procedural search users need to explore and to assemble pieces of information to reach a comprehensive understanding and build knowledge. Exploratory search [12] is defined as a set of tasks that goes beyond simple search, and in which the user has to apply a greater cognitive effort to be able to investigate and learn from the retrieved information.

Investigation and learning are also the focus of Searching as Learning (SaL) [15, 17], for which the research agenda aims to address issues related to four main objectives: to understand search as a human process; to measure learning performance and outcomes during search; to establish relationship between learning process and search context; and to design functionalities and search system interventions to promote learning [6].

Search engines should assume a more supportive role by presenting the content that satisfies learning needs. Thus, they might be able to identify learning intent and reorder indexed content based on this assumption. Page results order could satisfy learning needs through instructional design principles. We consider cognitive relevance criteria to reorder the retrieved information in a way to better attend educational aspects that characterizes an exploratory search. From the SaL context, the focus of the current study lies on how the information is presented to the user, in an attempt to customize results to inexperienced users.

This paper is organized as follows: Sect. 2 presents learning theories in which this study is grounded; Sect. 3 presents the related works; Sect. 4 presents the relevance sorting criteria to reorder SERPs to support learning; Sect. 5 presents how the survey and online interview were planned; Sect. 6 shows the results and discussions; and Sect. 7 presents the final remarks.

2 Learning Theories

This study is grounded on learning science. Learning does not necessarily imply in a behavior change, however since an outcome is usually required for assessment, we take into account the following statement: "Learning can be defined as changes in behavior resulting from experience" [9]. Considering search engines as supporting tools to learning, the experience cited by Lefrançois [9] comes from user's interaction with information. Two main approaches are predominant in this study: cognitivism and constructivism. While cognitive theories address issues of how information is received, organized, stored and retrieved by the mind, constructive theories equate learning with the creation of meaning from experience [1].

The value of what is learned is measured by how good it allows the learner to go beyond the information already given [5]. Bruner [5] explained that learning derived from the understanding of concepts and categories and from problem-solving procedures. Besides that, his theory of discovery learning represents an important influence on education, it means that the most effective way to construct knowledge is through discovery. In this manner, search engines should provide conditions for it.

A depth relationship between learning and development is established by addressing how learning actually occurs, not focusing on what influences learning [14]. As for the theory presented by Vygotsky [18], one of the founders of constructivism, in one of his main works - the zone of proximal development - defined the necessity to consider the difference between what a learner can do without help and what he/she cannot do without assistance. As an educational approach, the search engine could present the content in different knowledge contexts.

The zone of proximal development [18] may also be organized according to the domain underlying concepts to be discovered [5]. Concepts are represented by symbols (e.g. a text is composed by a set of words) that depict abstractions of fundamental attributes about what is referenced [2]. In SaL, this symbolism could be represented by document indexing which is retrieved during the searching process. This work bases the relevance sorting criteria on categories and concept chaining in order to enhance comprehension and learning.

Self-efficacy plays a major part in determining our chances for success. It is the belief that you are capable of carrying out a specific task or of reaching a specific goal [24]. A perception of complete lack of control in mastering a task may lead to the behaviorist theory called learned helplessness [25]. In an educational endeavor, learned helplessness acts as a vicious cycle reinforcing itself as the student perceives that there is nothing he/she can do to improve his/her learning outcome, thus making less and less attempt to do so. As his/her effort dissipates, failure is almost certain. In a Web search with exploratory characteristics, learned helplessness influences inexperienced users to avoid reformulate their queries to improve the results, to settle for useless or not-so-good results and to dropout from search sessions.

These premises should be considered to highlight the necessity to motivate users whose search literacy skills do not allow them to effectively reach learning goals. Search systems have the potential to decrease the sense of information dispersal, which could assist the user to handle the flow of information easier.

3   Related Work

There are two steps required to provide an educational content ranking: (i) search query classification to identify learning intent from query formulation and reformulation and (ii) the arrangement of the retrieved content based on relevance criteria [19]. Educational objects (search results) may be sorted through strategies within three categories [13]: ranking based on text similarity; ranking based on user profile; and ranking based on human review.

Since we do not present an automated solution yet, as text similarity review, we consider a human review in order to investigate the main implications of this approach. Human review approaches can be seen in solutions based on curatorship by specialists, as it occurs in Learning Management Systems' content sequencing [11] and knowledge graph, with the goal of organizing relevant factual associations and entities [20].

However, neither a curriculum in educational platforms nor a knowledge graph are completely available for any domain in a reliable manner. Therefore, we look for criteria of sorting relevance to handle the SERPs and reorder them, for instance based on the learning theories cited in Sect. 2. An idea to support the categorization is presented in [10] and further studies could go in direction to interface customization [22] and information visualization [23]. Although, we focus on reordering the retrieved results as an alternative before advance into more sophisticated solution.

An extended and enriched knowledge-context, which is the case for an adequate strategy of ordering the query results, can enable and motivate users' development and use of information-literate action, thus using the query engine and learning. Knowledge-context may be designed not only to enable the searcher's selection of the most relevant and useful results, but also to positively influence the searcher's confidence in the accuracy and reliability of the system's comparison, evaluation, and differentiation of query results and accessed sources [8].

4   Relevance Criteria to Support Learning Through Search Results Sorting Reorder

We propose a set of relevance criteria to reorder the first page of search results based on the relationship between concepts. This customized sorting reorder is based on the Smart Insights[2] research that indicates the importance of the first page as the most accessed of SERPs. Hence, we considered that a new arrangement of the results based on different content categories might be effective for learning purposes. As a teacher has the role to motivate and clarify a subject by organizing the lecture in a flow that allows thoughtful learning, we believe that somehow it could be reproduced by information systems when assembling information pieces into logically chained and sorted content.

The proposal, represented in Fig. 1, is based on relevance sorting criteria that bring the idea of content sequencing as a way to intentionally present a "learner friendly" SERP and also based on learning of concepts and its relationships as Ausubel's theory of meaningful learning [2]. It is structured according to the following disposal:

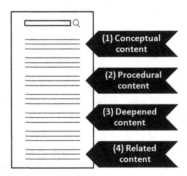

Fig. 1. Representation of relevance criteria embedded in a SERP.

---

[2] https://www.smartinsights.com/search-engine-optimisation-seo/seo-analytics/comparison-of-google-clickthrough-rates-by-position/.

- Conceptual content: it starts with chained concepts in order to enhance the identification of requirements, so that the learner does not access too complex content in the first interaction with sources. Sometimes we need to understand how concepts are related to each other in order to comprehend it. According to the concept of zone of proximal development [18], a person develops a skill by maturing his/her awareness within a particular internal context that includes the person's actual level of knowledge about the target domain, the types of help being offered and the sequence that these help types are offered. The choice to show first conceptual concepts – especially content which provides the user with an overview about the searched domain – is a way to avoid a learned helplessness situation. Retrieve sequenced information showing the relationship between the subject's topics could be a guide to develop search engines that are able to intervene in order to promote learning.

- Procedural content: allowing users to have access to guides and step-by-step material aid them to be fully engaged with the content by providing tips on to how apply it. Users can then organize the information based on what it relates to in order to create the associations necessary to better understand through the general notion-application relationship, consequently supporting learning and empowering them to be active in the process by choosing directions to explore. This process is grounded on Ausubel's theory [2] of meaningful learning and intends to relate the retrieved online content as meaningful signs, symbols and concepts that could be more easily incorporated within the user's cognitive structure. The choice to show procedural after conceptual content is an attempt to promote the feeling of "all pieces fitting together", in which the contents read are meaningful and made sense. Focusing on applied concept as a second level of organization has the purpose to present the information as useful and not limited to memorization but as a way to build a conceptual framework regarding how the searched subject can be interpreted and applied by the user.

- Deepened content: results capable of fetching specific information from what was searched (in an implementation, it may be used specialization of query reformulations from searches with similar topics). Based on Piaget [14] and Vygotsky [18] theories, the user will handle more complex content after the previous steps, in a process similar to constructivism's assimilation. As users assimilate new information, they can incorporate it into an already existing framework (provided by the conceptual content) without changing that framework (incorporating the deepened content into the conceptual framework about the searched subject).

- Related content: aligned to Bruner's assumption [5], the user needs to go beyond the information given. Here a variation of the spiral curriculum approach is applied, in which each subject is revisited at intervals, with a more sophisticated level being focused each time. Instead of deepen the subject; the idea is to retrieve related information about the searched subject to provide a better understand on how they mold together. The proposed approach aims to reveal concept chaining in a wider perspective instead of requiring a more focused search to avoid duplicate content. One goal is to reduce the effort to identify related concepts that is required to increase users' comprehension, by means of assisting users toward possible exploration paths and serving as a guide to query reformulation. It represents an educational view that could be applied whenever is identified a learning intent from the user. It may also represent an attempt to present the content in a flow that could contribute to motivation reinforcement.

5 Survey Setup

The success of information systems is influenced by the intent to use it; thus, the user's opinions are important [7]. To understand users' point of view, a qualitative investigation was conducted to inquiry a group of participants, which were selected based on their search literacy skills. We take in account that a search literacy expert's judgment may reveal issues regarded to technical side on learning supported by search tools. Seven experienced users were volunteers to an online interview, based on the following script:

1. How do you describe your searching and learning skills (i.e.: search literacy) and what makes you good at it? – We want to identify which skills a customized search engine could provide.
2. What kind of search strategies do you use to learn on the internet? – This question intends to map suitable approaches used by experienced users to increase their awareness about a subject.
3. While searching for the information what kind of problems do you face when you have to learn something new? – We want to know which challenges an experienced user face.
4. Comparing the following images of search engine results pages, which pages you would visit, which pages you would not visit and why. – This question seeks to provide a better understanding about results' usefulness through the indication of the pages that would be accessed or not, and to explain why.

The images of SERPs of the fourth question represented procedural search. The search subjects were chosen based on their classification[3] of most asked questions on Google (88th and 131st respectively): "how to start a business" and "how to create a website". These subjects represent a type of questions that do not match simple answers, it requires some information-literate actions in order to satisfy (learning) user's intent. The results of the first page were reordered according to the relevance criteria presented in the previous section.

6 Results and Discussion

The seven users chosen to be interviewed were selected from the group of people who claimed to have excellent search literacy skills. Their answers brought some insights regarding what could be expected from a learning driven search engine and also to the applied relevance criteria:

---

[3] https://www.mondovo.com/.

- Experienced users can properly formulate queries to find online whatever they are looking for from the first search query used. It indicates that even the first queries at the beginning of a search session can indicate if the user is an experienced or inexperienced one. The recognition of a user's struggle to formulate a query might take place in this early search session timeframe by mapping the user's behavior to identify searching behavior patterns. An example of such mapping was handled by [16], in which the user's search behavior is seen as exploratory and modeled as a Knowledge-intensive Process (KiP).
- Experienced users follow strategies like focused search in academic repositories and reliable sources and semantic search. This kind of user's decision-making also may help to distinguish a novice from an expert user. An aggregated search, as described in [3] could help novice users to envision wider possibilities and properly adopt the best strategy.
- The main problems any kind of users face concern to the type (documents not related to education) and content depth (superficial or incomplete). As a reflex of the huge number of documents on the web, novice searchers take the risk of not finding the most suitable document for learning purposes. As the most suitable document may vary according to the user's intent, the challenge is to identify the intent first rather than to tune an algorithm's document-query matching.
- Users worry more about sources than content. Reliability is pivotal and also should direct educational content indexing. Categories of information and content usefulness based on source reliability can be used to organize the documents, as indicated by [3] and [10]. According to participants' impressions the awareness of categories of the results would make the approach more acceptable.

Although the above topics could help to detect learning needs that search engines do not assist properly; to promote strategies to intervene in a Searching as a Learning process; and to highlight challenges faced by SaL agenda, still remains a lack of formal models to SaL and a lack of grounded theories that could better connect search process to the learning sciences.

7 Conclusions

The understanding of users' acceptance of SERPs sorting reorder and further analysis about the reasons why a document link is considered useful will help to improve our understanding about the requirements needed to customize a search engine able to support educational searches. It was the major motivation behind this research and we took into account search literacy user's opinion in order to reveal critical issues on the perspective of the search tool that even an expert could not overcome to satisfy his/her learning needs.

As the current search engines sorting relevance criteria of referenced page links, users search history and bookmarks and document-query matching does not necessarily improve results suitability for learning purposes (e.g. a professor's blog might be more useful than an article from The New York Times), an alternative strategy to reorganize SERPs, such as the one presented in this paper, is a necessary step. Using the searching experience of skilled users seems a reasonable alternative to aid novice searchers while performing searches with learning intent.

This work was limited to aspects related to SERPs sorting reorder; however, we could notice how important are users' behavior and interaction with sources to advance SaL research agenda. As future work, we envision:

- The implementation of an automatic detection of categories to sort, arrange and reorder results;
- The implementation of multimedia and aggregated search to search engines could be a reasonable path to enhance searching engines capability as tools to support learning;
- Since experienced users claimed the preference for direct answers to what they look for, we understand that the disposal of information should be split into frames so that users can see primarily direct answers and then related categories or multimedia;
- The identification of user's behavior in order to recognize profiles and perhaps present the content according to it, as expert users have different needs compared to novices;
- The assessment of human behavior changes as a result of search tool intervention and grounded on learning theories could provide important contributions to the field;
- Another work that could be done similarly to Smart Insights research, where the informational intent (inferred as learning purpose) could be analyzed from a dataset to provide a quantitative overview from real scenario.

Acknowledgments. This study was financed in part by the 'National Council for Scientific and Technological Development (CNPq) - Brazil' - Process 315374/2018-7, Project 'Searching as Learning: the information search as a tool for learning' and by the 'Coordination for the Improvement of Higher Education Personnel' (CAPES) – Brazil – Finance Code 001.

References

1. Ertmer, P.A., Newby, T.J.: Behaviorism, cognitivism, constructivism: comparing critical features from an instructional design perspective. Perform. Improv. Q. **6**(4), 50–72 (1993)
2. Ausubel, D., Novak, J., Hanesian, H.: Educational Psychology: A Cognitive View, 2nd edn. Holt, Rinehart & Winston, New York (1978)
3. Kopliku, A., Pinel-Sauvagnat, K., Boughanem, M.: Aggregated search: a new information retrieval paradigm. ACM Comput. Surv. **46**(3) (2014). 31 pages, Article 41. https://doi.org/10.1145/2523817
4. Belkin, N.J., Oddy, R.N., Brooks, H.M.: Ask for information retrieval: part I. Background and theory. J. Doc. **38**(2), 61–71 (1982)
5. Bruner, J.S.: The narrative construction of reality. Crit. Inq. **18**(1), 1–21 (1991)
6. Collins-Thompson, K., Hansen, P., Hauff, C.: Search as learning. Report from Dagstuhl Seminar 17092 (2017)
7. DeLone, W.H., McLean, E.R.: Information systems success: the quest for the dependent variable. Inf. Syst. Res. **3**(1), 60–95 (1992)
8. Smith, C.L., Rieh, S.Y.: Knowledge-context in search systems: toward information-literate actions. In: Proceedings of the ACM SIGIR Conference on Human Information Interaction & Retrieval (CHIIR 2019), pp. 55–62 (2019)
9. Lefrançois, G.R.: Theories of Human Learning: What the Professor Said, 6th edn. Cengage Learning, Wadsworth (2011)

10. Huurdeman, H.C., Wilson, M.L., Kamps, J.: Active and passive utility of search interface features in different information seeking task stages. In: Proceedings of the 2016 ACM on Conference on Human Information Interaction and Retrieval (CHIIR 2016), pp. 3–12. ACM, New York, NY, USA (2016)

11. Manrique, R.: Automatic learning content sequence via linked open data. In: International Semantic Web Conference (DC@ ISWC 2017) (2017)

12. Marchionini, G.: Exploratory search: from finding to understanding. Commun. ACM **49**(4), 41–46 (2006)

13. Ochoa, X., Duval, E.: Relevance ranking metrics for learning objects. IEEE Trans. Learn. Technol. **1**(1), 34–48 (2008)

14. Piaget, J.A.: Equilibração das estruturas cognitivas: problema central do desenvolvimento. Trad. Álvaro Cabral. Rio de Janeiro, Zahar (1976)

15. Rieh, S.Y., Collins-Thompson, K., Hansen, P., Lee, H.J.: Towards searching as a learning process: a review of current perspectives and future directions. J. Inf. Sci. **42**(1), 19–34 (2016)

16. Tibau, M., Siqueira, S.W.M., Nunes, B.P., Bortoluzzi, M., Marenzi, I.: Modeling exploratory search as a knowledge-intensive process. In: 2018 IEEE 18th International Conference on Advanced Learning Technologies (ICALT), Mumbai, pp. 34–38 (2018)

17. Vakkari, P.: Searching as learning: a systematization based on literature. J. Inf. Sci. **42**(1), 7–18 (2016)

18. Vygotsky, L.S.: Mind in Society: The Development of Higher Psychological Processes. Harvard University Press, Cambridge (1978). (Edited by Cole, M., John-Steiner, V., Scribner, S., Souberman, E.)

19. Yilmaz, T., Ozcan, R., Altingovde, I.S., Ulusoy, Ö.: Improving educational web search for question-like queries through subject classification. Inf. Process. Manage. **56**(1), 228–246 (2019)

20. Voskarides, N., et al.: Weakly-supervised contextualization of knowledge graph facts. In: The 41st International ACM SIGIR Conference on Research & Development in Information Retrieval (SIGIR 2018), pp. 765–774. ACM, New York, NY, USA (2018)

21. Liu, C., Gwizdka, J., Liu, J., Xu, T., Belkin, N.J.: Analysis and evaluation of query reformulations in different task types. In: Proceedings of the American Society for Information Science and Technology, vol. 47, no. 1, pp. 1–9. ACM (2010)

22. Marchionini, G, Geislerand, G., Brunk, B.: Agileviews: a human-centered framework for interfaces to information spaces. In: Proceedings of the ASIS Annual Meeting, vol. 37 (2000)

23. Singh, J., Zerr, S., Siersdorfer, S.: Structure-aware visualization of text corpora. In: Proceedings of the 2017 Conference on Conference Human Information Interaction and Retrieval (CHIIR 2017), pp. 107–116. ACM, New York, NY, USA (2017). https://doi.org/10.1145/3020165.3020182

24. Bandura, A.: Self-Efficacy. The Exercise of Control. W.H. Freeman and Company, New York. Emory University, Division of Educational Studies, Information on Self-Efficacy: A Community of Scholars

25. Maier, S.F., Seligman, M.E.: Learned helplessness: theory and evidence. J. Exper. Psychol. Gen. **105**(1), 3–46 (1976)

How Do Search Engines Shape Reality? Preliminary Insights from a Learning Experience

Davide Taibi[1(✉)], Giovanni Fulantelli[1], Luca Basteris[2], Gabriella Rosso[2], and Elisa Puvia[1]

[1] Istituto per le Tecnologie Didattiche, Consiglio Nazionale delle Ricerche, Via Ugo La Malfa, 153, 90146 Palermo, Italy
{davide.taibi,giovanni.fulantelli,elisa.puvia}@itd.cnr.it
[2] Liceo Scientifico e Classico Statale "Giuseppe Peano - Silvio Pellico", Corso Giovanni Giolitti, 11, 12100 Cuneo, Italy
{luca.basteris,gabriella.rosso}@liceocuneo.it

Abstract. More and more often, search engines are used by students as a tool to access information on the Web. This has the potential to affect the learning activities conducted by students. In this paper, the project "In WWW veritas?" is presented. The project has the following objectives: (1) to investigate how searches carried out on the Web through search engines can lead to different results based on different criteria; (2) to increase students awareness on how search engines "filters" can work and thus lead to a different perception of reality; (3) to stimulate critical thinking in the use of searching tools on the Web to fully exploit their potential. The project involved students of a high school in northern part of Italy. They examined the results presented by a popular search engine on selected controversial topics and tried to support or contrast the different points of view through a role-playing game. A qualitative and quantitative analysis of results showed an increased students' awareness on the presence of filters through which the search engines provide information. Moreover, the activities undertaken into the project were also effective in developing critical thinking processes.

Keywords: Search as learning · Filter bubble · Critical thinking

1 Introduction

Increasingly, search engines are used by students as a tool to acquire information, also in support of learning. On the one hand, the use of search engines has facilitated the retrieval of information on the net making it possible to access a multitude of contents. On the other hand, search engines act as a filter between users and the Web, defining the most relevant information which has to be proposed to the users.

The algorithm that determines the relevance of a given website in relation to a specific search is based on several criteria. Although each search engine adopts a different approach to determine the relevance of the results, and such approaches are generally

© Springer Nature Switzerland AG 2020
E. Popescu et al. (Eds.): SETE 2019, LNCS 11984, pp. 370–377, 2020.
https://doi.org/10.1007/978-3-030-38778-5_40

covered by trade secrecy, some of the parameters that significantly influence the results are now known, and common to the most popular searching tools [1].

Furthermore, the same companies that develop search engines tend to make public some of these parameters (albeit in an abstract form avoiding to specify the implementation details), highlighting the advantages for the users who can thus receive customized answers; specific to their needs and habits.

The location from which a person connects, the language set in the browser, the type of device used (desktop or smartphone), and navigation history are just some examples of factors that can influence the behaviour of the search engines. Consequently, it is quite common that people who query the same search engine with the same keywords in different conditions, will get different results. As mentioned, these differences are very often motivated by the introduction of improvements in usability namely, the user experience. A user perceives useful to get as results on his smartphone only those sites that are correctly displayed on the device; likewise, obtaining results for hotels or restaurants that are nearby (therefore based on the user's position) is a very useful feature for travelers. Similarly, a user who connects from Italy and who has set the language of his browser in Italian, will find useful to obtain pages mainly in Italian [2].

This ability of search engines to filter the contents of the Web has paved the way for new research opportunities on social dynamics. Researchers from the Digital Methods Institute of Amsterdam [3, 4] have shown how search engines provide different results on particularly sensitive topics based on the country in which the search is conducted. In [4] Rogers analysed the search results in different localized versions of search engines in relation to the theme of "rights". The results of this study showed that, in general, different types of "rights" have different relevance in the various countries, certain types are significant only in some specific countries, thus reflecting a different sensitivity to the different type of "rights" in the world context. In this perspective, search engines provide an effective analysis tool to support social research [5, 6].

One of the key features that influence the presentation of results is the number of times a specific page, listed amongst the results, has been visited by the users. Also, the previous search activities carried out by the user play a fundamental role. Indeed, users can benefit from the behaviour of the algorithm implemented by the search engine. In the first case, the user will have access to the most popular pages, those that are chosen by the majority of users. In the second case, the user will be able to obtain personalized search results, since the search engine will be able to infer what s/he already thinks about a topic (according to her/his previous navigation history), and consequently it will filter only the contents of interest of the user, thus contributing to strengthen the "bubble" effect [7].

These mechanisms make search engines not only tools for retrieving information, but environments in which the user interacts with content and information. In these terms, it is simplistic to consider the outcomes of the searching process merely a list of results. Students, who increasingly use the search engines as a first approach to the Web and as a tool to forge their understanding on a new topic, are very often unaware of these mechanisms, thus taking the risk to access polarized information on a specific point of view, which does not support the development of critical thinking.

The present project "In WWW veritas?" aims to study how search engine "filters" can literally "lead" students to misleading conclusions and theses; thus, inducing different perceptions of reality.

Providing greater awareness in the use of search engines, they will enable students to exploit the full potential of these tools, controlling them, avoiding to be controlled by them. In parallel, from a didactic point of view, the project allows teachers to introduce issues related to the reliability of Web sites and information on the Net, and "fake news", thus promoting the key competences necessary for media literacy [8].

2 Methodology and Tools

"In WWW veritas?" is a project that combines both didactic and research aspects. The project involved four classes of the last three-year of the high school located in a city in the northern Italy for a period of about 3 months. The project involved 10 teachers and about 100 students, for a total of 10 h of activity, 5 in classroom and 5 at home.

The project activities have been designed by researchers and teachers in order to define:

- research methodology,
- technological tools to be used for the searching activities,
- tools for tracing students' activities,
- questionnaire to collect students' opinions.

In particular, the questionnaire aims to stimulate some reflections on the search results in order to acquire awareness about the way in which filters, applied by search engines, shape reality.

The project activities were organized in three phases, each divided into specific actions as shown in Fig. 1.

The first phase involved the preparatory activities of the project, in which the teachers illustrated the project objectives and tasks to the class. In the preparatory phase the teachers, along with the students, chose the topic on which the search on the Web would be focused. Students of each class performed searches related to this topic by using their computer at home with the popular search engine Google. In the second phase, the search activity was conducted at the school laboratories.

In this case, the searches were carried out with different devices (PC, tablet, smartphone), and these search activities were traced through a specific designed software that acts as a Web browser. In particular, this software is used to trace the page visited by students, the link of the search results they clicked, and the time spent by students on each Web page.

In the third phase, the results were discussed with students. The tracking of the activities was initially used to reflect on students' "searching style" and to analyse the "influences" that the search engine can generate on the results. The phases of the project, schematically shown in Fig. 1, are described in detail in the following paragraphs.

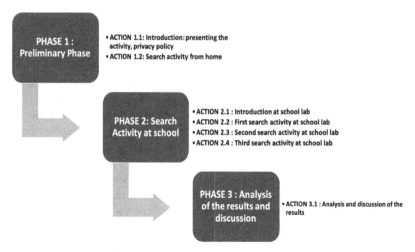

Fig. 1. Phases and actions of the project.

2.1   Phase 1: Preliminary Phase

In the initial phase, teachers presented the activities to be carried out, then they provided technical instructions on the use of the tools, and finally they informed the students about the data related to their online activities that would be collected. A privacy statement indicating data management regulations has been delivered to students (Action 1.1).

Afterwards, the teachers discussed with students the topics under examination. Controversial topics were selected in order to foster a debate amongst students. Examples of keywords and topics on which the searches have been carried out were as follow: selfie syndrome, holocaust, vaccines, homeopathy, N.G.O., horoscope, flat earth. Once the topic to be explored online was chosen, the students carried out a search with their computer at home (Action 1.2).

2.2   Phase 2: Search Activity at School

Phase 2 started with teachers discussing the individual results obtained by students during their search at-home, highlighting:

- differences in the results obtained by each student;
- polarizations that emerged from the result pages.

The presence of different points of view was highlighted, and students were invited to report and discuss some of the results they assumed to be of particular interest. The teacher also guided students in the "critical reading" of the search engine results, by providing examples based mainly on the results obtained by the students themselves. At the end of this task, students were divided into two groups. Each group has to support a point of view about the topic and to argue with the other group, sustaining an opposite perspective on the same topic. It is important to note that students did not have to agree necessarily with the point of view "sustained" by the group, but they have to play a proper role-playing game (Action 2.1).

In the next action (Action 2.2), students used the devices (computers, tablet and smartphones) available at the school laboratories to perform online searches by using the same keywords used at home. At the end of the search sessions, students filled in an ad-hoc questionnaire, designed to annotate different aspects of their search (e.g. how many search results sustaining their point of view they obtained). The ultimate goal was that of promoting a critical reading of the results. Subsequently, the teacher presented various strategies to modify the keywords to be used in the search, such as: the use of synonyms that have a relationship with the starting word (e.g.: vaccines and diseases), or the use of keywords that describe concepts belonging to the same category (for example in the case of vaccines, immunology). In Action 2.3, the teacher invited students to carry out new searches by changing the keywords according to the strategies suggested, with the aim of finding Web pages containing information in favour of the hypothesis supported by the group the student belongs to. At the end of this search session, students filled in another questionnaire to compare the results with the ones obtained in the previous search sessions. Finally, in Action 2.4, students were asked to perform the search using exactly the same keywords used at home and in the first search session at the school laboratory. This task had the aim of highlighting the potential polarization of the results. Indeed, the search activities performed by the two groups of students aimed to sustain a specific point of view, led the search engine to produce polarized results. A final questionnaire was filled in by the students in order to annotate any of this condition.

2.3   Phase 3: Analysis of the Results and Discussion

The third and final phase of the project consisted in data analysis. In this phase, the teacher guided students to reflect (initially within the group) on the differences between the first and second search sessions and the changes detected at the end of the third search session. Finally, the students had to defend the point of view supported by the group they belong to. At the end of this phase, the teacher stimulated reflection together with the class on the reasons why different search results come up while using the same search engine (in this case Google). Other search engine alternatives (e.g. Duck Duck) were also presented to the students, in order to induce them to compare the differences in the algorithms used.

3   Discussion

3.1   Strengths and Weaknesses

The analysis of the results has been used to highlight the strengths and weaknesses of the experimentation. Strengths include the flexibility of the activities carried out. Indeed, the online search activity can be adapted and modelled on the specific needs of the teacher, in relation to the class involved, by taking into account the specific interests of the students, the timing of the experimentation and the most appropriate assessment methods. In the project "In WWW veritas?" most of the teachers personalized their activities, by adapting the actions proposed to their didactic objectives. Furthermore, this type of activity can provide valuable support even in those disciplines in which the use of information technology is often very limited, as in the case of subjects in the humanities area. Another strength to be noted, is the different skills that this type of activity can stimulate in students such as: creativity, critical thinking, and digital literacy.

The main weakness of the project, highlighted by some teachers participating in the experimentation, is the difficulty in assessing the activity carried out by students. Since these are non-traditional activities, based on non-formal learning approaches, it is necessary to implement appropriated evaluation strategies that take into consideration the different skills that are stimulated in the students. Technical difficulties when using the tracking software on the different devices were also met. Another point of weakness, encountered during the activities, is related to technical difficulties in using the tracking software on the different devices. Moreover, even if the software used by students worked as a browser showing the results produced by the Google search engine, the graphical interface was not exactly the same as the one of the browsers commonly used by students. This can even indirectly, influence user interactions. Finally, some considerations arose during the experimentation process concerning the motivation of the teacher with respect to the topics proposed for the search. The selection of the search topic is crucial for the success of the project, both to capture the interests of the students and to analyse and emphasize the differences in the results produced by the search engine. In fact, the most critical phase of the project is the choice of the topic to be searched.

3.2 Results

The analysis of the results highlighted interesting data regarding the navigation style of the students. During the experimentation 40% of students visited only one of the results proposed by the search engine, and only 24% visited six or more results (Fig. 2).

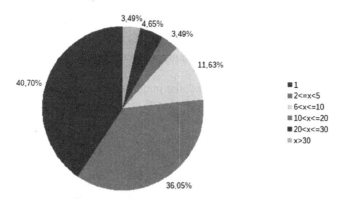

Fig. 2. Numbers of results visited by students

Regarding the number of result pages viewed by students: 82% of students viewed only the first page (up to 10 results as shown in Fig. 3). This means that the majority of

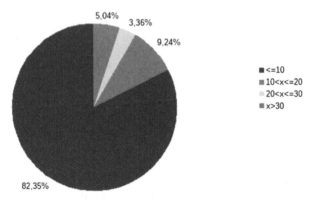

5,04% 3,36%

9,24%

■ <=10
■ 10<x<=20
20<x<=30
■ x>30

82,35%

Fig. 3. Number of results viewed by students

students did not go beyond the first 10 results proposed on the first page by the search engine.

These preliminary results are particularly interesting from the educational point of view, because they lead to a reflection on the limits of student interactions with search engines, thus pointing out the needs for a more effective literacy on the use of search engines.

4 Conclusions

The project "In WWW veritas?" has the aim of promoting a more aware use of search engines for finding information on the Web. Specifically, teachers identified the following key points that stimulated reflection within the classes:

- the "bubble" effect: the type of search engine response varies according to different parameters (place from which the search is performed, language used for the search) and in relation to the "history" of previous searches
- the reading style: which element of a singular page the students look at and in which order
- the searching style: the keywords used, the number of pages viewed (less than ten or more) and/or explored, and the time spent exploring a singular page
- the reliability of the source that is based on specific descriptors such as authorship, frequency of the update, graphical quality
- the propagation of information on the net.

Furthermore, the search styles of students were analysed, highlighting how very often they do not interact with the search engine results properly, thus increasing the risk of accessing only that part of contents filtered by the search engine.

The interviews conducted at the end of the project activities with students and teachers, resulted in a considerable interest. This result encourages to widen the number of participants, extending the experimentation to schools of different order and types and in different areas (in order to take into account also the localization of the results). The involvement of a greater number of students, along with the introduction of appropriate tools for the evaluation of competences, will support further investigations on what students learn by using search engines which filter reality, with particular reference to the retrieval of information on controversial topics.

Finally, it will be of great interest studying which search strategies are mostly implemented by students when they have to sustain specific opinions, and which changes to the search styles are induced by experiences like the one conducted in this project.

Acknowledgments. Students and teachers of the high school "G. Peano - S. Pellico" in Cuneo (Italy).

References

1. Langville, A.N., Meyer, C.D.: Google's PageRank and Beyond: The Science of Search Engine Rankings. Princeton University Press, Princeton (2011)
2. Zhang, J., Lin, S.: Multiple language supports in search engines. Online Inf. Rev. **31**(4), 516–532 (2007)
3. Rogers, R.: Digital Methods. MIT Press, Cambridge (2013)
4. Rogers, R., Jansen, F., Stevenson, M., Weltevrede, E.: Mapping democracy. In: Global Information Society Watch 2009, pp. 47–57. Association for Progressive Communications and Hivos (2009)
5. Fulantelli, G., Marenzi, I., Ijaz, A., Taibi, D.: SaR-Web – a tool to support search as learning processes. In: Proceedings of the 2nd International Workshop Search as Learning (SAL) 2016 at the ACM SIGIR 2016 (2016)
6. Taibi, D., Fulantelli, G., Marenzi, I., Nejdl, W., Rogers, R., Ijaz, A.: SaR-WEB: a semantic web tool to support search as learning practices and cross-language results on the web. In: IEEE 17th International Conference on Advanced Learning Technologies (ICALT), Timisoara, pp. 522–524 (2017)
7. Cardon, D.: Che cosa sognano gli algoritmi. Le nostre vite al tempo dei big data. Mondadori Università. De Carolis, C. (Translator) (2016)
8. Averame, M.C.: Riconoscere le fake news in classe. Percorsi per una comunica-zione consapevole in rete. Collana "insegnare nel XXI secolo". Pearson (2018)

Correction to: A Teaching Experiment on a Knowledge-Network-Based Online Translation Learning Platform

Yuanyuan Mu and Wenting Yang

Correction to:
Chapter "A Teaching Experiment on a Knowledge-Network-Based Online Translation Learning Platform"
in: E. Popescu et al. (Eds.): *Emerging Technologies*
for Education, **LNCS 11984,**
https://doi.org/10.1007/978-3-030-38778-5_35

The original version of this chapter was revised. The authors' affiliations were corrected to:

Yuanyuan Mu
1. School of Foreign Studies, Hefei University of Technology, Hefei, China
2. Center for Translation Studies of Specialized Corpora, Hefei University of Technology, Hefei, China

Wenting Yang
3. School of Foreign Languages, Anqing Normal University, Anqing, China

The updated version of this chapter can be found at
https://doi.org/10.1007/978-3-030-38778-5_35

© Springer Nature Switzerland AG 2020
E. Popescu et al. (Eds.): SETE 2019, LNCS 11984, p. C1, 2020.
https://doi.org/10.1007/978-3-030-38778-5_41

Author Index

Printed in the United States
By Bookmasters